Right Rev. JOHN N. NEUMANN, D.D.

OF THE CONGREGATION OF THE MOST HOLY REDEEMER.

FOURTH BISHOP OF PHILADELPHIA.

From the German of

REV. JOHN A. BERGER, C.SS.R.,

BY

REV. EUGENE GRIMM, C.SS.R.

SECOND EDITION.

APPROBATION.

By virtue of the authority granted me by the Most Rev. Nicholas Mauron, Superior-General of the Congregation of the Most Holy Redeemer, I hereby sanction the publication of this translation of the "Life of Right Rev. John N. Neumann, C.SS.R."

ELIAS FRED. SCHAUER,

Sup. Prov. Baltimoriensis.

Baltimore, Md., *January* 3, 1884.

RIGHT REV. JOHN N. NEUMANN, D.D.,
Of the Congregation of the Most Holy Redeemer.
FOURTH BISHOP OF PHILADELPHIA.

LETTER ADDRESSED TO THE AUTHOR

BY THE

MOST REV. JAMES FREDERICK WOOD,

ARCHBISHOP OF PHILADELPHIA.

REVEREND AND DEAR FATHER:

It was to me a source of great gratification when I heard that you were preparing for publication the Life of your illustrious uncle, the Right Rev. John Nepomucene Neumann, my venerable predecessor. I thought that it was but right and proper that a record should be made of his many virtues, that they might serve to all as an example worthy of contemplation and imitation.

I also rejoice that the work was undertaken by one who has had at his disposal solid material derived from the annals of his time and from the traditions of his brethren in religion.

My first acquaintance with the Right Rev. Bishop Neumann began in Cincinnati in 1857, when he kindly came there to assist at my consecration as his Coadjutor. As the Bishop died in 1860, I had a little less than three years to enjoy his society, yet long enough to be edified by his example and aided by his advice. I became convinced that he had all the learning and virtue necessary to adorn the high position which he occupied. I still admire his lively faith, his firm hope, and his burning charity, his fortitude, and his constancy in the discharge of all his apostolic duties.

I am, therefore, fully persuaded that his Life will be interesting, instructive, and edifying; that it will serve as a model for our youth, as an example for priests and religious, and as an ornament of the episcopal office.

I could record many incidents that happened during the life of the venerable prelate, but his biography will contain them as well as other facts that will show forth his noble character, and will stimulate its readers to imitate his virtues. Hoping that there may also be an English translation of the Life,

I am, reverend and dear Father,
With much esteem and affection,
Your servant in Christ,
JAMES F. WOOD,
Archbishop of Philadelphia.

CATHEDRAL, PHILADELPHIA, October 4, 1881.

AUTHOR'S PREFACE.

ALTHOUGH twenty-two years have elapsed since the death of Bishop John N. Neumann, he still lives in the hearts of all that knew him; and many have expressed the wish that his memory should be preserved, his biography written for the edification of posterity.

For this reason, Superiors several years ago entrusted to me the task of compiling his Life — a task whose accomplishment was by no means easy. For although the servant of God performed many great deeds, his extraordinary humility enabled him to conceal them, in a measure, from the eyes of all save God alone. The diocesan archives of his time record nothing calculated to throw light upon the subject; and the missionaries who labored with him, comparatively few in number, were too much occupied with the care of souls to record a history of their trials and labors. Sufficient material was, however, soon collected from which the Life of the holy Bishop could, to some considerable extent, be faithfully portrayed. From the members of his immediate family, his brother and sisters, many interesting and reliable communications were received; but his own letters and, above all, his own journal have proved valuable sources of information. They afford a consoling glimpse into his noble heart and elevated soul.

Thanks are due to all that have aided me in the fulfilling of my task. Any additional communications will be gratefully received and used in a subsequent edition.

In compliance with the decree of Pope Urban VIII., I declare that to the miracles, revelations, graces, and wonders recorded in this book, as also in reference to the titles *Saint* and *Blessed* given to persons not yet canonized, it is not my intention to ascribe any other than a purely human faith, excepting, however, in those cases which the Roman Catholic Church has confirmed by her judgment.

If this Life of Bishop Neumann should stimulate the reader to a more fervent practice of the love of God, I shall be richly compensated for my labor. May it serve to edify the faithful and encourage my brethren in religion in the discharge of the onerous duties of their state of life!

BALTIMORE, FEAST OF ST. WENCESLAUS, 1882.
Fiftieth Anniversary of the Arrival of the Redemptorists in America.

CONTENTS.

	PAGE
Letter of the Most Rev. James Frederick Wood	5
Preface	7

PART I.

NEUMANN'S YOUTH.—1811–1836.

CHAPTER
I.	Birthplace and Childhood	11
II.	Student-Life	26
III.	The Seminary at Budweis	39
IV.	At the Archiepiscopal Seminary of Prague	45
V.	His Piety as a Seminarian	50
VI.	Trials and Sufferings	72
VII.	Preparations for Departure to America	95
VIII.	Departure from Home	110
IX.	Voyage to the New World	141

PART II.

JOHN N. NEUMANN AS A SECULAR PRIEST.—1836–1840.

I.	John Neumann is Raised to the Dignity of the Priesthood	150
II.	Rev. Mr. Neumann Starts for the Scene of his Future Labors	155
III.	Father Neumann's Field as a Missionary	159
IV.	Father Neumann's Zeal in the Discharge of his Ministry	166
V.	Trials and Sufferings in the Ministry	182
VI.	Father Neumann and Non-Catholics	191
VII.	Father Neumann's Missionary Plans	201
VIII.	Father Neumann's own Sanctification	208
IX.	Father Neumann's Vocation to the Religious Life	216

PART III.

FATHER NEUMANN A REDEMPTORIST.—1840-1852.

I. The Redemptorists in America.................... 222
II. St. Philomena's Church, Pittsburg, and St. Alphonsus', Baltimore......... 238
III. Father Neumann a Novice among the Redemptorists..... 246
IV. Father Neumann Superior of the Redemptorists, Pittsburg... 260
V. Father Neumann Vice-Provincial of the Redemptorists in America................................ 282
VI. Father Neumann's Labors as Vice-Provincial............ 290
VII. Father Neumann is Raised to the Episcopate... 320

PART IV.

FATHER NEUMANN AS BISHOP OF PHILADELPHIA— 1852-1860.

I. The Diocese of Philadelphia..... 323
II. Bishop Neumann's Arrival in Philadelphia............. 326
III. Bishop Neumann's Pastoral Charge.................. ... 334
IV. The Establishment of Catholic Schools in the Diocese of Philadelphia...................................... 342
V. Bishop Neumann's Solicitude for his Clergy............ 350
VI. Bishop Neumann's Solicitude for the Religious of his Diocese.. 361
VII. Bishop Neumann's Reverence and Devotion in the Performance of Sacred Functions..................... 371
VIII. The Building of the Cathedral....................... 381
IX. Bishop Neumann visits Rome and his Native Place...... 386
X. Bishop Neumann is Assigned a Coadjutor.,............ 414
XI. Some Traits of Bishop Neumann's Saintly Character..... 420
XII. Death and Obsequies of Bishop Neumann.............. 430
XIII. Bishop Neumann's Reputation for Sanctity. Extraordinary Effects of his Intercession.................... 450

PART I.

NEUMANN'S YOUTH.
1811–1836.

CHAPTER I.
Birthplace and Childhood.

IN a rich and highly-cultivated valley in the south-western part of Bohemia, lies the ancient city of Prachatitz. The surrounding mountains, towering up to a considerable height, their summits clothed with dense foliage and pine-forests, afford a grand and imposing view.

The natural beauties of this charming region, as well as its historical associations, attract thither during the summer months visitors from all parts, who, having inhaled new vigor from its fresh mountain-breezes, leave with regret so delightful a spot.

As early as the year 1036, Prachatitz was an important little city, the chief depot of trade between Bavaria and Bohemia. The road leading from it to Passau is called, even at the present day, "The Golden Path," since from the intercourse between these two places, the inhabitants derived great gain.

Some of its edifices, though centuries old, are still so well preserved as to suggest the probability of their outlasting many a modern structure. Their frescos are still bright, and the inscriptions in Hebrew, Greek,

Latin, Bohemian, and German, are not only discernible, but may be readily deciphered. On the city brewery is an excellent fresco representing a hard-fought battle of the olden times from which the inhabitants came forth victorious. On the town-hall and several private houses are portrayed in vivid colors the kings and patron saints of the country, as also allegorical representations of Faith, Hope, and Charity, whilst numerous texts from Holy Scripture suggest the practice of justice, prudence, and patriotism. The finest and most important monument of the city is the old parish church, built at the beginning of the fourteenth century, which was destined to become in after-years the scene of distressing events.

Under the reign of Sigismund (1410–1437) the German Empire was exposed to various religious and political disturbances. It was at Prague that Huss made himself notorious, publicly announcing his errors from the pulpit and the professorial chair. Obstinately persisting in his heresy at the Convention of Kostnitz, he was, by order of the court, burnt alive on July 6, 1415. One year later a similar fate befell his disciple and friend, Jerome of Prague.

Their followers, exasperated by such treatment, gathered around their daring leader, John Zizka, and attacked the Government House at Prague. Then these fanatics, who called themselves Hussites, or Taborites, rushed upon the Catholics, whom they plundered and murdered, and set fire to convents and churches. One of their unjust demands was that laymen should be allowed to drink out of the chalice at Holy Communion, and in their processions they often bore the chalice before them like a banner. In November, 1420, Zizka appeared with his enraged followers before the town of Prachatitz. The gates had been locked, the drawbridge raised, and the citizens ranged on the walls to defend their city. Zizka, in a friendly tone, called out to them to surrender: "Open the gates that we and our priests may enter with the Most Sacred Body of Christ. We promise to do you no harm." The besieged, with Christian boldness, answered, "We want neither *your* Body of Christ nor your priests. We have our own Body of Christ; we have our own priests!" Enraged at this answer, Zizka cried out, "I swear by the Almighty, not one of you shall live; I will put you all to death!" The Catholics defended themselves heroically, but were vanquished, at last, by the superior force of the enemy. The savage Hussites scaled the walls, massacred the defenders, beat down the gates, poured into the city like a devastating flood, and slew two hundred and thirty-five of the inhabitants in the streets. Still thirsting for carnage, they forced their way into the houses, dragged the frightened occupants from their hiding-places, butchered the men, and drove the defenceless women and children from the city.

After this cruel massacre, the Hussites remained in undisturbed possession of Prachatitz. To crown his impious deeds, Zizka caused eighty-five of the citizens to be locked up in a side-chapel of the principal church and, deaf to their cries for mercy, ordered straw soaked in pitch to be lighted and thrown down upon them from above.

In their death-struggles these martyrs for the faith vainly tried to force the iron window-grating, which even at the present day is pointed out in its bent state, as a memorial of the terrible event.

For nearly two hundred years the heretics occupied the city, whose beautiful church they abused and profaned. The Thirty Years' War (1618–1648) brought a change in affairs. As the first religious disturbances had broken out in Bohemia, under Huss, one hundred years before the so-called Reformation, so, too, did the Thirty Years' War take its rise in the same country. During the reign of the Emperor Mathias, Protestant tenants of the Archbishop of Prague, relying on the imperial rescript given them by the Emperor, Rudolph II., erected churches at Klostergrab, whilst those of the Abbot of Braunau did the same. The rescript had, however, been granted only to the Protestant lords and knights, and not to the Protestant tenants of Catholic landlords, as was decided by both the court and the Emperor.

On the 23d of May, 1618, Count Thurn, with a body of Protestant Bohemians, made his way into the royal castle, seized the imperial councillors and hurled them out the windows. Daily increasing in numbers, the malcontents expelled the Jesuits, and placed the supreme authority in the hands of a regency composed of thirty directors.

The Protestants had, in 1608, formed a compact called "The Union," at the head of which was Frederick of the Palatinate, who sent the insurgents auxiliary troops under the command of Count Mansfeld. And now the flames of revolt burst forth. The Emperor Mathias was succeeded by Ferdinand II. The rebels discarded the new Emperor, and at Prague solemnly crowned Frederick of the Palatinate leader of the Protestant Union. With the aid of the brave Tilly, the usurper was, however, defeated at White Mountain, near Prague, November 8, 1820, by Maximilian of Bavaria, head of the Catholic League.

In 1619, Mansfeld's troops occupied the city of Prachatitz as a frontier fortress; but on September 27, of the following year, they were vanquished after a bloody battle with the imperial forces under Count Boucquoi.

Peregrin, in his Chronicles, gives a sad picture of that fearful combat in which eighteen hundred soldiers lost their lives. Hundreds of cannon-balls may still be seen in various openings of the city wall, striking proofs of the sanguinary attack.

While Mansfeld held Prachatitz, its Catholics numbered only eighty-eight. They assembled for divine service in the side-chapel of St. Barbara. Six years later, however, all the inhabitants returned to the faith which St. Adalbert had preached to their forefathers. The church of Sts. Peter and Paul is said to have been dedicated by the same holy Bishop.*

In this ancient and memorable city, on Good-Friday, March 28, 1811, the subject of the present biography was born. On the same day his soul was regenerated to the life of grace in the church of the Apostle St. James Major. His sponsors, John and Barbara Marek, a truly Christian husband and wife, named him John after the glorious protector of Bohemia.

To the new-born child was granted the inestimable blessing of good and pious parents. Philip Neumann, his father, born at Obernburg, Bavaria, October 16, 1774, had come to Bohemia and settled in Prachatitz in 1802, making choice of this city because into it his business of stocking-weaving had not yet been introduced. Here he married Agnes Lebis, the virtuous daughter of one of the citizens.

God blessed their union with six children, to whom the pious parents imparted a truly Christian education. John, whose birth and baptism we have just recorded, was the third child. The eldest daughter, Catherine, married Mathias Berger, who left her a widow in 1848, when she chose a life of seclusion devoted to God alone. Her only son entered the religious state and became a priest. Veronica, the second child, was united in marriage to Anthony Kandl, and died in 1850 without offspring. Joanna, the fourth child, entered at Prague, in 1840, among the Sisters of Charity of St. Charles Borromeo, and took the name of Sr. Mary Caroline. These religious had recently been introduced into Bohemia from Nancy, in Lorraine. At present they are laboring

---

* St. Adalbert died a martyr in 997.

successfully in various communities, in prisons and orphanages. Since her profession, Sr. Mary Caroline has constantly exercised the office of Superioress, and for a long time that of Superioress-General. The fifth child, Aloysia, has, since the death of her much-loved father, been with the same Sisters of St. Charles Borromeo. The youngest child was a son, named Wenceslaus. He learned his father's trade, and was destined to succeed him in the business; but Almighty God had ordained otherwise. He followed his brother John to America, where he has been since 1841 a lay-brother in the Congregation of the Most Holy Redeemer. Such were the consoling fruits of conscientious and religious training on the part of parents whose earnest endeavor was to give good example to their children.

The fear of God reigned in their household, and the works of a genuine Christian life were zealously performed by all its members. It was soon well known in the little town that if one of Philip Neumann's workmen dared to utter an improper word on his employer's premises, he would be suffered to make his appearance there no longer. Morning and evening, before and after meals, prayer was made in common, the head of the family presiding. Business ceased earlier than usual on Saturday afternoon, that the workrooms might be cleaned and the employees free from labor on Sunday.

Philip Neumann was a man of very active habits. He was never seen idle. "Early to bed and early to rise" was his motto; and his whole life was an exemplification of the proverb, "Eat little, live long."

His eminent virtues, above all his prudence, rendered him conspicuous among his fellow-citizens, who elected him to several public offices, the duties of which he conscientiously discharged to the satisfaction of all. It was as city-almoner that he especially distinguished himself; for during his administration of that office a beggar on the streets was a rare sight. He levied a poor-tax, and with the proceeds established a fund for the relief of the indigent according to their needs. Here he acted with his usual discretion. To the destitute through their own improvidence or extravagance he furnished food and fuel, but withheld money lest they should squander it; and he provided that young journeymen should be supported by the guilds. The general esteem for Mr. Neumann was so great that not unfrequently the people, young and old, would kiss his hand when they met him on the street.

Passion never influenced his actions, as the following instance will prove. His little daughters, it seems, were great admirers of scalloped dresses. One of them, in her childlike simplicity, conceived the happy idea of affording her father a most unexpected pleasure, a most agreeable surprise. Watching her opportunity, she slipped unnoticed to the wardrobe where hung her father's holiday suit, took down the coat and, as skilfully as she could, scalloped the skirt. Next Sunday, the unsuspecting father donned the coat, and was about starting for church when some one drew his attention to its unusual ornamentation. Convinced that one of the little girls had been trying her skill on his coat, he called them together and inquired which of them had done it. But no answer came from the startled group; no acknowledgment of guilt was made. Displeased at their want of candor, the father quietly changed the coat for another, and went to church. On his return, he tried again to discover the author of the mischief. "If I could find out who scalloped my coat so beautifully," said he, "I would give her a twenty-cent piece." Instantly one of the children cried out, "Father, I did it, I did it!" The little offender did, indeed, receive the promised reward; but, at the same time, she underwent a suitable punishment, not because she had spoiled the coat, but because she had delayed to confess her fault.

The following incident portrays Mr. Neumann's Christian sentiments. He had been frequently warned that a certain poor man was in the habit of committing petty thefts at his expense. At first Mr. Neumann would not credit the report, his charity inclining him to think well of all. But finally the thief was caught in the act, and Mr. Neumann himself sought an interview with him. In trembling tones he thus addressed the offender: "You know, my friend, that God sees even our most hidden thoughts. How dare you, then, offend against the Almighty?" The poor man was so affected by his words and manner that he began to shed tears. "Forgive me!" he cried, "I was driven to it by necessity." Mr. Neumann replied: "Had you mentioned your needs to me, I would gladly have relieved them. For the future, come to me when you are in want, but never resort to theft again." The poor fellow was deeply humbled. He received a large alms on the spot, and, to fill up the measure of his forgiveness, Mr. Neumann forbade the two witnesses to speak of the affair, that the man's reputation might not suffer.

Let us here record the testimony of the venerable Father Schmidt, at that time Catechist and Director of the city school. In a letter dated February 27, 1872, he says: "The parents of Bishop Neumann were plain people of Prachatitz, but highly distinguished for their thoroughly Christian conduct and industry. The father was specially noted for his activity as city-councilman and city-almoner. The Christian education which their children received was truly exemplary. So well trained were they that a look from their parents had more effect upon them than corporal punishment on other children."

In the practice of all good works, Mr. and Mrs. Neumann were models for imitation. Their biography, written by their illustrious son himself, records the following: "Our education was conducted in accordance with the good old Catholic method, for our parents were thorough Christians. After morning prayers, our father superintended his workmen until evening. Our mother daily heard Mass, to which she always took one or other of the children. She received Holy Communion and fasted on certain days besides those prescribed by the Church. That one of us who had been so fortunate as to be chosen to accompany her to Mass, to the Rosary, or to the Way of the Cross, generally received a penny or some other trifling reward." This circumstance gave rise to the following ingenuous remark on the part of one of their young companions. His mother was exhorting him to imitate John's assiduity in attending church, when the little fellow replied, "Mother, give me a penny every day, and I will do the same; I'll be just like him."

It was an acknowledged fact that when Mr. Neumann no longer held the office of city-almoner, beggars began again to frequent the streets. Certain days, Fridays especially, were set apart by Mrs. Neumann for the distribution of alms. Then, prayer-book or rosary in hand, a bag of flour and a basket of bread at her side, she would take her seat near the door and deal out to the poor according to their needs. Her donations were always accompanied by a few kind and instructive words. Others received a breakfast or a dinner on specified days. To relieve the wants of the poor was her delight, and, like a wise and prudent mother, she strove to instil into her children an active love for their neighbor. She taught them that virtue, to be of value, must spring from the heart; and, to accustom them to its practice, she often placed in their tiny hands the alms to be distributed among the needy. She lost no opportunity of instructing them, and a few simple words from her lips sufficed to incline them to good. One day her daughters complained of their own plain clothes, whilst other girls of their age were dressed according to the fashions. "If there is any good in you," replied their mother, "it needs no finery to show it off. If you think to make yourselves something by wearing fine clothes, you clearly show that you are nothing."

She greatly disliked to hear the faults of others discussed, and if any one so far forgot himself in her presence as to lessen the good reputation of his neighbor, she met the indiscreet remarks with words like these: " Such talk can do no good. We all have our fault , and yet God is so patient with us."

The upright, straightforward principles of this family failed not to attract the attention of every beholder. Mr. Neumann abhorred flattery and deception. His instructions to his sons and nephew on their departure from home he terminated by this warning: " Beware of flatterers! The flatterer is a deceiver, a wily thief whose aim is to obtain something from you to your detriment. Never trust a flatterer!"

The above brief remarks go to show what an example John Neumann had in his own venerated parents, outside of whose home he found no pleasure. Let us now pass on to our proper subject.

Almighty God usually surrounds His chosen souls from their very childhood with His special providence, and endows them with peculiar aptitude for the acquisition of virtue—a fact clearly exhibited in the subject of this biography. The child was not yet three years old, when he was saved by some invisible influence from a fatal accident. He fell through an open door into a cellar fifteen feet deep without sustaining the least injury. His mother always felt that God had protected her child, and she frequently recurred to the fact in the presence of the other children, to stimulate them to gratitude to their Creator, and confidence in the divine assistance.

At an early age, the Christian virtues, and especially the love of God, sprang up in the heart of the favored child. His fervor in attending divine service was, as we have already remarked, of such a nature that he was held up by the neighbors as a model to their children.

The thought of sin filled him with alarm; to offend God was his greatest horror. Only once, as his eldest sister testifies, was he punished by his father, and that was for telling an untruth. This punishment he never forgot. In later years he used to say, "That correction did me good, for I never after told a lie." When, years after, he visited his native city as Bishop of Philadelphia, he again thanked his father for that long-remembered punishment.

In November, 1818, at the age of seven, John began to attend the city school, where, for the next six years, he was always the same gentle, pious, diligent lad, holding among his school-fellows the highest rank in class. During his first year at school an incident occurred which though apparently trifling, yet shows the boy's extraordinary conscientiousness. His little five-year-old sister begged one day to be taken to school, and John humored the childish whim. But when he saw his companions losing time in chatting and amusing themselves with the little girl, he resolved that in future she should stay at home. "I'll not take you to school any more," said he, on their way home. "You distract the scholars; they do not attend to the teacher."

A short cut through the city square led from his home to the school. But when John found that it was a rendezvous for mischievous boys, he took another route to escape witnessing their noisy games. He preferred amusing himself at home in the company of some young companions with whom his parents allowed him to associate.

The Catechist of the parish church speaks of him in these words: "I admired John Neumann even as a little boy. When I looked at him I thought of what is written of St. John the Baptist: 'What an one, think ye, shall this child be?' (Luke i. 66.) He was always so gentle, so good, so excellent a pupil, that by my advice, even when he was in the lowest class, his teacher, Mr. Chlauda, appointed him monitor of the new scholars. Later on, in the upper class, I gave him the duty of correcting his companions' exercises. The task of tendering public thanks to the trustees, and of making the address to his schoolmates, usually devolved upon him."

He was nearly always monitor over the other boys, who both esteemed and loved him for his invariable justice toward them. He highly appreciated his school-duties; he was never known to be late, and he never voluntarily absented himself. If, in the morning, his parents required any little duty or errand of him, he cheerfully set about its fulfilment, mindful all the while, however, that school-time was drawing near.

His vocation of after-life early manifested itself. He erected a little altar, decorated it with lights and flowers, and, assisted by his young companions, he frequently "said Mass."

During his last year at school he was, on account of his modesty and recollectedness, admitted to the honor of serving in the sanctuary of the parish church. So great was his reverence for the Holy Sacrifice that he would not break his fast before serving, even at High Mass.

His darling inclination, the one which followed him through life, which gained strength as years rolled on, was an intense yearning for study and reading. Books were the joy of his heart. His parents procured him a book-case well supplied with good and useful matter for his perusal; and who can say how often these treasures were handled, their leaves turned? This was the boy's greatest pleasure. He tells us in his journal: "From my good father, who well knew the value of books, I had inherited a passion for reading. Whilst the other boys were romping, catching birds, etc., I was poring over my books. My mother used to chide me, sometimes, and call me book-mad, a bibliomaniac."

Here we discover in the boy of ten or twelve that thirst

for learning which was never content with a superficial knowledge of things. He dived into first principles, and not unfrequently his abstruse questioning puzzled both parents and teachers. About this time John and his little brother Wenceslaus roomed together. One night the latter ran to his mother complaining that John would not go to sleep. The mother anxiously arose and hurried to see if anything ailed her boy. What was her indignation, on entering the room, to hear her young philosopher propounding to her the question: "Mother, how is it that our earth floats in the air without falling?" "Let it float! You have not to hold it," was the curt answer. "God takes care of that. All you have to do is to go to sleep and not disturb your brother." And the obedient boy turned on his pillow to follow the maternal injunction.

The education of his heart kept pace with that of his mind. His neighbors' woes aroused his deepest sympathy. Once he saw a poor little child going from door to door with a bag on his back. His heart was touched, and in his childish compassion he exclaimed, "Oh, if I only had a bag, I could go about begging with the poor boy, and then he would get more!"

He could never be induced to keep for himself any little present he might receive. Gifts from his godparents were so distributed among his brother and sisters that the smallest share always fell to himself; and he would often run away lest a larger portion would be forced upon him.

One day whilst amusing himself with several companions at a game, in which each of the players mentions what he desires to become in after-life, John was the only one who kept silence. His mother, who was quietly noticing what was going on, questioned her boy afterward as to what he would like to be. "Mother," he answered, "I *would* like to be something, if it did not cost so much money."

We shall soon see that God so ordained that money should prove no obstacle to the fulfilment of the boy's pious desires.

It is customary among the Bohemians to make on some occasions three small crosses on the forehead, lips, and heart, respectively, instead of the large Latin cross. It so happened that one day at table John inadvertently signed himself with the latter, whereupon an old maid-servant cried out, "Look at little John! he wants to be a priest!" His mother often adverted to this apparently insignificant circumstance in her son's presence, for she dearly longed to see him enter the service of God. John's secret aspirations seconded his good mother's desires, but his notions of the dignity of the priesthood were so elevated that he believed it far above his efforts to attain.

In his seventh year he made his first confession, and in his ninth, as an exceptional favor, he was permitted to receive the Sacrament of Confirmation. Scarcely was he ten years old when he was familiar with the so-called Large Catechism, and was deemed sufficiently instructed to receive First Communion with boys two years his senior. From this period his fervent piety made him long for the Bread of Angels, and he communicated as often as his confessor permitted. In after-life he sometimes reverted to the care with which he prepared for Holy Communion in those innocent childhood days.

The good old Catholic custom of teaching Latin, during their last year at school, to those boys who intended to pursue the study of the sciences still existed in his native place. When John was asked whether he too did not wish to study Latin, the boy at first hesitated to speak his mind on the subject, lest he might afterward prove a burden to his family. The Catechist, however, soon calmed his fears, his parents' consent was obtained, and from that time forward, with ten or twelve others, he daily spent a considerable time in the study of the classics.

Whilst still a boy he evinced great love for the beauties and wonders of nature. His leisure moments were spent in the garden of the Catechist, where he loved to work among the flowers. Here he began the study of botany, in which he afterward became so proficient that even at the present day we may marvel at the advance he made in it.

CHAPTER II.
Student-Life.

AT twelve years old John was ready to enter a gymnasium, and it was decided that he should be sent to Budweis, the episcopal see, distant one day's journey from Prachatitz. Toward the close of October, 1823, the young student presented himself as a candidate for examination, through which he passed successfully. In every branch he received the note "Very good," and was found worthy of admission to the "First Class with distinction."

Again we meet his considerate affection for his parents. To reduce his expenses he clubbed with three other students for a room, an arrangement which he afterward regretted when he found himself deprived of that quiet and seclusion so necessary to successful study. He complained of this later, and to it attributed the little headway he made in his studies during his first two years at Budweis. He learned very little, but in fact he had little to learn at the time. His good Catechist must have instructed him well, since he so readily gained admittance to the Third Grade of the gymnasium. The days of his childhood had flown by unclouded and happy, leaving their sweet remembrance to brighten after-years.

But now Almighty God, who had great designs over the pious boy, allowed various trials and annoyances to cross his path; not yet launched into life, he was to taste some of its bitterness. He was confided to the care of a teacher who reflected little honor on his calling. Of this period John writes as follows: "We had for professor a very old, very good-natured man, who was unfortunately addicted to liquor. We made, as may be imagined, no progress in our studies. I even forgot much of what the Catechist at home had taught me. During the third year, our professor came, intoxicated as usual, to the examination presided over by the Reverend Superintendent. The unfortunate man was of course compelled to withdraw. He soon after died by his own hand. His successor was as strict as he was learned, and wished us to crowd into six months the studies of two years and a half. This was, however, requiring too much of most of the pupils, especially as we had contracted habits of carelessness under his predecessor. The result was, as might be expected, that many of them remained behind. I was even more dissatisfied with our teacher of Christian Doctrine. He was the very personification of dryness and a great stickler for *verbatim* recitations. But, as I had no memory for words, our two hours of religious instruction became very irksome to me."

John Neumann soon suffered the consequences of this faulty method of teaching. At the close of his fourth scholastic year he returned home worn out in body and mind. His friends noticed with regret the absence of his wonted amiability and cheerfulness. In former years he had at once produced his certificate for inspection; but now things were changed, and not till called upon did he place it in his father's hands. With a heavy heart he awaited the paternal comment, for in two branches, Latin and mathematics, he had received only "two." After quietly and attentively scanning the report, Mr. Neumann turned to his son: "It seems that you are no longer interested in your studies. You may stay at home and choose a trade"—stern language for the boy's tender heart, more afflicted at his parent's disappointment than at his own trials. And so poor John actually resigned himself to exchanging his books for the tools of a workman. . Let us quote his own words on the subject. At the close of 1827 he writes: "I was thoroughly disgusted with my studies, and I resolved during the vacation to discontinue them. But my good mother's persuasion, joined to that of my brother and sisters, finally overruled my objections. Besides, just at that time the study of the humanities had grown less irksome to me, as we had a professor who, though even stricter than his predecessor, yet showed some consideration for us poor boys." These words disclose the real cause of his discouragement; for John, during the same vacation, avowed to his father, after long deliberation, that he had not deserved the unfavorable notes; that there were outside influences bearing upon the discouraging result. Mr. Neumann immediately spoke to the Reverend Dean and to a professor who was at that time staying at Prachatitz. Both asked for an interview with his son. After questioning him closely in the branches in which he had failed, they unhesitatingly advised Mr. Neumann to demand a second examination for his son. It took place, and John stood it most successfully.

When the new term began, he requested to be allowed a room to himself, that his studies might be pursued in quiet. The first three years he passed almost unnoticed by either professors or schoolmates. The wish to live unknown was his life-long characteristic. To this quality, perhaps, he is chiefly indebted for his progress in the sciences and his growth in grace. We shall soon have opportunities of admiring both.

Rev. Adalbert Schmidt, Spiritual Director of the Episcopal Theological Seminary at Gratz, was John Neumann's most intimate friend. Concerning those years of student-life he writes as follows: "When a boy, not yet twelve years of age, I became acquainted with John Neumann at Budweis. During the first three or four years we entertained friendly relations of mutual respect, though we were not intimate; but our fourth and fifth scholastic years found us on more confidential terms. We used to study and walk together. John's progress in the sciences astonished me then, and arouses my admiration even now when I reflect upon it. As to the labor he performed and the answers he gave, he never advanced beyond the middle grade; but his quiet study probed every subject. He contrived to procure books in all branches of learning, and, like an indefatigable bee, he laid up a store of knowledge for future use. His reflections on what he had read afforded ample matter for conversation during our rambles after study-hours. Summer and winter, sunshine or storm, we traversed the environs of Budweis in all directions, quite forgetful of aught else in the heat of our discussions. Neumann's conversation, as might be expected, was never frivolous or superficial; his learning was many-sided and thorough. He was well versed in languages, sacred and profane history, geography, geology, and poetry. During his philosophical studies he occupied himself with physics and astronomy also. In this last-named branch two companions shared with him his labors and successes, and without the aid of a teacher, even with slender pecuniary resources, they attained an extraordinary knowledge of the heavenly bodies and the laws by which they are governed. What one read or discovered by investigation was enthusiastically accepted and noted down by the others. Their attainments in astronomy, if we consider their circumstances and their little leisure, we must designate as truly splendid."

We here subjoin the testimony of some other ecclesiastics, former schoolmates of John Neumann. They all express themselves in praise of their illustrious friend. The Rev. Dean Iglauer, born at Prachatitz, writes: "I knew John Nepomucene Neumann when I was a boy. I saw a good deal of him at the Budweis gymnasium and during the vacations which we spent in our native place. As a boy he was exceedingly industrious. He was fond of drawing and natural history. He had an excellent microscope, and in his study of created things he saw and admired the omnipotence and greatness of the Creator. To these divine attributes he frequently drew the attention of his young companions. He received a solid and thorough education, and was well versed in the classics."

Rev. Mr. Laad, another of his schoolmates, writes: "It is a pleasure to me to recall that, for thirteen years, I was a fellow-student of the Right Rev. Bishop Neumann. Born in the little city of Wälschbirken, about two hours' walk from Prachatitz, I met the deceased at the city school of the latter place, to which my parents had sent me, and I was not separated from him till the year 1836. The school at Prachatitz enjoyed a high reputation, especially under the management of Rev. Peter Schmidt, Director at that time. . John Neumann was endowed with superior mental gifts. He was also a hard-working student. I never saw him idle; he even took his walks book in hand. The branches discussed in the class-room were not the only ones that occupied his attention. He found time for other useful pursuits, among them the study of languages, to which he early devoted himself. In the lowest class of the gymnasium he began Italian; in the upper class, French was his favorite. During his course of philosophy I remarked some Protestant books in his room; but I soon found that he read them only to discover in what they differed from the truth, to be able to refute their errors, and, above all, to strengthen more and more his attachment to the true faith."

Rev. Father Krbecek testifies as follows: "I studied at the gymnasium at Pisek, and so became acquainted with John Neumann only in the class of philosophy. I noticed how well he employed his time. We used often to walk together after school-hours. Sometimes I brought my little scholars to see him. He always gave us a cordial welcome, and to my boys a treat of nice white home-made bread out of the large chest that stood in his room. Then he let the little fellows play on his zithern, showed them his microscope, and laughed heartily at their exclamations of amazement. Their eagerness to see his wonders made them push and jostle one another, sometimes, to his great amusement. Once I accosted him with, 'Well, what progress have you made to-day?' 'You mean in Littrov?'* he answered, and at once set about giving me the results of his careful experiments, calculations, etc. I became greatly interested in the study, especially after he had pointed out to me, one night, the different constellations. One evening in autumn we were standing together with our telescope viewing the heavens, when a soldier passing by exclaimed, 'What ill-mannered people to smoke so late!' 'Oh!' we cried, 'come closer and look at this.' He did so, and said, 'Ah! that's something else! You are not so ill-mannered, after all.' Neumann was greatly amused. I never look at the starry heavens now without a grateful remembrance of my dear friend.

"On another occasion we were trying to prove a theorem, but could not succeed. Neumann went to the professor of mathematics, and asked for an explanation; but all the information he received was, 'I never came across such a thing before!' Upon this, he returned courageously to the task, and on the following day showed us the proper solution of the problem. He labored unremittingly. It would seem that he had laid down for himself the rule never to rest.

"One day as I entered his room to invite him to a walk, he closed his book in a serious mood. I ventured to take it up, and found it an Italian grammar. I expressed my admiration for that beautiful language, whereupon he offered to instruct me in it if I would give him lessons in Czech. We mutually promised to do so, and during the vacation we gave each other lessons and

---

* Astronomy (Littrov's).

corresponded in Czech and Italian. In this way we became quite proficient in those tongues. When, years after, he visited us as Bishop Neumann, he gratefully told me what benefit the Bohemian language had been to him in America, since by its aid he was able to master other Slavic dialects. His active mind was ever in search of solid information. He disliked nothing so much as want of depth; a thorough insight into whatever he undertook alone satisfied him. Although naturally reticent, he knew how to give clear and satisfactory explanations when called upon."

In the Bishop's journal we find the above statements corroborated by himself: "During our two years of philosophy many changes took place in my surroundings. There were at least a dozen students who showed great aptitude for the different sciences. We employed all our free time, even our days of recreation, in communicating to one another what we had acquired, each in his separate department of learning. While improving ourselves in this way, we were greatly assisted by the good Cistercians, our teachers in philosophy. They received us kindly and answered all our questions satisfactorily. These good Fathers ever showed themselves stern enemies of deceit or ill-will. During these two years I followed perhaps a little too much my inclination for the natural sciences. Natural history, geography, physics, geology, astronomy kept me busy, whilst algebra, geometry, trigonometry, which I had formerly disliked, were now my favorite studies." John seemed to possess the art of finding persons suitable to give him assistance in the commencement of any new branch. In Joseph Jüttner, Artillery Commander, he found a friend who gladly instructed him in higher mathematics. His thirst for secular knowledge did not, however, lead him to neglect the sacred sciences, nor did his demeanor become gloomy or repellent from close application to study. His companions remember him as invariably bright and cheerful, not unfrequently surprising them by his modest but clever display of wit.

On the summit of Mount Libin, in the neighborhood of Prachatitz, stands a chapel dedicated to "The Patriarch," and which contains a large picture of St. Philip Neri. Neumann visited this chapel once with some of his young friends, one of whom inquired what patriarch it was who was there venerated, Abraham, Isaac, or Jacob. John smiled and said, "Why, there are patriarchs in Europe. This is St. Philip Neri, the founder of an Order, and one who has as much right to the title of patriarch as St. Benedict, St. Francis, St. Dominic, and others." Then his friend remarked that *Philip* is derived from the Greek and means *a lover of horses;* to which John laughingly replied, "Indeed, you are Greek with a vengeance!"

After a certain tedious examination in history, John began to skip about and shake his head, as if to shake something out of it. His companion, astonished at so unusual a demonstration, inquired, "What is the matter? Is there water in your ears?" "No," was the laughing rejoinder, "but I want to get rid of that hard-studied history."

The students of that period were required to learn *verbatim* a history impregnated with the errors of Josephism. This was a task highly repugnant to our young scholar. He studied the Holy Scriptures, also, at this time, and set a high value on the apologetic method so well calculated to refute the errors of Protestantism. On one occasion he said: "Protestants allege that we Catholics change the passage *hæreticum devita* and write the word *devita* in two words thus, *de vita;* for, as they say, it was on account of this word that Huss and his adherents were condemned to death by the secular authority. Have these gentlemen so slight a knowledge of Latin?"

John was most considerate in his behavior toward his

fellow-students. Once during vacation they had made arrangements for a ball. Our young friend, not wishing to offend any by a refusal to attend, withdrew during the dancing to the refreshment-room, where he zealously attended to the wants of all who presented themselves. Next morning one of the students twitted him on his not joining in the dance, when John laughingly compared himself to Saul taking care of the garments of the Jews while they stoned St. Stephen. His studies proved no hindrance to the care of his soul. His most earnest aim was to become daily more pleasing to God. At the early age of sixteen he already understood that mortification of the senses is absolutely necessary for advancement in virtue.

He was, therefore, scrupulously careful to mortify his senses and chastise his body. In childhood we meet with mortifications that betoken an extraordinary spirit of self-denial, surpassing the natural powers of tender age. In his sixteenth year he took but one meal a day, his breakfast and supper consisting of only a piece of dry bread. A fellow-student who, on account of family affairs, was compelled to give up his studies writes of him as follows: "As a mere boy, I admired in Neumann his remarkable strength of character, his perseverance, his resolute will in mortifying himself, a disposition which increased with years. I remarked in him a spirit of self-control and self-denial. He was always ready to sacrifice even the most lawful worldly pleasures to spiritual ones. When, in the fourth year of my studies, I was obliged to discontinue them on account of ill-health and certain family reasons, he wrote me in so consoling a strain that I was encouraged to support the trial with resignation. Whilst others aggravated my troubles by urging me to continue my studies in spite of all difficulties, from him alone I received consolation. He constantly wrote me letters full of piety and encouragement."

Another fellow-student renders the following beautiful

testimony of him: "Heart and mind were benefited by intercourse with John Neumann, though the impression produced was wholly involuntary on his part. The principal trait of his beautiful character was his unassuming, childlike piety. Obliging in his demeanor, ever ready to perform an act of kindness, he was at that time at which I knew him a pious student, living only for God and for his studies; a youth according to God's own heart." Selfishness formed no part of John Neumann's character. To help one to advance in the love of God gave real joy to his heart.

"One day I went to see him," a fellow-student writes, "and found lying on his table a small Latin book. I opened it, and was deeply affected by the very first lines. It was a copy of Thomas à Kempis, of whom I had never heard before. Seeing my interest aroused by the little volume, he at once offered me the use of it. This incident contributed not a little to strengthen and spiritualize our friendship. On another occasion I noticed in his room two small volumes, of which he made me a present. They were Louis of Grenada's 'Sinner's Guide.'"

We would fear fatiguing our readers were we to insert the many beautiful and edifying communications received from his fellow-students. We cannot, however, omit that of his most intimate friend, who writes: "Even now I dwell with pleasure upon that time when we were but one heart and one soul. On the paths which Neumann trod in childhood and in youth was met only disinterestedness. Those worldly goods and advantages which others eagerly crave possessed no charm for him; they proved no snare for him, they gained no hold on his affections. Toward his fellow-students he was affability itself, a model of true fraternal charity. He was always ready to lend his books and manuscripts, or give assistance to students who were backward in their studies. His manner on such occasions was marked by the most charming willingness to be of service; no shade of ostentation could be observed in him. His life was one of great mortification. True, he practised no unusual penances at the time, but his whole life was one of self-denial. He never visited saloons or theatres, never indulged in games for money, though sometimes, for recreation, he would take part in the amusements of his companions. In his food he was not hard to please. He never tasted liquor. A glass of beer, at most, was all he allowed himself when setting out on a long journey on foot. Heat and cold, rain and storm, were all the same to him, and by their patient endurance he added new vigor to his naturally strong constitution. Vanity, hidden under a thousand forms, often attacks, to their incalculable injury, the intellect of the most promising youth. But in the heart of Neumann were found, in its stead, only modesty and humility. Unlike other young men of his age and talents, he never made any display of his learning, never boasted of his feats of courage and daring. His dress was plain and betrayed no attempt at prevailing fashions. Calm deliberation reigned in all his actions. His memory was retentive; his imagination lively, but always under the dominion of his cool, correct judgment. From extravagant enthusiasm he was quite free. With him all things were regulated by weight and measure. Modest and cautious in speech and action, one could readily detect in him the well-ordered mind. His calm and prudent deliberation was his shield against undue excitement or outbursts of passion; a fact which rendered intercourse with him easy and pleasant."

We have now followed John Neumann to his twentieth year. May we not, from all we have learned of him, conclude that the dangerous period of youth had cast no stain on his baptismal innocence? His love for God, his humility and mortification—virtues necessary for the preservation of purity—secured to him that precious treasure. Like three stanch bulwarks, they enclosed his innocent heart. His intimate friends admired his modesty, and his fellow-students unanimously concur in testifying that from his lips even an equivocal word never issued. Until he began his theological course he lodged at the house of a widow, whose daughter received the addresses of her affianced a long time previously to marriage. One of his friends said to him: "Do not the frequent visits of that girl's lover annoy you? Is she not herself a subject of distraction to you?" John answered: "Not at all. That girl occupies my thoughts no more than any other woman. To me they are all beautifully bound books which I know not how to read." The same friend tells us: "In his love for the holy virtue, John Neumann shone a model for all. His whole demeanor was modest; his glance never rested on dangerous objects. He never jested with females, nay, I am certain that he never exchanged a useless word with any one of them. When questioned, he answered, and that was all. Not even under the pretext of piety or edification did he lay aside his reserve in his communications with the opposite sex. Few knew the nobility, the elevation of Neumann's soul. He was a diamond which from lack of outward polish was all the more precious in the sight of God, all the dearer to those privileged ones who enjoyed his friendship." The reminiscences of another friend end with these words: "The more deeply versed in human nature were our professors, the more able, just, and pious, the more was Neumann respected and honored by them."

Another dangerous rock against which many young men suffer shipwreck John Neumann carefully avoided, viz., the neglect of the Sacraments. In those early years he often approached the Heavenly Banquet, for which he prepared with extraordinary care. "I aimed most especially," he says of himself in the sketch of his life, "at deriving the greatest possible benefit from Holy Communion. The recollection of the piety that reigned in my father's house, of the devotion with which my mother prepared for Holy Communion, was for me the best guide. I was thus protected from those dangers and sins which cause the ruin of so many souls. I heard Mass daily, and never neglected my evening visit to the Most Blessed Sacrament. This was the pious custom of many of my fellow-students."

CHAPTER III.
The Seminary at Budweis.

WE have seen that John Neumann in the course of his studies was in danger of losing his vocation, not indeed by his own fault, but through unfair treatment on the part of his professors. Almighty God, however, who had marked out for him a very high destiny, had regard to the uprightness of his intentions, and made use of the pious mother to protect the docile son.

After eight years of diligent study he completed his classical and philosophical course, obtaining to his own and his parents' satisfaction the highest testimonials of exemplary diligence and irreproachable conduct. The joy of his friends was further enhanced by the thought that in four years more he would leave the theological seminary a priest. But a great and unlooked-for trial was in store for the young graduate. The youth so highly privileged by God, who had been marked out, even in early boyhood, for the clerical state, must now prove that vocation and strengthen his natural inclination to virtue. The Christian mother, ever watchful over her boy's interests, was still to be the guiding star to light him on to his high destiny. We cannot but rejoice in beholding young Neumann following, despite all obstacles, the path marked out for him by Divine Providence. With the docility of a child he allowed himself to be led by the hand of his Heavenly Father. In his autobiography he speaks as follows: "When, at the close of my philosophical course, I had to make choice of theology, jurisprudence, or medicine, an incident occurred which made me incline toward the last-named. Out of eighty or ninety applicants for theology but twenty were to be accepted, and that only on the best testimonials, the highest recommendations. Now, this offering of recommendations for such a purpose I regarded as an innovation; consequently I would use no effort to obtain them. In this uncertainty as to the choice of a profession, I arrived home in the autumn holiday of that year, and found to my surprise that my father was not disinclined to my going to Prague for the study of medicine, although such a step would entail considerable expense. My mother, however, was quite dissatisfied with the arrangement; the very thought of it saddened her. I represented to her my inability to procure recommendations, as I was not acquainted with any prominent personages. But she would not listen to such reasoning. She urged me to send a petition to the Episcopal Consistory, saying that God would help me. In compliance with her wish I drew up a petition for admission, and sent it by a special messenger to the Council. Without recommendations, simply at my own request, I was admitted to the seminary, and from that moment the temptation to devote myself to the study of medicine disappeared. Even my favorite pursuits, physics, astronomy, etc., I gave up almost entirely and without regret."

Thus did God reward Neumann's childlike obedience. But the evil spirit, not discouraged by the failure of his plans, approached the youth with other temptations, and sought to seduce him by earthly joys. The children of the world, under the mask of friendship, tried to dissuade him from choosing the clerical state, a state fraught with pain, void of pleasure. Let him, they said, employ his talents and acquirements for the world, which alone holds out prospects of a position of ease, honor, and happiness. But these and kindred illusions had no other effect upon him than to call up a smile. Enlightened from on high, he understood the vanity of the transient things of earth.

On All-Saints, 1831, Neumann began the study of the sacred sciences. The seminary was small and could accommodate only the alumni of the last two years' theological course; so Neumann during his first two years had lodgings in a private family.

And now his soul, thirsting for knowledge, drank deep draughts from the clear fountains of theology; his zeal for study increased. The natural sciences were still pursued, but only as secondary objects; for, following the dictates of conscience, he applied first of all to what he knew to be of obligation. Hence his efforts were crowned with success, and his professors praised his diligence. That they were pleased with his progress may be gleaned from the fact of his being allowed to engage in other studies. He tells us in his journal: "My favorite occupation during my first year of theology was the study of the Old Testament, ecclesiastical history, Hebrew, etc., which afterward proved of incalculable benefit to me. My professors encouraged me, and, to their credit be it said, they all had, with the exception of one who was inclined to Josephism, a good spirit; they were stanch adherents of Holy Church. They were, also, competent instructors. With great facility and in a short time one might acquire under their direction much useful and practical information."

That his superiors were satisfied with their young student is also clearly manifest in the fact of their permitting him in his first year of theology, July 21, 1832, to receive the tonsure and minor orders.

A fellow-student, speaking of this period, says: "His acquirements in every theological department were thorough and comprehensive. The Holy Scriptures were his daily bread. He had a copy of the Vulgate in several small volumes. No fact of the Old Testament, no biblical character, was unfamiliar to him; there was no passage of Scripture that he could not quote. The students used to amuse themselves in cross-questioning one another on dates, localities, personages, facts mentioned in the Bible, upon which they raised objections, debated on the proper application of different passages—in a word, engaged in animated discussions. Their enthusiasm was enkindled by Professor Koerner's practical explanations of the Sacred Text. In these discussions Neumann showed himself fully equipped for every encounter, ready for any question that might be proposed. By such practices his stock of knowledge increased like a stream swollen in its course by the inflowing of many tributaries. But with it all he was ever the modest, retiring youth, aiming only at the acquisition, not at the display, of learning."

Behold another communication from one of his contemporaries: "Neumann sustained, in Budweis, a theological discussion of several hours with the Professor of Moral Theology, a man justly esteemed the most able in the seminary. At the close of the disputation the professor remarked: 'Had a stenographer taken down Neumann's defence, any theological journal might insert it in its columns.' Next to the Holy Scriptures, dogmatic theology was his favorite study. He had a copy of Peter Canisius' "Summa Doctrinæ Christianæ," with notes, which he studied until he made it entirely his own. In questions involving an explanation of some scriptural text the students unanimously appealed to him; for he either knew it by heart or could point to the page on which the solution might be found."

At the beginning of his second year of theology the designs of Almighty God over young Neumann became more manifest; he was gradually being prepared for his high vocation. Grace illumined his intellect and inflamed his heart. He understood that he was called to labor at the salvation of souls in the far-off regions of America. He lent an attentive ear to the voice of God; his noble and generous soul responded to the call of grace. The Professor of Holy Scripture, Rev. Father Koerner, to rouse in his pupils a love for the study of the Bible, was accustomed to speak in enthusiastic terms of the Apostle to the Gentiles. In glowing words he depicted his labors and sufferings for the glory of God and the salvation of souls.

It so happened that one of John's friends, fired with the desire of imitating the Apostle, and his attention being directed by the reports of the St. Leopold Society to the vast field offered the missionary in America, resolved to devote himself to that work. He soon made known his resolution to Neumann. The latter, to prove his friend's earnestness, bantered him a little on the subject. But no long time elapsed before he, too, expressed his determination to accompany him. "Do you know that I am going with you to America?" he said one day. "Yes, such is my fixed intention."

This most important resolve is thus noticed in his journal: "In my second year of theology I began to read the annals of the St. Leopold Society. The letters from Rev. Father Baraga and other German missionaries in North America charmed me. One day, as G—— and I were walking along the banks of the Moldau, the thought came to us to set out for America as soon after ordination as we should have obtained some practical knowledge of our priestly duties. We invited two or three of our fellow-students to take part in our enterprise; but, though admiring our resolution, they were unwilling to accompany us. I suppose it was not their vocation. From that day my resolution was so firm, my desire so lively, that I could think of nothing else."

Such a resolution we must pronounce grand and heroic, when we reflect on the time of its adoption and weigh well the circumstances connected with it. In 1833 America was looked upon as little more than a vast wilderness, a land of privations, sufferings, and persecutions, offering to the missionary no other prospect than that of sacrificing health and life for the glory of God and the salvation of souls. Bohemia had not yet sent out its priests, its young seminarians had not yet crossed the Atlantic, and the fact of emigrating to America as a laborer in the vineyard of the Lord was thought equivalent to seeking martyrdom. Though the actual state of things in America was not quite so bad, still there existed for the Catholic missionary many hardships and privations. From this time the most engrossing thought of the two young friends was their missionary project and the means of carrying it out. Prudence demanded secrecy. Their plans were disclosed to only a few special friends, and Mr. and Mrs. Neumann for nearly three years had no suspicion of what was almost exclusively occupying their son's mind. Henceforth all Neumann's aspirations aimed at one object—to become a worthy and efficient missionary. This object, he thought, could be accomplished only by courageous self-denial, by assiduous prayer, by diligent study, and unlimited trust in the help of God.

He began to prosecute his studies with still greater zeal, and to devote himself to prayer with such fervor and perseverance that both students and professors looked on in wonder.

Young Neumann was of the opinion that a missionary should, as far as possible, be able to speak all living languages; consequently he eagerly sought every opportunity to perfect himself in the same. The right to allow some of his seminarians to study at the Archiepiscopal Seminary at Prague had been conceded to the Bishop; and, as the students of this institution frequented the university, Neumann hoped that there he would find superior advantages for acquiring English and French. He petitioned for a transfer to the Seminary of Prague, which favor was readily granted.

CHAPTER IV.

At the Archiepiscopal Seminary of Prague.

JOHN NEUMANN left the seminary at Budweis after two years of successful study, and went to Prague in 1833, there to spend two years more in theology. Soon, however, he regretted the change. "The Right Rev. Bishop," he says in his journal, "permitted me to leave Budweis in order to finish my studies at the Archiepiscopal Seminary of Prague. But at the latter place I met a great disappointment. I had just begun to visit the French school at the Clementine, when an order was published by the Archbishop prohibiting seminarians attending the lectures. I could not study English, for this language was not taught at the university. Nor was I satisfied with the professors of dogmatic, moral, and pastoral theology. The first was more against the Pope than for him; yet, as the objections which he advanced were most absurd, he could do but little harm. The second was too philosophical to be understood by his hearers. The third was a thorough Josephist. I had to do violence to myself even to listen to them, for the absurdity of their treatment of those subjects I fully understood; much less could I accept their opinions, which I regarded as heterodox. It is a matter of regret that in such institutions so much is done to preserve the splendor of learning instead of diffusing good Catholic and useful knowledge. I was, therefore, heartily glad when, after the examinations, I was, in August, 1835, allowed to return to Budweis."

Among the papers written at that time by Neumann we find a dissertation on the infallibility of the Pope, which point he defended most strenuously, though his professor favored the views of Fabronius and the Gallicans. This paper is an answer to a former fellow-student of Budweis who asked Neumann's opinion on Papal Infallibility, which at that time was not an article of faith. From this document we see that Neumann, even in his third year of theology, set forth his arguments plainly and solidly; that he was imbued with childlike docility, and that his judgments in questions of mere opinion were decided.

As we have gathered from Neumann's own words, he hoped to find at the University of Prague an opportunity of perfecting himself in French and English. His disappointment we have seen. English appeared to him indispensable for one who would labor successfully as a missionary in America, and now he had no other resource than to apply to these languages by private study. He did so, and attained so great proficiency that all who knew him were astonished. A fellow-student relates that, at the close of the school-term, Neumann applied for examination in French. When the professor turned to him with the words, "You never attended my lectures," Neumann replied in excellent French that he had studied in private and now wished to be examined. The professor admitted him to examination, from which the young candidate came forth with the certificate "First Class with distinction." "Every theologian," Neumann used to say, "should learn French, if only through respect for the ascetic and theological works written in that language."

English also engrossed his attention, and, in his eagerness to speak it correctly, he went so far as to call upon some English workmen in a factory. They were delighted with the student's great desire to learn their language, and they did all in their power to help him in its attainment. It was not long before this assistance was unexpectedly withdrawn, and he was again thrown on his own resources. His efforts, however, were soon crowned with success, as his aptitude for languages was very great. His journal of that period furnishes us with a proof of this, for a large part of it is in French and much of it in English. It contains but few errors in the construction of those languages, errors which are usually overcome only after long and continued practice. He had begun Italian years before at the gymnasium, and he soon made such progress that he both spoke it and wrote it with ease. He loved to read the works of St. Alphonsus in Italian.* He made numerous extracts from them, some of which we find among his papers. The beautiful work entitled "The Way of Salvation" he translated into German with the twofold intention of benefiting himself and others. It was published by Rev. Father Dichtl. He afterward mastered Spanish, in which he read with profit the works of St. Teresa and the letters of St. Francis Xavier. From these, also, he made copious extracts. At the time of his theological studies they comprised at least thirty-eight books.

The study of Latin and of Greek was obligatory at the gymnasium, and by continued practice he attained facility in the use of both languages, as his journal and scientific treatises on different subjects testify. Whilst at the seminary he undertook the study of modern Greek, and skilfully translated the Greek text of the Bible into three and even four modern languages at one and the same time. In his fourth year of theology he turned his attention to Hebrew, and with such success that he was soon able to meet every difficulty and give clear explanations to all that sought his aid. Add to these his own native tongues, the German and Bohemian, and we find Neumann, even as a student, familiar with eight languages.

With good reason could he make the following asser-

---

* The saint at that time had not yet been canonized.

tion in a letter written in 1834 to his family: "If I do not mistake, it is Catherine's turn to write me a letter. Let her begin very soon. The letters need not be painted; as I am familiar with eight languages, I shall undoubtedly be able to read hers. She always wrote a neat hand. Let her set to work at once."

It will not be a matter of surprise to us if, with so ardent a desire for knowledge, young Neumann scarcely allowed himself sufficient time for corporal needs. When at home in vacation he not unfrequently had his book before him at meals, and so preoccupied was he that he forgot to eat. When addressed by his parents or any other member of the family he was often at a loss as to the subject of conversation, and for this he received many a reproof.

It happened once that, after spending, according to custom, the greater part of the night in study, all around him suddenly grew dark. He groped for the candle in order to relight it, but scorched his hand in the flame. The light was still burning, but his sight had failed. The strain upon his eyes had been too great, and from that time he was forced to use glasses.

Neumann understood the art of landscape-painting both on paper and glass, and great was his delight when able to present one of his own productions to his friends. He displayed some talent also for portrait-painting; and several excellent pictures of his friends painted by him are carefully preserved to this day, treasured memorials of the reverend artist. He cared not to have his own picture taken, and to the entreaties of some of the students to that effect he answered that it was sufficient for him to be remembered in their prayers. The largest and most important painting he has left us is a faithful representation of his native city and its environs. With this piece of genuine art is associated an act of virtue far more valuable than the picture itself. The young artist had bent perseveringly over his work during an

At the Archiepiscopal Seminary of Prague.

entire vacation, had laid on such colors as best corresponded to the reality, and had earnestly watched the effect produced by each new touch of his brush; at last the work was completed, to the great admiration of the beholders. Long and approvingly did they gaze upon it, now in the whole, now in its parts. It so happened that, in his too great eagerness, one of its most sincere admirers broke the glass and very seriously injured the picture itself. Not the least sign of anger did he exhibit who for so many hours had devoted time and skill to its perfection, but, stepping quietly forward, he gently set about protecting his work from further accident. As long as that picture exists, the marks of the damage it then sustained will bear evidence to John Neumann's patience and self-control.

CHAPTER V.

His Piety as a Seminarian.

LET us now speak of the interior life which Neumann led as a seminarian. His fellow-students have recorded many beautiful traits of his piety. His friend A—— gives us the following:

"Although humility, meekness, and mortification, all the virtues, in fact, seemed natural to him, and for the same reason less meritorious; yet, at the beginning of the year 1833, when he knew that it was his vocation to become a missioner, they assumed a more perfect character. To his lively faith was joined heart-felt piety. Both were genuine; he knew not hypocrisy; both sprang from the depths of his soul, and both were concealed as much as possible from the eyes of men. No one ever remarked in John Neumann the least singularity, not even in prayer. He entered and left the church at the specified hour; he punctually performed whatever was prescribed for all the faithful in general; but in secret he practised many mortifications, especially during the last two years of his student-life. Many an hour of the night, even during the depth of winter, did he spend on his knees in fervent prayer. His obedience to his superiors and professors was sincere; but he never cringed, never flattered, never displayed any noticeable attachment toward them. Had they been asked what they thought of him, they must have answered: 'We know nothing particular of him. He does not distinguish himself in any way from others.' The order prescribed the students he kept most faithfully; the keenest observer would have failed to detect in him the least infringement of rule. 'It is the rule, it must be kept!' clinched every difficulty on the score of college regulations. In the absence of superiors, he spoke and acted as he would have done in their presence. If I review those ten years during which I was on intimate terms with him, to discover what were Neumann's faults, I should find only one imperfection, and that was a little obstinacy in clinging to his own opinions. In the case of a young man, clear-sighted and given to deep thought, whose conclusions are generally correct, this failing is quite natural. Indeed, without such adherence to one's views there can be no thorough work, no surmounting of difficulties; in a word, the practice of virtue itself becomes almost an impossibility."

The foregoing statement is fully endorsed by others of his fellow-students. One writes:

"As John Neumann increased in knowledge, he treated his body with a severity that often excited our astonishment; for instance, he frequently denied himself food and watched entire nights in the open air. Such severity on his part appeared to me, I must confess, asceticism altogether too strict. It was only at the close of his theological course, and when he was preparing for missionary life, that I understood his object in devoting himself to the study of languages and the practice of such mortifications."

Another friend testifies:

"Unaccustomed as he had ever been to a life of ease, yet Neumann strove to inure himself to still greater mortification. When others loudly complained of the seminary fare, he was never heard to utter a word of dissatisfaction; he even shared his portion of food with one of the poor students. If the day proved insufficient for the tasks assigned him, a part of the night, yes, even entire nights were stolen from sleep and devoted to their accomplishment. When at last he found himself actually overcome by sleep, he would put several chairs together and rest for a few hours on this uninviting couch. He also passed many nights in prayer and meditation before the Most Blessed Sacrament, especially before and after Holy Communion. Daily meditation he never omitted. In the year 1835 some gentlemen presented themselves at the seminary, to offer on the part of the government the position of Foreign Secretary to any one of the aspirants to holy orders who possessed the requisite qualifications, viz., a knowledge of languages. All eyes turned toward John Neumann, who, however, betrayed not the least desire for a post at once honorable and lucrative. Astonished at his unaccountable indifference, I begged him to inform me of his intentions for the future; what career had he mapped out for himself. He looked at me smiling, and answered, 'Guess.' 'Well,' I replied, 'I suppose it is nothing less than the life of a missionary in America.' He made no comment on my conjecture, but requested me to remain with him in the study-hall after evening prayers. I was all impatience for the appointed moment, so eager was I to hear what he had to communicate. At last evening came, prayers were said, and, after the other students dispersed, Neumann and I stood together at a western window looking out on the clear starlit sky. Like an experienced astronomer, he pointed to the worlds above us; but I paid little attention. His delay in coming to the point only increased my curiosity. Then he spoke of America, of the actual state and the future prospects of the Church there, remarking that the harvest was great, the laborers few. He referred to the missionaries, and at last acknowledged his own settled resolve to labor in that portion of his Lord's vineyard. I could not repress my tears of joy as I leaned over to press my lips to his hand. He begged me to keep his secret, as the fulfilment of his desires depended upon his parents' consent; meanwhile he would pray God to incline their hearts to the sacrifice."

Though Neumann's contemporaries offer us so much to admire in his life and labors, yet we find in his own journal subjects for still greater edification. Therein are noted down his secret thoughts and aspirations, the interior life of his soul. It is to be regretted that only a part of this journal is extant, and even of this part we must, in order not to exceed the limits of our task, give only a few extracts. His record refers to the last two years of his student-life, and affords us a glimpse of the interior workings of his mind and heart.

His two years at Prague proved a true novitiate of suffering which prepared him for his subsequent career.

From earliest boyhood, his most earnest desire had been to love and serve God; and as years passed, and the conviction of being called to the missionary life in America took possession of his soul, he felt that his first and holiest duty was to confirm himself in the practice of virtue. None other than a high degree of divine love could satisfy the longings of his soul, and the persevering efforts he made for its attainment find a parallel only in the lives of the most saintly.

By serious meditation upon the infinite perfections of God and his own miseries he arrived at true and solid humility. This virtue he recognized as the foundation of all others, and many were the prayers he uttered for its acquisition. One day he thus addresses his own soul: "O my soul, where wast thou twenty-five years ago? No one then knew that, created to the image of God, thou wast to have an existence; where, then, wast thou? Not in heaven, not in the abyss. Thou didst not exist, neither couldst thou call thyself into existence. Almighty God created thee! Thou wast *nothing;* thou couldst not even cry to God to call thee forth from nothing. Thou wast less than a drop of water, less than a grain of sand. God could have made thee a blade of grass, a plant, a worm, a bird, to exist for a time in His honor and then to fall back into thy original nothingness. But this He did not do. Thou canst turn to thy Creator, thou canst love Him, thou canst thank Him, since thou dost exist, since thou wilt exist to glorify Him forever. Ah, with what docility ought I not to correspond to the end for which I was created! Teach me, O Lord, to praise Thee!"

Let us hear the cry of his heart when he petitions for humility, when he invokes the blessed in heaven for the same: "O Jesus, my divine, my most amiable Teacher, teach me humility and resignation to Thy most holy will! I ask with confidence. Thou didst grant me temporal favors when I called upon Thee; Thou wilt not now reject my prayer for spiritual ones. True, the favor I now beg is infinitely superior to any temporal one, and I am altogether unworthy to receive it; yet it is Thy will that I should be humble, be really humble with sincere, heart-felt humility. Grant it, dear Jesus, that I may be more conformable to Thee! Grant it, my beloved Saviour, my most amiable Teacher! O Mary, Mother of mercy, whose help I so sensibly experienced to-day, pray to thy Divine Son for me, a poor sinner; beg Him to make me humble! Oh, how humble thou wast! thou, the purest of virgins; thou, my powerful mediatrix! Thou, O most holy among the children of Adam; thou, Immaculate Mother of God, thou didst declare thyself the handmaid of Him whose Mother thou wast! Behold, my dear heavenly Mother, how gladly I would devote myself to thy Divine Son that His will may also be mine! But my pride, my self-esteem, my vanity, are always against me. I fear them, and yet I allow them to surprise and deceive me so often. Oh, how this afflicts me! O Mary, O refuge of sinners, if I were only sincere when I beg of thee to obtain for me humiliations! But alas! whilst praying for such helps to humility, I fear the granting of my prayer. I clearly see the better things, I even desire their possession, and yet I shrink from what alone can give me true humility! Behold my trials, my combats, in this valley of tears! O my dearest Mother, if to be freed from this body of death would give God glory, how gladly would I not lay down my life! Yes, and gladly would I lay it down for the attainment of humility. But what do I say? My life? Is it anything praiseworthy to give as a ransom from the slavery of sin, that existence which sin renders burdensome to me? O Jesus, meek and humble God-man, my Teacher, teach me to be humble! Regard not the rebellious struggles of him who has been confounded! Pardon his vexation when insulted, his tears when neglected! Let me everywhere know and adore Thy holy will! O my Guardian Angel, lead me to the practice of humility! Help me to become more like unto thee, more like unto my best friend, my most merciful Lord Jesus Christ! And ye, my holy patrons, St. Joseph, St. Francis Xavier, St. Vincent, pray for me! Ye taught humility by word and deed. Take me for your disciple, that I may become worthy of being the least and last of the servants of my Lord Jesus Christ. Amen!"

Neumann not only prayed for humility; he was, moreover, careful to repress every craving after honor or distinction. The following lines betray the feelings that dictated them:

"The happy events of last week, the scene at the house of Professor M——, my meeting with the Englishman, very greatly excited my ambition and vanity. There is, perhaps, a great struggle in store for me. O God, have mercy on me! O Jesus, grant the victory to humility! Grant that I may, at last, obtain this fundamental virtue, for I dread humiliations, the only means of destroying in me my thirst for fame!"

Mindful of his Divine Master's words, "He that hath My commandments and keepeth them, he it is that loveth Me,"* he put forth his best endeavors toward their fulfil-

---

*St. John xiv. 21.

ment in deed as well as in word. From childhood he had scrupulously avoided sin; and in early manhood his whole aim was to divest himself of his faults and imperfections. Sincerely, and with exactitude peculiar to himself, he daily examined his conscience, calling himself to account for all his thoughts, words, and actions, scrutinizing his inclinations and desires. He spared self-love in nothing. He deplored even his involuntary faults, which, in the light of God's infinite sanctity, he called his sins, his crimes, his sacrileges; and, with heartfelt sorrow, he begged for grace and pardon. To propitiate God's mercy, he imposed upon himself penances which were scrupulously performed; and, having discovered the cause of his relapses, he made firm resolutions for the future. Conscious of his own weakness, he called the angels and saints to his aid, but most frequently he had recourse to the Blessed Virgin. "O my Mother Mary," he cried, "Mother of my God, turn not thy eyes from me on account of my sins! I desire to love thee like a little child, but I am not worthy that thou shouldst think of me. How can I say that I love thee, when my sinful life proves the contrary? I weep; but what do such tears as mine avail? Do they console me, a sinner? Are they tears of penance? Alas, how insignificant is my penance compared with my sins! O Mother, help me whose sins crucified thy Son!"

Thus did he struggle courageously and perseveringly against his inclinations to sin, against his real defects. He complains in strong terms of his deviations from truth, as he termed certain involuntary inadvertencies of speech.

"O my God," he writes, "do Thou accept, at least for the present, my earnest desire not to offend Thee, instead of the well-merited penance from which my obstinacy still recoils. Hear, O my Divine Teacher, hear my prayer! Teach me how to speak, for I am ignorant of the art! Permit me not to fall into temptation! My conscience shrinks from falsehood, but alas! my God, how can I avoid such faults? O Thou, the All-Holy, the All-Wise, direct my speech! If it be Thy will, O my Jesus, that I should communicate with my fellow-creatures, grant me the necessary qualifications for gaining their confidence; but if such be not Thy holy will, grant me patience to bear the confusion in store for me!"

On October 4, 1834, he made a vow to fast one day for every exaggeration in speech of which he found himself guilty. A day or two after, he purchased some fruit; on returning with it to his rooms, he encountered the president of the seminary, who playfully accosted him: "Are you going to eat all that yourself?" "No," answered Neumann, "I am going to share with L——." Now, previously to the president's remark, Neumann had formed no actual intention of sharing the fruit; the resolve to do so was made only when unexpectedly interrogated. He did, indeed, divide the fruit with his friend, but that evening his remorse found vent in such lamentations as these: "O my soul, how hast thou fallen to-day! How deeply hast thou fallen into the sin of falsehood! Oh, how hateful is this vice! To-morrow will be for me a fast! O God, grant me grace to fulfil my resolution!"

One day the prefect questioned each seminarian as to the number of languages he understood. Neumann, taking the word in its strictest sense, answered in his turn, "Three." But soon after he reproached himself with having exaggerated, and begged pardon of God for his two offences, one of exaggeration, the other of pride.

How great were his fervor and devotion in celebrating the festival of Christmas! Daily did he hold long colloquies with the Infant Jesus. One year, about three days before Christmas, to his great confusion he failed in an address he had been chosen to deliver. In excusing himself he made use of an expression which, according to his ideas, was not strictly truthful. Intense was his sorrow, and many are the lines of his journal we find devoted to its expression. Among other things, he says:

"Dear Infant Jesus, I must give Thee back to Thy Mother; I am no longer worthy to bear Thee in my arms! Ah, miserable indeed I would be, were I to die in this sin! The dear little Jesus in His crib weeps over my offences."

All are familiar with the fact that students occasionally amuse themselves at the expense of their masters. One day Neumann joined in a laugh raised against a certain professor; but soon recovering himself, he resolved to do penance for his fault. "My penance for this sin is far too trifling," he writes. "I feel that divine love has been diminished in my soul. I perceive the abyss opened by it, O my God, between Thy glory and my ever-increasing malice. Have mercy on me!"

Although every page of his journal is a proof of Neumann's indefatigable zeal, yet he sincerely regarded himself as an indolent, useless servant. "My predominant passion," he says, "is sloth in the fulfilment of my duties. I perform them only from dread of remorse. O Spirit Sanctifier, grant that never more may I insult Thy presence and degrade myself by sloth! Give me, O Jesus, more earnestness in striving after perfection; give me more humility! I ought willingly to relinquish everything that might prove a hindrance to me in imitating Thee." Here follow resolutions to devote the time after morning prayers to his prescribed studies. Soon, however, we meet fresh self-accusations on account of new failures:

"I resolved to devote myself after prayers to my regular duties, and an interior voice urged me to the fulfilment of my promise; I also begged Thee, O my God, for the grace to overcome my self-love to-day: and yet, behold, something quite the opposite of my good resolution! My sinful conscience knows no rest. O my Jesus,

I have rendered myself unworthy of Thy grace!" Next comes a resolution to deprive himself of bread both at breakfast and supper whenever he failed in his duties. Again he laments:

"O my Jesus, once more I have separated from Thee by my disobedience. I have again broken my resolution to study at fixed hours. Pardon me, my God, pardon this my great sin!"

Later on he accuses himself: "To-day I neglected my morning prayers. My God, to what may not this lead me! O my God, change my joy into bitterness, that I may weep over my sins!"

Once he fell asleep whilst preparing for confession. "O God," he cried, "will not this disrespect be the cause of my eternal damnation?"

Such tenderness of conscience greatly displeased the evil one, and he endeavored to check young Neumann's ardent zeal. But Satan's efforts proved fruitless, as the journal testifies: "God often permits me, for my greater humiliation, to fall into despondency. Then rise up before me all the sins of my past life, my hardness of heart, the thought of God's justice, etc., and I feel as if I should die of grief. This gives place, in turn, to hellish pride and vanity, which whisper, 'You do not commit so many faults; your sins are not so great as those of others. You perform such or such a good work; you avoid such and such evil ones. Do not be so troubled; be not so discouraged!' Ah, Satan, how foolish thou art! True, I am not a murderer; but am I not constantly committing great sins in little things? God has enlightened me. He has taught me how pleasing virtue is to Him, and how hateful vice, though to thee, O wicked spirit, the latter is more acceptable! Heaven and hell lie open before me; and yet I crucify Christ anew, I persevere in my wickedness, I heap crime upon crime! O merciful God, whither shall I flee from Thy wrath? Thy immensity fills heaven and earth, whilst I disgrace both. Where shall

I hide myself? Thou heapest graces upon me, and I continue a malefactor, a monster in human form. Alas, my Jesus! Thou didst pray for Thy executioners. Behold at Thy feet one of them! Have mercy on me! Thou art peacefully enthroned in the hearts of Thy saints, but my heart is the foul haunt of Satan. O Lord, my God, have mercy on me! Break the hard rock of my heart, but be merciful to me! Pardon the work of Thy hands! My soul, where art thou? How far removed art thou from salvation! Woe is me! O Jesus, I have driven Thee from Thy own possession, I have cast Thee out of my heart! Oh, what misery! My God, be merciful!"

His contrition, being true and supernatural, was also effective. Hence the following petition: "Since Thou art so good, O my Jesus, grant me true compunction for my sins! Give me to taste the bitterness of Thy chalice! Let one drop of Thy baptism fall upon my head, that in some small degree I may experience the pain my sins have caused Thee!"

His untiring supplications were at last rewarded. The love of God, which, as we have seen, early possessed his heart, began to take new increase in the midst of trials and temptations of divers kinds.

We have already stated that his sojourn at Prague was for Neumann a time of suffering; but, though the thought of those two years was a bitter one in after-life, yet they were, on the whole, of inestimable advantage in the formation of his character.

The opinions of his fellow-students were entirely too liberal for one of Neumann's pious turn of mind, and their mode of life was little in accordance with the spirit of Jesus Christ. This diversity of sentiment rendered him an object of contempt and ridicule in their sight; they regarded him as one given to eccentricity. The unkind treatment he experienced from them pained young Neumann's sensitive heart, and the pleasing reminiscences of Budweis, where, as a student for ten years, he had made so many friends, only aggravated his present position. He writes:

"The thought of Rev. Father Dichtl and my friend A—— only increase my desolation; my tears flow every evening. Here I live in the midst of sloth and tepidity, which are a hindrance to my own advancement; and among the pious directors of Budweis no one is thinking of me. They have all forgotten me; I am sad and alone! Willingly would I bear it all, could I only advance in the spiritual life. My heart bleeds; I have no remedy. Abandoned and despised by all, I turn to Thee, O Lord! Oh, let me be ever, ever Thine, though Thou be deaf to my prayers, unmindful of my tears!"

Again we read: "X—— will have nothing more to do with me, he thinks me idle and unfaithful; and for this, O Jesus, mayest Thou be ever praised! The good despise me for my awkwardness, and the wicked for my apparent rigor, which they take for false enthusiasm. Gladly do I throw myself at Thy feet, O Jesus! Trample upon me; I deserve it, but do not cast me off from Thee!"

On December 10, 1834, one of the students read aloud in the study-hall a letter ridiculing Neumann's extravagant orthodoxy, as they termed his firm adherence to Holy Church. Its effect was to alienate many of his companions from him. In his examen that evening he thus alludes to the affront: "My self-love was roused. My God, what will become of me if I continue so sensitive? I am not yet ready to suffer with Jesus. O God, pardon me!"—and then and there he resolved to be revenged, but in a manner worthy of a Christian. "I find," he writes, "that pride, even on account of some seeming spiritual advantages, begins to show itself; a kind of jealousy gnaws at my heart. To humble myself, I will on every occasion offer my services to my brethren. Every time I meet any one of them I will, in spirit, lovingly kiss his hand as I would that of our

Lord Himself. I will also defend and excuse them whenever I possibly can."

We must conclude from these words that his love for his neighbor was true and sincere. In his humility he seeks and finds the cause of their unjust treatment, not in their ill-will, but in himself; he turns the insults heaped upon him to his own greater humiliation.

Quite differently, however, did John Neumann judge of things when God or His Holy Church was made the object of contempt.

"O Mary, my Mother," he one day exclaimed, "pray for me in this affair with D—— regarding Canisius, that, if it be God's holy will, our contention may cease!"

On another occasion he remarks: "A dispute arose at table which filled me with disgust. H—— ridiculed certain saints whose canonization he regards as the result of ignorance and superstition. I will withdraw as much as possible from all who love not Thee and Thy Church, O Jesus!"

Our straightforward and unpretentious student was generally misunderstood by his professors, who often, though unintentionally, increased his interior sufferings at this period. We have already caught a glimpse of his opinion of these gentlemen, and much of his suffering was due to the fact of his own inability to treat with the president as a child with its father. Daily do we find him lamenting this want of confidence in his superiors, though, in his humble estimate of himself, he seeks the cause in his own shortcomings.

"The president and all good people despise me," he writes. "My Jesus, my uncertain relations toward the president cause me great anxiety." And again: "My aversion for the president increases. I regret that he knows my most important secret, my intention of going to America. If I mistake in his regard, pardon me, O my God! I will be obedient to him, I will shield him from derision, I will try to bear him a Christian love."

May 10, 1835, he writes: "O Jesus, Thou didst permit me to-day to become better acquainted with the president through his criticism of Father Dichtl's article in the *Katholik*. Ah, my Father, do Thou win him to Thyself! He is Thy son. Hear my prayer in his behalf!" "To-day the president entered the museum whilst I was reading the Meditations on the Gospel. He glanced at the book and asked, 'Why do you occupy yourself with such reading?' 'You know the reason,' I answered. Then he continued, 'Are you serious in your resolve to be a missionary?' I replied in the affirmative. Now I must speak to him on this delicate matter; for, should he mention it to others, he might do much harm to the cause."

On April 13th he wrote with still greater freedom: "If sometimes I seek his company, he avoids me; he seems to despise me. Perhaps more than appearances are against me. Were it not for this misunderstanding, I would not feel as I do toward him, and he could give me much assistance. But his maxims, his guarded behavior, his carefully concealed intentions, his want of forbearance toward the erring, his apparently unsympathetic nature, which seems only to feign compassion,—all prevent my opening my heart to him. My God, forgive me if I sin against this zealous man! My own bad heart may be the cause of my unfavorable judgment of him; yet, so far, I have not been able to understand things otherwise, and I dare not act against my conscience. To consult another would infringe upon the respect due to him, and would help me little. The judgments of others might be still harsher, since, perhaps, even less than myself can they form an opinion of him."

Despite his reluctance, however, we find young Neumann a few days after disclosing his plans to the president, who, so far from discouraging him, suggested his entering the Society of Jesus. But soon again we meet the lines: "The president's sermon has wounded my heart. I like him now less than ever. O Jesus, Thou knowest my sad condition! Here I am without a guide, without an adviser. Lord, teach me how to pray that I may obtain what is so necessary for me, a guide in the spiritual life. I have none to console me in my falls, to counsel me in my doubt as to whether I should enter an Order or Congregation where I might live in perfect obedience; none to direct me in my efforts to amend my life, none to point out how I may become more pleasing to Thee. O my Jesus, in my desolation I cry to Thee! Hear my prayer, send me a good confessor!"

Neumann recognized the necessity of a spiritual guide in order to make progress on the road that leads to perfection; but no such director was to be found to assist him in his scruples and doubts. This uncertainty, this feeling of abandonment, added greatly to his mental sufferings at this epoch. With what fervent supplications did he not entreat God to send him an enlightened director! "To-morrow," he writes at the beginning of the scholastic term, "to-morrow I shall go to confession. I pray God that I may meet a confessor who will understand how to apply a remedy to my passions!"

His preparation for confession always comprised a prayer for his confessor: "O Jesus, enlighten my confessor that he may make known to me Thy will!" Again: "O Jesus, enlighten my confessor that he may understand the state of my soul! Oh, see how I wander without a guide in this labyrinth of doubt! To whom shall I apply for counsel? Where shall I find relief? O Lord, Thou knowest my heart with all its faults, but Thou also knowest that it is resigned to Thy holy will! Aid me in my misery!"

His temptations increased daily, whilst his efforts to attain perfection became more earnest.

"Would that I had some one to point out the sure way to Thee, O my Jesus! O my Divine Master, if Thou wert still on earth, I would seek Thee out, cast myself at Thy feet, and abandon to Thee my life and my soul! But, alas, I wander here an exile, far from my country, far from Thee! Thou hast established Thy Church, and she teaches me that if I fulfil Thy holy will, Thou wilt love me. Thou seest my heart, O Jesus! I am firmly resolved to follow Thee. Have mercy on me, O good Saviour!"

This spiritual guide whose assistance would have been of such benefit at this time was not to be found. John Neumann was to attain perfection without human aid and by the royal road of the cross. This was God's most holy will. His daily examen was always followed by an act of heart-felt contrition, which was greatly intensified when about to approach the tribunal of penance.

"My Lord Jesus," he cried, "behold me defiled by sin! Again have I stained the holy garment of purity which Thy Blood has so often cleansed. O Father, hear my prayer! Give me the true spirit of penance, that, through the humble supplication of my contrite heart, I may again receive pardon. Since my last confession, O my Jesus, I have fallen more frequently than usual! My incessant combats, my unholy desires, my tepidity and discouragement, have made me forget many great sins. My Jesus, I have not kept my word! I promised to advance, and lo! I have gone back. But do not Thou forsake me, though I have richly deserved to be rejected as obstinate and incorrigible. But what would become of me if Thou wert always angry with me? Behold me prostrate before Thee, O my God! My sinfulness weighs me down. My anguish Thou, the Omniscient God, alone knowest. Alas! Jesus, my God-Saviour, I dare not raise my eyes to Thee! How can I presume to ask pardon? I who have so often violated my word, so often returned to the mire of iniquity whence Thy love had drawn me! O my soul, my poor, cowardly soul, thou art crushed by thy load of sin! Take courage; thy Redeemer will console thee in thy wretchedness! Come, let us again approach His throne; let us again crave forgiveness. Jesus, my Lord and my God, I beg pardon for all my sins! Reject me not, although I have miserably broken my resolution of amendment. Mercy, my Jesus! I have no one to help me. Thou alone art my Lord and Saviour. Cast not off Thy wretched, sinful child, or he will be forever lost! From my heart I grieve for having offended Thee, O Jesus, and yet I am so cold that I fear my confession will not be a contrite one! O holy Mother of God, my guardian angel, my holy patron, intercede for me with my Judge, obtain for me the pardon of my sins! O Jesus, grant me the true spirit of penance; permit me not to make a bad confession! Pray for me, ye blessed spirits! My Jesus, have mercy on me! Amen."

His desire for weekly confession was real and sincere. He was impatient for the appointed day to arrive, for in the Sacrament of Penance he found calm for his troubled heart. Yet even this consolation was often withheld, as we discover by the following lines: "I long to confess to-morrow that I may regain my peace of heart, for my sins are continually before me. But Thou, my Lord and my God, Thou art my law! Do with me as is pleasing to Thee; I resign myself entirely to Thy will. Dost Thou wish me still to bear the pain of the withdrawal of Thy grace, be Thou forever praised! I will be more watchful, I will never forget Thee, I will love Thy Law as Thy gift to man; and since Thou art the best of fathers, I will be faithful in keeping Thy commandments. Teach me Thy will, O dearest Lord, that I may never waver but, trusting in Thy assistance, may begin and end all my works to Thy greater glory!"

On the following day, so eagerly longed for, so ardently hoped for, no confessions were heard. For this privation our pious student thus consoles himself: "No confessions to-day. What a disappointment for me! Now for eight days more I shall be restless and miserable. But I must not lose courage. Thou, O my most amiable Jesus, Thou dost sleep in the poor crib of my heart. Art Thou, perchance, weary of my incessant weeping over my sins? Forgive me, O Divine Babe! Whilst Thine eyes are closed in slumber, I will adorn Thy crib with the most lovely flowers. When Thou awakest, Thy little eyes will be delighted; Thou wilt be better pleased with Thy new home. Dearest Mother Mary, teach me how to adorn the dwelling of thy Divine Child! Thou art full of grace; the Lord is ever with thee! Angels and saints of God, help me! With the blue forget-me-not I will surround Thee, little Jesus; they are blue as Thine own loving eyes. Oh, do not Thou forget me on the great Day of Judgment! I will keep Thee alone before my eyes, for Thou art my God! On Thy breast, O Divine Infant, I will lay the white lily of purity and innocence, for Thou art the All-Holy. I will become like unto Thee. To it I will add the rose of love, as a proof that I sigh for Thy love alone. Oh, let me love Thee with my whole heart! It is a blood-red rose. Deign to purify me from my sins, cleanse me in Thy own precious blood! And, because of its sweet fragrance, I place beside the lily and the rose the humble little violet! Jesus, my Teacher, I am Thy slave, Thy disciple! Be Thou merciful to me! Grant me true humility; make me advance in Thy love! Sweet Babe, scarcely hast Thou begun to live when Thy cheek grows pale and on Thy eyelids tremble the glistening teardrops. Thou sufferest for me. Ah, do not reject me! I will never more offend Thee! What shall I do to regain Thy favor? Thou art my God, my Creator; I have nothing but what Thou hast bestowed upon me; but, behold, what I have I return to Thee! For Thee only will I live, Thee only will I love! What causes Thee joy shall be my joy, and all that Thou dost hate I will hate. See, my soul, how sweetly the Divine Infant slumbers! do thou watch and pray that He may love thee! Fear not that He will reject thee. Children are kind, they have no guile. But take care not to cause Him pain by any disobedience on thy part, not even by some slight carelessness; for He is also a God who has it in His power to punish thee!"

On February 14, 1835, Neumann made the general confession for which he had so long and so ardently sighed. He prepared for it with the full persuasion of its being one of the most important actions of his life. Urgent were the prayers he poured forth to his Divine Redeemer, and repeated his invocation of the saints, that he might accuse himself of all his transgressions with profit to his soul. We find him recording the momentous affair in the following words:

"O my God, it is accomplished; a Christian life has been begun! I have confessed all the sins of the past. Henceforth I will ask consolation neither of the world nor of Thee, O my God! Thou, my Divine Teacher, knowest whether consolation is useful to my soul or not. In dryness I will no longer be disturbed, but do Thou, my God, preserve me from presumption! Take entire possession of me. To Thee I consecrate all the powers of my soul and body, my whole being!"

After each confession we find a grateful and loving acknowledgment of the graces received.

"O my Jesus, Thou hast cleansed me from my sins! For this I rejoice, as I can now again love Thee as I once did. But yet, my God, my poor heart is not joyful, though it is contented. Yes, it is satisfied, since Thou dost treat it according to Thy mercy. Come, O my Lord, come and inflame my heart with love! Thy love raised Lazarus from the dead; Thy mercy has roused my soul from the lethargy of sin. Thy priest has loosened the bonds which bound me fast. Ah, truly, Thou must love me! Thou dost heal all the wounds of my soul at once. O Jesus, accept my thanks! Though they come from an arid, tepid heart, I know that Thou wilt not reject them. From this day I begin a new life! With the help of Thy grace I will be patient, diligent, and devout. Remind me, dear Lord, on occasions in which I may practise my good resolution. Hear my prayer, O Jesus, to love and praise Thee with my whole heart, with my whole soul, with all my strength! Mother of Jesus, pray to thy Son for me! Jesus, be with me! Jesus, stay with me!"

Almighty God was all in all to John Neumann. Several days previously to the happy one on which his Lord and Saviour, his only Love, was to enter his soul in Holy Communion he spent in devout preparation. The thanksgiving which followed was not less lengthy or fervent. No expressions seem adequate to depict his transports during this happy period. Sufferings and joys, consolation and desolation, were alike laid as a holocaust at the feet of his Divine Redeemer, to whom he again consecrated himself an obedient disciple and slave. To record the one-hundredth part of his edifying thanksgivings at such times would far exceed the limits of our work. A few will suffice to convey some idea of all. On November 22, 1834, he writes:

"My Lord and my God, once more am I to approach the altar of Thy Most August Sacrament; once more am I to receive the Almighty Creator of heaven and earth; once more receive the Most-High God in whose all-seeing eyes the seraphim are not pure; once more receive that Just Judge who knows my crimes better than I do myself; once more receive Him whose garments alone healed the sick! My God, what shall I do, since in Thy sight the angels themselves are not pure? What shall I, a sinner, do that I may not eat judgment and damnation to myself? O my God, my Redeemer, how is it that Thou dost desire to confer on me this great favor? Behold, I offer Thee my tears of penance and of love! I have naught else to offer. Deign to accept my heart and my will. Enlighten me, O Eternal Wisdom, that I may practise Thy teachings, that I may concur in the salvation of those whom Thou didst purchase at so great a price! Do with me what Thou pleasest, for all my desire is to fulfil Thy holy will. Ah, I know that Thou lovest me! Thou didst grant me to-day tears of love and of penance, for which, O Jesus, mayest Thou be ever blessed! I would ask Thee for many things, but, alas, I know not what to ask! O Father, give Thy children daily bread; forgive us our sins; lead us not into temptation, but deliver us from evil! Preserve Thy Holy Church, our good Mother! Direct our Holy Father the Pope; be merciful to all the faithful; enlighten unbelievers! Bless my parents, my brother, my sisters, my friend Schmid, and all my friends and enemies. And thou, my Heavenly Mother, accept my thanks for thy wonderful intercession! Be forever my refuge, my consoler! My loved patrons, whom I have chosen as intercessors at the throne of the Most High, come to my assistance! My holy guardian angel, my faithful guide, thou hast seen the tears that have flowed from my eyes—those eyes which were before so long without a tear; to thee I give them, that thou mayest present them to my Judge and Redeemer. Amen."

Neumann's love for God suffered no decrease even in seasons of great aridity. Behold the proof of it in the familiar language he addressed to Almighty God:

"True, I feel but little devotion; my soul is dry and sluggish; but yet, O Lord Jesus, I believe in Thee, I hope in Thee, I love Thee, and I grieve for having ever offended Thee! Behold my resolution to live entirely for Thee, to be patient in sufferings, diligent in the fulfilment of my duties, humble before Thee and my neighbor, and devout in Thy service. O my God, accept the sacrifice of my lowliness! Holy Immaculate Mother of my Jesus, pray for me, a poor sinner, that I may worthily receive my God!"

Here follows a prayer for the day of his Communion.

In it we see his love inflamed, his will strengthened by contact with his Eucharistic God: "O my Jesus, Thou hast come into my heart! I cannot weep for joy, because of the aridity of my soul, but I can protest that I love Thee above all things, O Jesus, Thou God of my heart! Before all the angels and saints, I promise that in trials and sufferings I will love Thee as much as in joy and consolation. Bless my work, rouse my courage, and, should it be Thy most holy will, help me to announce Thy divine teachings to the ignorant."

CHAPTER VI.

Trials and Sufferings.

ALMIGHTY GOD, finding His youthful disciple willing and capable of being received into the school of trial and purification—a school frequented only by His special favorites—treated John Neumann as a hardy soldier, or rather He sought, by severe discipline, to fashion him into such a soldier. For this end, his virtues were, one by one, to be tested and ennobled by temptation; consequently he began about this time to experience great disgust for prayer and the performance of daily duty. His soul entered into that utter darkness where faith and hope and love seem totally extinguished. He felt that God had forsaken, had entirely rejected him; and yet he bravely struggled on, resolved to love Him, and Him alone, as his Lord and Sovereign Master. But the anxiety he felt as to the reality of his love filled up the measure of his misery. In this painful state, with no one to direct him, God allowed him to remain a considerable time. It was precisely along this rough road, however, that he was to attain a high degree of humility and love. His journal now teems with amorous complaints: "Alas, I am in great distress! Last evening, after prayers, I lingered in the museum, reflecting on the love of Jesus for me and my own ingratitude toward Him. Tears of bitter sorrow fell from my eyes. In my misery I turned to the Blessed Virgin for aid; and I also addressed Jesus, whom I fancied by me. I besought Him to teach me how to act in order not to cast obstacles in the way of grace. But I waited uneasily for the sound of His voice in my soul; nay, my whole soul seemed to revolt against it. In my heart, I wished to hear nothing; my corrupt nature shrank from its whisperings. Then came the bitter thought that I do not love my Saviour, that I do not esteem Him, seeing that I do not receive Him oftener in Holy Communion. I was perplexed and uncertain as to whether this was an inspiration from God or a suggestion of the evil one. Now I believed it from God, and again I doubted. I was cast about in anguish of spirit. But, O my God, of this I am certain: I do feel a great desire to receive Thee more frequently. This is now my dearest wish, and yet I dread to enter upon a closer examination as to how I may effect it, in view of my relations to the president, to my confessor, and to my fellow-students. This unceasing attraction of grace on the one hand, and my own resistance on the other, cause me unspeakable pain. In my anxiety, I do not consult my love for Thee, O Jesus, because it would demand of me a firm resolution and a generous correspondence. Or does the evil one seek to place obstacles to my love for Thee? Ah! he will never succeed; for behold me, dearest Jesus, behold me awaiting Thy decision!"

After spending the Lent of 1835 in the devout meditation of our Lord's Sacred Passion, Neumann made, on Palm-Sunday, a cross of blessed palm, which he placed on his breast in memory of his suffering Redeemer. The enemy of salvation, enraged at his tender devotion, raised on the instant a storm of revolt in the heart of the young man, though he did not succeed in making him omit any of his penitential practices. The following effusions of love sufficiently express his sentiments at this period: "My dearest Jesus, to suffer something for Thy sake, and to bear Thee in constant remembrance, I placed on my breast a cross of blessed palm. Oh, what joy to suffer something for Thee, my suffering Saviour! But, alas, such things are trifles! Oh, that I could be burned alive, if only to love Thee more perfectly! O Sovereign Lord of my life, my mind, my soul, my whole being, O my Saviour and my God, send me great sufferings, that I may thereby better love and praise Thee! Ah, behold! since I placed that cross on my heart there have sprung up within me diabolical emotions and desires. But wherefore should this trouble me? Ought I not rather rejoice that, by despising their importunity, I may prove to Thee that I love Thee better than my body and its miserable pleasures? Thou, my Jesus, art my joy! My heart longs for Thee! Come, my Love, my All! If it be to Thy honor, let me become a missionary, that I may suffer for my sins and die for Thee, my Divine Master; nevertheless, not my will, but Thine be done!"

His tender and persevering supplications at last drew upon him the merciful regards of Almighty God, and obtained for him a favorable answer. The trials and sufferings which purify the soul on its road to perfection, which lead to the acquisition of perfect love, were freely bestowed upon him. The childlike narrative, culled from the daily record of his passing thoughts, tells us of his struggles and his love:

"Remorse pursues me!" he exclaims. "My Jesus, banish the demon of despair! My devotion has vanished, my tears are dried up, thoughts of my angel and of my patron no longer soothe my troubled soul! Even Thy remembrance, my Saviour, and that of Thy Blessed Mother, grow dim before my mental gaze. O Jesus, do not forsake me! Help me! help me! I am resolved not to omit a single one of my devotions!"

The greater his sufferings, the greater his struggles, the more fervent his prayers. "Hear me, O my God," he cried; "strengthen and increase my faith! Lead me not into temptation. O Jesus, Thou who hast said, 'My yoke is easy, My burden light,' have mercy on me! for wheresoever I turn my eyes, I see naught but obstacles and difficulties. Lord, pardon my impatience!"

A few days later we read: "O my God, this dreadful state has come on me again! O my Divine Teacher, make known to me the faults that have merited such punishment! Were my faith strong, I would thank Thee for my sufferings; but, alas, I feel only impatience, doubt, and discouragement!"

We cannot behold young Neumann's immediate recourse to his Heavenly Father in the midst of his mental sufferings without sentiments of edification; but still more are we touched by his childlike, trustful supplications when freed for a time from temptation:

"I am still incapable of meditation, but I feel the necessity of speaking to Thee, my highest Love! Do thou, my heart, open thyself to thy Lord. Receive Him; do not offend Him; do not force Him to separate from thee again. I foresee shame and disgrace, and the prospect fills me with dread; but Thou, my Jesus, art my strength! Thou wilt not permit him to pine away whom Thou hast once rescued from death. I am assaulted by the demon of discouragement and despair; but do thou, my soul, hold fast to Jesus. He will have mercy on thee! This temptation is like remorse of conscience; with difficulty is it distinguished from it, and with still greater difficulty is it overcome. Jesus, Thou knowest how much I love Thee; protect me from my enemy! How faint-hearted, how childish I am! Thou art all-powerful, my Jesus, and yet I am afraid! But I feel that Thou wilt soon grant me many great graces, since I have so little consolation on earth! All my comfort, all my joy must come from Thee. Worldlings may call me unhappy, but I will rejoice in Thee alone. Thou wilt free the poor sinner from his burden; Thou wilt receive him again into Thy favor. My heart longs for Thee! O my Jesus, if it be Thy will that these terrible temptations against faith should again assail me, I beseech Thee suffer me not to fall! Let me taste their full bitterness, but let me not fall! O my Lord, my God,

I cast myself entirely into Thy hands! Worn out by the struggle, I will rest beneath Thy cross; I will embrace it; I will kiss it as the symbol of my victory! O Mother Mary, pray for me, a poor sinner; pray for me in my desolation of soul! Jesus, be merciful to me! Amen."

On the following day he thus expresses himself: "All despise me, but I have deserved it. All avoid me,—the bad because I cannot countenance their wickedness; the good because they find in me only sin and imperfection. I am alone, despised by men, and in thy sight, O my Supreme Good, a most sinful creature! The joys of this world I hate, and of heavenly joys I am unworthy. My life is a joyless one!"

After several weeks of such spiritual desolation God enlightened and strengthened his soul, but only to prepare him for fresh sufferings. June 11, 1835, seems to have been a day of unusual spiritual gladness. That evening he wrote: "The study of the rubrics of Mass, and especially that of Canisius, warmed up my heart. True, I am not yet entirely relieved from my fears, but I feel far nearer to Jesus Christ. Ah, how sad has been my state for the past three or four weeks! I might have committed any sin, even the most horrible, had not God's mercy protected me! Truly the soul without God is nothing. My Jesus, my God and my King, to Thee do I return, since Thou dost call me!"

These sorrowful outpourings of a desolate spirit strongly remind one of St. Francis de Sales, who during his career as a student neared the brink of despair through a similar state of soul. And, like that great saint, we find young Neumann protesting in accents of love that he will never abandon his God: "The spark of faith and love is almost, if not wholly, extinguished in my soul. What shall I do without faith, without hope, without love? To whom shall I turn if my God casts me off,—if, on account of my sins, He withdraws from me the graces necessary for my salvation? My soul, what wilt thou do? Thy Redeemer has forsaken thee, perhaps forever. His merits are lost to a soul hardened in malice. Thou mayest knock at heaven's gate, but it will not be opened. Thy crimes have barred it against thee. Thy God loved thee, but thou didst flee from Him, and now He leaves thee to thyself—alone, alone, alone! No friend, no consoler will rise up to aid thee, for thou hast sinned against the whole world. O my Lord Jesus Christ, Thou hast indeed forsaken me on account of my sins, but I will never abandon Thee! My observance of Thy commandments will still be pleasing to Thee, and I will keep them as far as I am able. To transgress them would be to increase my misery."

The nearer Neumann approached the end of his desires, the sharper and more frequent became his trials. God permitted all kinds of temptations to combine their force-in order to torture his soul. Disgust for his vocation to the priesthood first assailed him. He speaks of it in these terms: "Self-love demands that I should renounce the priesthood, since its uninterrupted round of duties calls for the sacrifice of every earthly comfort and pleasure. Cowardice whispers that Jesus did not die for me, that I am a reprobate, that I shall be eternally unhappy; then, wherefore devote myself in this world to such a life of privation? Would that I could find some one to understand the state of my soul! If I felt sure of its being only a passing temptation, I would bear it patiently."

And now came the tempter, holding out as a snare to the young student's innocence the thought of carnal gratifications. His journal at this time records the following:

"Temptations against the holy virtue assail me. It is long since I was molested on this point. I imagined all such inclinations dead within me. Thank God! this temptation is more easily vanquished, since it is less subtle than pride, vanity, sloth, anger, etc., etc. O Queen of those virgins that follow the Lamb, intercede for me that I, too, may remain pure, that I, too, may one day gaze upon Thy Divine Son! Ye saints of my God, have compassion on me, a poor sinner! Pray for me that God may free me from my sins, that the garment of innocence and purity of heart may be mine!"

His earnest prayers and supplications were abundantly rewarded, not by a release from sufferings and temptations, but by the bestowal of that strong and dauntless love which always and in all occurrences seeks only the greater honor of God. Wherefore his actions from this time were performed with a spirit of greater generosity which sprang from a heart inflamed with purer love. No desire now animated him but that of loving and serving God, suffering and laboring for God; no other desire than that of being forever united with Him. He multiplied his penances and exercises of devotion; he spent much of his leisure time in church, heartily lamenting the sins of his life. He cries out in loving accents:

"How much do I not love Thee, O my Jesus! I love Thee with my whole soul, but yet 'tis not enough. The fear of being condemned on account of my sloth still haunts me. Would that I could die in fulfilment of Thy good pleasure, O Thou sweet Bridegroom of my soul! I have only one desire, that of being with Thee. My Lord Jesus, my Love, my All, gladly would I endure hunger, thirst, heat, and cold to remain always with Thee in the Blessed Sacrament! Would that I might unceasingly weep over my sins at Thy sacred feet!"

The following lines afford a beautiful example of his disinterested love for God:

"My joy of heart, my *feeling* of love for my Jesus, were very moderate to-day. When I felt my soul trembling under their influence, I asked Thee, my Jesus, to take such sweetness from me, and to give me instead the grace to avoid sin. And yet perhaps I was wrong in making such a request. Is it for me to determine which grace is the more advantageous to me?"

His communications with Almighty God were those of a loving child with an indulgent father:

"Where art Thou in my heart, O Jesus? Art Thou pleased with me? Do I not often pain Thee by my imprudence? Teach me how to amend my ways. Ah, how foolish I am! I forget that Thou art the Physician of the sick; wilt Thou not take pity on my fainting soul? Have patience with me still. I will aim at rooting out my bad habits. I rejoice to see others love Thee. Would that I could infuse into all hearts a burning love for Thee! How glorified wouldst Thou be on earth if every human heart were an altar, on which every human will were laid in perfect conformity with Thine, to be consumed by the fire of Thy love!" Again: "O Infant Jesus, I desire to love Thee, to love and embrace Thee with my whole soul! I desire to love Thee as Thy Holy Mother, Thy foster-father loved Thee! Oh, that I had their humility, their fidelity, their purity, confidence, and love! My Divine Redeemer, grant me these virtues!"

If our perfection depends upon our love for God, and if both are in proportion to our conformity to the Divine Will, we must conclude that John Neumann, even as a student, attained a high degree of sanctity. The accomplishment of God's good pleasure formed the object of all his aspirations. "O my God," he exclaims, "I have consecrated myself to thee! Do with me whatever is most pleasing to Thee!"

The gift of tears was again bestowed upon him, as we see by the following ingenuous remarks: "I cannot understand how it is that the fire of divine love, which is enkindled every evening in my long communings with Almighty God, can become extinguished during the night. The tears which I shed in such abundance after evening prayers must quench its flames, for in the morning I feel nothing but dryness." And yet we know how faithfully, even during the periods of his greatest interior troubles, he had embraced every opportunity to make himself worthy of that precious and exceptional grace, the gift of tears! With admirable tenderness of conscience he sought out the cause of any interruption to his childlike intercourse with God; and with deep contrition he deplored the same, firmly resolving to amend. Once after the usual lamentations respecting his spiritual aridity he added these words: "But I richly deserved it for reading a sonnet that was not quite proper. I should not have read it."

His great love for poetry led him to purchase a volume of Petrarch's sonnets, which, however, he afterward regretted in these terms: "Of what use will this work be to me? I did not invoke the light of the Holy Ghost; therefore I fell into the occasion of sin." For the same reason he resolved to give up the reading of Shakespeare, although he found it of great service to him in acquiring English. Horace came under the same ban, as we see by the following lines written on another occasion: "I was faithful to all my resolutions to-day until the evening, when I read one of Horace's satires. Its rhetorical beauty pleased me. But all profane books, especially if no mention is made in them of God, distract the soul and render it unfit for meditation. I am resolved, therefore, to give up such reading, or to indulge in it only when some real advantage is to be gained from it."

He had, on the other hand, a high appreciation of the benefit to be derived from the use of good books. On a certain occasion, after the erection of a raised seat for the reader in the refectory, his comments on the same end by these significant words: "It is truly wonderful how the reading of a good book revives piety, infuses the love of well-doing, and affords subject-matter for conversation on the infinitely good God."

Neumann was, as he tells us himself, passionately fond of painting; "But," he adds, "I will give it up, for time is too precious to be so employed." One evening, after his examination of conscience, he wrote the following:

"O my God, how I offended Thee by my distractions during evening prayers! Ought I not to give up playing checkers? The distractions that follow those games seem to demand the sacrifice. I will not, for the future, play until I become excited. I would like to engage in a game occasionally, in order to overcome temptations to envy at the success of others, or pleasure at their failure. By limiting myself in this particular I shall gain more time for my studies. Pardon me, dear Lord, my sin of this evening. I will no more offend Thee in this way."

A few days after penning the above, we find him again accusing himself in the same strain: "The dryness I experienced to-day prevented my recalling Thy Divine Presence as frequently as I should have done. No doubt it arose from my indulgence in chess. I will play chess no more. Heavenly Father, bless my resolution!"

Now his immortification at table gives rise to the following remarks: "Although to-day I felt somewhat devout, and fulfilled all my duties diligently, yet I have not been free from a certain interior trouble. Doubtless it arose from my excess in eating, for during breakfast I was inattentive to the reading of the Word of God."

Again, he rejoices in having complied with God's will: "To-day, after our walk, I felt hungry, and I thought of buying some apples. But, my God, Thou didst not permit me to carry out my intention, and yet the hunger I felt did not prevent my getting through all the work I had intended. Now I know that I can fast and work at the same time, and I will often mortify my appetite." And, in fact, he at once imposed upon himself a privation by making over to one of his needy companions half the bread, fish, and soup destined for his own meal.

Not satisfied with the punctual observance of the seminary rules and regulations, his love of God and desire for perfection urged him to map out for himself a still stricter mode of life. His great object was to spend every moment of the twenty-four hours in the manner most pleasing to his God. And here again he felt the need of a director. His stock of self-confidence was not very great. He dreaded going astray; but, after invoking the Holy Spirit, he formed his resolutions, which he committed to writing. Five o'clock was the regular hour for rising, but Neumann determined to advance it an hour for himself. One morning he failed to rise with his accustomed alacrity; and we find, in consequence, these lines recorded in his journal: "My soul, what a miserable day! We have displeased our God by our inconstancy in good resolutions. Although awake at four, I failed to rise promptly, owing to sloth and carelessness. The thought of my unfaithfulness haunted me even in prayer, and I found no consolation. O my soul, acknowledge thy sloth and ingratitude! If the Divine Master should reject so sluggish and disobedient a disciple, thou wouldst surely forfeit eternal happiness. How easily thou mightest have fallen into some great sin if His grace had not shielded thee! What wilt thou do with this poor soul of mine, O Jesus?"

Here are the resolutions above referred to: "On rising I will recite the morning prayers from 'La Journée du Chrétien' ['The Christian's Day'], and in the evening I will say the seven penitential psalms, with the usual prayers. I will meditate on a verse of the Holy Scripture every day. O Holy Spirit, give me Thy grace to perform all this well. O my Jesus, I will every day receive Holy Communion spiritually, and offer it up for the prevention of sacrilegious communions. Lord, increase in me the effects of Holy Communion. In my visits to the Blessed Sacrament I will recite the psalms xiv., xxvi., and lxxxiii. At the beginning of every sacred function I will say: 'O good God, incline unto me a favorable ear!' In church I will sing the hymns with the people. Every day I will read a chapter of the 'Following of Christ,' one of Canisius, or one from the 'Catechism of the Council of Trent.' At every change of occupation I will make the sign of the cross, in order not to lose sight of God's presence. I will be more punctual in the fulfilment of the duties of my state; I will labor with more love and confidence. Every quarter of an hour I will offer myself to God and make an act of love."

Whilst our fervent young seminarian was aiming with all his power to serve his Lord and Master well, he could not banish the apprehension that he might possibly be in error. The desire for a guide in the path of perfection still pursued him, and led him at one time to entertain the idea of becoming a Jesuit. "It is," he says, "a strict Order; yet if I live piously, Almighty God will grant me the grace to comply with its rules." Again: "O my Jesus, enlighten my confessor that he may make known to me Thy holy will. Behold me ready to fulfil it! The desire to be a Jesuit haunts me again to-day, for certain reports have so inflamed my soul that I long to consecrate myself entirely to God. My God, give me to know Thy will; direct my steps! St. John, pray for me that, like thyself, I may become a holy priest. I resolve to lead the austere life of a missionary." Again he says: "The wish to be a Jesuit is stronger than ever to-day, and I desire especially to remain here several years more. The time spent in the novitiate and the year of probation would greatly conduce to my spiritual advancement. Doubtless there are many good confessors among those fathers, and I would be wonderfully assisted by the society of so many saintly men. Thy will be done, O Lord! Thou seest that the resolution to serve Thee is firmly fixed in my heart. I am resolved to suffer every torment of soul and body for Thee, my Jesus; yes, even death itself. Do Thou prepare the hearts of my beloved family and friends, that our separation may not afflict them too deeply. Indemnify them for the pain which my obedience to Thy commands will cause them."

The president of the seminary had on several different occasions strongly urged the young seminarian to enter the Society of Jesus. His motive in so doing was, perhaps, the thought that, in an Order which was accomplishing so much for the Church, Neumann could more easily carry out his project of becoming a missionary in America. His advice, however, produced just the opposite effect upon the young student, as we see by the following remarks: "The president spoke to me to-day of the Jesuits. He praised their institutions, and showed me a letter just received. The writer recorded, as an instance of obedience, the account of a certain Jesuit who, on his death-bed, expired only after having obtained leave from his Superior to do so. Then, with a significant look, the president went on to say that he had been instrumental in obtaining an entrance into the Order for several who had so distinguished themselves as to authorize his proposing others; that a letter of recommendation from him would open the doors to a candidate, etc. But I feel very little inclination to accept his services, for the way in which he offered them makes me doubt his sincerity. If I knew it to be Thy holy will, my Jesus, I would willingly take the step. I beg Thee, O my God, to let me see clearly what I ought to do!"

To be a Jesuit was not, however, his vocation. Some circumstances about this time diverted his attention to a certain undertaking which, unfortunately, was never carried out. In May, 1835, Rev. Father Dichtl contemplated the establishment of a mission-seminary. In this pious and enlightened priest Neumann had unbounded confidence. The hope that under his prudent guidance light would dawn upon his soul, and anxiety as to his future career cease, was a powerful inducement for the young seminarian to view the plan with an eye of approval. But this was not the only motive that enlisted his sympathy; his far-seeing glance discovered other and more cogent reasons for wishing well to the projected institution. May 30, 1835, the journal records these remarks: "For me, O Jesus, to enter the mission seminary which Thy servant, Rev. Father Dichtl, thinks of establishing will, I think, contribute more to Thy glory than my joining the Jesuits would do. To see me a secular priest and a missionary might encourage many young students of theology to follow my example. Besides, would not the contributions to the St. Leopold Society increase in Bohemia if a missionary were to go forth from this country? May Thy light, O my Jesus, enlighten my soul!"

Here we discover the object dearest to young Neumann's heart, the only undertaking which he strove to promote to the best of his ability—the glory of God, the salvation of souls. His journal of May 23d of the same year is still more explicit on these points. Moved by the consideration of the pressing needs of the times in which he lived, he casts around for means to rouse the dormant zeal of his companions. Behold his words: "It would indeed be well if our young seminarians who really aspire to being good priests, to educate a new generation pleasing to God, would unite more intimately, would form a close if not a distinct society whose members would severally labor under the wise direction of some one leader. True, the priesthood was instituted for this general object; it has the same ends and the same obligations. But the spirit of Christ and His Apostles, by which they should be animated, has grown cold. Many have but little faith, and others are wanting in that zeal which quickened Christ and stimulated the Apostles to bear all sorts of trials and hardships. Religious Orders of priests were soon formed. As long as the spirit of the founders animated the sons, they accomplished an extraordinary amount of good. But, however strict, elaborate, or determinate the rules drawn up by the founder may be, human artifice, or rather diabolical cunning, can discover loop-holes through which the religious may communicate with the world.

"If Superiors are not in harmony with the spirit of the founder, abuses, defects, scandals will constantly creep in, to convert an asylum of godliness into a home for the lowest passions of man. How fatal has not State influence been upon the internal well-being of religious Orders! Where now is your spirit, St. ——?" (Here follow the names of several religious founders.) "What do the religious in your monasteries think of you? The rules of an Order should never be tampered with, even in the smallest particular, by the members of a community, much less by State officials. What is holy should be respected as such. Why, in so many religious houses whose duty it is to send forth missionaries filled with heavenly piety and wisdom, is there so little knowledge—indeed, no knowledge at all—of that striving after perfection, that sanctity which should characterize them? And look at the wretched state of the confessional! Who goes to convents nowadays to become perfect? Poverty drives some, the hope of a comfortable life attracts others, ambition is perhaps the motive that impels others. How does it happen that the ——" (here follow the names of certain Orders, male and female) "are nearly the only ones that harbor saintly souls? Ah! it is because they are the most lowly. They are despised by the world on account of their poverty and rigid discipline. O Humility, thou dost effect this!"

Joys and sorrows and trials served only to draw John Neumann more closely to his God. His life now became one continued meditation on heavenly things, one series of uninterrupted prayer. Once whilst enduring some physical ailment, he wrote: "For nearly a week the pain in my right shoulder has been constant. But, notwithstanding its intensity, I would rather bear it than the hopelessness of suffering in vain." Again: "Dear Lord, my throat is very sore to-day, but I thank Thee for it! Bodily ills keep Thy remembrance ever before me, my Supreme Good! Pardon me, O Lord, if I have done wrong in applying remedies! I have only myself to blame for it. Punish me if Thou wilt, but forgive me likewise. Thy displeasure would be for me a far greater evil!" The laughter and ridicule which he sometimes had to endure from his companions he knew how to turn to good account, by offering all to God. Behold the proof in the following lines, written with charming ingenuousness on some such occasion:

"My God, Thy hand lay heavily upon me to-day! Shame, sadness, and vexation were mine. My cassock came home, but it did not fit around the neck. The students all laughed at me. My neck was the source of greater vexation to me to-day than my sore throat some time ago. But I thank Thee, O my Jesus, for this opportunity of mortifying my vanity! I see now that I ought to have recourse to Thee more frequently."

In order to have the means of procuring good books, Neumann imposed upon himself numerous privations, as well in clothing as in other things. The following is an instance of this. On a certain New-Year's Day the students of the seminary went, as usual, to offer their greetings to the Archbishop. Young Neumann could not form one of the number, as his old torn cassock was no longer presentable. He bore the humiliation with characteristic resignation, exclaiming, as he turned to his beloved books, "My God, do Thou comfort me!"

He prepared by assiduous application, and still more by earnest prayer, for his examinations, whilst at the same time offering to God, in the humility of his heart, any possible failure that might follow. Such a result with its attendant disgrace he was willing to endure if it were more agreeable to God, more salutary to his own soul. One day he thus addressed himself to God: "Our new professor will examine us to-morrow. O my God, give me skill and courage! But should my desire proceed from vanity, hear not my prayer! Yet, Lord, my heart still bleeds from former wounds, have mercy on me now!"

On June 3, 1835, we find him delivering his first trial-sermon. As usual, he prepared for it by imploring assistance from on high, and begging to be preserved from discouragement should his effort prove a failure. "My God," he cries, "I have indeed deserved but shame and chastisement. But of what use would be a disheartened missionary?" The sermon, however, turned out well, as we infer from the usual evening record: "My Jesus, who didst shield me to-day from disgrace, who didst infuse into my soul courage to preach Thy holy Word, what thanks can I render Thee? By this Thou hast given me a sign that I am chosen to announce Thy Gospel to souls redeemed by Thy Blood. My first trial-sermon was preached to-day in presence of Professor M——. He found some fault with my reading of the last part of the Gospel, some fault with the connection of certain words. He also criticised one of my gestures. The expression *carnival* he did not like, because of my youth. The composition, however, as well as the delivery, met his approbation. Jesus, keep me in holy humility!"

True love for God begets a corresponding love for one's neighbor. As John Neumann's love of God may be termed magnanimous, so also may his love of his neighbor be judged worthy of our highest admiration. His was a charity which sought to help and console wherever help or consolation was needed. When the bestowal of active aid was not in his power, his heart's best sympathy, his earnest prayers, were freely poured out on his suffering brother. His own heaviest trials, his aridity and desolation, even those most painful temptations against faith which shrouded his soul in darkness, could offer no hindrance to his sharing in his neighbor's griefs. "My God!" he exclaims, "how are they not to be pitied who have no faith, or who are weak in their faith! They believe not in Thee, O my Jesus! Enlighten them, I beseech Thee! For this end I offer Thee the troubles I am enduring in my own wretched state!"

Sometimes we find the journal recording loving complaints to God of his being forgotten, forsaken by his friends. Letters from his loved companion Schmid, to whom he so often alludes, seem not to have been forthcoming as frequently as he desired. Witness the following: "I would gladly write to dear Schmid, could I refrain from chiding him for his silence. It would not do to reproach him on his feast-day; rather should I seek to give him pleasure. I will wait, O Lord, if it so pleases Thee, till I am in a brighter mood."

On October 23d the good friend above referred to made known his intention of entering the Collegiate Society of Hohenfuhrt, a piece of information which was far from gratifying to Neumann. Both had agreed to labor together in America, and here now was a cloud overcasting that bright prospect. In his chagrin and disappointment Neumann turned to God: "If I did but know it to be an inspiration from Thee, my God! Have mercy on him! Oh, that it be not vanity or discouragement which has induced him to take this resolution! A resolve to change one's state, to give up a pious design, ought not to be the result of one day's reflection."

Among all his college companions we find mention made of only one, of L——, who seems to have been a man after his own heart. He rejoices on one occasion that L—— had acquitted himself creditably in a certain discourse before Professor M——. And again, he remarks: "I spoke to-day with my good friend L—— on the subject of the priesthood, the confessional, etc. My

God, strengthen him that he may become a good priest, a consolation and guiding angel to Thy people!"

Rev. Father Dichtl, of whom we have already made mention, was stationed at the cathedral of Budweis. With evangelical freedom he rebuked the soldiers, and especially the officers, for their habitual vices, earnestly reminding them of their obligations as Christians. This frankness on the part of the zealous priest so exasperated certain unruly spirits among them that it was deemed necessary for him to seek safety in flight. On hearing of the affair, Neumann rejoiced at the opportunity offered his friend to suffer for Christ's sake, and thus alludes to it in his journal: "This day will ever be a memorable one to me, since it brought me the news of Father Dichtl's having to flee from the revenge of the soldiers whose vices he had reproved. O my Jesus, Thou knowest how my heart beat for joy when I learned that Thy faithful servant had had an opportunity to display his courage and fidelity in Thy service. O Jesus, grant me, also, and grant to all Thy priests, the courage to resist the world!"

In proportion to his joy at seeing God glorified by word or deed was his sorrow on witnessing any offence against Him. "I experienced a sweet feeling of devotion," he writes, "on visiting the holy relics in the churches of Prague; but I was indignant on seeing the disrespect shown to holy-water."

Neumann, as we may believe, paid few visits of ceremony. The world and its formalities had no charms for one whose thoughts and aspirations soared to a higher level. Once only do we find his journal recording such a visit. He seems to have been unable to avoid it; but, as was his wont, he turned it to good account by referring it to God: "Dear holy patron," he exclaims, "Madame C—— has sent for me. I must call upon her. Do thou procure, if it so please God, that I may be put to shame. My God, if such be Thy will, I will visit this lady. Lead me as Thou didst lead Lydia to St. Paul; yet, if it be Thy good pleasure for all to despise me, may Thy will be done!" Next day he wrote: "I have been to Madame C——'s. She received me like a mother. Oh, how good, how pious and charitable she must be! Be merciful to her, my Jesus! She showed me some writings of the Empress Caroline Augusta, and of our Emperor Francis who now sleeps in the Lord. My God, grant our present Emperor the spirit of piety, for they say that he suppressed the convent at Welk."

As Neumann approached the term of his desires, the greater became the obstacles to their execution. Hope held out to him her flattering promises, yet only to increase his disappointment when they remained unfulfilled. His confidence, however, firm as the basis on which it rested, God Himself, no difficulty could daunt. On June 22, 1835, he received a cheering letter from his friend Schmid. Its effect upon him we may gather from the lines which noted its reception: "O my Jesus, I know not whether to weep for joy or grief! Yesterday, after the procession of Corpus Christi, I received Schmid's letter asking whether I did not want to accompany him to Strasburg and thence to Philadelphia. Thou knowest, O my Jesus, that I would willingly suffer and die for Thee, though I am all unworthy of such a grace! But my poor parents—how will they endure the separation? I wish to be entirely Thine. Strengthen them, I beseech Thee, since Thou callest me!"

On the following day Neumann discovered that the news conveyed by his friend's letter was ill-founded. He says: "I was speaking to the president to-day, and I told him, among other things, that Father Dichtl intended to take seminarians to Strasburg, thence to sail next spring for America. But he replied that Father Dichtl had written to him contradicting the rumor. My God, Thy will be done! My own plans are ever before my mind; and the thought of Jesus, the Almighty One, who will aid me to fulfil His blessed will, is never absent from me."

The separation from family and friends, the dangers and hardships consequent on a missionary life in America, offered prospects far from seductive to nature. The difficulties of such an undertaking were fully comprehended by Neumann, for he says, June 29, 1835: "Whilst pondering, last evening, on my resolution, separation from home appeared to me so bitter that I burst into tears. My Jesus, if it be Thy will, increase my sufferings, but hear my prayers! Let my resolve be put in execution! With no other guide than Thyself, O Lord, I stand on the outskirts of an immense region full of dangers and difficulties. The final step once taken, there will be no looking back. No fond parents, no devoted brother and sisters, no kind friends will greet my landing on those far-off shores. I shall meet none but strangers. There, indeed, I shall find unbelievers who scoff at Thee, my Jesus, but many souls, also, who hunger to know Thy Word, O most merciful Saviour!"

Neumann had hoped to be ordained before his departure for the scene of his future labors. To bestow the priestly benediction upon his beloved parents, to celebrate his first Mass in the midst of his family and friends, would have gone far to assuage the grief of parting. But on July 3d he learned through his friend that they would be deprived of this consolation; that they would be obliged to start before their ordination.

As usual, Neumann had recourse to God: "My Lord and my God, how sad Schmid's letter made me to-day! I must set out on my journey without giving the priestly blessing to my dear parents and friends, without offering the Holy Sacrifice for their spiritual welfare. This thought grieves me to the heart. It will render the separation more difficult, O my Jesus! But I am Thine, my parents are Thine! Multiply my sorrows, but pour out on them Thy consolations. I have consecrated myself entirely to Thee; Thou art my only Lord! Be merciful to my parents, as also to those of my friend Schmid! I will bless Thee for every blow, since Thou dost deal it in mercy! As I have recognized Thy holy will, so will I conform to it!"

On the following day, July 4th, he learned that holy orders were to be conferred upon all the seminarians, with the exception of those belonging to the diocese of Budweis. The reasons for this exception we shall meet further on. Neumann's humiliation at having been put off was faithfully recorded in his journal of this date:

"I am quite disheartened to-day. The seminarians of Prague and Königgratz will be ordained, though those cities have a larger number of priests than Budweis."

The last day of his stay at Prague was one of intense anxiety to Neumann. The final examinations after a twelve years' course naturally claimed his time and attention, whilst his soul was a prey to interior sufferings, perplexity, and doubt. His journal of the 7th runs as follows:

"How gladly, O my God, would I thank Thee for the innumerable benefits Thou dost heap upon me! Yesterday my examinations ended happily, even more happily than I dared to hope. But my approaching departure from Prague, the postponement of my ordination, and the arrival of my brother and cousin Janson from Munich, distract me. I feel discouraged. My cousin came to be present at my ordination, not knowing of its having been deferred. His affection for me brought him to Prague, but I can now afford him no gratification."

Finally, on July 8, 1835, the moment of release arrived, and he set out from Prague homeward-bound, his feelings very foreign to what might be expected from the successful termination of a twelve years' course of study. The truth was this: the young seminarian felt very uncertain about his ordination, the first and necessary step toward the attainment of his noble ambition. Added to this was the humiliation of receiving a certificate with "Moral Conduct, First Class."*

In allusion to this circumstance he says: "I left Prague feeling pretty calm, although with a foreboding of unpleasant things. That 'Moral Conduct, First Class' embittered my joy at the completion of my career as a student. Only in resignation to the will of God did I find comfort. I thank Thee, O my God, that during this time my faith did not waver, else I might have perished!"

---

* It would appear from this that there was a higher testimonial awarded at the seminary which Neumann failed to attain.

CHAPTER VII.

Preparations for Departure to America.

ON the morning of July 10th Neumann arrived at his father's house dispirited, as we have seen in the last chapter, and far from certain as to his future. And indeed, viewed in the most favorable light, his prospects were not cheering. The great object of all his desires, the work of the missions, was still far from his grasp; the diocese of Budweis possessed more than a sufficient number of clerical workmen for all its needs, and the Right Reverend Bishop, with his eighty years and feeble health, was in no hurry to ordain supernumerary priests. Permission to leave the country could not easily be obtained, the episcopal consistory opposing determined opposition to such departures. As to his travelling expenses, Neumann, not wishing to tax his parents, hoped to have them defrayed by the St. Leopold Society of Vienna. Supposing all the above obstacles cleared away from his path, there still remained the most painful and difficult of all, that of breaking the news to his family. He shrank from causing them pain, whilst his own heart bled at the thought of separation from home and friends.

This delay and uncertainty caused him much uneasiness, as appears from his journal of the first days of vacation. "I am in a most embarrassing position," he says, "and to disclose my resolution to my parents seems almost impossible. That note, 'First Class' in moral conduct, fills me with dissatisfaction. God knows my efforts. I detest this delay to my eager wishes, and I doubt if my application for the needed travelling funds will be successful. My parents and family will surely oppose my project, and my own heart sinks at the thought of separation."

Meanwhile Neumann failed not to improve, as far as he was able, this tedious period of hope and fear. He took counsel of several pious and learned men, who severally approved the resolution which Divine Providence appeared to sanction in the following remarkable manner. About this time, Right Reverend Francis Patrick Kenrick, Bishop of Philadelphia, empowered the director of the Strasburg seminary to engage young priests or theological students for the American missions. The director applied to Rev. Father Dichtl to know if such candidates could be found in Bohemia. Father Dichtl was the confessor of Neumann's personal friend, and was well acquainted with the desires and plans of both. It was, consequently, highly gratifying to him to be able to name the two young seminarians to the director as aspirants for the American missions. He took a lively interest in the realization of their long-cherished intentions, and to him, under God, must be attributed its success, as well as that of many other good works.

But as there was no prospect of their receiving holy orders under five or six months, the zealous priest advised them to set out at once and await their ordination in America.

In the interim, Neumann had recourse to prayer. He spent much of his time in pious pilgrimages to the various shrines in the neighborhood of Prachatitz, with an occasional visit to one or other of his fellow-students.

On the second day after his return home he went to Gojau, a well-known sanctuary of the Blessed Virgin, and thence proceeded to Krumau and Goldenkron, little towns in the neighborhood. The last-mentioned place made a deep impression upon him, as he tells us in his journal:

"The sight of the empty church and the dilapidated, desecrated convent drew tears to my eyes. What little Christian sentiment do these words express, 'Work is more pleasing to God than prayer!' Men seek to justify the suppression of monasteries on the plea that they foster idleness."

On July 14th he went to Budweis, hoping to push forward the affair nearest his heart. Here he met some encouragement from his friends, as we learn from the following remarks: "I arrived in Budweis on the evening of the 14th, but felt too despondent for any conversation with Schmid. Next day, however, I met him, and a talk with him did me immense good. Together we called on the rector of the seminary, Father Dichtl, who received us most kindly. His words, 'In your certificate I have given you *distinguished* in every branch,' cheered me considerably. The reception from my old companions was cordial. I do not know whether they have been informed of my project or not. May our example inflame their charity more and more! P—— is a perfect Christian. His humility shines forth in word and deed. S—— was depressed: mental troubles. May God be with him! The Right Reverend Bishop gave us hopes of being ordained soon, though he said nothing definite as to the time."

Nearly three weeks had now elapsed since his return from Prague, and he had not yet ventured to disclose his hopes and desires to his family. At last, however, a favorable opportunity presented itself, of which he hastened to make use. In a few words, clear and decisive, he unfolded to his mother and sisters his views and intentions, his ardent desires to labor in the American missions, and his firm resolution to do so. His pious mother, who may have suspected her son's design, exhibited neither surprise nor disapprobation. With maternal solicitude she set forth in lively colors the dangers and hardships of the missionary life; but in such a tone and manner as to reassure her son and give him to see that from her, at least, he would meet with no violent opposition. His sisters, however, were not so easily won over to his views. It was hard to reconcile themselves to the thought of giving up so dear a brother, perhaps forever. They left no means in their power untried to dissuade him from so perilous an enterprise. The sequel shows with what result.

Six days later, June 26th, his presence in Budweis was necessary, and at his friend Schmid's notification he immediately set out. Before doing so, however, he summoned up courage to inform his father of the object he had in view. His journal records briefly this victory over self, and then goes on to mention the business that had called him to Budweis:

"July 26th," he writes, "before setting out for Budweis, I made known to my father the project I have in view. I could see that his distress was intense, though he tried to conceal it by a smile. The morning after my arrival in Budweis, I went to confession and communion, in honor of St. Anne, in the parish church. I was by turns depressed and joyous. My anguish of heart is unspeakable, and yet I feel relieved, for I think Jesus has heard my prayer. He has laid the sorrow of my family on my shoulders. With Schmid I visited the Right Reverend Bishop, the Canons, and Professors Leo and Kosel. We are anxious to win them over to look favorably on our enterprise."

Whilst Neumann's desire for the missionary life took new increase day by day, and whilst hourly awaiting the happy conclusion of preliminary negotiations, he received from his friend a letter containing the vexatious intelligence that further delay was in store for them. It stated that the St. Leopold Society had refused to advance the necessary funds, alleging that not the two young seminarians, but the Right Reverend Bishop of Philadelphia, for whose diocese they were bound, should present a formal petition to that effect; besides this, the episcopal consistory had refused to sanction their departure until they could present their parents' permission in writing; and, lastly, passports were withheld on account of some want of formality in the application for them.

This was bad news for the already sorely-tried student; but by recourse to prayer, his never-failing remedy in affliction, peace and courage were restored. Next day he went for the second time to Budweis. On this journey he took with him his father's written consent to his leaving home. "Early in the morning, just before setting out, I asked my dear father for his consent in writing. He gave it unhesitatingly, though the effort cost him visible emotion. I thank Thee, my most merciful Jesus! We started together, my father and I, for he was going as far as Schwarzbach, where he had some business. On the way I laid before him all my plans. From Schwarzbach I went on to Krumau. Beyond Gojau, I prayed toward evening in the chapel of the Holy Virgin, for her protection over our undertaking. God granted me here special devotion. In Krumau, Rev. Father Pfeifer introduced me to the Right Reverend Prelate. Such scenes humble me. I feel embarrassed, and I cannot conceal it; and yet I have to put on an air of self-confidence.

"The Bishop received me most kindly, and told me that a priest of his diocese would accompany us as soon as certain obstacles would be removed. Arrived, at length, at Budweis, I went in quest of Rev. Father Dichtl. I found that Krbecek had gone to Gmünden, and Schmid had not yet arrived; so I was forced to go alone to the Right Reverend Bishop. I presented him the document containing my father's consent, authenticated by the city Dean. His reception was exceedingly cordial and condescending. I returned to Prachatitz the same day, though the heat was oppressive and violent thunderstorms succeeding one another in rapid succession."

Drenched with rain and worn out by fatigue, Neumann reached home toward midnight. He found, of course, the house closed and the family retired. Unwilling to disturb any one at that late hour, he made his entrance through a kitchen-window which, fortunately for him, happened to be open. Great was the astonishment next morning when he issued from his room, and in answer to the questions as to what kind of supper he had had the previous evening, he replied with a smile, "Oh, a piece of bread is enough for me!"

Whilst efforts were being made to facilitate his departure, and his friends were endeavoring to raise the requisite funds among the priests of the diocese, Neumann was employing his time, as we have seen, in furthering the interests of his soul. We know from his journal that he paid frequent visits to the various places of pilgrimage in the neighborhood, at whose shrines he received many graces. Uniting mortification to prayer, he applied himself to the acquisition of the virtues most pleasing to God. These pilgrimages were always accompanied by the reception of the Sacraments of Penance and Holy Communion, for which he prepared with laudable fervor and devotion. During a considerable time he confessed daily, for his tender conscience, or rather his love for God, gave him no rest until he had removed every obstacle to the divine intercourse. His heart yearned for the closest possible union with his only and dearly Beloved. These pious journeys were made alone and on foot; consequently we are in ignorance of many particulars which might redound to his praise. On one occasion, however, he was accompanied by a fellow-student, to whom we are indebted for the little we do know of the piety and zeal with which he performed these exercises. The following is from the pen of this student, now the Rev. Father K——:

"In the middle of September, 1835, I visited Neumann. Next morning he received Holy Communion, and we started for Strakonitz, a pilgrimage dedicated to 'Our Lady of Victory.' We both went to confession and Holy Communion next morning at Podsrp, in the church of the Seven Dolors. It was then almost noon. After partaking of some refreshment at the inn, we returned home. It was a very warm day, and I was bathed in perspiration. I took off my coat, but Neumann with a smile only buttoned his more closely. The sun was darting his fierce rays down on my head, which I did my best to protect, whilst Neumann walked on coolly, hat in hand, leading in the recitation of the Rosary. In this way we reached Skocic, where stands a shrine of 'Our Lady of Help.' We asked the pastor for the church-keys, but he declined trusting us with them; and so we were obliged to adore the Most Blessed Sacrament outside the door. Then we recited together the Profession of Faith of the Council of Trent, and turned our steps homeward. It was about seven o'clock in the evening when we reached my parents' house, where a good supper was soon set before us. Neumann smiled, but would not touch anything. His conduct puzzled me, and I exclaimed somewhat impatiently, 'Why do you act so? You are always tantalizing me. Sit down and eat!' 'I must go,' he replied. 'Where are you going?' I asked. 'Don't you see that it is already late?' He sat down, and I began to help myself, for I was hungry after our day's journey. But in a few moments up he sprang, saying in a cheery tone, 'I can easily find my way as far as Prachatitz,' and seizing his hat, he was off. I ran after him and insisted on accompanying him. He permitted it for a short distance, and then urged me to return. It so happened that, in spite of his confidence, he lost his way, and reached home only on the following morning. 'God punished me,' he remarked some days after. 'I should have passed the night with you.' From his conversation that day I discovered his knowledge of the interior life. Among other things, he made clear to me the words *apex mentis*, and explained the way in which the soul acts."

The pilgrimage referred to in the above account is thus briefly noticed by Neumann: "On the same day I went with good K—— on a pilgrimage to Podsrp and Strakonitz. Next morning I went to confession and Holy Communion again, and peace was restored to my soul. To thee, O my Mother, Our Lady of Podsrp and Skocic, I owe much! I love thee with my whole heart."

The poor souls in purgatory claimed alike his sympathy and prayers. He often visited the cemetery outside the city and St. Peter's Church adjoining. One evening the "good K——" accompanied him thither, and thus alludes to the visit: "One evening in autumn we went out to St. Peter's, where we prayed till eleven o'clock. As we were returning, Neumann, pointing to the cross in the starry sky, said, 'As often as you see that cross, think of me, as I will of you.'"

The last day of September was devoted to a pilgrimage to Our Lady's shrines at Klattau and Nepomucene, the latter the birthplace of Neumann's patron. His account of this visit is highly edifying.

"I was greatly distracted," he writes. "On the 23d of September I made a sincere confession at the Capuchins in Schüttenhofen. But I went to Communion with a scruple which assailed me shortly before receiving. This disturbed my devotion. Perhaps it was a punishment imposed as a penance. At Klattau, where I arrived on the 24th, at half-past seven in the morning, I prayed earnestly in both the churches, though without any sentiment of devotion. No opportunity for confession presented itself. I was greatly disappointed, for I would gladly have rid myself of my doubt. I had, moreover, to abstain from Holy Communion, a most painful privation. With a sad heart, though not without a certain mixture of consolation, I went to Nepomucene, where God was waiting to visit me in a special manner. I think that, with the exception of the time of my general confession, I never entered the confessional with greater fervor or a more upright intention than I did here. This was Thy work, O Jesus! Thou didst hear the prayers of my holy patron. The kind reception given me by the deans was quite in contrast with that of the curates, though indeed that of the latter was well merited. I love those curates, however, and from this day forward I will look upon every priest, without exception, as the representative of God. I reached home on the 26th, richly rewarded for the bodily fatigue and mental suffering I had endured. Now, O my God, I belong entirely to Thee!"

Another of these pious pilgrimages led him through Chrobold, where Rev. Anthony Dichtl, brother of the aforementioned Rev. Herman Dichtl, was pastor. He invited young Neumann to preach on the Feast of the Nativity of the Blessed Virgin. The invitation was cheerfully accepted. The devout son of Mary rejoiced in an opportunity to publish the praises of his good Mother, the fair Queen of Heaven. To his act of contrition that day he added these words: "O Mother of my God, how can one as unworthy as I announce thy praises? O pray for me, a poor sinner!"

On the eve of the feast he says: "To-morrow I shall preach at Chrobold my first sermon in honor of the Blessed Virgin Mary. No doubt curiosity will attract many. Thy will be done, O Jesus! If success will not elate me, help me worthily to announce the praises of Thy Mother! But if failure be more conducive to my spiritual advancement, may Thy holy will be done! Withdraw Thy hand but for one moment, and I shall be covered with shame and confusion. O Jesus, I am Thine!" The result of the sermon we may gather from his notes: "My sermon was not so successful as I had hoped it would be, but I bore my failure with passable resignation."

We cannot peruse his journal of this time, nor, indeed, of any other period of his holy career, without being edified by the constant manifestation of his one great desire, viz., to seek and adore in all things the honor of God and the accomplishment of His most holy will. We find also in that faithful record of his inmost thoughts numerous occasions to admire his ever-active and disinterested charity toward his neighbor. On one of his journeys to Budweis he met a well-known free-thinker. Neumann lost no time, but, engaging him in conversation, satisfactorily defended the truths of religion. That evening we find him thanking God for throwing such an opportunity in his way, and begging a blessing on his efforts for the spiritual good of the deluded man.

A certain Mr. F—— with whom he had lately become acquainted calls forth the following remarks: "He is a very pious man. Thy Church, O my Jesus, has some faithful sons after all!"

A visit from one of his fellow-students is noticed in these words: "Would that I were able to contribute something toward his perfection! He suffers greatly. But I am presumptuous in my wish. I am far more imperfect, more sinful than he." Of another he says: "It is my opinion that he carries his mysticism too far. May God grant us His grace!"

Neumann often accompanied his friend to the hospital in charge of the Gray Nuns. The sight of the care bestowed upon the poor sick by the good Sisters and their postulants charmed him. His admiration of their work, so pleasing to God, finds expression in the following lines: "Oh, how great must be the fire of divine love enkindled by the spirit of God in the hearts of these spouses of heaven! I long to become as perfect as they. Oh, how charming their heavenly sentiments, their resignation, their holy joy, their maternal care! How consoling the patience and cheerfulness of the sick! O God, Thou hast poured into my arid, sinful heart a fulness of grace for which I cannot even in thought stammer my thanks!"

Neumann knew how to defend God's honor on proper occasions; and his words, brief and to the purpose, rarely gave offence. When his missionary project to America was rumored abroad, many were the representations and entreaties of friends and acquaintances to dissuade him from it. His only reply was, "If God gives me the grace, I shall remain faithful to my resolution."

One friend in particular was untiring in his importunities. Among other arguments, he alleged that the sciences which Neumann had acquired with so much labor and application would be useless to him in America. To this Neumann replied by the question, "Why do you ship your goods to foreign markets?" "Because," answered his friend, "in foreign markets they command higher prices." "For the same reason I intend to go to America," returned Neumann, thus putting an end to further remonstrance.

One clear, cold December morning, about half-past four o'clock, the stillness of Prachatitz was broken by the sharp clanging of the fire-alarm. Neumann sprang from his bed, threw open his window, and saw flames rising from a neighboring village only a few miles distant. Dressing hurriedly, he hastened to his father's room. "Pfefferschlag is on fire!" he cried. "I'm off!" And soon he was on the scene of action. One house was already enveloped in flames, whilst the frightened villagers stood in a crowd uncertain what to do. The danger was imminent as the houses were all of wood and close together. "A ladder!" cried Neumann. "Form two lines and pass up buckets;" and up he darted, followed by several others. Water was passed from hand to hand, by which the flames were kept under until assistance arrived from Prachatitz. With God's help the fire was soon extinguished and the homes of the poor villagers saved.

This village belonged to the sovereignty of Prince Schwarzenberg, who, some days later, forwarded to Neumann a commendatory letter of thanks, inviting him to apply confidently for any favor he desired. Neumann quietly slipped the letter into his pocket without even breaking the seal. His mother, however, with true feminine curiosity, questioned him on its contents. Then only did he draw it forth, break the seal, and read. "Very probably I shall never make use of this," he remarked, as he folded it and returned it to his pocket.

In his violent efforts to extinguish the flames he received a severe wound in the hand. The cold weather aggravated its grievousness to such a degree that when, two months later, he set out for America it was not yet healed. The villagers of Pfefferschlag often inquired after him, expressing their desire to have him for pastor. When they were informed quite recently that his biography was being compiled for publication, they insisted that the above-mentioned fact should not be forgotten. They forwarded a statement of it, signed and sealed by their chief men, with the request that it should be inserted in the said biography. The account contained in this document informs us that Neumann worked so hard that not a single garment on him remained dry. His coat was encased in icicles. He continued his exertions until he sank from sheer exhaustion, in which state he was taken to a house near by and provided with dry clothing and refreshment. A few modest words in his journal record this event: "On December 13th a fire broke out in Pfefferschlag. I helped to put it out. To Thee, O my God, our first thanks are due! By calming the winds Thou didst check the fire and save Thy poor people from misery!"

John Neumann was silent with regard to whatever might redound to his own honor; consequently we find him merely touching upon those extraordinary favors with which God at times rewarded his fervent prayers and mortifications. His tender conscience gave him no rest until again and again he had confessed his faults and imperfections. He loved God truly, he loved Him above all things, and his only dread was to offend his only Love. Notwithstanding the violence he was forced to offer his pride and self-love, he confessed every week, and sometimes even more frequently. One day he writes of himself as follows:

"I wanted, in honor of the Most Blessed Virgin, to go to confession to the Piarist Fathers (Budweis), but I was disappointed. I could not make up my mind as to the choice of a confessor. I was not resigned to the will of God. It was only on the next day that the Blessed Virgin granted my wish. Through her gracious intercession I resolved to confess to that priest whom I should happen to meet first. It turned out to be the prefect of the gymnasium. Then I received Holy Communion in the parish church. Heavenly peace, resignation, and joy were restored to my desolate soul. Ah, how I long to meditate on the immense sufferings of my dearest Jesus!"

We are astonished on beholding young Neumann's diligent employment of those hours of vacation, his assiduity in caring for his spiritual welfare, whilst his friends in Budweis pushed on preparations for his projected journey. And yet he regarded himself as an indolent servant in his Divine Master's vineyard. "Yesterday," he writes, "I resolved most earnestly to lead a strict and retired life. Both to-day and yesterday, O my Jesus, I have had to ask Thy pardon several times; yet, so far, Thou hast not answered me as Thou art wont to do!"

On November 1st he laid down for himself a rule of life in which the hours from four in the morning till eleven at night were to be conscientiously divided between prayer and study. So high was Neumann's appreciation of the sanctity of God that, notwithstanding his rare gift of tears, his mortified life, and his regular reception of the Sacraments, he never thought his penance adequate to his sins. He exclaims in his journal, "Ah, woe is me! Of what avail are my tears, O God, when I offend Thee by my deeds? Oh, that these tears might lessen my pain and wash out my sins! O Jesus, behold me here by Thy cross! Hear my prayer! Alas, I have so basely crucified Thee! Forgive me! O Cross, I tremble before Thee! Far rather would I kneel at Thy crib, O Divine Child, were I less sinful! I offer Thee only desires, no works; therefore how can I hope for pardon? On Thy heart my hot tears have fallen; do Thou soften my hard heart, dear Infant Jesus! Oh, that I had never come into this world, since I am in it only to give Thee pain! O Divine Child, did I know that my tears would reconcile me to Thee, they should flow till sight would fail! But what are tears without works?"

About the middle of December a letter from his friend Schmid bore him the welcome intelligence that the long-expected passports had been received by the episcopal consistory, and that a collection was being taken up among the priests to meet the expenses of the journey. Rejoicing at the happy progress of his affairs, Neumann, as usual, confided his emotions of joy and gratitude to the pages of his faithful journal:

"My God, pardon me for not thanking Thee with all my heart as I should! My will is bound up with Thine; I desire only what Thou dost desire! Oh, what pain this leave-taking will cause my poor heart! My grief borders on despair; it draws from me these supplications. O Jesus, upon me, the wretched malefactor, let the whole weight of this bitter trial fall! Brand me, Thy penitent, with Thine own hand, but soothe my parents' grief! With the assistance of Thy grace I will be able to endure the blows of Thy merciful justice, for they come from Thee, most amiable Jesus, my Love, my Treasure, my All! Have mercy on me!"

At last the final preparations were made, the moment

for departure was at hand, and the struggle going on in the breast of our noble young student may best be depicted in his own words: "I tremble at the thought of parting from my parents, my brother, my sisters! My heart is torn with anguish! O Jesus, Thou who hast inspired the resolution, grant me strength to fulfil it! All things urge upon me the necessity of doing so. Oh, what sacrifices have to be made in Thy service! The Brothers of Mercy must constantly sacrifice many things in order to follow out their vocation in the care of the sick—and *I?* what am I doing here? Cannot I, too, resolve to do something for God? O my Jesus, give me strength!"

And yet, it must be allowed, the result of this long preparation, this waiting and hoping for six weary months, was far from satisfactory. Only after repeated petitions and negotiations was a passport granted which was to hold good for three years; Neumann's undertaking was approved neither by the Bishop nor his chapter; and the St. Leopold Society absolutely refused to supply funds for the journey. Through Rev. Father Dichtl's efforts, however, a sum was raised among the priests of the diocese, but it was scarcely sufficient to defray the expenses of one individual. It was decided, therefore, that Neumann should set out alone, and that his friend should follow as soon as practicable. The director of the seminary had promised to every missioner going to America the sum of four or five hundred francs to supply any deficit in travelling expenses. Availing himself of this kind offer, Neumann saw at last the obstacles to his long-cherished desires removed. We shall, however, see, as we follow him step by step in his career of self-sacrifice, that the removal of present obstacles did not mean immunity from those of the future.

CHAPTER VIII.

Departure from Home.

ON February 8, 1836, John Neumann bade farewell to Prachatitz, his native place, though not to his parents and family. Mr. Neumann, in giving his consent to his son's leaving home, had made use of these words: "If you believe yourself called by God, we shall put no obstacle in your way, but you must not take leave of us." The father was visibly affected at the thought of losing this first-born son, who had never before caused him a moment's pain. As the young student frequently absented himself from home, either to go to Budweis or to make a pilgrimage to some hallowed shrine, his doing so at this particular time called forth no special comment from any member of the family. Merely signifying his intention of going to Budweis, he set out with the pain at his heart all the more poignant from his efforts to conceal it under an appearance of indifference. His farewell letter to his beloved parents, dated from Budweis, February 11th, affords some intimation of the feelings which prompted it:

" MY VERY DEAR PARENTS:

"By my sudden and unexpected departure I designed to lessen our mutual pain of separation, as much on your account as on my own. Convinced that your parental blessing will follow me wherever I go, I forebore for the reason stated to ask it before leaving you. I feel assured, also, that the thanks I owe you for so many and so great benefits, and which I now express in writing, you will accept as if tendered by word of mouth. I am persuaded that the career in which I am about to embark, and which, with God's blessing, I shall faithfully pursue, will be conducive to your spiritual good also.

"You have, my dear parents, the right to lay claim to whatever return my affection could possibly make you, and, God knows, I would have done my duty in this matter! But the unalterable resolution cherished for three years, in spite of so many hindrances, and which was so near being fulfilled; the ease with which I acquired the knowledge necessary for my future career, with many other circumstances, combine to assure me that it is God who calls upon me for this sacrifice, however painful, in behalf of the ignorant and abandoned. These considerations, added to the conviction that my sacrifice will be beneficial not only to my own soul but to yours likewise, determines me not to relinquish the end in view. My dear parents, may you bear patiently and resignedly this trial imposed upon us by God! The greater our sorrows now, the greater our joys hereafter. God would not demand such a sacrifice, did He not deem it salutary to us and were He not willing to impart the necessary strength. May His holy will be done!

"I thank you for all you have sent me. You have furnished me too abundantly; less would have been sufficient. In a few days I shall set out by way of Linz. To-morrow I call on the Bishop.

"I embrace you with all my heart, and beg you to present my regards to the Reverend Dean and the other priests of my acquaintance. My heart-felt thanks to the charitable ladies of Prachatitz for all their very acceptable gifts. From Nancy I will write soon again.

"Begging your prayers, I remain your devoted and grateful son,   JOHN N. NEUMANN.

"BUDWEIS, February 11, 1836."

His separation from home and friends was a bitter pang to Neumann's sensitive heart, one too keen for endurance, perhaps, had not his intense love for God come in to rectify natural feeling. He thinks only of his Jesus; he sighs only for union with Him. "Ah, Lord Jesus," he cries, "Thou must tear my heart from this world that it may be healed! O Jesus, be my Saviour!"

On February 18th he left Budweis, though not till he had implored a blessing from the Right Reverend Bishop. The favor was indeed accorded, although his lordship plainly intimated dissatisfaction at his going abroad. Distressing doubts and disappointments awaited him; but trust in God's providence buoyed him up to bear them manfully.

"The thought of the journey before me," he says, "banished every other care. I became almost insensible to other considerations."

The road to Linz led through the Bohemian forest, and snow lay on the ground to the depth of from fourteen to fifteen feet. His friend Schmid accompanied him a considerable distance. The journal informs us:

"At Einsiedeln my dear Schmid and I parted. But few words had been interchanged by us in the stage-coach, for we had little to communicate. The thought that now I have so many for whom I must pray weighs upon me. My unworthy prayers can do my benefactors little good, and still I yearn to show my gratitude."

On arriving at Linz, Neumann's first care was to visit his Lord in the tabernacle of some church, and there to pour out his heart in praise and prayer. Thence he repaired to the seminary, where a cordial reception was tendered him by the rector, Rev. Father Stolzenthaler. Next day he was introduced to Bishop Ziegler, who honored the young missionary with an entertainment and a Latin address. Neumann thus records these items:

"Yesterday I prayed, with many tears, in the beautiful parish church. My heart grew strong, and my resolution of last week revived. Then I went to the seminary, where I was received by the rector with the greatest courtesy. This roused my courage. To-day I called on the Bishop. What an apostolic man! 'Have you not the Holy Ghost to enlighten and teach you?' he said to me with fatherly kindness. O God, how holy and mighty art Thou!"

On the morning of February 20th he arrived at Munich. Under this date we find the following expressions of gratitude, the outpourings of his noble heart:

"The rector, the spiritual director, and the sub-rector of the seminary at Linz provided for me in a truly paternal manner. May God reward them! The Bishop was extremely kind, and told me to write to him at once should I be in any need. He assured me of his readiness to come to my assistance. May God reward him for his charity!"

Young Neumann's next visit was to his cousin Janson, who resided in Munich, after which he attended to some business for his friends of Budweis and Linz. While thus engaged he met Rev. Father Henni, a missionary from the diocese of Cincinnati, later Archbishop of Milwaukee. Through this reverend gentleman Neumann learned that German priests were indeed badly needed in some parts of the United States, though not in Philadelphia just at that moment; that Bishop Kenrick had revoked the order given to Dr. N——, director of the seminary, but that admission might, perhaps, be secured to the diocese of New York, Detroit, or Vincennes. Right Rev. Bishop Bruté, of Vincennes, he further stated, was then in Rome, but was expected in Paris at Easter. There he might meet him, confer with him upon the subject nearest his heart, and perhaps cross the ocean in his company. Father Henni, moreover, strongly advised the young student not to start for America without a permit from his Bishop. These communications were not very encouraging. They might, perhaps, have shaken the resolution of one less dauntless than John Neumann. But in his case they had only the effect of sending him to the source of strength and courage—resignation to the holy will of God. His journal of this date runs as follows:

"The information just received casts me down. Why? Will Canon N—— furnish funds for my travelling expenses? Will he give me a recommendation? Shall I receive the written discharge from my Bishop? How shall I be received under the circumstances? I am almost disheartened. What is worse than all else is that in these trials I cannot encourage myself with the thought that my heart is pure. I know full well that I have naught but sin. Perhaps God has forsaken me on that account. Prayer has grown irksome; my efforts seem vain and fruitless. O Jesus, have mercy on me! Jesus, living God, make haste to help me! The waters of tribulation are rising, my feet find no solid resting-place. My God, I am sinking! Save me, O Lord; I perish! Say not, 'Thou art not deserving of pardon.' Lord, hadst Thou willed to glorify Thy justice in me, I should have died a million deaths! But I implore Thee to show forth in me the greatness of Thy mercy; forgive me my sins! Behold, my bodily strength is well-nigh exhausted by my journey; how will it bear up against the mental trials that now assail me? Jesus, my Jesus, Son of David, have mercy on me! My dear Mother Mary, St. Joseph, my guardian angel, my holy patron, pray for me!"

As there was little room for hope of his being received into the diocese of Philadelphia, Professor Philipps offered to interest himself to secure him admittance into the diocese of Vincennes. It was therefore decided that Neumann should await in Strasburg an answer from Bishop Bruté. On his journey thither he stayed two days at Augsburg, where he received hospitality from Rev. Father Fischert, of the cathedral-chapter, and his curate, Dr. Schmidt. He had a letter of introduction from Dr. Stadtler of Munich to Mr. Charles Brug, editor of the *Sion*. Some of the citizens of Prachatitz had, shortly before, forwarded through this gentleman a pious gift to Sweden. This circumstance, joined to the letter of introduction, secured for our traveller a most flattering reception, cordial beyond expectation. On taking leave, a number of prayer-books and religious works were presented to him for the American mission. Before quitting Augsburg he made the following note in his journal:

"I have indeed arrived thus far safe. But I feel dejected, owing in part to the state of my soul, the delay in my journey, and the visits I have been obliged to pay. O my Jesus, truly present in Thy Blessed and Most Wonderful Sacrament, help me! He will!"

At last, February 27th, he reached Strasburg, and with his letters of introduction repaired to the seminary. Here he was most graciously received, although disappointments seemed to await him at every turn; one disappeared only to give place to another. Philadelphia, he was again informed, needed no German priests, and the funds promised him had been given to other missionaries from Alsace and Lorraine. Dr. N—— consoled Neumann by promising to apply for his admission into the diocese of New York. He further assured him that funds would be forthcoming on his presenting a letter of introduction from himself to a certain merchant in Paris. The latter, he said, was a friend of the missions and would, without doubt, advance a considerable sum in their interest. He advised him also, in consideration of his slender means, to set out immediately for Paris and there await an answer from the Bishop of Vincennes. These incidents gave rise to the following notes in our young student's journal:

"Perhaps I shall be received into the diocese of New York. No money to be had in this place. Dr. N—— has received no letter, and I no written discharge from my Bishop. Yet all this troubles me little. God does not afflict me with all these evils at once, but only one by one; it is a salutary school for me. Reasoning from the past, I shall, doubtless, have many more crosses to endure. I rejoice at the thought, for thereby I shall be able to atone for my sins. Help me, O God! Be not Thou far from me when tribulations come upon me! I have a presentiment of approaching sorrow; my heart grows restless and uneasy. My soul is dry and parched, as if a tempest were about to burst upon it. Thank God that I can raise my eyes to Him with confidence!"

On the afternoon of the following day, March 3d, he left Strasburg with a heavy heart.

"March 3d.—I will start at four o'clock to-day for Nancy. I received no pecuniary assistance here at Strasburg, though I was told I might have better success in Paris. Now I plunge into the uncertain. It seems to me that Dr. N—— is not well informed in this matter; the truth is, it looks like some underhand game. But no evil can befall me, for I am Thine, my Jesus, and Thou art mine! Men cannot injure me, for Thou art omnipotent! Out of my poor purse I have to pay the freight of other people's books. But if they only serve to glorify Thy name, dear Jesus, I am willing to hunger and to pay, for I love Thee in my poverty!"

On arriving at Nancy, Neumann's first care was to despatch a second letter to his parents, to acquaint them of his movements up to that time and relieve their anxiety on his account. After describing the various incidents of his journey, he says:

"Almighty God, who confirms me more and more in my resolution and gives me the physical strength necessary to accomplish the work I have begun, will surely recompense you for the sacrifice demanded of you. He always helps us to do what He requires of us. Let this thought, which inspires me with courage, console you. I embrace you," etc., etc.

Neumann hoped to meet in Strasburg Rev. Father Schaefer, who, like himself, was bound for America; but he had not yet arrived. Behold the journal of this date:

"I was disappointed more than ever here at Strasburg. How will affairs turn out in Nancy? Will Father Schaefer come? On Monday I leave for Paris. Admission to either the diocese of New York or Vincennes is uncertain. O Jesus, I am under Thy protection! The greater the struggle, the more glorious the victory. Thy will be done, O Lord, on earth as it is in heaven! I shall very probably experience some perplexity in Nancy, where French is the spoken language. But I shall be no loser thereby, for God is present when distress is greatest. Lord, show Thy love for me, that, in return, I may love Thee more confidingly! Jesus, have mercy on Thy poor servant who for Thy sake has left father and mother and all things dear to him! For Thee, my Jesus, I live, for Thee I die, in life and in death all Thine!"

He remained four days at Nancy, awaiting Father Schaefer's arrival. During this interval he prepared himself, as usual, for the worthy reception of his Eucharistic God, from every one of whose visits he gathered innumerable graces and laid up a new increase of strength against future trials.

He writes, March 5th: "My stay here has been so prolonged that my funds are becoming low. It can be of no possible advantage to me. But Thou art powerful, O my Jesus; in Thee will I confide. I will never despair, however uncertain my position may be. Lord, permit me not to be distracted by the bustle of this world! Recall my wandering soul to thoughts of Thyself whenever the things of this life have turned it away from Thee. To-morrow I shall again venture to approach Thy sacred Banquet."

"March 7th.—Yesterday I experienced great devotion in my Communion, which I received at the Cathedral, and I made a vow to recite daily the 'Little Hours' of the Church. May it be agreeable in the sight of God, and may He grant me the grace to fulfil it whenever it is possible! I went to the Sisters of Charity of St. Charles

Borromeo. They gave me a little book entitled 'Novena to St. Francis Xavier.' I will make the novena at my first opportunity. The confessor of the sick presented me with some relics of the blood of a martyred missionary of Cochin China. This good priest, along with two others, greatly approves my undertaking, though all three think it rash to set out without a written discharge and recommendation from my Bishop."

Neumann took special interest in the Congregation of the Sisters of Charity of St. Charles Borromeo, Nancy. Two considerations influenced him: first, because shortly before three postulants from Budweis had been sent thither by Rev. Father Dichtl with the view of introducing those pious and zealous religious into Bohemia; and secondly, because his own sister Joanna was to enter among them as soon as a house of their Congregation should be opened in Prague.

On March 11th, to Neumann's great joy, Rev. Father Schaefer arrived. At 4 P.M. of the same day they set out for Paris, which they reached late that night. Next morning they sought hospitality at the seminary of St. Sulpice, but were dismissed with the remark that strangers could not be admitted. They then turned their steps to the house of "Foreign Missions." Here, also, they were regarded with a sort of suspicion. It was only after repeated entreaties that a room was assigned them for which they were to pay twenty francs a month. This unusual conduct on the part of those otherwise hospitable gentlemen may have been prompted by the odium cast upon the German priesthood in consequence of the question of clerical celibacy agitated by the clergy of Wirtemberg and Baden.

Disappointment and chagrin attended Neumann's every step in Paris. The rich merchant whose generosity toward the missions had been so vaunted was nowhere to be found; no letter was forthcoming from Bishop Bruté; and his slender purse of only two hundred francs was already considerably reduced. Reluctantly following advice, he resolved to await the expected answer from Bishop Bruté, into whose diocese both he and Rev. Father Schaefer had applied for admission.

Neumann's impressions of Paris are found in his third letter to his parents:

"I arrived in Paris about the middle of Lent, and the first walk I took showed me this city in glaring colors. I met a procession of masked fools. *Carnival clowns* I cannot call them; for, as I said, it was mid-Lent, and *Lenten clowns* would be an appellation not only quite inadmissible, but among Christians altogether unchristian. Some were on foot, some on horseback, and others in chariots. Their behavior was simply scandalous. I marvel that the earth did not open and swallow them alive. However sad this picture, that of the great devotion in the churches was consoling. I was indeed surprised to see in this so-much-decried city the crowds that filled the sacred edifices. Not only are the poor and the aged there to be seen, but multitudes of the higher classes. This proves that the apparently impossible is possible to God. He can cause a camel to pass through the eye of a needle. He can harmonize riches with piety. During Holy Week, especially, the churches presented the sublime spectacle of divine life in God. Here may be seen the faithful of every condition in life kneeling during the consecration, kissing the floor, frequenting confession and Holy Communion, etc. In short, Paris can display the two extremes of piety and wickedness."

As usual, we behold Neumann making good use of his stay in Paris. He frequented the various churches, daily heard Mass in one or even several, visited the Blessed Sacrament, recited the Rosary, made the Via Crucis, and performed many other exercises of devotion. Several times in the week he approached the Holy Table, his heart burning with the purest love, springing from his lively faith. Behold a few extracts from his journal:

"March 18th, eve of the Feast of St. Joseph.—I should like to receive Holy Communion to-morrow. Would that my soul were purer, that my God might be better pleased with me! O Jesus, I long to receive Thee! Thou knowest the yearning of my soul after the Bread of Angels; but if, by communicating, I should be so unhappy as to commit a sin, rather let me die to-night than live to offend Thee!"

The feast of the following day was spent in the spirit of the Church, and was in consequence fraught with graces for the fervent young student. On the evening of the 19th he thus records the events of the day:

"Our Lord has given me to-day innumerable blessings through the intercession of St. Joseph, whose feast we celebrated. I made the earnest resolution to recite matins daily, though I made no vow as yet regarding this part of the breviary. I will strive to keep my resolution in honor of St. Joseph. I went to Notre Dame, the church of Our Lady, the spouse of St. Joseph. There the Lord led me to the privileged altar of the saint, at which I received Holy Communion."

It was Neumann's good fortune frequently to be present at the Abbé Lacordaire's sermons. He loved to listen to the eloquence of the great Dominican preacher, though his notes record the fact in very brief words: "It has become fashionable for the young people here to attend Père Lacordaire's sermons. The church is always crowded."

He appears to have been particularly impressed by the example of the Sisters of Charity, of whom he repeatedly makes mention. Under date of March 30th he expresses the edification the mere sight of them caused him: " The presence of these saintly religious in a church, their modest demeanor on the street, enkindles in my heart the love of Jesus. Would that it were in my power to introduce them into other cities! What joy that would be to my heart! Happy Prague! A great blessing is in store for thee! Mayest thou be ever blessed, for I owe thee much!" At Prague, as we have before intimated, a foundation of these Sisters was to be established through the efforts of Rev. Father Dichtl.

The house in which Neumann and his reverend companion resided whilst in Paris offered to the ardent soul of the former food for reflection and multiplied aspirations to God. It was the house of the "Foreign Missions," and the thought of the brave hearts that had gone forth from its hallowed precincts, that had toiled and suffered for the glory of the Heavenly Master, everywhere suggested itself.

"O ye glorified friends of God," he exclaimed, "ye who once dwelt under this roof, who occupied this very room, ye who gave your life-blood for Jesus, pray for me, a poor sinner, that the Almighty may deign to make me like unto you!"

The beautiful church of St. Genevieve, converted by the Revolution into a pantheon, exerted a saddening influence on Neumann's mind. His indignation finds vent in these words:

"Alas for Christians changed to Pagans! O God, have mercy on us! Permit not these multitudes of Thy creatures to perish forever! They are Thy creatures; for them Thy well-beloved Son shed His Blood."

One day, whilst returning from the church of St. Roche, he lost his way and wandered into one of the picture-galleries of the Louvre. That evening he records the following: "Too great liberty of the eyes. Perhaps purity of heart has suffered thereby. So will it ever be when one runs wilfully into dangerous occasions." And here follow heart-felt expressions of self-condemnation. He looks upon himself as impure, unfaithful, an outcast, the greatest of sinners. Peace of heart was restored only after having unburdened his conscience in the tribunal of penance. Behold his resolutions of amendment:

"Henceforth I will be more on my guard. I will use my glasses only when absolutely necessary, that my soul may be less open to the attacks of Satan, who enters through the eyes. I will remain more in my own room, and study French and English. This will give Thee greater honor, my Jesus, than the gratification of my curiosity would do. On Fridays I will make the Stations and recite the Rosary. O Jesus, assist me to keep these resolutions according to Thy holy will! Thou hast already taught me how to fast and pray; the former I must practise more diligently, that my flesh may not become rebellious."

Father Schaefer and Neumann often took long walks together. On returning from one of these rambles, Neumann records the following significant remark: "Thanks to Thee, O my Jesus, the picture-gallery was closed! Had it been otherwise, matters might have gone badly with me."

The privation on which he so heartily congratulated himself was, however, amply compensated by the pleasure derived from a visit to the zoölogical and horticultural gardens.

Another temptation, more difficult for one of Neumann's inclinations to resist, was that held out by the bookstores. Many were the purchases there made of what seemed to him at the time either absolutely necessary or, at least, very useful; but after-thought generally brought with it the conviction that such outlays were not for one of his limited means. Whilst in Paris, he purchased at different times "Theotymus;" a Greek Bible; a Spanish prayer-book; Fleury; the "Works of St. Francis de Sales;" "Devotion to the Passion of Our Lord Jesus Christ;" "Entretiens avec Jésus;" "The Spiritual Combat," etc., etc. Now he rejoices at having possessed himself of some coveted treasure, and again he accuses himself of bibliomania:

"Before God, it is high time for me to put an end to these purchases. For the future I shall avoid temptation by staying either at home or in church."

Not many days go by, and we again read: "My greatest temptation is to procure beautiful books. I begin by imagining that such or such a book would be useful to me, and that I must have it. This desire is so vehement that it seems to penetrate my very soul, and yet I ought to entertain myself with Jesus Christ alone. To-day brought me a fresh struggle, another temptation in the form of a magnificent Greek-English dictionary. I have wanted one like it a long time. I was on the point of asking the price, but, with God's help, I resisted the temptation and hurried into a church. I must struggle against this enemy which I find ever ready to attack me."

On another occasion a small ivory crucifix attracted his attention. It was very beautiful, and Neumann, ever alive to all that is lovely in nature or art, felt that he must have it. It is needless to say that it was soon transferred to his possession. The cost, indeed, was not so great in itself; but when we consider our young hero's slender purse, we catch, as it were, an insight into the elevated soul whose happiness lay in the gratification of such tastes. Nor is it without a certain sense of appreciation that we recall the fact that he who knew so well how to deny his body the usual quantum of food and rest could not resist the attractions held forth by books and beautiful specimens of sacred art. The circumstance of the ivory crucifix called for the following note in his journal. We cannot read it without a sympathetic glow in our own heart, and we congratulate him on the possession of his treasure: "My little crucifix has given me the greatest pleasure. I have long wished for such a one. Seven francs do not seem so much for what affords such gratification."

Neumann's stay in Paris soon grew tedious. To the silent pages of his faithful journal he confides the uneasiness and misgivings aroused by Bishop Bruté's long delay in replying to his letter:

"March 22d.—Still in Paris, almost two hundred German miles from my loved country, where the tender care of friends and relatives would lighten the burden of my existence. My funds have dwindled to one hundred and twenty-five francs, and here must I stay till the Sunday after Easter. O my God, what shall I do if Bishop Bruté does not come, or if he will not receive me?"

Again: "My soul is in distress as to the future. My want of means, the uncertainty of my reception in America, and even the voyage across the ocean—all combine to destroy my peace. Several vessels have been wrecked lately, and I shrink from the dangers of the ocean. My want of confidence undoubtedly springs from my want of mortification. I am too much given to idle thoughts and desires. I must rise out of all this. St. Francis Xavier had unbounded confidence, and therefore God worked miracles through him. After his example, I will love Jesus more by deeds, and then I, too, shall have more confidence and courage. O Jesus, Thou hast indeed much to bear from me! My rudeness heaps upon Thee a thousand insults, even before it is conscious of the wrong it inflicts."

On March 20th he felt interiorly urged to make a review of all his confessions of the past year. The inspiration fell upon good soil when it entered the soul of John Neumann, as we may conclude from the following note:

"Whilst saying my Office, the thought occurred to me to make another general confession. I will do so at Montmartre in honor of St. Dionysius and the saintly priests Ignatius, Francis Xavier, etc., who there entered into a holy covenant for the greater glory of God. I will go at once and inquire the regulations of the church at Montmartre, that, cleansed from my sins in Thy Precious Blood, O Jesus, my prayers may be heard, and I may receive Thy grace! St. Ignatius Loyola, St. Francis Xavier, St. Francis de Sales, St. Genevieve, all ye holy souls who in Paris once lived and still live, all ye whose holy relics rest here, obtain for me, a sinner, the grace of true repentance!"

Thus resolved, he set to work to note down his sins, which he did all the more carefully, as he distrusted his own proficiency in the French language. He feared being betrayed into a want of clearness in expressing himself. Four days were thus spent. He says: "To-morrow I will try to finish my examination of conscience. Then I shall have but one desire, that of making my general confession as soon and as perfectly as possible. My God, direct me! To Thee do I cry from the depths of my wretched heart! Have mercy on me! I weep, but what kind of tears? If they were tears of love for Jesus, I would gather them up as precious pearls. But, alas, they fall on account of the unhappy state of my soul!"

His examination, lengthy and minute, finished on March 24th, the eve of the Annunciation: "I have just finished my examen since my last general confession of February 14, 1835. O my God, Thou knowest that I have reopened those wounds of my soul only for the greater security of my conscience! This is Thy work, O my God, for I used to think such an undertaking beyond my strength! Thy yoke is sweet and invigorating! O my Jesus, I fear nothing now, excepting that I may recall some sins either this evening or to-morrow morning, and so my work remain only half done! My most amiable Jesus, Thy wisdom and power have given me new life, Thy goodness has strengthened me! O Jesus, look down upon my sins here laid at the foot of Thy cross! Alas, they are wicked deeds! They nailed Thee, the Most Holy, my most amiable Lord, my Master, my God, to the cross! Oh, would that my heart could melt with sorrow! Ah, it is a bitter thought! My Jesus, perfect Thy work, give me contrition equal to my sins! Give me Thy love, that my sorrow may be true and sincere!"

Circumstances prevented his making his confession at Montmartre, so he confessed and communicated, on the Feast of the Annunciation, at the church of Notre Dame. On the following day he received Holy Communion at Montmartre, in honor of St. Ignatius. His general confession was made with the greatest devotion, fervor, and childlike sincerity. But, as if to try His servant's courage, Almighty God permitted him to fall almost immediately into profound desolation, which state continued throughout the entire day. Let us listen to him as he describes this severe trial:

"O Lord," he exclaims, "there is naught but gloom and misery in my soul; the staff on which my hope rested is broken. I am like a plank at sea dashed about by the winds and waves. Chaos more dreary, more desolate than reigned in my soul to-day, could not have existed before creation."

That evening he again writes: "The storm that raged in my soul all day has somewhat abated; still I cannot pray. This morning, full of courage and good resolutions, I entered a confessional at Notre Dame, and confessed my sins most carefully. My soul was at peace. But scarcely had I left the confessional when I was overwhelmed by a sense of my own utter unworthiness, such as I had never before experienced. As for several days I had looked forward most eagerly to a devout reception of the Holy Eucharist on this feast, this unexpected trial fell upon me with crushing weight. It was with difficulty I repressed a cry of pain. I moved on to another altar at which Mass was about to be said. Regarding the storm so suddenly raised in my soul as a passing temptation, I was still resolved to communicate. But when the moment arrived, my conscience was in such a state of revolt that I refrained from Holy Communion, notwithstanding the sacrifices I had made in preparation. On my return home, Rev. Father Schaefer received a letter from Bishop Bruté, promising him a position in his diocese, but making no allusion to me. I yielded to the bitterness of my soul. I had not the strength to control it, though it would have been better for me had I done so. Worn out with the struggles of the day, I fell toward evening into a deep sleep, from which I awoke refreshed and somewhat comforted. I had been afraid to pray; it seemed to me so utterly useless. But now I must say my Office and other prayers, and await better times."

Next day he writes: "Comparative peace of soul is again mine. In spite of my little devotion and feeble desires, I went to Holy Communion. Thanks to God's grace, I kept perfect guard over my eyes all day. This morning I copied the protestation from 'Philothea,' which on the day after to-morrow, my birthday, I will sign in the church of Montmartre, in honor of the founder of the Society of Jesus. I will also go to Holy Communion, if possible. I feel more cheerful to-day."

The day following happened to be Palm-Sunday. Consolation and encouragement seem to have returned, in some degree, to Neumann's pious soul: "I went at an early hour to the church of Notre Dame, and communicated with some little feeling of devotion. I did this in comparative peace, despite certain doubts which often deprive me of my greatest good. I wonder to find myself so full of courage. I feel ready for any cross, even if accompanied by disgrace. My greatest trial, however, would be to have to return home. I should certainly feel that keenly. But were Almighty God to allow such a termination to my project, He would not fail to sustain me by His grace. If it be for His greater glory and my own salvation, I am resigned to His holy will. Our Lord sent me to-day an opportunity of fasting. I gladly availed myself of it in honor of St. Francis Xavier, who, as is related in the 'Novena,' abstained from all kinds of food for three and four days at a time during his retreat. To-morrow, March 28th, my birthday, I will perform my devotions at Montmartre, and sign the protestation which I am resolved to read every day, or at least before every Holy Communion. I have now been saying my Rosary daily for some time, and many are the graces it has brought me. I feel that to it I owe the inspirations which prompted my confessions and good resolutions. I will continue to recite it with still greater devotion for my own benefit, as well as for my dear parents, relations, benefactors, friends, and enemies—in short, for all who have ever recommended themselves to my prayers. Forsake me not, O God, to-morrow! Have mercy on me!"

The morning of the 28th, Neumann's twenty-fifth birthday, broke dark and lowering. The rain fell in torrents, but, faithful to his resolution, he set out for Montmartre, to perform his devotions in honor of St. Francis Xavier. During the Holy Sacrifice he signed the protestation which he had previously made in spirit and in truth. Whilst thus holily engaged, he felt inspired by Almighty God to receive Holy Communion more frequently. The incalculable benefit that would accrue to his soul therefrom was clearly shown him. In the following words he expresses his gratitude for the light vouchsafed him:

"O Jesus, with all my heart I thank Thee for teaching me that only in the frequent reception of Thy Most Holy Body can I find spiritual nourishment and salvation!"

That same day, as he was returning from church, he found an opportunity of helping a little child, though in what he does not tell us: "On my way home, our Lord granted me the happiness of rendering a trifling service to a little child." In this remark we discover more than the words themselves imply; for we see how every circumstance of life, even the seemingly indifferent, was by Neumann directly referred to Almighty God.

Many favors appear to have been bestowed upon him on this day, in reward, no doubt, of his fidelity. Behold his own words:

"O my Lord, I thank Thee for the love Thou hast begun to plant in my heart! I will cultivate the precious germ; I will cherish it as coming from Thee, my Heavenly Spouse! I will guard it day and night that nothing may injure it; that its delicious fragrance may greet Thee on Thy entrance into my heart. But do Thou, O Lord, water it with the dew of Thy grace; do Thou cause it to flourish, else it will wither and fall to the earth. O Mary, Mother of my Lord Jesus Christ, in union with all the saints and angels, pray for me that I may become a perfect disciple of Jesus!"

Neumann clearly recognized and keenly deplored what he called his moral infirmities, his lack of energy for good, his proneness to evil; and heart-felt was his humiliation before God when he contemplated his want of correspondence with grace. "Lord Jesus," he cries, "do not punish me by detaining me here in Europe, as I have a thousand times deserved! Poverty and disgrace I am willing to bear, O my Jesus; but, ah, do not punish me by holding me back from the sublime and life-giving struggle for souls! My severe headache prevents my praying or studying long to-day, though I feel great need of both. But if my patience will now be more acceptable to Thee than study or prayer, may Thy holy will be done!"

Here lay the secret of his strength, the holy will of God. It sustained him in trial, enlightened him in doubt, soothed him in anxiety, calmed him in the rudest storms. Confidence in God, the total abandonment to Him of self and of everything pertaining to the future, shone forth conspicuously in Neumann at this time.

"My old courage," he writes, "has revived. Our Lord

has never permitted utter discouragement to assail me, though the prospects for my journey still cause me considerable anxiety. Surely an answer must soon be forthcoming from Bishop Bruté. He must have received my letter in Lyons. O Jesus, I thank Thee with all my heart for having placed me in so difficult, so perplexing a position! O God, my longing for virtue grows more earnest, more fervent! Grant me, I pray Thee, faith, the foundation of the Christian life; hope, which sustains in every combat; and the holy virtue of charity! But, above all, dearest Jesus, give me Thyself! To-morrow I will again present myself to receive Thee, my Creator, my Redeemer, my Sanctifier!"

The last three days of Holy Week were devoted in a special manner to the consideration of the sufferings of our Redeemer. On Wednesday evening of that week he records the following: "Ah, my Jesus, the bitter-sweet days of Thy Passion and death draw near! Could I rightly meditate upon their mysteries, I would do so. But Thou hast bestowed upon me only the gift of vocal prayer and the simple consideration of Thy life and sufferings, for which gift I thank Thee from the bottom of my heart. To-morrow, Holy Thursday, I will receive Holy Communion in the parish church; then I shall adore Jesus in His Passion, and visit some of the other churches."

"Holy Thursday.—On returning home, the thought of fasting till eight that evening presented itself; but I waived it, as I intended visiting Father Fischer at noon, and doubtless he would have invited me to breakfast with him. But I was prevented. When about to leave my room, I found that the servant had inadvertently locked me in. My mishap caused me more satisfaction than regret, since by it I understood that the inspiration to prolong my fast actually came from God. I comforted myself with Bourdaloue's sermons. They inundated my soul with joy and devotion. During the evening I received a letter from Rev. Father Räss of Strasburg, which contributed very much to brighten up my spirits. Father Räss held out to me the hope of being received by Right Rev. Bishop Bruté, and mentioned, likewise, his having applied for my admission to the diocese of New York. My effects are now being forwarded to me. Full of interior joy, I went to Notre Dame, heard a sermon, and visited the Holy Sepulchre. O my Jesus, how is it that on the days that commemorate Thy great sufferings I receive such graces, taste such joys, whilst on the glad festivals of the Church it is just the reverse? Ah, my Jesus, Thou dost wish to encourage me to bear joy and sorrow equally for Thy sake!"

Good-Friday was spent by Neumann in church, meditating upon Jesus in His Passion, death, and burial. That evening he accuses himself of having prolonged his fast only till four o'clock. Then he adds: "My longing for the Blessed Sacrament has increased since I have experienced how much it weakens my bad habits, inclinations, and passions, gives me strength to combat, and fills my heart with joy and peace. The love of Jesus sweetens what is bitter. Temptation is often a subject of congratulation to me, since it affords me an opportunity of proving my fidelity to God. Ah, my Jesus, how glad I am that Thy death-agony is over! The thought of Thy sufferings gives me pain; and does not every sin I commit torture Thee, crucify Thee anew? Help me, O my dearest Mother Mary, to fulfil in all things the most holy will of Thy Son Jesus! Help me, that I may never more offend Him!"

Holy Saturday found the pious young student still occupied with thoughts of his Saviour, now resting in the sepulchre, now risen from the dead. Nearly the whole day was passed in church, as we read in his own account of it, which closes with the following childlike petition:

"Ah, my Jesus, stay with me! Or wilt Thou abandon

me to-morrow, as Thou dost generally do on festival-days? May Thy will be done! Let me not fall into sin; teach me to detest and avoid it. Hark to Our Lady, the angels and saints! They cry in ecstatic joy, 'Alleluia! The Lord is risen!' O glorified Jesus, have mercy on me!"

On this day certain individuals of the house behaved in a rude and insulting manner to young Neumann, who, as was his wont on such occasions, took little notice of their conduct. He merely remarks:

"I will pray for all who have offended me, or rather I will pray for humiliations. I will ask that they may come upon me in such a way that God may not be offended by them, and that I may become more like my Saviour in patience and meekness. Do I not deserve severer reprimands, greater punishments? Truly I do, O my Jesus! Were the whole world to tread me under foot, I should still be forced to acknowledge that I deserve such treatment a thousand times."

The want of correspondence between the ceremonies he witnessed in the churches of Paris and those of the Roman ritual, to which he had ever been accustomed, was by no means agreeable to Neumann. It evoked from his pen the following remark: "The difference in the ceremonies made a very disagreeable impression upon me. It can scarcely be the spirit of Christ that has introduced such changes; consequently there is wanting, even in the hymns, that simple, tender, elevating character so noticeable in the Roman liturgy. I prefer in obedience to accomplish something less perfect than, through self-seeking and vanity, to attain greater perfection."

The festival of Easter was in fact, as he had anticipated, a joyless day to Neumann. Although he had devoutly received Holy Communion, he grieved over his tepidity in the performance of other spiritual exercises. He ascribes his indignation at the changes introduced by the Gallican church into her liturgy to his own pride, for which he imposed on himself a penance. Finally, we find him resolving no longer to await Bishop Bruté's answer, but to continue his journey on the following Tuesday.

On Easter-Monday he communicated, made his thanksgiving till nine o'clock, and then began the necessary preparations for his voyage. Five P.M. the next day was fixed for his departure from the great French metropolis. Twenty-nine francs were expended for fare, the transportation of baggage and the box of books received from Dr. Räss. That evening he writes:

"O God, my undertaking is still marked by unlooked-for incidents, failures, humiliations, and disappointed hopes. I see, my God, that Thou dost will to do Thy work alone. My good God, willingly and cheerfully do I abandon myself to Thy care! My own designs never lead to anything good. Be Thou, therefore, my constant guide and protector! My Jesus, soon shall I embark upon the sea of Thy Almighty Power! But joyfully will I accept whatever Thou hast marked out for me, even death itself if conducive to Thy glory and my own salvation!"

Tuesday evening, as previously arranged, he bade farewell to Paris, no letter having as yet been received from Bishop Bruté. The resolution to confide wholly in Divine Providence was to be the guiding-star of our courageous young student, and to it he entrusted the vocation that was to be his in the New World. Arrived at last at the station whence the stage-coach was to start, fancy his dismay on being informed that it had left just five minutes before! To overtake it he hired a cab, at a cost of five francs; but on reaching the city limits the driver refused to proceed further. These incidents the journal thus records:

"I would not turn back; so, trusting to my strong limbs, I trudged coolly along the road toward the sea, though the sun had already set. It grew darker and darker, and rain began to fall. The end of this night-ramble found me thoroughly drenched, though not unusually fatigued, and so I arrived at Nanterre."

Here he was accosted by a good old Frenchman, who, noticing the perplexity of the young stranger, conducted him to the station and assisted him to mount to the top of the stage-coach, on the point of starting for St. Germain. For the good old man's services Neumann had to pay seventeen sous. At St. Germain he found time to make a pencil-note of the condition of his soul:

"Ah! what is this, my dearest Jesus?" he asks. "Thou dost tighten the reins, that I may not wander from the right path. Dear Lord, I thank Thee for it! My present position is full of the most painful uncertainty, yet this, too, is Thy most holy will. Mayest Thou, O my Jesus, be forever blessed! Bright and early to-morrow I will go on foot to Rouen. I shall reach it in good time. I had better spend the nights in travelling, for then I shall not have to pay for lodgings. However, may Thy holy will be done, my Jesus! I will practise resignation in adversity for the love of Thee, that Thou mayest have mercy on me and on all my loved ones. Lord Jesus, how sweet dost Thou not make my painful position! Lord, stay with me now and ever! Amen!"

Early next morning he set out on foot for Meulan, where, for ten francs, he purchased a seat on the stage-coach bound for Havre. At Rouen he entered the following note in his journal: "My dearest Jesus, I thank Thee for this day of suffering! Since my journey began, this is the first day Thou didst try me sharply! But, with the help of Thy grace, I have overcome my enemy. I have been far from well; my head ached all day; the past and the future lay like a hundredweight upon my heart; the conductor's rudeness aggravated my distressed position; but, because I turned to Thee, my Jesus, or rather because Thou didst turn to me, I bore all patiently for Thy love! O Jesus, I renew my morning offering of the sufferings of this day. I offer them for Thy glory, for the good of my own soul, and for the souls of those to whom I am related as son, brother, relative, subject, and client. My God, I now near the term of my journey in this part of my native land. Soon shall I leave it. O Jesus, forgive the sins I have committed here in the Old World! Help me, O Almighty Lord, to overcome, to root out the wicked passions that have taken possession of me! Nowhere am I better off than with Thee, my Jesus! While crossing a marshy tract to-day, I lost my crucifix. I certainly regret my little treasure; but what does it signify, provided I lose not Thee, my Jesus? Since Thou hast permitted this loss to befall me, I beseech Thee, for the sake of the tears with which I so often bedewed the little crucifix, to allow it to fall in the way of some pious soul who will embrace it with greater love, shed over it tears of truer contrition than I ever did! Oh, that I, miserable sinner as I am, could proclaim to all the world the sweetness of Thy love, the happiness hidden in suffering with Thee and for Thee, my dear Redeemer! Ah! this privilege will indeed be mine when Thou hast received me into Thy holy service. Come to my aid, O my Lord; strengthen me in good that I be not a sounding bell, calling others to devotions in which it never joins itself! Ah, Lord, I am now alone! no friend, no acquaintance, and in a strange land! But, surely, Thou dost ordain this, in order to prove that Thou Thyself, the strong God, will combat for me! Oh, lead me safe to-morrow into the haven [Havre de Grace], as Thou once didst lead me into the haven of grace! Jesus, Mary, Joseph, mercy!"

A very pleasing little incident occurred to our young traveller on his journey to Havre, which we cannot but ascribe to the loving care of Divine Providence in his regard. At one of the stations on the road the coach halted, and Neumann's travelling companions alighted to take dinner. Neumann, also, began to feel his strength giving out; nature called for food. Alighting with the rest, he followed the direction of the crowd, but at a slower pace, mentally revolving the question as to how with the least outlay he could procure some refreshment for his weary frame. Just at this moment a friendly voice fell upon his ear, as if calling to him. Turning his eyes in the direction of the sound, he beheld a tidy-looking little woman, who proved to be the innkeeper's wife, beckoning him into one of the eating-rooms. He obeyed the sign and entered almost mechanically. He soon found himself at table with several dishes set before him. But here he paused embarrassed. and excused himself from partaking of the food on the plea of want of means. Such variety, he said, was not necessary; he could do with less. "Eat, eat," said his kind-hearted hostess encouragingly; "we will not quarrel over the bill." Neumann waited for no second invitation, and, after a hearty meal, the words, "Pray for us, pray for us!" was all he heard by way of settlement.

On April 7th our travellers arrived at Havre. Neumann's first care was to visit his Lord in the Blessed Sacrament, after which he satisfied his desire for a sight of the mighty ocean. After making inquiries concerning the departure of vessels for New York, he returned to his lodgings and, according to custom, spent a part of the evening recording in his journal the events of the day.

"My situation here at Havre is beset with difficulties. With my imperfect knowledge of both French and English, I am likely to be imposed upon, and even a small loss is more than I can afford just now. I saw the ocean to-day for the first time. It is not exactly what I imagined. O my God, will this voyage of mine end successfully? I saw the vessel in which very probably I shall embark for New York. The thought of travelling alone, without an acquaintance or friend, is not very cheering. But why this fear, as if there were no God! But I am not worthy of His protection. Be at peace, O my soul! To-morrow the Lord Jesus Christ in Holy Communion will again strengthen thy weakness. I will try to spend the whole of the forenoon in church to-morrow, and in the afternoon I will make inquiries about my voyage, etc. O God, be Thou my guide, my interpreter. Remember that my undertaking pertains to Thy glory. For two days I have been prevented from saying my Office, but I will now resume it."

Next day, after a long search, Neumann found the ship Europa. The price of passage-tickets ranged from ninety to one hundred and twenty francs. This piece of information greatly relieved our young traveller's mind, as he still had funds enough to cover his expenses. A letter from Rev. Father Schaefer, who was still in Paris, came most opportunely about the same time, and contributed largely to his satisfaction. It contained a check for his baggage, which was being forwarded to him from Paris. His journal says:

"Father Schaefer's truly fraternal letter came like a gleam of sunshine. My God, reward this good man who has shown me so much kindness! He is the only one in France who seemed to take an interest in me, and he has shown it even beyond his means. May God reward him in heaven!"

Neumann's stay at Havre was far from pleasant. Every day brought him some new trouble. On April 8th he writes: "My spirits ran unusually low to-day. My boots are nearly worn out; the weather is rainy; the prospect of remaining here till the 16th and even longer —all this depressed me. I became almost home-sick. But I offered all to God; I prayed, and my sadness was somewhat dissipated. Our table is in style, but for the future I will only breakfast here. Bread, with the addition of butter, perhaps, will satisfy me for dinner. Could

I go aboard ship at once, I would do so; but I hardly think that would be allowed. God seems to ordain that, like Gideon, I should be deprived of all natural succor, that His divine power may be more strikingly manifested in me. I shall, however, try what I can do, and if not successful I must be resigned to the will of God. In the morning I shall communicate, that in this 'Haven of Grace' I may find much grace. My God, this poor heart of mine yearns for home to-day. What are my loved ones, my parents, my brother, my sisters, now doing? Ah! they often anxiously think of me. I will write to-morrow and try to console them. O my God, lay my parents' sorrow on me! Give them peace now in their old age. Oh, how I love them! My God, have mercy on us all! Grant us to meet again in heaven and, with no fear of parting, to be happy with Thee for all eternity! The loss of my ivory crucifix, and portfolio containing relics, has cost me tears to-day; they were my dear treasures. Now I am poor indeed. I had no idea how near they were to my heart. O Jesus, I deplore their loss! P——'s leaflet; the blood of the Cochin-China martyr; the scrap of linen belonging to Blessed Electa, etc., etc.—all gone! Ah, my Jesus! I did not deserve to possess those sweet mementos. Thou shalt have the love I once bestowed upon them. Help me to persevere in good, to be humble, courageous, meek, pious, holy!"

Thus did Neumann spend those tedious days in Havre, praying, communicating, visiting the churches, and pouring out his whole soul to God. At last, to his great joy, he was told that the moment of departure would soon arrive. Urged by his eager desire to reach the land of his hopes, the scene of his future labors in God's service, he let no day pass without inquiries respecting the vessels bound for America. In answer to his questioning, he learned that besides the ship Europa there were two smaller vessels, the Sully and the Troy, to sail about the same time as the first-named, and for the same destination. This circumstance had the effect of lowering the Europa's tickets, and allowed young Neumann to secure for himself a second-class passage. April 12th was the day fixed for departure, and on the eve we find the following remarks in that fruitful source from which we have drawn so largely for the foregoing pages:

"My Jesus, I recognize this favor as coming from Thee! Thou hast heard my request; Thou hast granted my prayer. Oh, how I may now rejoice! Mayest Thou be forever praised! After so many struggles, I am again at peace. O Jesus, I will never forget Thee, since Thou hast so graciously remembered me! Bless my enterprise! May it tend to Thy greater glory! My soul is full of joy. I will bless Thee, O Lord, all the rest of my days! To-morrow I shall inform my parents and Father Dichtl of my success thus far. They, too, will rejoice. They, too, will praise Thee, O my Jesus! Now I must see to having my baggage conveyed to the vessel, on which I am to embark to-morrow. Lord Jesus, stay with me, assist me, grant me success! Ah, I must be diligent in my project, since the Lord blesses my plans! O Jesus, remain with me, and grant me ever to remain with Thee!"

Contrary to expectation, the Europa did not sail till the 20th, eight days later than previously arranged. Those eight days, as we may readily conjecture from the past, were not blanks in the life of our pious young student. The weariness of delay he relieved by prayer and good works. Day followed day, and finally the morning of the 20th dawned. For the last time in many years he had the happiness to receive Holy Communion on the soil of the Old World. Noon brought the long-sighed-for signal; the Europa weighed anchor and stood out for sea, bearing with her under the guiding hand of God one who was to be, at a later period, one of the brightest and holiest ornaments of the American hierarchy—John Nepomucene Neumann. Nineteen years later we shall find him returning to his native land under circumstances very different from those that surrounded his lonely and unnoticed departure, though the heart beating under the pectoral cross remained unchanged. It was still the humble, devoted heart in love with that God for whose honor and glory alone it throbbed.

CHAPTER IX.

Voyage to the New World.

AT last, after the numerous difficulties and multiplied disappointments above recorded, sufficient it might seem to daunt the bravest heart, Neumann found himself on board a vessel bound for the New World. What cared he that, among the multitudes hurrying to and fro, not one familiar face met his anxious gaze; that most of his fellow-passengers were of the humblest walks of life; that of the two hundred German emigrants most of them were Protestants, some from Berne in Switzerland, others from Alsace, Lorraine, and Baden? The love of God that glowed in his heart, that animated his every action, that nerved him to set out alone, friendless and almost penniless, in answer to the voice that called, ignored all such considerations. God, and God alone, was the end, the object of all his desires, in comparison of whose attainment all things else sank into insignificance. Forty long days did that voyage last. We must remember it was in the year 1836; and not till two years later, 1838, did steamships make regular passages across the Atlantic. Then the Sirius and the Great Western began to run between London and Bristol and New York. Each day of this long ocean-trip was duly recorded by Neumann. Four days of storm greatly retarded their progress, as the ship was driven back by adverse winds. Neumann suffered only slightly from sea-sickness; after the first three days he was wholly free from its attacks. During one of the storms above alluded to his life was saved in a truly providential manner. The time not spent in his devotions, which, as we know, were many, was devoted to study and reading, or in musing upon the designs of Divine Providence in his regard. One day the storm raged so fiercely as to drive the passengers below deck. Neumann, absorbed in anxious speculations on his uncertain future, alone remained above. Lost in thought, he took no heed of the rolling billows and the tossing ship now rising, now sinking on the foaming waves. Suddenly he started as if touched by an invisible hand, and lo! scarcely had he stepped forward, when with a terrible crash down came the sailyard upon the very spot on which he had stood one instant before! That moment witnessed Neumann's unconditional surrender of himself into the hands of Divine Providence. Long years after he loved to revert to this incident as to the one which awakened in his soul unbounded confidence in the paternal protection of Almighty God.

Some days later a change of atmosphere betokened the vicinity of icebergs, and on the following morning Neumann gazed in admiring wonder on those floating mountains of glittering crystal. Again did he raise his soul in gratitude to God for averting from himself and his fellow-voyagers this formidable danger. In all that met his eye, the ocean's broad expanse, now rising and swelling in mighty billows that threatened destruction to the huge vessel riding on its waves, now reposing like some potent monster in the proud consciousness of its own strength, the never-ending sky lit up by the dazzling rays of the noonday sun, or anon wrapped in angry, lowering clouds, or sparkling at night with myriads of glowing gems whose scintillations were mirrored in the waters beneath—all, all spoke to our hero's loving heart of the omnipotence, the wisdom, the goodness of God. "My God!" he cries out, "how great Thou art, how wonderful in all Thy works! Ah, what graces hast Thou not heaped upon me since I left my native shores! Speak to me, my God; let me know Thy will; for behold me ready to fulfil Thy every command! The difficult, the irksome, I will patiently endure for love of Thee. Behold me in Thy hands! My heart exults in the manifestations of Thy power. O dearest Infant Jesus, what joy to contemplate Thy infinite greatness! O dearest Child, Thy tiny hands have hollowed out the ocean's vast abyss!"

A weary calm of several days, at another time, retarded our voyager's progress. Neumann remarks: "A calm of three days has kept us back. Here we lie on the waves, neither advancing nor receding; meanwhile our provisions are getting low. Alas, my God! is it not thus with my poor soul? Thanks to Thy grace, I fear sin; but how is it with regard to my progress in the spiritual life? Lord, have mercy on me! I am spending the precious time which should be consumed in Thy service in doing absolutely nothing. I would like, on reaching America, to devote myself, at least for a while, to the care of the sick, or rather to God in the person of the sick. It seems highly improbable that I shall be received into the diocese of New York. Still, my Jesus, I am in peace; nay, I even rejoice in the anticipation of sufferings. They will, doubtless, procure for me many graces. Humble me, purify me more and more, that Thou, my Lord and my God, mayest find an acceptable resting-place in my heart."

Again he writes: "This is the third of the rogation-days. Oh, what a consoling thought! Were I at home, how joyfully would I not assist at the processions of this day and supplicate Thee, my God, to bless the fruits of the earth! But now it is Thy holy will that I should be cut off from all such consolations; that I should live, as I hope to die, only for Thee. I offer Thee, dear God, as a substitute for those processions, my sufferings, my misery, my loneliness."

"Feast of the Ascension.—O holy day of my Lord's ascension, thou art welcome! The thought that my

Jesus has left our earth has moved me to tears. Yesterday and to-day I made many good resolutions for my future. God gave me, also, an opportunity of practising humility under contempt and insult. I bore it patiently, though with violence to my feelings."

The gentle, retiring, and religious demeanor of the young traveller, so different from all around him, did not fail to attract the attention of his fellow-voyagers, who sometimes greeted him, in consequence, with derisive laughter and cutting remarks. To this he seems to allude in the sentences just quoted.

"I have learned by experience," he continues, "that the daily reading of 'Philothea' is a powerful means of fostering devotion. It renders the practice of virtue easy. Give Thyself to me, O dearest little Jesus, and give me, also, Thy most amiable Mother!"

"Pentecost.—My wants here at sea are easily satisfied; but if, on reaching New York, I shall have to continue my journey, uncertain whither to turn, I fear my courage will fail. If not received in any diocese of America, I shall seek a hermitage in some vast forest, or on some plain. There, my God, if it be Thy will, I shall serve Thee alone and do penance for my own and others' sins. Oh, how greatly would not such a life contribute to my spiritual good! My God, permit it to me, and teach me the best way of setting about it! Mary, my guardian angel, my holy patrons, all ye saints of heaven, pray for me!"

On the Monday after Pentecost, Neumann was quite sick, the effect of a sudden change of temperature. It was not, however, a very serious indisposition, for we again find him using his pen: "Though sick, yet I feel somewhat more disposed to piety. My sufferings should be pleasing to me, dear Jesus, since they afford me a chance of practising patience. From the quantity of sea-weed we saw yesterday we may conclude that land is near. Soon, O Jesus, the dreaded voyage will be accomplished. What happiness for me! Whether I shall become a priest or not, I shall now have hourly opportunities to atone for my sins. Oh, how have I deserved such a favor!—I who have so often rejected Thy graces! My fancy loves to dwell upon the solitary life I purpose leading, if it be the will of God that I should not be ordained. This question will soon be decided. Confiding in Thee, dearest Infant Jesus, I dread not the future. My Lord, my God, what am I doing? Am I not pondering too much on the future, which is still beyond my grasp, and too little on my present opportunities of perfecting myself by the practice of virtue? O God, grant that I may soon purify my troubled conscience by a good confession and regain my strength of soul in Holy Communion!"

On the eve of Trinity Sunday a light fog partly obscured the horizon, through which the crew of the Europa caught their first glimpse of the New World. Twenty-four hours later, Trinity Sunday evening, the ship anchored at quarantine, about three miles below Staten Island. What were now the feelings of those weary voyagers, for forty long days and nights beaten about by the winds and waves! What, above all, were young Neumann's emotions on finding himself after so many struggles, so many disappointments, at the term for which he had so ardently sighed! But fresh obstacles, new delays, were in store for him before setting foot on those far-famed shores. On the eve of Corpus Christi he writes:

"Since Trinity Sunday we have lain at anchor within sight of New York. O my God, with Thy assistance so near to my destination, and yet with so little hope, so little consolation! I tried at least six times to-day to find some means of reaching the island, whence I might cross over to the city by steamboat. I am so anxious to celebrate in church the great love-feast of my Redeemer to-morrow. I could have spent the night praying in the open air. But all my attempts, my entreaties, were vain. My God, why hast Thou forsaken me? O my soul, thou of little faith! Poor and friendless, I will present myself to Thy Bishop, dear Lord. His heart is in Thy hands. Thou art the Almighty God; do Thou incline that heart to Thy own glory, to my good and that of my dear family! Alas, I am not wise; I know not what is profitable to me! Graciously accept the sacrifice of my resignation! Ah! I know well that no one is less worthy than I to enter that land in which I am resolved to serve Thee. Still the desire to land haunts me. The captain's knavery incenses me, and the incessant humiliations to which I am subjected almost crush me. My Jesus, behold the burden that rests upon me! My loved parents, my brother and sisters, the priesthood, worldly honors, ease — all these I have renounced for Jesus Christ. What will my future be? What is in store for me?"

Neumann's first letter from America describes his own feelings and those of his fellow-voyagers at the sight of land and the city of New York:

"How grateful to the eye, after a long voyage, is the sight of land! The sensation is indescribable; it must be experienced to be understood. Forty days after our departure from Havre we hailed land. Oh, the glad sight! In spite of the drenching rain, we stood on deck as long as the waning light permitted anything to be seen. We gazed with delight on the charming green banks dotted with light red houses and gayly painted cottages. They produce a most pleasing effect. All hands, even the poor sick, came up on deck, forgetful of suffering and hardship. Some shouted for joy, some sang snatches of song, all were jubilant at the thought of setting foot on land once more. Oh, what happiness must inundate the heart of the just man when, stretched on his dying bed, he sees the end of his trials and miseries approaching, and heaven, the land of his desires and affections, opening out before him!

"But our joy was soon checked. The captain announced that, owing to the unfavorable wind and the presence of sickness on board, we would have to remain at sea some days longer, perhaps even a whole week. Most unwelcome news was this, as the water for drinking had grown offensive, and provisions were becoming scarce."

Neumann's eagerness to reach land induced him to apply once more to the captain. The latter, overcome by the young man's earnestness, consented at last to having him conveyed next morning to Staten Island. Eleven o'clock next day, the Feast of Corpus Christi, saw the promise redeemed, and Neumann landed on the island, whence by steamboat he reached New York about 1 P.M.

"What emotions were mine at that moment," he goes on to say in his letter, "you can imagine. My first care was to hunt up a Catholic church. The rain fell in torrents. Up one street, down another; but no Catholic church could I find, though I searched till evening. I indeed came across numberless meeting-houses, but nowhere what I sought. I had to call all my philological skill into play to decipher the inscriptions on those edifices informing the passer-by to what particular sect they belonged. One had only a plain flat roof; another was surmounted by a vane; a third had a cross, above which turned a weather-cock. The devil, I thought, may array himself in fine garments, but the cloven foot will be sure to appear. These places of worship were all locked; only from one, a Wesleyan meeting-house, did I see several men coming out, their hats on and each with a cigar in his mouth. My search was fruitless, and at last I turned to look for lodgings at an inn kept by a Swiss. Next morning my host pointed out the direction to the nearest Catholic church. I soon reached it, and recognized it by its simple cross. It was a church for English-speaking Catholics. There I received the address of the Right Reverend Bishop and the German pastor who lives with him. An hour later I arrived at the Cathedral, where the first one I met was Rev. Father Raffeiner. He showed the greatest astonishment at my unexpected appearance. He informed me that Dr. Räss had applied for my admission into the diocese; that I had been accepted three weeks before, and a letter to that effect despatched to Europe. Father Raffeiner then took me to Bishop Dubois, who, in his surprise and joy, knew not whether to welcome me in Latin, French, or English. After examining my testimonials, he repeated that I had been accepted, but that he had expected several theological students, and he very much regretted their not having come with me. He added that his need of a German priest was so great that he was on the point of sending to Philadelphia for one. He promised to ordain me on his return from his pastoral visitation, which had already been mapped out. Though eighty years of age, he never omits his duty."

The emotions that now held sway in young Neumann's heart on this happy fulfilment of his long-cherished desires we must leave to his own pen to depict. In his usual childlike manner he turns to God, the Author of all his success:

"Thanks, a thousand thanks to Thee, my Jesus, for having prepared a place for me in Thy sanctuary. Now free from anxiety, I can enter into myself. This I do the more gladly as I know it to be my duty. Oh, what emotions were mine when, on the Feast of Corpus Christi, I set foot on American soil! I felt interiorly urged to look for a church. I wandered about in the rain till evening, but in vain. The next morning I met Father Raffeiner. My God, how can I thank Thee for Thy goodness in sending me to so paternal, so pious a man! Here I am at last! Doubt and uncertainty have vanished like mist before the rays of the sun. I may now look forward with confidence to the speedy attainment of my hopes. Silently, O my Jesus, silently but surely hast Thou disentangled the knot which once appeared to me so difficult. Three weeks even before my arrival here was my reception agreed upon. Very likely my friends have been apprised of it by this time. Oh, what an apostolic man is our Bishop! Whenever I think of him, St. John the Evangelist rises up before me. My God, I am seized with fear when I consider the sanctity of the office that awaits me and compare with it my own unworthiness. Lord, punish me not in Thy anger! Take from me the burden, or, dear Lord, increase my strength and faith, my hope and charity, a thousand-fold! Enkindle in my heart charity toward my neighbor. In such sentiments I would be willing to die; I would not care what might happen to me. Oh, joyful thought! now I shall really be Thy servant; now I shall be able to receive Thee, my Jesus, often, often! O Jesus, I must henceforth labor for the salvation of others. Do Thou strengthen my weakness! Be Thou forever praised, dearest Jesus, my Lord and my God! Behold, my life, my strength, my whole being, all that I have, all that I am, I devote to Thy greater glory."

PART II.

JOHN N. NEUMANN AS A SECULAR PRIEST.
1836–1840.

CHAPTER I.

John Neumann is Raised to the Dignity of the Priesthood.

CANDIDATES for holy orders are, as a general thing, allowed several days of retreat in preparation for the worthy reception of the Sacrament. During those days an experienced director superintends their exercises and imparts to them a practical knowledge of the various ceremonies of the Church. This privilege, so grateful to a soul seeking God, was not to fall to John Neumann's share. Circumstances arising from the imperative demand for a German pastor did not permit him such an advantage. Father Raffeiner lost no time in charging young Neumann with the duty of giving regular instructions in Christian Doctrine to the German congregation of St. Nicholas' Church, and of catechising the children of the school in preparation for their First Communion, which duties were most cheerfully and zealously performed. No assistance that he could possibly render his neighbor was ever withheld by our pious student. To prepare young souls for the worthy reception of Holy Communion, and to awaken in them the liveliest devotion toward the Most Blessed Sacrament, were his greatest delight. He frequently declared it his conviction that a subsequent virtuous or vicious life depends upon a worthy or an unworthy First Communion. His efforts in behalf of the little ones entrusted to his care were always accompanied by fervent petitions to Heaven imploring grace for them. "Jesus, Thou Friend of children," he would exclaim, "have mercy on these poor little ones whom I am preparing for Thy Banquet of love!"

On June 19, 1836, in St. Patrick's Cathedral, Neumann received, from the hands of Bishop Dubois, the first of the holy orders, that of subdeacon. How devoutly and earnestly he prepared for its reception we may gather from his own words recorded that same evening in his journal:

"O my Jesus, how I glory in belonging to Thee! how I glory in being Thine, in possessing Thee without reserve! Yesterday Thou didst pardon me my sins, and to-day—be Thou eternally praised!—Thou didst not only visit me, but Thou didst also confer upon me the sacred order of subdeaconship. O Lord, Thou hast graciously accepted the vow of perpetual chastity which Thy Holy Church requires of me, and which I most gladly make to Thee. O Jesus, I promise, with all my heart, to obey Thee in the person of Thy pastor, in simplicity, in love, and in veneration. I will love Thy Church. She is now my spouse, since I have bid farewell to the world; and I will serve her because she is Thy spouse, O my Divine Affianced! Thou hast wedded her by Thy sacred Incarnation, purified and sanctified her by Thy holy doctrine, Thy life, and Thy bitter Passion, that, stainless, she may be like unto Thee, my dearest Lord. O my Jesus, Thou hast received me, a most miserable sinner; Thou hast graciously admitted me to the service of Thy Church. Oh, draw me powerfully to Thy holy Cross, that I, too, may become pure and pious and holy; that, as a devoted servant of Thy holy Church, I may walk without blemish before Thee and before men in the way of Thy Commandments! Thy death, O Jesus, has made all men my brethren. Come Thou, O Holy Ghost, come Thou upon me, a wretched sinner, that, placed on the candlestick by the unfathomable decrees of Thy mercy, I may show forth to the world the way of eternal salvation! Grant me, O Thou the Light of souls, not only to teach Thy holy Word to others, but do Thou come upon me, Thou Strength of the weak, that my life and my works may exhibit faith made fruitful by Thy grace! I shall be ordained under the title of the American Missions; my conduct must henceforth be a living expression of my gratitude. Until my final ordination, I will remain, as much as possible, in retirement and prayer. I shall map out my future in accordance with the rules of St. Francis de Sales. O Holy Spirit, direct me in all my ways! To-day or to-morrow I must write to my loved parents. They will rejoice with me, and thank Thee, the Giver of all good gifts. Oh, what joy will not my letter give the Reverend Dean!"

On the following day he again gives vent to the holy emotion of his soul in such words as these:

"The order of subdeacon has exerted an extraordinarily beneficial influence upon my soul. I am now separated from the world: and what could be more salutary to sinful man? The reception of this order has filled me with courage, increased my confidence in God, and inflamed my love for Him. The Divine Office is now of obligation for me, and I am released from the vow made at Nancy. O Jesus, I promised Thee yesterday to say the Rosary every day in honor of Thy dearest Mother, my mediatrix, to secure her assistance in the discharge of my duties, and to beg her protection over my dear ones at home. To-day I renew this vow. Grant me ever, O my God, Thy holy grace!"

As the time for Neumann's final ordination and first

Mass drew near, the more ardent became his familiar colloquies with his Lord and Saviour.

"June 23d.—My Jesus, I know not how to spend this day, the eve of that on which I shall receive the great Sacrament! My God, what shall I do? Ah! nothing else than remain here by Thy lowly but glorious Crib, near to Thy delightful Banquet, by Thy holy Cross. Ah, how confused is my poor soul before Thee! My God, how couldst Thou love us so much? Alas! wretched sinner that I am, I can only cast myself into the dust before Thee! With the Blessed Virgin Thy Mother, and with St. Joseph, I kneel at Thy Crib to weep over my sins and to supplicate Thy grace. Oh, how near am I to the object of my desires! Thou art my All, my Lord, my God, and I shall receive Thee every day. Oh, how this union with Thee will strengthen me in good, will sanctify me! O Jesus, Thou Searcher of hearts, Thou seest my soul inflamed with desires; Thou knowest how it longs to be holy, to be united with Thee! And, O Holy Ghost, hast Thou not infused in my soul a great devotion to St. Teresa?"

On the following day, June 24th, Feast of St. John the Baptist, young Neumann received deacon's orders, and on the next day, June 25th, he was raised to the dignity of the priesthood. His feelings during the ceremony we find recorded in his journal, embodied in such acts of thanksgiving as the following:

"At last, my dearest Jesus, I have attained to that for which my soul has so long sighed! Ah, behold Thine own work! O God, I am amazed at the grandeur of this grace, at my own high dignity and its responsibility! O Jesus, Thou hast conferred upon me the power of offering Thee, my God, to Thyself—my God to my God! Oh, far too high a privilege for me! Angels of God, ye saints of heaven, descend upon earth and adore my Jesus, for the stammerings of my poor heart are only imperfect echoes of what our Holy Church bids me say!

O grace of the Holy Spirit, how I glory in exalting Thee to-day! how I glory in being able to thank Thee, my Creator, my Redeemer, for Thy three great gifts, Creation, Redemption, and our Holy Church! O joy above all earthly joys, I am a member, a servant of that same Holy Church! I pray Thee, grant to me and to all the living and the dead forgiveness and sanctification. Now I can efficaciously pray for myself, my parents and relations, my dear friend N. N., ———, and for all in Bohemia who have recommended themselves to my prayers." Here follows a long list of individuals, confraternities, etc. In his love and gratitude he forgot none with whom he had in any way been connected; all mankind shared in his prayers. On the next day, June 26th, he offered up the Holy Sacrifice of the Mass for the first time. It was a Sunday, and the day on which the Church celebrates the Feast of the martyrs John and Paul. The young priest, now Rev. Mr. Neumann, sang his first Mass in the German church of St. Nicholas, Second Street, New York.

In a letter to the Reverend Dean of his native place, this memorable event in his opening career is thus described:

"The feast was celebrated with as great pomp as is usual here. Father Raffeiner preached after the Gospel to a large congregation drawn together by what is as yet an unusual occurrence in these parts, the celebration of a first Mass. I gave First Communion to thirty children whom I had myself prepared. Oh, how gladly would I not have hailed the presence of the various members of my family! With my whole heart I prayed for them that God's blessing might descend upon them. A great and unexpected pleasure was mine after Mass. My little First Communicants, accompanied by their parents, called upon me to offer their thanks for the pains I had taken to instruct them. Before taking leave, each presented me a little token of gratitude."

CHAPTER II.

Rev. Mr. Neumann Starts for the Scene of his Future Labors.

RIGHT REV. BISHOP DUBOIS, even before Mr. Neumann's arrival, had destined him for the missions around Niagara Falls. He was now anxious for him to set out at once for his destination; so the third day after his first Mass found Father Neumann on his way. Travelling in those early days of American civilization was not what it is in our own time, as railroads were few. Father Neumann proceeded by steamboat to Albany, where, on the Feast of Sts. Peter and Paul, he offered the Holy Sacrifice in St. Mary's Church. On July 4th he reached Rochester. Here, by order of his Bishop, he was to tarry a few days in order to administer the consolations of religion to the German Catholics, at that time without a pastor of their own nationality. The zealous pastor of St. Patrick's, Rev. Bernard O'Reilly, gladly welcomed Father Neumann, and extended to him the hospitality of his own house. He had long been in quest of a German priest to break the Word of God to the German Catholics of Rochester, and now that Divine Providence had sent one in answer to his heart's desire, great were his joy and satisfaction. Father O'Reilly was made Bishop of Hartford, November 10, 1850. Sixteen months later, March 28, 1852, he assisted at Father Neumann's own consecration. Bishop O'Reilly was one of the passengers of the ill-fated steamer Pacific which was lost on her midwinter trip to America, January, 1856. The Bishop was returning from Europe, whither he had gone the previous year on affairs connected with his diocese. His loss was mourned from Georgia to Maine. In him the American hierarchy was deprived of one of its holiest and most laborious pastors. No tidings of the missing vessel were ever received.

Conversing with two of his fellow-priests here in Rochester, Father Neumann happened to revert to the circumstance of his unsuccessful application for a written discharge from his diocese. His companions discussed the matter, and decided that his ordination, though valid, yet was illicit. Father Neumann's tender conscience was not a little troubled at this information; but he acted wisely under the circumstances. He says in his journal:

"To-day I said Mass with a great scruple. But, according to Blessed Liguori, I may be tranquil, since no doubts assailed me at the time of my ordination. Is a *written* discharge really essential? Had I not an oral one? As soon as I meet either Father Pax or Father Prost I will lay the case before him and abide by his decision. Thank God, Blessed Alphonsus' 'Moral Theology' does not condemn me!"

Though his stay at Rochester was to be brief, yet he manifested the liveliest interest in the spiritual welfare of the German Catholics. A true disciple of the Divine Friend of childen, Father Neumann's chief care was bestowed upon the catechetical instruction of the little ones.

"July 6.—I began yesterday to instruct the children. Things are in a sad state. The poor little creatures have had few advantages. They speak both German and English badly, and have little idea of religion. From lack of care and instruction, many weeds have sprung up among them; and yet a school cannot even be thought of. O God, how melancholy is the spectacle in this part of Thy kingdom! Ah, do not punish our disobedience to Thy Church in this way! Take not away the good seed; suffer not the spread of heresy and infidelity! Oh, hearken to the voice of Thy priest weeping over the sins of Thy people, supplicating pardon and grace! My God, forsake us not! Good Shepherd, permit not the wolf to tear Thy sheep to pieces! Enlighten me, strengthen me with Thy powerful grace, that I may snatch from Satan his unfortunate prey, and lead them back to Thee."

On July 7th Father Neumann administered the Sacrament of Baptism for the first time, which circumstance the journal records in these words: "If the newly-baptized child dies to-day, in the grace received from this holy Sacrament, my journey to America will have been richly rewarded; yes, richly rewarded, even if in the future I accomplish nothing more."

The Sunday appointed for Father Neumann to celebrate divine service for the Germans drew near. In the humility of his heart, our holy young priest wrote: "I feel anxious, for to-morrow I shall hear confessions for the first time, and preach twice; as yet, I am not prepared. I must not lose courage, however. My Jesus, I am a worthless instrument, but do Thou glorify Thy power and grace, not only in me, but in those, also, who will come to hear me. O my God, I cannot ask Thee to put me to shame, to let me fail in my sermon to-morrow. But I will resign myself to Thy will. Put me to shame, if so it please Thee, but do not allow me to fall into sin."

One year previously, in 1835, Rev. Father Prost, Visitor and Superior of the Redemptorists in America, arrived at Rochester on his journey from New York to Ohio. At the request of Rev. Bernard O'Reilly, he remained awhile to preach to the numerous German Catholics and hear their confessions. These good people, duly appreciating the benefits of religion, implored Father Prost to stay with them and assume the charge of their parish. He could not then accede to their proposal, but he promised to return soon and make arrangements for their spiritual good. Shortly after this, Bishop Dubois formally requested Father Prost to undertake the care of the German Catholics of Rochester. Father Prost readily accepted the charge, and arrived in Rochester at the close of the same Sunday which witnessed Father Neumann's labors in behalf of his own future parishioners, July 10, 1836. And thus Father Neumann met for the first time a Redemptorist Father, a son of St. Alphonsus. On Father Prost's invitation, he remained in Rochester a few days longer. Father Neumann describes his new friend as a saintly, amiable priest, whose acquaintance awoke in him the first desire to enter the Congregation of the Most Holy Redeemer.

On July 12th Father Neumann left Rochester, and arrived in Buffalo at five that evening. Here he found Father Alexander Pax, to whom the Bishop had directed him. The following day, having celebrated Mass in the frame church erected by the venerable Father Mertz, he repaired with Father Pax to Williamsville, about ten miles distant, where he was to take up his abode in the family of one Philip Jacob Wirtz. An humble apartment was here placed at his disposal. Such were the temporary arrangements made by Father Pax for our young and ardent missionary. That they were perfectly in accordance with his own ideas we may gather from his record of the day:

"Father Pax is just the man for me! O God, my desires are now accomplished! I am in America; I am a priest, a missionary; and I have a flock! My Jesus, Thou must have strengthened me by Thy grace, since Thou dost entrust to me so dangerous a post."

CHAPTER III.

Father Neumann's Field as a Missionary.

AT the period which now engages our readers' attention, about the year 1836, the state of the Church and of society in the United States presented aspects very different from the present. In western New York the missionaries were Rev. John Nicholas Mertz and Rev. Alexander Pax, the founders of the German congregations of that region. We cannot pass over these venerable priests without a short sketch of their labors. It will doubtless prove interesting to the reader of to-day to glance at the missionary life of those primitive times.

Father Mertz was born April 26, 1764, at Bondorf, in the diocese of Luxemburg. Obeying the inspirations of the Holy Ghost, he devoted himself to the service of the Church, and was ordained at Treves, March 23, 1791. At the beginning of the present century he made a journey to Rome with the intention of entering the Society of Jesus. The venerable Pontiff, Pope Pius VII., however, directed his attention to the vast missionary fields of North America, and urged him to labor in those regions. Docile to the wishes of His Holiness, Father Mertz abandoned his first intention of becoming a Jesuit, and from 1805 labored zealously amid the numerous hardships attendant upon the new apostolic missions of Pennsylvania and Maryland and, lastly, of western New York. In his sixty-fifth year his health and vigor were unimpaired. The last twenty of these years had been spent, as we have said, in America; and yet he always appeared clad in the clerical costume common to his own country in the last century. It consisted of a three-cornered cap, black cravat, long brown coat, knee-breeches, and shoe-buckles. His extraordinary appearance often subjected him to the laughter and ridicule of the godless youth of the place; but little did the good priest heed the taunts that occasionally met his ears.

His dwelling was a small frame house on the west side of Pearl Street, between Court and Eagle streets, Buffalo. He celebrated divine service at first in a poor frame building. But later on, a Mr. Le Conteulx, having donated a plot of ground for the purpose, Father Mertz erected on it a neat little church, also of wood, and dedicated it to "The Lamb of God." The tabernacle of the altar was bronze, and on it rested a small image of the Divine Lamb. The English, German, and French Catholics of Buffalo all assembled in this pretty little church for the various acts of public worship practised in their holy religion. Although extremely poor himself, the good pastor employed every means in his power, and did not hesitate to expend what he could command in the adornment of the house of God.

This venerable priest occasionally visited Eden, Lancaster, Sheldon, North Bush, Williamsville, etc., which little towns then consisted of only a few scattered houses. His only conveyance to these distant places was an ox-cart, and he often made the journey on foot, carrying with him whatever was needful for the service of the altar. The frequent insults he received from the non-Catholics among whom his duties called him demanded on his side the practice of heroic patience. On one occasion he had ordered a table to be placed in the District Hall at Eden; but one of the most prominent men of the place bade his son go pitch the table out. The young man obeyed, but—strange to relate!—at that very moment he fell into a state of mental and physical disorder, and shortly after died. The avenging hand of God was recognized by all in this event, and the father of the unhappy youth was often heard to say that he would take care not to meddle with a Catholic priest again.

To children and the poor Father Mertz was a true father. For the former he provided instruction both in the church and the school-room, whilst to the latter he furnished means to supply their needs. His conduct toward Protestants and unbelievers he regulated by this principle: "Let us take care to make Catholics what they ought to be; the rest will come of itself."

In his own humble dwelling Father Mertz when not engaged in prayer was never seen without a book in his hand. The centre of all his devotion was Jesus in the Blessed Sacrament.

This pious priest was not spared by certain proud spirits who aimed at governing both church and pastor. On one occasion, during an episcopal visitation, several of these men appeared before the Bishop as delegates of the congregation. Their complaints were chiefly of their pastor's want of confidence in them: he did not entrust them with the financial affairs of the church, etc., although the funds collected belonged to them. The Bishop listened patiently to the end, and then quietly asked how much each one had contributed toward the erection and support of the church. This unexpected question was soon answered, though to the confusion of the disaffected parties. Not one could name any particular sum as the amount of his donation; for, in truth, not one had contributed a cent.

When Father Mertz had reached his seventieth year, failing strength obliged him to procure an assistant. Rev. Alexander Pax, in every respect a most estimable priest, was the one destined by Divine Providence to share his labors. Born in 1799, in the diocese of Metz, he was elevated to the priesthood in 1823. For twelve years he labored successfully as pastor at Sucht and Vliesbrücken, but, being informed of the great want of priests in America, he left home and friends for the New World.

In that same year, 1835, Father Mertz made a journey to Europe in behalf of the American missions, leaving his extensive and laborious charge under the sole care of Father Pax. With courageous activity the latter set about erecting a large church, which his zealous efforts brought to speedy completion. It is still in existence, and is known as the church of St. Louis. His cares and sacrifices were, however, repaid with the greatest ingratitude by many for whom he had so untiringly labored, for whom he had undergone so many hardships.

In this noble priest Father Neumann found his nearest neighbor, his most devoted friend. They exchanged visits, took counsel of each other in important matters, and found mutual support under numerous trials.

Two years before Father Neumann's arrival the erection of a new church had been urged by a Catholic named Furniss. With Father Mertz's approval, a collection was begun in the neighborhood for that purpose. The proceeds amounted to four hundred dollars, besides seventy loads of building materials. The building was immediately begun on a site which had been donated by a Protestant named Schmidt. The conditions attached to the donation were that the church should be of stone, one hundred and fifteen feet long, thirty feet broad, and twenty-five feet high. At the period of Father Neumann's arrival the walls of the church were already up. Though the Catholics themselves took the matter in hand, yet a considerable debt had accumulated, which debt was swelled by the unjust claims to compensation put forward by many who had promised assistance gratis. Father Neumann's method of proceeding in this embarrassing conjuncture succeeded in calming the storm so far that several withdrew their claims, whilst others donated to the church money already advanced.

The building could boast neither roof nor floor when Father Neumann began to hold service within its naked walls. A temporary altar and a few rough benches alone betrayed the use already made of it.

The non-Catholics of the district were at that time greatly disaffected toward the Catholic Church. The services held by Father Neumann and his little congregation were frequently disturbed by the noise and clamor of a lawless crowd without; stones were thrown over the walls, and one even struck the altar during the celebration of the Holy Sacrifice. Rude boys used to call to one another: "Come on! Let's go to the Catholic church and have some fun!"

After the first public service at Williamsville, Father Neumann noted in his journal: "My first sermon to my parishioners was well received. I ascribe its success to the intercession of the Blessed Virgin Mary, to whom I have promised to introduce among the children the Confraternity of the Most Blessed Sacrament."

Besides his parochial duties at Williamsville, Father Neumann attended the following stations: North Bush, five miles distant; Lancaster and Transit, six; Batavia, forty; Sheldon, twenty; Niagara, fifty; and several other places in that locality.

On July 18th the new pastor went for the first time to Lancaster, to administer the last sacraments to a dying person. He heard several confessions that evening, and next morning celebrated Mass in the village church. Of this visit he thus writes: "The church at Lancaster is more like a barn than a church. Whilst preaching, after Mass, on the humility of Jesus who deigns to dwell in that poor hut as He once did in the stable of Bethlehem, my tears would not be restrained, and I was forced to discontinue my sermon."

On July 20th he rode to North Bush. Here the Catholics had constructed a log chapel in which they assembled on Sundays and holy-days to recite the Rosary.

Father Neumann clearly recognized the responsibility of his post, but, convinced of his own weakness, he prays for help: "O my Jesus, I, a poor, ignorant young man, have become a shepherd in Thy sheepfold! Lord, regard not my sins. Give me an ever-increasing love for Thy redeemed ones, that I may labor at their salvation in wisdom, patience, and holiness. Grant that not one of those whom Thou hast confided to me be lost through my fault. O my Jesus, help me to sanctify my children! O holy Mother of my Lord and my God, pray for me and my flock! Holy guardian angels of my dear children, teach me how to act toward them in order to instil into their hearts principles of pure faith and the love of God! Lord, teach me how to live, and, if needs be, die for my people, that they may all be saved, that they may all love and praise Thee in eternity, that they may love Thy dear Mother! Ah, through that infinite love Thou didst exhibit toward us in Thy Incarnation, have mercy on those poor souls whom Thou hast redeemed, have mercy on my poor children! Mother Mary, Thou who art ever victorious over heresies, pray for all who are walking in the paths of accursed error! Open their eyes, touch their hearts, that they may begin to love Jesus and His Holy Church and bring forth fruits for eternal life! O my poor Jesus, why do not all men love Thee? O Holy Spirit, have mercy on us who do not desire to taste how sweet is the Lord! Sanctify us, poor, wretched creatures, who constantly offend our Creator and Lord! O sweet sufferings of my little Infant Saviour, sweet pains of love! Oh, that these tears of mine could blot out my own sins and the sins of my people! My Jesus, what shall I, a poor creature, do to lead many souls, yea, *all* souls to Thee? Oh, pity my ignorance! Teach me, sanctify me, a wretched sinner. Holy Mother Mary, St. Joseph, all ye holy virgins, caress the dear Infant Jesus for me; beg Him not to be displeased with my poor children! Holy guardian angels, holy patrons, cease not to pray for me and for them! Obtain for us light; obtain for us the love of God; obtain for us perseverance!"

CHAPTER IV.

Father Neumann's Zeal in the Discharge of his Ministry.

NO duty awakened livelier interest in Father Neumann than the instruction of youth. Before his arrival in Williamsville, a teacher had come from Buffalo to take charge of the Catholic children; but his conduct was such as to render his dismissal necessary. Father Neumann then assumed the duties of teacher himself, a post which he filled during seven months. "For," as he says in his journal, "the debt contracted in the building of the church and school, added to the actual poverty of the congregation, made the maintenance of a teacher at that time impossible."

As soon as divine service was concluded at the various stations under his charge, he administered the Sacraments, attended to the other duties devolving on a parish priest, and ended by assembling the children for instruction. The little ones of his flock he looked upon as the favorites of his Lord and Master, and his first thought after that of the church was to provide for them a school as commodious and well-disciplined as possible. Such improvements soon sprung up at most of his stations; but wherever this was still an impossibility, Father Neumann, as at Williamsville, instructed the children himself in the most necessary branches, and this for several weeks and even months of the year. He knew well how to suit his words and demeanor to the age and capacity of his scholars, among whom he ever appeared with a smiling and affectionate countenance. As soon as he arrived at one of his stations, the children would flock around him in eager, loving salutation, the younger ones, bolder than their more advanced companions, pressing on all sides, even slyly examining his coat-pockets for the little gifts he was accustomed to bring them. To encourage their good behavior and diligence, he used to bestow upon them such rewards as medals, rosaries, pictures, and even candies.

As may be imagined, with such a teacher and such rewards, Father Neumann's school was well attended. The scholars made rapid progress in Christian Doctrine, as well as in reading, writing, arithmetic, etc. To this day, the old residents of those places recall with pleasurable emotions the kind, fatherly instructor of their children, and often are they heard to exclaim, "He was a real saint!" Pictures and medals received from him in those early days are still treasured up as most precious mementos. One of the good Catholic mothers used to say familiarly to her children, "Our pastor deserves to be framed in gold."

Father Neumann loved to hear his young pupils sing in church the hymns he himself had taught them; and if, at times, one or other would offer as an excuse for not joining in with the rest hoarseness contracted in coming so far to church, he would be met with the cheery reply, "Oh, that is nothing! I can easily cure that"— and in fact a spoonful of sugar, the usual remedy on such occasions, joined to the pastor's kind, genial tones, soon had the effect of dissipating all such ills.

Sunday afternoons were devoted to the young people's catechetical instruction. For illustrations of his subjects, Father Neumann was in the habit of drawing upon the examples contained in Holy Writ, thus combining sacred history with doctrine, to the greater advantage of his hearers. As an incentive to attention and improvement, he rewarded with a picture, or some other trifling object of devotion, all who could repeat the principal points of the last instruction.

Ever anxious to counteract the fearfully pernicious effects of immoral books, Father Neumann exerted himself untiringly to diffuse among his parishioners good and useful reading matter. Donations in the shape of manuals and books of piety were often sent him from his friends in Bohemia, and most thankfully were such valuable gifts received for his poor missions. A donation of this kind was thus acknowledged: "All contribute largely to the diffusion of our holy religion who, like good children of our Holy Mother the Church, not only pray for her welfare, but prove their love and attachment to her by pious gifts. The sympathy and support which the American missions find in my native land prove that Bohemia is not willing to bury the inheritance bequeathed her by Cyrillus and Methodius; but, thankful to God and charitable to all the redeemed of Christ, she seeks to return blessing for blessing. If you have collected any money, be so good as to send it to Augsburg or Strasburg for the purchase of the following books in German: the works of St. Teresa, of Catherine Emmerich, of Goffiné, etc.; also those of Blessed Alphonsus and the publications of the Mechitarists, etc. They cannot be obtained here, and they are valuable aids in the acquisition of piety."

In a letter to a friend, Father Neumann describes the way in which divine service was performed in the early days of his mission. "I am very much encouraged," he says, "when I reflect that within a few short years churches and schools, poor though they be, have been erected in many parts of our district among the woods and swamps. Even an humble temporary building for divine worship or instruction is a consoling spectacle. The altar is usually nothing more than a table furnished with a pair of wooden candlesticks, a crucifix, a missal, two tumblers, and a plate. From the woods around, frequently from a distance of five to ten miles, flock groups of worshippers, natives of Alsace, Lorraine,

Baden, France, Ireland, etc., some on horseback, some in wagons, all in the costume of their own nation. The more courageous among them assemble in the nearest churches on the Sundays on which they have no priest, and try to sing a hymn together. But this is difficult for some, on account of the variety of language and melody. Truly, my dear friend, did I not know that Jesus Christ was born in a stable and died on a cross, I should doubt the lawfulness of celebrating the Holy Mysteries in such poverty. May God compensate us by giving us hearts rich in virtue and grace!"

Father Neumann, besides the pious books previously referred to, received also, on several different occasions, donations of vestments and other religious articles for his churches. Such gifts brought joy to the heart of our fervent young missionary.

"The many precious things I have received," he says in one of his letters, "add splendor to our ceremonies, and stir up even our most indifferent members to contribute a mite toward the beautifying of our altars."

Before the great feasts of the Church, he often labored with his own hands at the decoration of the altar and sacred edifice. He desired that everything appertaining to divine service should be arranged with exquisite neatness and all the magnificence possible, and this with the twofold intention of honoring God and saving souls, as we may gather from his own words:

"In respect to our holy religion affairs are progressing. Catholicity is spreading, and the zeal of the faithful is considerably on the increase. Many of my good people have acknowledged that they consider their soul's salvation furthered by their immigration to America; for in Europe, where churches and schools abound, where the facilities for practising our holy religion are so numerous, they did not feel half the earnestness and zeal that now animate them. In fact, under the inspiration of God, these good people may be seen at work for days and even weeks at a time in the construction and adornment of their churches. God strikingly manifests His goodness in them. The thought of a church which they may call their own is to them a most consoling one. Thank God, they have not labored in vain, nor are they likely to absent themselves from divine worship in the future! When we consider, besides, that most of them, especially those who live remote from the cities, are miserably poor, we must regard their readiness to help in the good work as an evident sign of divine co-operation. Laboring in the sweat of their brow, amid the turmoil of the world, their heart still hungers for something higher and holier, and in their poverty they turn to the Lord, who alone can satisfy their cravings for happiness. Labor and privation then grow sweet, and they are filled with childlike faith and love for God. Like Simon of Cyrene, they are, in some sort, forced to carry the cross, and in it they discover graces hitherto unknown."

After a stay of seven months at Williamsville, Father Neumann removed to North Bush. Here he remained for the next eighteen months in the family of the devout Catholic above mentioned, Mr. John Schmidt; meantime, adjoining the log chapel, a small frame house was commenced for his accommodation. Whilst the building was in progress, the reverend pastor walked daily to his church, the distance of a mile and a half through a marshy forest. But he consoled himself for this hardship and the many others that it entailed by the tender and loving aspirations he poured forth to his God in the solitude of the woods.

The summer of 1837 found Father Neumann still a member of the Schmidt family. During this period, the Bishop, making the rounds of his pastoral visitation, included the parishes confided to the young priest's care. He was received with all the honor possible on his arrival from Buffalo, accompanied by Father Prost, C.SS.R., Superior of the Redemptorists. The male portion of the congregation, old and young, in holiday attire, awaited for hours, in anxious expectation, their distinguished visitor's arrival; and when the carriage drove up they crowded around it, eager to offer their cordial welcomes and expressions of joy.

After the Sacrament of Confirmation had been administered, the pastor conducted the Bishop and his companion to Williamsville and his other stations. The Bishop was astonished on beholding everywhere such fruits of the young priest's zeal, nor was he slow in giving expression to his unlimited satisfaction. Father Neumann proposed some difficulties that had arisen in the discharge of his pastoral duties, and received the Bishop's decision on the same. That evening he wrote in his journal:

"Lord, enlighten my doubts respecting my parishioners of North Bush and Lancaster. I will be obedient to the voice of my Bishop, regarding it as Thine own."

From a letter to his parents, dated February 5, 1837, in which he explains to them his mode of life, we glean a few passages which afford a glimpse of his noble heart, his effective love of God, and his deep filial love. It runs:

"Though determined to await an answer to my last before acquainting you with my present situation, yet the thought of your anxiety haunts me, urging me to write again. No doubt you well remember my promise to give you a true account of myself. This I can do the more readily as I have no reason to fear the intelligence conveyed by my letter will cause you to die either of joy or of grief.

"Like an old German emperor followed everywhere by his court do I carry with me all needful church articles when visiting my three parishes of Williamsville, North Bush, and Lancaster. From an American citizen here I have received two acres of land for a church. The large number of French and Irish Catholics at Niagara Falls renders a church, or at least a chapel, necessary. Do you remember our examining together a fine steel engraving of the Falls? You little imagined then that I would one day establish a parish in the neighborhood. I am so near to them that I can hear the roar of the cataract in my room. It sounds like the noise of a distant hail-storm. I have not yet visited the Falls."

One of Father Neumann's intimate friends assures us that it was the love of mortification alone that could lead him to deny himself a sight of that widely-famed spectacle. To such a lover of nature it must have been no trifling sacrifice.

To resume: "I am living here at North Bush with a native of Lorraine who, in consideration of payment in the next life, furnishes me with board and lodging. My furniture consists of four chairs lately purchased with some money I had laid by, two trunks, and a few books. For your consolation, I will tell you that the timber for my future residence has already been cut, and my people are rejoicing in the prospect of supplying me with corn, potatoes, etc. I have never yet suffered from hunger; and as for clothes—when one garment grows too shabby for wear, some one or other of my good people provides me with another. So, you see, my dear parents, things fare well with me. If it were otherwise, this wandering life that I lead would soon become impracticable; but, as it is, every house is my home."

After entering into a detailed description of the country, its people, its animals and plants, he continues:

"I am becoming more and more engrossed in my duties. It is likely I shall never have a chance to go sable-hunting as Commissioner Herbst predicted. As much as I would like to spend a few days with you and give you an oral account of my short experience in America, I shall have to defer the realization of that desire for several years. The want of priests is so great that it is impossible for the few who are here to take long journeys. Ah, how often have I not wished for the strength to multiply my exertions, in order to meet the innumerable spiritual wants!

"Be persuaded, my dear parents, that I often think of you, of my brother and sisters, and of all my friends; all are daily remembered at the Holy Sacrifice. Whatever good Almighty God may will to effect here through my instrumentality will redound to your benefit, as well as to my own; for that I am now a priest is owing to you, under God. What joy would be yours could you see the affection entertained for me by my good parishioners! And again would you rejoice at the sight of our holy religion planted and cultivated, with the help of divine grace, in the midst of these dark forests. Oh, that my former fellow-students and their parents could behold the need of missionaries here! Could they but see the tears of those who, like the children of Israel in the Babylonian captivity, are cut off from the consolations of religion; the children eager for instruction, yet growing up in ignorance and infidelity, the dying passing to another life unassisted by priest or sacrament—could they see these and many other things equally sad, they would surely renounce temporal satisfaction and comfort to afford assistance to their Catholic brethren in North America! Great would be their reward on the last day."

Father Neumann's letters to his parents and family always happily arrived at their destination; but the answers to them, though forwarded regularly, seem not to have reached him. This may have been owing to some misdirection or some fault of the mail. Whatever may have been the cause, news from home, though indirectly received, was always a great satisfaction to the young missionary in his far-off field of labor. When, in this way, he heard of his sister Joanna's entrance into the religious state, he expressed his satisfaction in a letter to his parents, as follows:

"Joanna's resolution to enter among the Sisters of Charity of St. Charles Borromeo is a subject of heartfelt joy to me. It has infused new courage into my own soul. May our merciful Lord enkindle more and more in my heart the fire of Christian charity toward my neighbor! God be praised for having inspired my sister with the good thought of consecrating herself entirely to His service, and for having strengthened her to overcome the numerous difficulties opposed to the accomplishment of such a resolution! I salute her with all my heart, and beg her prayers in behalf of the poor scattered faithful of America."

The actual hardships of his mission Father Neumann never hinted at in his letters to his family. He wished to spare them unnecessary anxiety on his account. Trials and sufferings of various kinds were not, however, wanting to him. The district in which several of his missions lay was marshy and unhealthy, thereby engendering much sickness. Whooping-cough was prevalent among the children, while gastric fever attacked the adults. This painful and tedious illness called for the daily services of the zealous physician of souls, and often was he seen in the depth of winter crossing the marshes, sometimes on foot, sometimes on horseback, carrying the Blessed Sacrament in hands stiff from the cold. During these long journeys he used to pray with head uncovered, and in summer he generally arrived home worn out from fatigue, his garments saturated with perspiration and bespattered with mud. When his kind-hearted host wished to brush and clean them, deeming it an honor to do so, the humble priest would not accept such a service. But if Mr. Schmidt, as sometimes happened, succeeded in doing so secretly, Father Neumann, not content with expressing his thanks in words, would offer his assistance for work in the field.

It not unfrequently happened that directly after Mass

he was obliged to answer one or more sick-calls, from which he returned in the evening fasting as he went; for he made it a rule never to ask for anything. His long journeys through the gloomy forests were not only very fatiguing, but often attended with danger from venomous reptiles and ravenous beasts. And not less than these were the attacks of wicked men to be dreaded, for the solitary and unprotected wayfarer might have been set upon with impunity. More than once Father Neumann escaped in such encounters owing to the manifest interposition of Divine Providence.

On one occasion his feet were so blistered and sore from walking that, unable to go further, he sunk down at the foot of a tree. Presently he saw several dark figures approaching. They gathered around him in threatening attitudes, and regarded him with a fierce air. The poor helpless traveller recognized in them a band of roving Indians, and inwardly recommended himself to God. But as soon as these wild sons of the forest discovered that he was a "black gown," they spread a buffalo-skin on the ground, placed him on it, and in this novel conveyance transported him to his destination. On another occasion, whilst returning from baptizing a child, at a sharp turn in the road the wagon made a sudden lurch, and Father Neumann was pitched out backward. In his evening record of that day he says: "O my Jesus, it was a miracle of Thy mercy that I was not instantly killed!" He did not, however, escape unhurt. His left arm was injured so seriously that it was feared it would have to be amputated. He suffered intense pain from the accident, and for two weeks had to forego the consolation of saying Mass.

One night as he was returning from a sick-call, a furious thunder-storm burst upon him and the rain fell in torrents. In the pitchy darkness Father Neumann lost his way in the swamps. He wandered up and down, now right, now left, uncertain what direction to take. In his perplexity he began to implore Almighty God to shed a ray of light upon his pathway, when suddenly his prayer was answered. Not far ahead he perceived through the waving branches a faint gleam as if from a solitary lamp. He followed the light and soon came upon a wretched hovel. His rap at the door was answered by the voice of a child crying, "We let no one in at night." Again he rapped, and again received the same response to his call for admission. It was only after repeated efforts and entreaties that the door was opened and he was ushered into a scene of misery. Off in one corner, with only a little moss between him and the bare ground, lay a man apparently in the agonies of death. The poor fellow, as Father Neumann afterward learned, had but recently lost both wife and children, the little girl who opened the door being the only one left to him. She, poor child, would soon have been an orphan, were it not for the priest's timely arrival. The man was an Irish Catholic, and intense were his joy and gratitude on finding himself so unexpectedly visited by one who could minister to him the helps of religion in his trying hour. Father Neumann, seeing his utter prostration, instantly brought forth the small bottle of wine he carried with him for the service of the altar, and poured some down his throat. Its effects were instantaneous. The man revived and was soon able to make his confession. When morning dawned and Father Neumann left the hut, the poor fellow, thanks to the kind ministrations of his guest, was in a fair way of recovery. He praised God whose providential care had furnished him with aid so timely, and ever after preserved the most grateful remembrance of his benefactor, Father Neumann.

That the sick whose poverty forbade the procuring of physicians and medicines might not be destitute of assistance, Father Neumann began the study of the healing art. His extensive knowledge of botany served him here, and his constant journeying through country and forest afforded an opportunity for procuring herbs suited to his purpose. We have met individuals who still remember their pastor's solicitude in searching for flowers and plants to be used in compounding medicines. In one of his letters to Europe he says:

"As I am obliged to roam the forests, I have made use of the opportunity thus afforded to extend my knowledge of botany. I gather the flowers on my way, many of them unknown in your country. Had I an opportunity, I would send to Bohemia specimens of the rare and curious plants I everywhere meet." Later Father Neumann found means to forward a very rare and valuable collection to Munich, where it was deservedly appreciated.

The exemplary conduct of their young pastor was a subject of great edification to the souls under his care. His life was to them a living and perpetual exhortation to good. To fervent prayer he joined assiduous study, and it was a subject of astonishment to many to find him, though otherwise so poor, the possessor of quite a choice little library. This circumstance may be regarded as a proof that in the solitude of the forest Father Neumann continued what he had ever been, a friend of study.

And now he began to comprehend the ever-growing magnitude of the work devolving on him, as well as his own inability to compass it unaided and alone. He multiplied his petitions for a German co-laborer to whom he might confide two of the largest and most important of his parishes, retaining for himself the smallest and most difficult. After some delay, the Bishop was able to grant his request and appoint Rev. F. L—— to the charge of Williamsville and Lancaster. But Father Neumann's zeal was not to be seconded by Father L——. This unfortunate priest proved himself a hireling and intruder in the sheepfold of Christ. Only a few days had elapsed after his appointment, when letters were despatched to the Bishop characterizing his conduct and teaching as very suspicious, to say the least. Father Neumann made repeated efforts to arouse the poor man to a sense of his duty to God, to his neighbor, and to himself, but all in vain. He was at last suspended by the Bishop, and Father Pax, of Buffalo, entrusted with the execution of the measure. Father Pax, accordingly, betook himself to Lancaster, but only to find the incumbent absent. He published the Bishop's writ of suspension against the unworthy pastor, and explained to the people the grievousness of receiving the Sacraments from the hands of a suspended priest. Father Pax then returned to Buffalo, carrying with him the consecrated altar-stone which he himself had lent to Father L—— on his appointment to Lancaster. Father L—— was at Williamsville during the transaction of these events, and, when the news reached him, he was so enraged that he set about inciting the people of that place to rebel against their lawful superiors. The unfortunate ecclesiastic happened to possess two qualifications which won for him the favor of his parishioners and secured to him unbounded influence over them: he was an eloquent preacher and a fine singer. Taking advantage of his popularity, he urged the building of a pastoral residence, etc. The circumstance of the altar-stone was no secret in the Catholic community of Lancaster; but Father L—— carried his audacity and impiety so far as to have a fac-simile of the first made, and went on saying Mass as before. To put an end to these scandalous proceedings, Fathers Pax, Mertz, and Neumann went together to Williamsville, assembled the congregation, and pointed out to them in presence of the wretched priest the abomination in the holy place. They explained it as the bounden duty of all who called themselves Catholics to avoid one who had been so unhappy as to have incurred the punishment of ecclesiastical suspension. The unfortunate object of their strictures was, at last, covered with confusion. He could utter no word in extenuation of his conduct, though, alas! he manifested no sign of contrition for the past. His flock withdrew from him, and he was compelled to leave the diocese. Father Neumann was thus obliged to resume his first charge.

As soon as the humble frame house at North Bush was ready to receive him, Father Neumann took possession of it. With the exception of a little boy of ten, one of the neighbors' sons whom he engaged to stay in the house during his own absence, Father Neumann was its sole occupant.

Scarcely once a week was smoke seen to rise from the chimney. His parishioners, who felt great sympathy for their gentle, patient pastor, often wondered how or on what he lived. Sometimes they ventured even to put the question, when, with a cheerful smile, he would answer, "Bread and butter and cheese are very nourishing." Occasionally he was urged to remind the people that they ought to provide him with good food properly prepared. "They know very well," he would reply, "what I need. If they wish to supply my wants, I am willing to receive."

The little ten-year-old companion received from his pastor, we may imagine, many a useful lesson. Among other things, Father Neumann once told the little fellow that he who would sleep soundly must take a light supper. This piece of information seems greatly to have impressed his young hearer. Not many days after, both found themselves seated at quite an exceptional meal for them, thanks to the bounty of some good parishioner.

Hunger lent a zest of its own, and the savory dishes were receiving full justice, when suddenly the child recalled the lesson lately received. He paused, and with the simplicity which so often amused the good priest he said, "Your reverence, if you stop eating now, you'll sleep all the better for it."

In his letters home Father Neumann frequently expressed the desire of having his brother Wenceslaus with him. The latter was not at all averse to accepting the invitation, provided his parents would give their consent. After repeated urging to this effect, Mr. and Mrs. Neumann generously agreed to part with their only remaining son; and on the 25th of September, 1839, the two brothers met once again, after a separation of more than three years. Father Neumann at once informed his parents of his brother's arrival in America. He says:

"I rejoice at being able to apprise you of the arrival of our dear Wenceslaus. He took me by surprise two days before the feast of his holy patron. Not having heard directly from you since my departure from Prachatitz, I was becoming very anxious. But the good news and loving messages he brings me dispelled all uneasiness and carried me back home. I thank God for giving you the strength to make so many and so great sacrifices, and that, renouncing temporal comforts and advantages, you serve Him in domestic seclusion."

Wenceslaus proved a great help to his reverend brother, who for over three years had had to manage as best he could for himself. Poverty, joined to his disinclination to employ strangers, had forced him to look after his own domestic concerns. Now, however, things took a turn for the better; the surroundings began to look more homelike. An air of comfort, never before seen there, began to pervade the lowly dwelling of the missionary; and, though plain as before, it now lost that general appearance of loneliness and desolation. Returning from a fatiguing journey, exhausted by heat or benumbed by cold, Father Neumann now found a devoted friend to welcome him and surround him with every care a brother's love could suggest. Wenceslaus soon became deeply interested in the schools, as Father Neumann informs us in a letter to a friend:

"My brother has excellent health here. During my absence he teaches in the school at North Bush, besides which he is general superintendent of our household affairs. I assure you he takes good care of me. As the parish of St. John Nepomucene at North Bush increases rapidly in numbers, though not in this world's goods, my brother intends giving instruction to the children of three or four localities. How glad I am to have him with me!—and still more delighted at finding him so willing to take upon himself the care of these abandoned children solely for the love of God and our Holy Mother the Church. He is now, by prayer and study, preparing for his new vocation. May God strengthen and enlighten him!"

CHAPTER V.

Trials and Sufferings in the Ministry.

WHEN our Lord Jesus Christ sent His disciples to teach the Gospel to all nations, like a good and thoughtful father He gave them some advice by which to regulate their conduct. This He did as much for their own benefit as for the speedy conversion of their fellow-men. Among other warnings is found the following: "Be ye therefore prudent as serpents and simple as doves."*

If in their time the Apostles and disciples of our Lord needed these rare qualities combined with solid sanctity, may we not conclude that in no less degree were they requisite for a missionary coming from Europe to the United States in Father Neumann's day?

The reason is obvious. Before his time the missionary in America might be said to have no home, or rather his home was everywhere—wherever a Catholic family dwelt, there might he seek and find a welcome. To perform his priestly functions he was obliged to travel incessantly over the vast district under his care. In the houses of his scattered flock he celebrated Mass, preached, and administered the Sacraments. A chasuble, a chalice, and a portable altar were all that he needed for such duties almost the whole year round. His position was precarious, his life one of fatigue and sacrifice. But he had the consolation of knowing that every member of his flock was as well provided with spiritual food as the circumstances of the time would permit.

---

* Matt. x. 16.

But this state of things could not continue forever. Catholics increased in numbers; the young could not be allowed to grow up in religious ignorance or indifference; churches, schools, and pastoral residences had to be erected; some fixed plan of action had to regulate the missionary's movements, etc. Such undertakings, though ever so poor and simple in the beginning, involved considerable expense. Hence arose the first difficulty. Most of the people of Father Neumann's district were very poor; consequently, although recognizing the necessity, they could contribute but little to these noble purposes. Again, the majority of his scattered sheep came from a country where they had found church and school ready for use and open to all; where priests and teachers received in common with state officials their salary from the government; and where, apart from the penny collection of Sunday, no demands were made on their purse.

Now they had to learn in their newly-adopted home that all this could not be done without their own co-operation. To many it was evident and reasonable. They saw their pastor poorer even than themselves; they understood that he could do nothing for them without their scanty contributions. To others, again, it was hard to understand why things should not be in America just as they had left them in their homes of earlier years. In the next place, these infant congregations consisted of members speaking, for the most part, the same language, though in many different dialects. They came from different provinces and dioceses of Germany. All brought with them some traditional customs and ceremonies which long usage had made very dear to them. They may, indeed, have known that such customs were not essential to their religion, but who is not aware of how tenacious some faithful Catholics are of these little observances, how unwilling to give them up?

And so it became the pastor's duty to reduce this chaos to order, to instruct and guide his poor sheep in prudence and simplicity, in patience and firmness, and to unite them in the little church which after a long struggle and with many sacrifices had been built and blessed for their use.

In the following letter to Rev. Father Dichtl the young pastor gives a detailed account of his missionary field:

"Only a poor priest, or one who is content to endure the hardships of poverty, can labor here with fruit. His duties call him far and near, and he is constantly on the go; he leads what might be termed a wandering life. The new settlers, on arriving in the district, choose a spot in the woods upon which, in a few days, there rises a log-cabin. Then they clear a certain space all round by felling or burning down the trees, where they plant potatoes and sow oats. In a few years these products give place to wheat. Our Germans all live this way in the woods, about two to twelve miles apart. The only pleasure allowable to the parish priest is that found in the care of souls. If he seeks comforts, honors, riches, he will seek in vain; he will lose both patience and courage; his usefulness will come to an end.

"Here all are expected to contribute toward the maintenance of pastors and teachers; and, no matter how trifling the contribution, there are some who think themselves entitled to a voice in parochial affairs. Others wish to see the non-essential customs of their own country, their own diocese,—yes, even of their own parish,—introduced and followed here in their new home. The consequences likely to flow from such a state of things may be readily imagined. Party-spirit becomes the order of the day, a spirit to be counteracted only by patience and prudence on the part of the pastor. The priest must love poverty also, since his parishioners are, with few exceptions, as needy as himself.

"The care of souls is, however, full of consolation, since the less the gratitude of those for whom he labors, the greater the reward the priest expects from God."

Calumny was one of the most inveterate of the evils prevalent at the epoch of which we write. It arose from the desire of certain individuals to insinuate themselves into the pastor's good graces and thus obtain a voice in questions relating to parochial affairs. Father Neumann was not long in detecting the unchristian spirit, to counteract which he invented a novel though effective mode of action. When he found himself waited upon by such persons, he usually interrupted their invidious remarks with the words, "Let us say the Rosary together and then talk the matter over," and, suiting the action to the word, down he would kneel and give out the prayers. Few could stand such a test, nor did they care for a repetition of the scene.

Although our young priest had from his earliest childhood given proof of the angelic soul within; though he so strictly guarded his senses against even the approach of evil; though naturally silent and through principle averse to all unnecessary conversation, particularly with the opposite sex, yet did the foul fiend dare to attack his reputation through the invidious tongue of the slanderer.

During the first year of his ministry at Williamsville Father Neumann lodged with a family by the name of Wirtz. Unavoidable as was this arrangement, it aroused the jealousy of one who thought "His Reverence" might just as well become a member of his own family and let him enjoy the benefit accruing from the same, viz., the weekly board. Not being able to attain his ends, envy and avarice incited the miserable man to spread a base calumny against the innocent young priest. "Wirtz," he said, "employs a young maid-servant. It is not proper that a priest should lodge in the same house with her." And he threw out sundry hints that matters were not just what they ought to be, etc. The vile suspicion was soon noised around and, through the market-dealers, found its way to Buffalo. Certain individuals affected to credit the report, and resolved to hold a meeting to sift the affair. The honorable assembly was convened in a tavern, and it was unanimously agreed that either the priest or the servant should procure other lodgings. These men carried their audacity so far as to cite Father Neumann to appear in their presence. He obeyed the summons, and was not a little astonished to find himself the subject of such gossip. When informed of the resolution adopted by the august assembly, his only reply was a withering smile which quite disconcerted his would-be judges. It was not long before his malicious calumniator found himself the object of universal contempt. Father Neumann alone, the innocent victim of his invidious accusations, pitied the poor wretch and tried to shield his reputation. When fifteen years after, clothed with the episcopal dignity, he visited this same locality, he made special inquiries for him and his family.

At Lancaster, also, the gentle and retiring priest found enemies, and once he was even threatened with assassination. A drover addicted to liquor followed him one day gun in hand, and crying out, "You cursed priest, if you do not turn round and answer me, I'll shoot you down!" Father Neumann, for whom death had no terrors, quietly pursued his way, allowing no threats to deter him from the discharge of his duty. The same lawless fellow made, some time after, a similar attack upon Father Neumann's successor, this time brandishing a huge knife. But a log of wood, hurled at him in the priest's defence, brought him to his senses. Had it struck him, it would have put an end to his disorderly career; a sudden spring aside alone saved him.

At another of his stations one of the parishioners brought Father Neumann an ostensorium, saying that he would present it to the church provided the latter were named after his patron. Father Neumann represented to him the impropriety of giving the church a title other than that which the majority of the congregation desired. Such reasoning was unintelligible to the owner of the ostensorium, who, however, offered to lend the vessel for use on the approaching Feast of Corpus Christi. To this Father Neumann replied that his offer could not be accepted unless the ostensorium became the property of the church. But again the stipulation was laid down that the sacred edifice should be named after the donor's patron; and so the matter ended by the ostensorium's remaining in the hands of its unreasonable owner. Some time after this, as Father Neumann was passing the man's house, he was assailed by a shower of mud and stones. Like others who had offended against the good young priest, this poor deluded fellow and his family were special objects of inquiry when Father Neumann visited those parts as Bishop. He even bestowed upon them the flattering appellation of *friends*.

Another fruitful source of annoyance to Father Neumann in his early missionary days were the drinking-saloons. Wherever a Catholic church was erected, in its vicinity immediately arose a drinking-saloon, in which noisy merriment prevailed with numerous offences against God. Father Neumann could not tolerate such disorders. He admonished, he warned; but all in vain. His remonstrances were answered with the threat that a ball should inaugurate the next holy-day. In his sermon on the Sunday preceding the said festival, he impressed upon his people the impropriety, the scandal, the sinfulness of such a proceeding, declaring that if these amusements did not cease, if they did not give up their present intention, he would abandon the parish rather than countenance such an offence against God. The people, however, trusting to the well-known indulgence of their pastor, would not relinquish their design.

The holy-day dawned. Extensive preparations had been made for the iniquitous amusement, and all were on the *qui vive* as to how the day would end. And behold! after Mass that morning a wagon was seen in waiting before the pastor's residence. The driver, a non-Catholic, being questioned as to what it all meant, answered frankly: "You must have offended your pastor very grievously. He intends to leave you." And now from all sides flocked men and women around the house. Father Neumann had packed his books and other effects, and was ready to start. To every appeal to the contrary he replied, in a decided tone: "I have implored you, I have warned you to remove this scandal. You would not listen to me. I will no longer be your pastor." The poor people entreated him to remain, promising that the saloon-keeper should give up the projected ball. The latter, hearing of what was taking place at the pastoral residence, hastened in dismay to ask "His Reverence's" pardon, but begging him at the same time to sanction the ball just this once, as he had made quite an outlay in preparing for it. But their otherwise gentle and condescending pastor was firm in his decision; there could be no compromise in a question involving sin. "No," he replied, "it must not be. I warned you in time, and now you must abide by my decision." The man was obliged to yield, and soon after he left the neighborhood.

Such encounters pained Father Neumann's kind, benevolent heart, though they failed to weaken his zeal for the honor of God and the salvation of souls. He was simply indefatigable in the enormous amount of work entailed upon him by the immense district under his care. He instructed the children, administered the Sacraments, attended the sick, and built churches and schools. Taught by his own experience, his good friend Father Pax often admonished him to spare himself a little. But Father Neumann would smilingly reply to such exhortations, "Oh, I'm a strong Bohemian mountain-boy! It will not hurt me."

Long years after, Father Pax used to delight in recalling the sayings and doings of his young friend and companion, the sharer of his labors in the painful beginnings of the western New York missions. More than once he spoke as follows: "It was something truly extraordinary to see that learned, pious, and amiable young priest, a little valise in his hand or a bundle, containing the requisites for saying holy Mass, over his shoulder, courageously journeying from one to another of his different stations. Sometimes the bad roads or the deep snow rendered it impossible to procure a conveyance; and very often, too, he would not use one, as he thought himself strong enough to go on foot."

How many interesting and edifying incidents must have occurred during these journeyings of the faithful priest! But, unfortunately, few have come to our knowledge, as Father Neumann carefully avoided everything in conversation that could, even in a small degree, redound to his own praise; and in his journal we find only the record of what he considered his infidelities to God.

One Sunday he arrived at Lancaster pale as death and fainting from exhaustion. He was obliged to go to bed immediately. He had said Mass that morning at a distant station, whence, laden as usual with altar requisites, he had started over a rough road to say Mass, preach, etc., at a second station many miles off. The tax on his strength had been too severe, and the condition to which it reduced him aroused fears for the worst. A physician was prompt in attendance, and, thanks to his skill joined to his patient's natural vigor and energy, a few days set all things right again.

About five miles from Williamsville, on the road to North Bush, lived a kind-hearted gentleman who had often been edified by the untiring zeal of our holy missionary. One stormy day he saw him passing, and he called out to him to come in and rest awhile. Father Neumann excused himself, saying that he was expected at Sheldon to perform a marriage-ceremony, and he named the groom. His friend endeavored to persuade him not to put himself to so much trouble, not to pursue his journey in such weather, assuring him that it would most likely prove fruitless; he knew the groom to be a lukewarm Catholic who would doubtless have contracted a civil marriage even before his arrival. But Father Neumann would listen to no such reasoning; he hastened on through wind and rain to the performance of his duty. What his friend had predicted was literally fulfilled. To Father Neumann's deep mortification and in spite of his earnest admonitions, the marriage had been contracted before a magistrate with as much publicity as possible, a band of music in attendance.

There was nothing left to the priest but to turn his back on the godless crowd and make his way home as best he could. But Divine Providence had some little indemnification in store for him, some little part of the hundred-fold promised to those who give up all for God. On his way through the woods, Father Neumann met some of the better-disposed of his flock, who, noticing the miserable condition of his shoes, insisted on his going straight to the shoemaker's hard by and leaving an order for a pair of good, stout boots. And so once more do we see an illustration of the truth that all things work together unto good for them that love God.

It is scarcely necessary to mention that the troubles here alluded to by Father Neumann, belong rather to the times in which the various congregations were formed out of many different elements. Later on, such difficulties disappeared.

CHAPTER VI.

Father Neumann and Non-Catholics.

AMONG the numerous obstacles which sprung up to oppose Father Neumann's apostolic labors, not the least inconsiderable was that which he experienced from the vicinity of the Mennonites, or, as they are known in this country, the Anabaptists. Their numbers in his parishes ran higher than those of the Catholics themselves. Bible in hand, they went from house to house, singing, praying, and exhorting to conversion. Many poor, ill-instructed Catholics were thus enticed to their meetings, and their hearts perverted. That our zealous young missionary was a target for their hatred and ridicule we may readily imagine. They nicknamed him "the little priest," and among them he went by no other title.

One Sunday morning in winter, Father Neumann was on his way to one of his most distant stations. The snow was on the ground, and with difficulty could a foot-passenger travel over the unbroken road. But such difficulties were easily surmounted by one like Father Neumann whose heart and soul soared above exterior things. On he plodded, patiently and untiringly, his bundle, as usual, slung over his shoulder. Suddenly the sound of bells strikes on his ear, and he recognizes the sharp ring of horses' hoofs on the crisp snow. Not many moments after, a well-filled sleigh dashes past him, and then comes to a sudden stand-still.

"Where are you going, little priest?" cries a cheery voice.

"To my station at ——," answered Father Neumann, the "little priest" addressed.

"Jump in with your load, and ride with us as far as our church. It is just on your road."

Father Neumann graciously accepted the kind invitation, and took the seat offered him. The sleigh belonged to a Baptist minister who with his family was on his way, as we have seen, to the meeting-house. Father Neumann's object in accepting the minister's kindness was the hope of benefiting souls, little dreaming that his own conversion was the motive from which the former acted. But so it was. We shall see how Divine Providence disposed this apparently casual meeting for Its own wise ends.

No sooner was the sleigh again bounding over the smooth snow, than its fanatical occupants opened their battery upon the "little priest;" each vied with the other in well-meant efforts to enlighten what they deemed his spiritual darkness. They pitied him because, as they said in sympathizing tones, he was laboring in vain, toiling on foot, bearing a heavy load for miles, cheerless and alone; whereas, if he were a Baptist preacher, he might have his own conveyance, might lead a comfortable, easy life, with a loving family to receive him when he returned home, etc., etc. "Besides," they triumphantly added, "*we* have the true religion, *we* have the Holy Ghost!"

Father Neumann, though inwardly amused, had all this time maintained profound silence. His opponents were highly elated, judging from his manner their cause as good as won. At the mention of the Holy Ghost, however, their wished-for convert took up the word and asked innocently, "Tell me how I also can be enlightened. How can I receive the true religion?"

The *enlightened* comforted him with the assurance that their ministers would fully satisfy him. Finally, it was agreed that on a certain day they would assemble at the house of one of their number and discuss matters publicly.

Father Neumann insisted upon the necessity of appointing some one, agreeable to both parties, umpire, to whose decision all would submit. Accordingly, to this office an aged and highly esteemed lawyer, a man who professed no form of religion, was named. His appointment gave general satisfaction. On that very day, Sunday, upon which the above incident transpired, the rumor spread like wild-fire that the Catholic priest was about to turn Baptist. Many even among the Catholics gave credence to the report, as is proved by the fact that one man was so enraged by what he heard that he lay in wait with a loaded pistol for the pastor's return. But Divine Providence interposed to avert from both the threatened calamity; for Father Neumann, without any special reason for it, went home by another route. He informed his parishioners of the projected conference, and requested their prayers for the triumph of Holy Church.

The looked-for day at last arrived, and, at the hour appointed, the ministers with their followers assembled. Then came Father Neumann, attended by several of the most prominent Catholics. The umpire took his chair, and proceedings began. Father Neumann opened the discussion by inquiring upon what authority his opponents rested their religious belief.

"Upon the authority of the Bible," was the answer.

Question—"Who wrote the Bible?"

Answer—"The Holy Ghost."

Question—"In what language and in what edition?"

Answer—"In all languages and in every edition."

Then Father Neumann, making a summary of the above, spoke as follows:

"The Holy Ghost cannot contradict Himself. If your Bibles do not perfectly agree, they cannot have been written by the Holy Ghost; consequently the authority of your religious belief is not divine."

Here the preachers asserted with one voice that their

Bible was the same in all languages; that different editions introduced no change. Then Father Neumann requested several Bibles to be handed to him, from each of which he read a few passages. The sense of these passages differed in each rendition, though the heretics obstinately maintained that it was not so. An appeal was made to the chosen umpire, who frankly owned that the passages in question differed so much from one another that the author of them could not be looked upon as worthy of belief.

Changing their ground, the preachers now declared that they were enlightened by the Holy Spirit; that He inspired them with what they ought to believe, and taught them how to interpret the Sacred Scriptures. Father Neumann replied by warning them against the spirit by which they thought themselves enlightened, quoting several instances in which the spirit of darkness in the form of an angel of light had deluded the minds of men.

"If you are enlightened by the Holy Ghost," said he, "where are your miracles?"

To this question they answered by another: "And can *you* work miracles?"

"Most assuredly," said Father Neumann, "I *can* work miracles. At every Mass I celebrate, at every absolution I give in the confessional, at every exorcism of the evil one, I work miracles. The Catholic priest can and does work miracles on these and any other proper occasions. Now tell me, if you have, as you say, the Holy Ghost, ought you not all to agree in your religious belief?"

"We ought," was the answer.

Here Father Neumann convicted them of inconsistency, showed them the glaring contradiction between their theory and practice, and referred to the innumerable variations which Protestantism had assumed and was daily assuming.

His opponents, confounded and ashamed, endeavored

to conceal their chagrin; and one of them, bolder than his brethren, boasted of his ability to prove to "the little priest" that he was enlightened by the Holy Ghost.

"Proceed, then," said Father Neumann. "But first answer me one question. Does the Holy Ghost dwell in you?"

"Most undoubtedly!" was the cool reply.

"Prove it, my friend," returned Father Neumann.

"My whole life proves it," began the preacher, with an air of righteous assurance. "Once I was a sinful man. I used to steal my neighbors' horses and cows; I often cheated them in many other ways. But since my conversion, I have been a changed man."

Father Neumann here turned to the assembly and, with a twinkle of amusement in his eye, asked:

"My friends, you have just heard one of your preachers confessing his past delinquencies. He assures us that he once cheated and stole, etc. Now can any of you inform me whether he ever made *restitution* for his ill-gotten goods?"

"No, no!" shouted a chorus of voices. "He *never* did!"

"Then," asked the priest, highly amused, "is his conversion a genuine one?"

"No, no, no!" resounded from all sides. "He is the same old rogue that he ever was!"

The reader is free to imagine the ludicrous effect produced by this unexpected conclusion of the religious debate. Filled with shame, the disputants slunk away from the hall, one to meet an engagement, another to return to his sick child, etc., and Father Neumann and his friends soon found themselves alone with the umpire. The latter shook hands with the victorious party, laughingly congratulating them on their triumph; whilst the preachers had nothing to bring forward in extenuation of their defeat excepting that "the little priest" was too shrewd, too cunning, had too much worldly wisdom in him. Religion must be pure.

Though vanquished in argument, the heretics did not return to that unity from which their forefathers had unhappily strayed. Pride closed the avenues to so great a grace, but thenceforth their fanatical attacks upon Father Neumann and his flock ceased. One blessed result of the conference was the return of the poor deluded Catholics whom the hope of worldly advantages had been mainly instrumental in seducing from the truth. Their repentance was sincere, and gladly did they find themselves once more in the fold of Christ.

From a remark in one of his letters to a friend we may gather Father Neumann's opinion of his opponents' argumentative abilities:

"How I wish B——'s admirers could dispute for a short time with our American heretics! It would be the very best means of removing his doubts. As soon as a man separates from the Church and her doctrines, even in one point, he becomes unreasonable, illogical, falls into doubt, and ends by obstinate heresy.

"As regards Protestantism, I must say that I have been undeceived. I used to think that its splitting up into innumerable forms had generated coldness and indifference; but it is not so. Their noisy preaching in the streets and public places, the obtrusiveness of those who distribute Bibles, their ridiculous prophecies respecting the Day of Judgment, etc., amaze us Catholics. If one enters a Methodist meeting-house during religious services, one might believe himself transported to the times of Elias and the priests of Baal. All are praying aloud, though not in concert. One shouts, another screams; some weep, some sing; whilst others, turning deadly pale, fall to the floor, foam at the mouth, groan as if in agony, roll about convulsively, having, as they blasphemously assert, received the Holy Ghost. It would be worth while to advise our European sceptics to attend one of these sensational meetings. They would, without doubt, carry away a belief in the existence of the devil. That the Catholic Church alone is *One, Holy, Catholic*, and *Apostolic* is convincingly brought home to our Catholics here, for the truth enters both by eyes and ears."

Father Neumann's fervent prayers for the conversion of infidels and heretics were productive of a rich harvest of souls. God granted him the consolation of leading many a wandering sheep back to the fold. If he happened to hear of some poor apostate Catholics among the Protestants of his locality, his heart was torn with anguish, and he redoubled his prayers and penances in their behalf.

"My God, my God," he cried, "sanctify me, that I may become a fit instrument of Thy graces and mercies to the souls Thou hast confided to me! If Thou seest that success will make me vain, do not, I beseech Thee, on that account allow me to fail. Humble me in some other way, but do not punish me through my parishioners."

Sometimes his journal speaks of whole families under instruction, either for baptism or reception into the Church. Here are some lines which initiate us into the secret of his success:

"The recitation of the Rosary for my stray sheep is always productive of abundant fruit. I will redouble my zeal in this sweet and efficacious devotion."

To prayer Father Neumann united study. One of his resolutions of this period was to prepare more diligently for his sermons, hoping thereby more easily to convince heretics of the truth.

His longing for the salvation of souls was so intense that he offered himself a victim to the justice of Almighty God, being willing to suffer and die for this end. We read in his journal, under date of September 14, 1836:

"To-day has been a very painful one to me. I have heard of the apostasy of one of my parishioners. My heart is pierced with sorrow. Lord Jesus, have mercy!

Ah, permit not that any one of those whom Thou hast entrusted to me should be lost! O my Jesus, I will pray, fast, suffer, and, with the help of Thy grace, sacrifice life itself! Lord, endue my words with power and unction that they may glorify the truth!"

Almighty God accepted the magnanimous offering of His faithful servant; for unspeakable were the mental tortures he endured to procure the grace of truth and faith for his flock. The same day on which his heart bled over the miserable defection of the poor soul mentioned above, he had the ineffable happiness of receiving back into the fold one dead to the faith for years.

On the evening of a day on which he had administered the Sacraments to the sick or dying, he always prayed especially for the sufferer. We learn this practice from the lines found in his journal:

"O Lord God, Heavenly Father, grant to my sick children a pure and heart-felt love of Thee! Give them contrition, patience, and, above all, heavenly aspirations."

Sick-calls at night were frequent, sometimes from a distance of ten or fifteen miles. His friends at last interposed, and begged the people to limit such calls, if possible, to the daytime. Mr. Schmidt, at whose house he lodged for a time, persuaded the young pastor to ride when the distance was great, and furnished him with a horse for that purpose. Now, Father Neumann, as we know, was no cavalier. Many a mile have we seen him journeying with no other conveyance than the "apostolic horses" provided him by nature. His was a life perfectly modelled upon that of the Divine Preacher who, footsore and weary, crossed mountain and valley in the hallowed land of Judea when He, too, went about His "Father's business." The first time, therefore, that Father Neumann mounted his spirited young horse, a groom had to lead the animal by the bridle. On another occasion, when about to mount, Father Neumann was exposed to imminent peril. He thrust his foot into the wrong stirrup, and that so far that it was impossible for him to withdraw it without assistance. Meanwhile the animal started, and, seeing that he was on the point of running away, Father Neumann flung himself into the saddle, when lo! he found himself seated backward. To secure his seat, he grasped the saddle with both hands. Off went the horse with his unskilful rider; and badly enough might it have fared with our reverend Gilpin, had not some men working near by run to the rescue. This horse seemed to be instinctively aware of his master's inexperience, and to take a malicious delight in trying his patience. Father Neumann was low in stature; consequently, to mount and dismount, he was obliged to make use of some neighboring fence or log. It often happened, especially on muddy roads, that the horse would plant himself obstinately in the middle of a swamp and refuse to move a step until his unfortunate rider had dismounted. Then he would advance nimbly enough; but let the master again seat himself in the saddle and, ten to one, the same tricks would recommence. Poor Father Neumann was often forced to foot it by the animal's side, his bundle over his shoulder. But no such freaks could disconcert the patient priest. In his holy simplicity, he used to praise the tantalizing beast, calling it his travelling companion, and sharing with it his bread, apples, etc.

One day a blacksmith was witness of the animal's capers. He prepared to administer a sound beating as a specific to its obstinacy, but Father Neumann hastily interposed: "My horse and I agree very well together. I cannot let him be punished."

"He needs to be broken in," said the man. "Let me train him for you;" and up he sprung to the animal's back.

Trot, trot, went the horse for a few paces, and then deposited his valiant rider on the ground, where he lay groaning from a broken arm.

Great as was Father Neumann's patience with his freakish companion, yet a day dawned on which it was put to a severe test. Father Neumann was, as we have before stated, a lover of Nature in all her forms, and a successful botanical student. He had long been in quest of a certain flower which at last, in one of his rides through the woods, he discovered. To get off his horse, make a foot-path through the swamp by means of some logs, was a labor fully repaid by the gratification he felt when gently holding the beautiful object of his exertions between his finger and thumb. Slowly he returned to where the horse stood. For an instant he paused intent on his examination of sepal and petal, stamen and pistil, when lo! it was suddenly snatched from his hand, and, looking up, he beheld the horse's head over his shoulder, and the animal in the act of swallowing it. Immense was his loss; but more quickly than the theft was committed went the *fiat* from the botanist's heart up to heaven. In the least as in the greatest events of life, our saintly priest recognized the finger of God. He felt sure that this little sacrifice was the one demanded of him at that moment. In after-years Father Neumann often recurred to this incident, and the remembrance of his horse's pranks never failed to amuse him.

CHAPTER VII.

Father Neumann's Missionary Plans.

FATHER NEUMANN had formed broad plans for the missions of America. One of his favorite projects, even while a seminarian, was the establishment of a mission-house in Bohemia especially devoted to the propagation of Catholicity in America. Under the direction of Rev. Father Dichtl, such of his fellow-students as were animated by a similar spirit were to open this institution so beneficial to the work of the missions, and by funds raised in Bohemia support the priests who would generously devote themselves to the service of poor abandoned souls.

Several of his letters to Father Dichtl and other friends bear witness to Father Neumann's adherence to these views, which, indeed, seem only to have gained fresh strength from his practical knowledge of missionary life. On June 4, 1837, he wrote in his journal:

"Thanks be to God! the obstacles to our missions in America augur good results. Our difficulties will vanish when God, as I sincerely trust He will, comes to our aid. If we resolutely set to work, resigned to the dispositions of Divine Providence, we shall soon attain the end of our desires.

"Doubtless you would like to hear my reasons for these fond hopes. Whilst at Munich I was informed by a priest from Philadelphia that my admission into that diocese was highly improbable; so I at once resolved to go among the Indians. God, however, disposed otherwise. I became a missionary in the diocese of New York, and was sent to the Germans living in the district between Lake Erie and Lake Ontario. Thus I was forced to abandon my design, if not forever, at least for the time being. But now I understand that this arrangement was for me the very best means of attaining my object, and I have constantly endeavored to learn the views of the various Bishops in the United States. For the Indians in the western part of the Union much has been done. By a decree of the Holy See the missions of this immense territory have been entrusted to the care of the Jesuits, though other laborers are not excluded. I now live scarcely half a day's journey from Upper Canada. I often inquire of the French Canadians who come here to make their Easter confession concerning the state of religion among them. The account they give is not cheering. True, there is a flourishing seminary at Montreal, but the labors of the Bishops are mostly restricted to the French and Irish. On the northern banks of Lake Huron and Lake Superior are immense forests peopled by Indians who, about once or twice a year, are visited by European fur-traders. Here is plenty of work for the missionary. Our projected institute, whose existence I trust is not far off, might also be of great service to the German settlers. Although I sometimes find myself in straits for the necessaries of life, yet I am quite satisfied that my district could easily support two or even three priests. But only poor priests, or those who are willing to lead a hard life, can get along in this part of the country. A permanent abode cannot be hoped for; the priest is continually on the go. Should any of your confrères be willing to devote themselves to missionary work among our northern Indians, they could not better prepare for it than by a temporary residence among our Germans. The body develops new powers of endurance from exposure, fasting, travelling, and other fatiguing exertions; one gradually learns the state of the country, the manners of the people, and becomes familiar with the

Indians, whom he constantly meets roaming about. Should you, Reverend Father, make any rules for the contemplated society, I give my consent to them in advance."

In another letter to the same reverend gentleman, Father Neumann says: "The second step toward the realization of our plan has, with God's help, been made. I enclose to you the written authorization of Right Rev. Bishop Dubois, of New York, securing the reception into the diocese of two or three zealous priests or theological students. Nothing is wanting now except that the Holy Ghost should inspire some of His servants to consecrate themselves to the spread of the Gospel in North America. The want of Catholic priests and the spiritual destitution of the people increase from day to day. Judging even from a human view, such a state of things must eventually lead to lamentable results. But God is the support of His Church. He will provide for her. Much scandal has been given in these parts by the arrival of unworthy priests who come here merely to lead a reckless life amid the confusion of heresies. But the vigilance of the Bishops over the teaching and conduct of their priests exposes these wretched creatures to greater opprobrium than they would be subjected to in Europe, and so they hurry off even before they have learned one word of English. Other priests, zealous and pious, return home on account of old age or ill-health; others, again, because of the corruption of morals, which appears to them incurable. That the evils existing among our people are very great is, indeed, only too true, and the reason of this is that many of them are mere adventurers, restless fanatics, sighing for what they call liberty; and some there are who have but narrowly escaped the outstretched arms of justice. Still, we must allow that apostasy from the faith, considering the evil influence everywhere exercised by heretics, is not so frequent as one might suppose; nay, the number of those who return to the bosom of the only saving Church balances the loss sustained by such defections. The gain would surely be greater if earnest priests were more numerous. If, humanly speaking, evils threaten the Church, they must be ascribed, above all, to the want of priests and the inadequate instruction of our youth. The education of the latter claims much of the missionary's time; but God's assistance is never wanting, it often interposes in ways most wonderful. The zeal of our young Catholics and their eagerness for knowledge are simply astonishing. Last year during my three weeks' stay at Williamsville preparing the children for First Communion, most of them had to come six miles to instructions, and this they did even in the worst weather. In that short time they learned not only the principal truths of Christian faith and morals, but they made greater progress in reading and writing than could be done in Europe in many years.

"The moment has now arrived for me to remind my dear friends in Bohemia of the words of Jesus Christ: 'Go into the *whole world*, and teach all nations.' From the seminaries of America no help for the Germans can yet be expected. Therefore do I beg my brethren who are resolved to come to this country to do so at once, to hasten to the assistance of our militant Church. If Rev. S——, of Verona; S——, of Vienna; P—— and S——, etc., are still inclined that way, I most earnestly entreat them to come. If any others entertain the same desire, I beg you to examine whether their religious principles agree with the teachings of the Roman Catholic Church; otherwise it would be well for them to provide the means for a speedy return. If my petition meets, as I hope it will, a favorable response, you would oblige me by letting me know at once. With the names of the aspirants, state also the time of their setting out for America."

In order to bring about more surely and speedily the

establishment of the Mission Institute, Father Neumann also addressed a letter to the Reverend Superior of the Archiepiscopal Seminary at Prague. In it he says: "Should your Reverence find among our confrères in the seminary of Prague (which I shall ever remember) one or more subjects who, in childlike faith and obedience to Holy Mother Church, desire to devote themselves to the arduous life of a missionary in America, I entreat you to give them every encouragement. If Father Dichtl should have the full number of applicants, you would oblige me by letting me know, that I may apply for their admission into the New York diocese. Right Rev. John Hughes, Coadjutor-Bishop of the diocese, told me recently that he would admit seven or eight candidates. It is not necessary for them to speak either English or French; they can easily learn both languages in this country, and that very quickly. Good health is a qualification very desirable in a priest destined for America; for the missions entail much travelling, fasting, and preaching. Still, indifferent health should not deter any one, since God supplies when strength fails.

"As for myself, I am fully satisfied with the labors of the sphere assigned me, for I came here to atone for my sins and to win souls to God. Nowhere, I think, can a better opportunity be found for doing both than here in America. May God grant me the grace to discharge my duties more worthily than I now do!"

Here Father Neumann enters into some details respecting his missions, and then continues: "From all that I have said, you will easily understand how much there is to be accomplished here, and how much more good might be effected were the workmen more numerous. The district, embracing about five hundred miles between the Erie Canal and the Hudson River, is peopled by Germans who, for the most part, are destitute of all spiritual assistance. Coming to this country after a certain age, a German scarcely ever learns English. He knows not even how to bid *good-morning* in that language. The words of the Lord, 'In strange tongues I will speak to my people,' are verified in them. May God vouchsafe to hear their prayers, and send them priests of their own nationality! Despite their entreaties to that effect, I can rarely visit them, as I am hardly sufficient for the wants of my own extensive territory.

"The Catholic population is continually on the increase; not that conversions swell our numbers, but immigration goes on rapidly. Conversions, however, are by no means rare. Many of our Catholics are in extreme poverty. They live in miserable shanties, some of which have not even the luxury of a window. As a general thing, chairs and bedsteads are unknown. I have seen the dying stretched on a bundle of straw or moss. To hear their confessions and prepare them for the Sacraments, I have to seat myself by their side on the ground. When the priest enters an Irishman's shanty, the whole family, young and old, make the sign of the cross and salute him with, 'Welcome, Father!' How consoling such a salutation from faithful hearts!"

Animated by the noblest sentiments of Christian friendship, Father Neumann invited his most intimate friend and fellow-student to join him in his labors for the glory of God. Here are his words: "May I not indulge the hope of seeing you again, of seeing you in America—in that land whose name, after the sweet name of Jesus, so often conjured up the brightest visions in the years we passed together? Yes, that name was so dear to us that it formed the theme of our daily conversation. Time never hung heavily with us, though we constantly interchanged the same sentiments. The idea of the American missions was at that time so closely interwoven with our one great thought, the service of God and our neighbor, that any other road leading thereto, how well known or secure soever it might be, appeared to us foreign and distasteful. You still sigh, if I may credit your own words, for America and your friend of by-gone days. Why, then, do you not come? Why are you not even now on the road to the New World? Of course, as you so well understand, there is question of vocation. But this, I believe, is not wanting to you. Your great desire to serve our Holy Church in America appears to me an undoubted call from Heaven."

As far as the present fulfilment of his ardent desires was concerned, Father Neumann wrote and pleaded in vain. The Missionary Society, whose formation he had so much at heart, was destined never to spring into existence; moreover, not one of Father Neumann's former companions ever found his way to the shores of America. Several of them did, indeed, make some futile attempts to follow him, but insurmountable obstacles arose to prevent the realization of their dream. Doubtless the vocation for foreign missions had not been vouchsafed to them by the Lord of the harvest. Many of those designated by Father Neumann in the letters just quoted are now zealously and successfully laboring in their own country for the honor of God and the salvation of souls.

CHAPTER VIII.

Father Neumann's Own Sanctification.

CONSCIENTIOUSLY and untiringly as Father Neumann attended to the spiritual wants of his flock, he yet found time for his own sanctification. His life was most exemplary. He made use of every means in his power to perfect himself in his high vocation. Hardships and journeys; the labors incidental to so extensive a parish as his; the building of churches and schools, to which, from the very beginning of his ministry, he energetically devoted himself—nothing could interfere with the one great object of his life, the sanctification of his own soul. As long years before, in the peaceful seclusion of college-life, so now, in the turmoil of active duty, do we find him faithfully recording the various impressions and emotions of his interior. His keeping of a journal was no idle formula, but conscientiously, in a way peculiar to himself, utterly regardless of the revolts of self-love, were all his entries made.

"I feel in myself," he writes, "an extreme desire to love Jesus Christ ardently, to be closely united to Him. The daily reception of His Sacred Body and Blood ought to bring with it immense graces to my soul. But I find that I am not sufficiently watchful over my eyes; I am indolent in the discharge of my duty; I say my Office with distractions. Every Saturday at five, I will recite the Litany of the Blessed Virgin in church. O my dearest Jesus, I can now visit Thee daily, as often as I choose. I receive Thee so frequently; I receive Thee every day—yes, even twice on Sundays and holy-days.

Oh, help me to grow in virtue, since I am so near to the fountain of living waters!"

Here are some resolutions made about this period. How clear an insight they afford into the interior state of him who formed them!

"1. I will always say my Office kneeling and as devoutly as possible. I will also try to say it at the stated hours.

"2. I will be very exact in making my preparation for Mass and my thanksgiving after it.

"3. Every day after dinner I will make a visit to the Most Blessed Sacrament.

"4. I will never eat out of mealtime, which will be at noon and in the evening.

"5. I will prepare more carefully for my sermons.

"6. I will speak only through necessity or for the greater glory of God.

"7. I will watch over my thoughts and senses. My God, help me through the intercession of Mary and all the saints. Amen."

That his prayers might be more efficacious, our good young Father addressed himself to those saints who were characterized here on earth by their intense love for God. "My dearest Lord and Master," he one day exclaimed, "behold my poor crushed heart! Oh, permit me to advance on the road of perfection, that road which leads to Thee, my dearly beloved Saviour, my only Treasure! O my Jesus, Spouse of St. Teresa, the thought of whom fills me with a longing desire for Thy love, delay no longer to shower upon my parched soul the consolations of Thy love! St. Teresa, whose heart was so inflamed with the love of Thy Divine Spouse, pray for me, that God may purify, justify, sanctify me! Behold my desires to love Jesus, to give myself entirely to Him!"

His sins, as he denominated those small imperfections from which even the "just man" is not wholly free, were to Father Neumann a source of constant and bitter self-recrimination. God alone knows the penances performed, the tears shed in expiation of them. Weighed down by the thought of them, he exclaims:

"I will weep over my sins even to the loss of sight. Lord, accept my tears, and grant me in this life true contrition."

In fact, page after page of his journal betrays abundant evidence of those tears which accompanied the outpourings of his love and sorrow. Meditation on the sorrowful mysteries of the Rosary was sufficient to produce in his soul emotions so lively that, as he himself states:

"My tears have so exhausted me that I have become almost senseless."

True love brings forth fruit; consequently we read, a little farther on:

"My Lord and my God, I vow to say every Friday, as long as I live, at 3 P.M., if possible, the Litany of our Lord's bitter Passion, and I promise, also, to teach my children to recite the Rosary in honor of the Blessed Virgin. This I resolve to do, O my God!"

Father Neumann was not exempt from those intense spiritual sufferings which usually fall to the lot of the elect. The salvation of those confided to him wrung from him many a cry of anguish. Witness the following:

"Mercy, mercy, my God! My God, infinite mercy! My faith in the Most Blessed Sacrament grows weak. Ah! when will this end? O ye tears, could ye but wash away the stains of my soul! Hopes and longings of my youth, how utterly have ye been blasted! Flowers of virtue in the garden of my heart, how have ye been rooted up and trampled upon! Ah, my Lord, would that I really loved Thee! Divine Master, how canst Thou permit my immortal soul, my soul which believes in Thee, to perish forever miserably?"

We see from the pages before us that whole months

passed in these mental sufferings; that no ray of consolation came from on high to alleviate their poignancy.

"That love, O my God, which once united me to Thee," he often exclaims, "has completely disappeared. O my Jesus, I am lost to heaven, I am dead to Thee! Oh, raise me up again to life, Thou who alone canst work wonders! Lord, what shall I do? Infant Jesus, how estranged hast Thou become from me! Am I to be forever banished from Thee? O my God, give me strength, give me back my love for Thee!"

Such were the mental tortures with which Almighty God visited His chosen servant; for such is the road trodden by souls from whom He, the wise and good Father, asks and expects much.

Harassed on all sides, trials, annoyances, and disappointments from without, anguish of spirit within, Father Neumann believed himself the cause of all the evils existing in his several parishes. More than once the thought of fleeing to the wilderness and there concealing himself suggested itself as a welcome release from his burden of responsibility.

"In my faint-heartedness," he says, "I indulged wild dreams. To escape the terrible responsibility resting upon me, I sometimes thought of abandoning my flock, of fleeing to some distant solitude where I might lead a hidden, penitential life, or hire myself as a laborer in the fields. The fear of creating suspicion in the minds of the faithful, and of affording the enemies of our holy religion occasion to blaspheme, alone prevented my carrying out this project. Dark thoughts constantly assailed me. Thou didst come to bring fire and the sword—yea, Lord, and both have fallen to my share! Holy guardian angel, blessed archangel St. Michael, strengthen me for the combat!"

Father Neumann's only refuge during these conflicts was fervent prayer to Jesus and His holy Mother. And therefore did his Lord and Master take the faithful servant by the hand that he might not suffer injury, might not succumb to temptation.

"God protected me," he goes on to say, "in all my terrible struggles. When clouds grew darkest, He arose to strengthen and to save. To-day I was several times on the point of being vanquished, but Divine Providence came to my aid."

His earnest strivings after union with God rises, at this period, to the inspired language of the Sacred Bard. Behold the following plaintive and beautiful aspirations of his loving soul:

"Jesus, my delight, has fled; alas, I seek for Him in vain! I have lost my Beloved. He hearkens not to my sighs, He heeds not my voice. My eyes are blinded by tears, my voice has grown weak from lamenting; but He is not moved. He does not show Himself to my poor soul. Jesus, Jesus, where art Thou? Because thou hast followed Baal, O thou priestly soul, thy Spouse has separated Himself from thee, He has wedded another. And behold! Baal wretchedly repays thee. He mocks thee, he repulses thee with scorn, and thou wanderest fainting and hopeless, tormented by thy reawakening love and fruitlessly sighing after thy Saviour."

Sometimes a ray of light seems to have penetrated his soul, and his aspirations assume a more trustful tone:

"O Heavenly Father, see, my poor heart opens up to Thee, touched by a ray of Thy divine grace. Drive from it, I beseech Thee, the evil one, for, of myself, I am unable to do so. O lovely Infant Jesus, Thou wilt live again in me! Oh, that on the glorious and joyous Feast of Thy Nativity I could prepare an agreeable dwelling for Thee in my heart! O Jesus, Almighty Saviour, hasten to my relief! O dearest Infant, wash me with the tears which my sins draw from Thy sweet eyes! Bless me, tiny hands of my Infant Saviour! Open, sweet lips of my little Jesus, and say, 'Thy sins are forgiven thee!' Oh, be not dead in my heart, dear Jesus! My sins have, indeed, put Thee to death; but do Thou, the Almighty One, be born again. Rise from the dead, and raise me with Thee to a new life! Bless me, O Jesus, with Thy little hands! Bless me, and give me simplicity of heart, humility, and obedience!"

Every assault of human passion was courageously combated by Father Neumann, everything carefully guarded against that might prove an obstacle to the attainment of the end of his priestly vocation. It seems to us almost incredible that he should accuse himself of avarice, he who had never lived save in the practice of the strictest poverty, cheerfully depriving himself of even the necessaries of life in behalf of a suffering neighbor. Still, we find the following ingenuous lines bearing upon this point:

"This hoarding up money for the poor-house" (Father Mertz had built one at Eden) "may end by making me avaricious. I must be on my guard." And again: "I fear I am becoming miserly. I take so much delight in counting money. I have begun to offer a little resistance to the vice of avarice by giving half a dollar to the servers at Holy Mass. I must repeat the donation in order to free myself entirely from such temptations; otherwise I cannot love Jesus with my *whole* heart."

And yet we know that at this time Father Neumann's circumstances were straitened enough for any apostle; there was neither room for the enjoyment of the comforts of life, nor even a thought of the same. His very self-accusation opens up to us some of the most charming secrets of his pure soul. Without such an acknowledgment, many of his heroic virtues would have remained forever concealed. The records of his humility redound to his own honor; for "without struggle no victory, without victory no crown."

Never hesitating to combat temptation by the most efficacious remedies, Father Neumann shrank not from employing, in what he considered his temptation to avarice, a means which, outside of a religious Order, would naturally give rise to innumerable difficulties. But "love casts out fear," and his was that perfect love which gives all to the Beloved. Here are his words:

"This incipient hankering after money prevents me from keeping my thoughts fixed on God. On the eve of St. Peter of Alcantara's Feast (1836) I was unusually discouraged and distracted. I took refuge from my cares with Jesus in the Blessed Sacrament, and as I prayed and wept before Him, the thought occurred to me to make the vow of poverty. I followed the inspiration in all sincerity. The reflection as to how I should practise it gave me some uneasiness; but, O my God, I trust to Thee for light and strength. Peace returned to my soul."

Father Neumann contemplated about this time the erection of a school-house at Williamsville; but, dreading the expense it would entail, the church-trustees opposed his plans. In one of his colloquies with Almighty God we find the following on this subject:

"This school-house will have to be my own work under Thee, O my God; but, for Thy love, I will spare nothing. My vow of poverty will now be of service to me. I shall have a chance to test the sincerity of my resolutions."

The disfavor in which some Catholics of Williamsville held Father Neumann the latter repaid in the coin of the saints. He left nothing undone to return the insults heaped upon him by the most disinterested works of charity in their behalf. During that bitter period of spiritual abandonment of which we have already made mention, he one day exclaimed:

"Will not even my love for my enemies move Thee, O Jesus? Witness my last expenditure, the stove for the school out of my private purse. Lord, I offer it to Thee."

This purchase, if the truth were known, was made at the sacrifice of Father Neumann's last dollar. Shortly after, we find him furnishing the same school with benches.

"The thought that it was for my Jesus, the Friend of children," he says, "for His love, has won me a victory over my hankering after money. Yes, my Jesus, all for Thee! I will teach my children to know and love Thee, but first do Thou make me humble, childlike, free from guile."

CHAPTER IX.

Father Neumann's Vocation to the Religious Life.

WHEN Easter of 1840 rolled round, it found Father Neumann completely broken down. He was seized with intermittent fever in its most violent and obstinate form, and for three months he was a prey to its weakening attacks, being often obliged to keep his bed. Now was the time for Wenceslaus to show his fraternal devotedness; nor was he found wanting in this hour of need. His thoughtful and gentle ministrations contributed in no small degree to the comfort and relief of his reverend brother. A very remarkable feature of this period was the fact that not one of his parishioners needed Father Neumann's priestly services during the whole time of his sickness, though previously to it scarcely a day passed without a sick-call.

When he began to convalesce he was advised by his friends to take a short trip for the sake of change of scene and air. Yielding to their advice, he went to Rochester for a few days. Here he stopped with the Redemptorist Father Sänderl; but though benefited by the change, no persuasions could induce him to remain over Sunday; he must be back for his missions on that day. Father Neumann's delicate health dates from this period; and though we shall still find him getting through an immense amount of hard work in the vineyard of his Lord, yet his pristine vigor was gone. His previous exertions regardless of his own corporal needs now told on his otherwise fine constitution. He returned, as we have seen, to his wide-spread missions to enter upon duties now far above his strength. One day when paying his customary visit to Father Pax in Buffalo, his first words after greeting him were: "Father Pax, I must give up; my health is gone." Such an admission from the "Bohemian mountain-boy" speaks volumes.

Dating from this epoch sprung up a closer intimacy between Father Neumann and the Fathers of the Congregation of the Most Holy Redeemer. About two years previously Father Neumann had had occasion to communicate by letter with Rev. Father Prost, C.SS.R., then at Norwalk, Ohio. He requested information respecting the German Catholics of Rochester, whose pastor Father Prost had formerly been. Father Neumann informed Father Prost that he now had charge of his former parishioners, whom he visited several times a year, and asked an explanation of certain difficulties which gave rise to dispute and discord. He praised the fervor of the people, and ended with the words:

"I must candidly acknowledge that my short stay among your former parishioners has afforded me much spiritual consolation. May God be praised! The zeal for decorating the house of God which you have infused into these good people, and much more the ardent desire which hundreds of them manifest for the Body and Blood of our Lord, filled me with astonishment. In my own parishes, which united count about the same number, I very rarely have the consolation of witnessing so great a love of God. I trust the Lord, after so severe a chastisement, will visit them again in mercy. If you could possibly arrange to come yourself, Reverend Father, or send one of your brethren, you would greatly rejoice these good people. They have several times asked to have me for their pastor; they have written to Bishop Dubois and his coadjutor, Bishop Hughes, to this effect. If free to choose, I could never resolve upon leaving my own people; for if they are once forsaken, they will, on account of their poverty, remain so. But the flourishing condition of the Rochester mission authorizes the conviction that no German priest will refuse the charge. The Rochester Catholics possess this advantage over my poor people, that, until the arrival of their own pastor, they can hear Mass and receive the Sacraments in the English church, as they have done since Father Czackert's departure; whereas in my districts there would be over a thousand souls who could get to Mass scarcely once a year."

A second reason which led to Father Neumann's correspondence with Father Prost was his desire of establishing the Confraternity of the Scapular among his parishioners. He says:

"I have been requested by some pious souls to bless their scapulars; but I have declined for the present, not thinking myself authorized to confer such a blessing. To whom must I apply for these faculties? For a long time I have been anxious to establish the Confraternity of Mt. Carmel among my people. I applied some time ago to Father Räss, of Strasburg, for the necessary faculties, also for the rules of the society; but as yet I have received no answer. If you can give me any information in this matter, I beg you to do so. I am unfortunately very ignorant on such points."

Father Prost, in his answer to the above, remarked that, as a member of the Congregation of the Most Holy Redeemer, he could establish the Confraternity of Mt. Carmel, though he could not empower another to do so. He closed his letter with these words of the Holy Spirit: "*Væ soli!* Woe to him who is alone!" He seems to have used the expression as an intimation of his desire of Father Neumann's joining the Redemptorists, for he had long been persuaded that such was the young priest's vocation. The thought, however, did not then occupy Father Neumann's attention; it was not till toward the close of 1840 that he felt drawn to the religious life. He tells us in his journal of the circumstances which combined to turn his heart in that direction.

"For four years," he writes, "I strove earnestly to animate my people to fervor similar to that which I remarked in St. Joseph's parish, Rochester, but I did not succeed. This, added to a natural, or rather a supernatural, longing to live in some society of priests, so as not to be left to myself in the midst of the thousand and one dangers incidental to the world, inspired me with the thought of entering the Congregation of the Most Holy Redeemer. On that same day, nay, at that same hour, September 4, 1840, I applied to the Superior, Rev. Father Prost, for admission. On the 16th of the same month I received permission to enter, with directions to repair to Pittsburg. Immediately on receipt of this letter I notified Right Rev. Bishop Hughes, administrator of the New York diocese, of my intention, begging his blessing, and requesting him to send a priest, or rather priests, to take charge of the different parishes. Reluctantly, and only after long deliberation and repeated refusals, did the Bishop grant me my discharge."

And well might the prelate hesitate to deprive his diocese of so faithful a missionary as Father Neumann, in losing whom he lost one of his most active and zealous priests.

Father Neumann kept his intentions secret until the day of his departure. Only his confessor, Father Pax, and his good brother Wenceslaus were aware of the loss they, in common with the parishioners of the several missions under Father Neumann's charge, were soon to sustain. When Wenceslaus heard from his reverend brother the design he was about to execute for the greater glory of God and the sanctification of his own soul, he exclaimed with vivacity, "I will go, too. I will follow you; I will enter the convent with you."

Father Neumann, we may well believe, was by no means averse to his brother's resolve; he accordingly petitioned for his entrance, also, among the Redemptorist Fathers, intending Wenceslaus to prepare himself in the Congregation for the holy priesthood. His request was unhesitatingly granted; but Wenceslaus, not feeling himself called to so high a vocation, chose rather to serve God as an humble lay-brother.

The grief of Father Neumann's parishioners at the loss of their good pastor was sincere and general. They felt that in losing him they had been deprived of a faithful father, friend, and guide. Father Pax wrote to the Bishop in the following strain: "It is my most painful duty to be obliged to inform your Lordship that my neighbor, good Father Neumann, left us a few days ago for Pittsburg with the intention of entering the Redemptorist novitiate. He was a most excellent pastor; the German missions have sustained a great loss. Father Neumann's charge extended over a wide and scattered district. It numbers three hundred German Catholic families with four churches, the fifth not yet completed. I beg your Lordship to provide these abandoned congregations with a good pastor."

The writer of the above had the consolation of extending hospitality to Father Neumann during the four days the latter spent in Buffalo prior to his final departure for Pittsburg. These were days of mutual satisfaction for both those noble souls, who regarded each other with an affection solid and lasting because founded in the unchangeable God. At 8 P.M. on the 13th of October, Father Pax bade a regretful adieu to his young friend, who embarked on a small steamer bound for Erie. The boat was crowded far beyond its capacity, nearly four hundred passengers being on board. Father Neumann could scarcely find standing-room, and right glad was he to land the next morning at the little town of Erie. A tedious journey of four more days took him to Pittsburg, his final destination, where,

Father Neumann's Vocation.

tired and exhausted, he sought admittance at the Redemptorist convent, October 18, 1840.

A hearty welcome was here extended to him by Rev. Father Tschenhens, then Superior. As it was Sunday morning, the good Father requested the new novice to sing High Mass. Though worn out by fatigue, the latter made not the slightest objection, but proceeded at once to obey the commands of holy obedience. Service for the German Catholics was held at that time in an old factory which went by the name of the "Factory Church."

Wenceslaus, whom Father Neumann had left behind to gather up his effects scattered in his different missions, arrived on November 13th, and began with his reverend brother a life to be thenceforward more than ever devoted to the service of Almighty God.

PART III.

FATHER JOHN N. NEUMANN A REDEMPTORIST.

1840–1852.

CHAPTER I.

The Redemptorists in America.

WE shall now, for the next twelve years, contemplate Father Neumann in his new character of Redemptorist; we shall follow him in his numerous and laborious missions as a son of St. Alphonsus. To form a correct idea of his life, it will not be superfluous to cast a glance at the early history of the Congregation of the Most Holy Redeemer in America, since they are so closely interwoven one with the other.

About the year 1827 or '29, Father Frederick Rézé, Vicar-General of the diocese of Cincinnati, made a trip to Europe for the purpose of procuring priests and contributions for the American missions. Whilst in Vienna he visited the Redemptorist Fathers at "Maria Stiegen." His glowing account of the immense fields in America in which the harvest was great, the laborers few, awoke in the heart of many a brave son of St. Alphonsus the desire to establish there the Congregation of the Most Holy Redeemer.

Venerable Clement Maria Hofbauer, that great servant of God who had been chiefly instrumental in procuring a colony of Redemptorists for Germany, used often to speak with enthusiasm of the possibility of establishing his brethren in those broad transatlantic domains. This idea had taken so firm a hold on his mind that, after his expulsion from Vienna in 1819, he resolved to go to America himself. To the inquiry of a government official as to whither he intended to betake himself, he responded, "*To America.*" It is even said that the venerable founder of the Congregation, St. Alphonsus himself, walking one day along the Bay of Naples, pointed out to his young students a ship bearing the words, "For New Orleans," and said, in a spirit of prophecy, "My sons will one day have a house in that place."

Very Rev. Father Passerat, Vicar-General of the Transalpine Congregation, set to work seriously to follow out the idea to which Father Rézé had given birth. In the spring of 1832 he despatched three Fathers and as many lay-brothers to form the nucleus of a Redemptorist foundation in America. The three Fathers were Rev. Simon Sänderl, Rev. Francis Xavier Hätscher, and Rev. Francis Xavier Tschenhens; the lay-brothers were Aloysius Schuh, Jacob Köhler, and Wenceslaus Witapil.

The little colony arrived in New York on the 20th of June, and on the following day, the Feast of Corpus Christi, the Fathers celebrated their first Mass on American shores.

After a short stay in New York, they went on to their destination, Cincinnati, where they were most cordially welcomed by their old friend, Father Rézé; the Bishop, Right Rev. Edward Fenwick, being absent at the time on his pastoral visitation. The diocese of Cincinnati embraced at this epoch an immense tract of country: the whole State of Ohio, the Territory of Michigan, and the eastern part of Wisconsin Territory. It was not hard to supply the newly-arrived Fathers with posts entailing a vast amount of missionary labor, which the Vicar-General did provisionally until the Bishop's return. Father Hätscher was despatched to Norwalk, Tiffin, and other small towns of northern Ohio, with directions to form the Catholics of those places into parishes; Father Sänderl and two lay-brothers were sent to Green Bay, on the northwest shore of Lake Michigan; whilst Father Tschenhens and Brother Jacob remained in Cincinnati, the former in quality of assistant priest to the Germans, the latter as cook and servant to the Bishop and priests. Soon, however, a serious obstacle arose to the establishment of the Congregation in America. The Bishops required that the Fathers should devote themselves to the religious wants of the Catholics scattered throughout their vast dioceses, a special district being assigned to each. However reasonable such a desire might seem in view of the state of the Church at that period, it could not be unconditionally complied with. The rules of the Congregation of the Most Holy Redeemer require absolutely that its members should lead the community life; and so strict was St. Alphonsus on this point that he seldom allowed any Father to reside out of his convent for an indefinite period. The Superiors in Vienna believed it their duty strenuously to uphold this point of the rule, claiming that, if the Redemptorists would work successfully for the salvation of souls, they must live in accordance with their vocation. This circumstance explains why the activity of the Redemptorist Fathers was, during their first years in America, necessarily and in many ways held in check.

Father Sänderl found a small log-church at Green Bay. He hired a neighboring house in which to open the first Redemptorist convent in the New World. Father Hätscher, who, as we have seen, had been ordered to the northern districts of Ohio, was now recalled by the voice of obedience, and sent to join the little colony at Green Bay. He set out immediately, but on reaching Detroit, where the cholera was raging, he found the Bishop occupied with the spiritual wants of the sick and dying. The saintly prelate was overwhelmed with work and far from equal to the task of caring for the many stricken down by the epidemic. He rejoiced, therefore, on seeing Father Hätscher, whom he regarded as sent by God to his distressed flock. Gladly acceding to the Bishop's request, Father Hätscher tarried in Detroit to aid in administering the Sacraments to the sick. Night and day saw him actively engaged in these heavenly ministrations. He left Detroit only after the epidemic had subsided, and continued his journey across the lake to Green Bay. The good Bishop Fenwick himself fell a victim to his zeal. He was attacked by the cholera at Canton, but started, nevertheless, to return to Cincinnati, intending to visit several congregations on the way; but the malady increased to such a degree that, on arriving at Wooster, he was compelled to retire to bed. He expired the next day, September 26, 1832, without those religious rites and consolations which he himself had so often administered to others. He fought the good fight, he finished his course, he kept the faith.

Meantime, Father Tschenhens had left Cincinnati to join his brethren at Green Bay; but on his way he was detained at Norwalk and Tiffin. The spiritual destitution of the poor Catholics aroused his compassion, for since the departure of Father Hätscher they had not seen a Catholic priest. The cholera was raging here also, and many were daily succumbing to its attacks; therefore Father Tschenhens resolved to remain in those localities whilst he could be of any assistance to souls.

The little colony at Green Bay had by this time discovered that their attempt to establish a convent in that district was altogether impracticable, and so the idea was abandoned. One priest would be quite sufficient for the wants of the small Catholic population; consequently a religious community, even if able to procure the necessaries of life, would be superfluous in such a place.

When Father Tschenhens was informed of this decision, he took up his abode for the time at Norwalk, built St. Alphonsus' Church, and visited the Catholics of the surrounding country, embracing a circuit of thirty or forty miles. Fathers Sänderl and Hätscher opened a mission for the Indian tribes of northern Michigan, and, from Green Bay and Arbre-Croche, extended their apostolic influence far and near. Their labors among the Indians were successful to a degree, though they effected little among the whites, who numbered few, and those few chiefly Protestants or indifferent Catholics.

The following brief yet striking lines we clip from the "Chronicles" which record the various trials and circumstances attendant on the efforts of the Redemptorist Fathers in their early American foundations: "Which of the Fathers suffered most, or which endured the greatest inconveniences, it would be difficult to say. The last day, the great Day of Judgment, will reveal many facts to their eternal honor and glory."

The lay-brothers, no less than the Fathers, were now in a position to try their fidelity. Necessity forced them to gain their own livelihood, and contribute likewise to the support of the Fathers whose clerical duties would not admit of their following secular avocations. Some of these good Brothers, sighing for the quiet and seclusion they had left behind them, became dissatisfied and returned to Europe. Divine Providence, however, provided for the emergency. Other young men felt within them a call to the religious life, and applied to the congregation for admission as lay-brothers. Among them we shall make mention of one who, without doubt, is now in the enjoyment of the crown promised to perseverance. We allude to Brother Joseph Reisach. He arrived in New York, January 8, 1833, in company with the well-known and highly distinguished Father Raffeiner, both having come to America intending to join the Redemptorists. They had, in fact, already been received in Vienna as candidates for the American missions. The German Catholics of New York were at that time, as was the case in so many other parts of the United States, totally deprived of spiritual assistance, having no priest to attend to their wants. Father Raffeiner thought it his duty to devote to them his time and strength for the glory of God and the salvation of souls. His companion, however, could not be dissuaded from his first purpose. He pursued his journey westward and, after undergoing many hardships and surmounting numerous obstacles, reached Green Bay, July 14, 1833.

In 1834 Father Sänderl removed to Arbre-Croche, taking with him two candidates, Brother Joseph (mentioned above) and Brother Vitus. During the Lent of 1835 it so happened that the altar-wine gave out. The Fathers were in some perplexity as to how the want could be supplied, when the two Brothers stepped forward and offered to undertake a journey beset with peril, in order to procure what was wanted. Their road led across the lake, which was still frozen. A sled was speedily constructed, a compass and materials for lighting a fire provided, and thus equipped the two Brothers set out briskly for the lake. The journey of the first day was a painful one. They kept along the shore, and only with the greatest exertions could they proceed; soon they found it absolutely necessary to abandon their sled, on account of the snow-drifts in their way. Hunger and thirst, also, began to make themselves felt, and, as our two travellers had neglected to provide themselves with fresh water, they were compelled to slake their thirst with snow. When night came on, they sought the shore, hoping to fall in with some friendly

Indians; but they found only an abandoned wigwam, of which a huge buffalo claimed prior possession. There was, however, plenty of room for them too; so, after kindling a fire and preparing some tea, for which purpose they again had to substitute snow for water, they threw themselves on the ground to rest. But in vain did they try to sleep. The intense cold and the howling of wolves precluded all ideas of repose.

Next morning at daybreak, they recommenced their journey, seventeen miles of frozen lake between them and the opposite shore. On they plodded, and, with God's assistance, reached Mackinaw in safety, where the pastor, Father Bondnell, extended to them the hospitality of his own residence. The glare of the sun on the ice had so affected the poor Brothers' sight that next day they could hardly see. But this did not prevent their rising betimes, for they had much business to transact and a long homeward journey before them. After making their purchases and executing the several commissions entrusted to them, they took leave of their reverend host to retrace their steps of the previous day. Both were heavily laden, Brother Joseph having three gallons of wine strapped on his back. And now, in real earnest, began the difficulties of their undertaking. They had scarcely proceeded five miles, when they found themselves exposed to a new and unforeseen danger from the sudden thawing of the ice. To their horror, they perceived that, despite their precautions, they were both standing on a block of floating ice which had broken away from the main mass. In their alarm, they turned to Mary, confidently invoking the aid of her who is never invoked in vain, when suddenly the floe approached the solid mass, ran a short distance under it, and there stuck fast. Our travellers were thus enabled to step from one to the other without so much as wetting their feet. For greater precaution, they now resolved to separate and keep some distance apart, in order to lessen the pressure. They had gone only a few yards in this manner, when Brother Vitus, who was in front, heard a cry of distress behind him. He turned quickly in the direction whence the sound proceeded, but all he could see of Brother Joseph was his hat just above the ice. He rushed to the spot, when *crack* went the ice on which he himself stood, and down he, too, splashed into the water. Several times, by clutching the edge, they succeeded in swinging themselves out on the ice, which each time again gave way and precipitated them once more into the water. Exhausted by their efforts, benumbed with cold, and poor Brother Joseph weighed down by his wine-keg, they were upon the point of abandoning themselves to what seemed to be their fate, when they turned again to Mary, the "Help of Christians." "O my Mother," cried Brother Joseph, "thou knowest that I have always loved thee, that I have made many sacrifices for thy sake! The time has now come for thee to help me. But do so quickly, else it will be too late." Here he turned toward his companion, as if to take a last leave of him, when the latter cried out in a hopeful voice: "Brother, hold on just a few minutes longer. When I shall have rid myself of this load, I shall be able to get out and help you." And so it happened. With renewed hope and wonderfully increased vigor, Brother Vitus struggled to the surface of the ice and hastened to his companion in distress. The latter, rousing his drooping courage and confiding in the help of his Heavenly Mother, moved slowly and painfully over to the spot where Brother Vitus waited to lend him assistance. His limbs were stiff with cold and scarcely could he grasp the edge of the ice with the tips of his frozen fingers. Little by little, calling upon God and His Blessed Mother, he moved along through the water until, at last, he reached the place where Brother Vitus stood and, with his assistance, succeeded in gaining a solid footing. The first impulse of both was to kneel in grateful homage to Almighty God and their loving protectress Mary. Then rising they proceeded on their way. They had not yet accomplished one third of their perilous journey, their garments clung like icicles to their benumbed limbs, and the day was fast waning. How the night of this eventful day was passed, the chronicler does not tell us; but next morning we find them once more on their march, each provided with a long pole with which to test the strength of the ice before setting foot upon it. In this way, slowly and cautiously moving forward, they reached at length the opposite shore, where they were met by some Indians who were on the lookout for them with horses. To counteract the bad effects of their long exposure in the water and prevent serious consequences, these rude children of the forest prescribed what seemed to their civilized neighbors a novel if not a hazardous remedy, viz., that the two wayfarers should stretch themselves in a running stream and allow the icy water to flow over their limbs. This, the Indians said, would take the frost out. The Brothers followed the advice, and actually experienced beneficial results.

The hardships attendant on the first foundations of the Redemptorists in America were generously shared by Brother Aloysius Schuh, of Baden, who in many ways rendered signal service both to the Fathers and the souls under their care. He taught the children in the schoolroom; gave catechetical instructions to the people during the Fathers' absence; read to them Goffine's Instructions on the Gospels; made with them the Stations of the Cross, and recited aloud the Rosary. His powerful voice did good service at Mass and Vespers during the absence of a choir; he was always on hand and served the Fathers with untiring fidelity, cheering and encouraging them in their labors by his own unvarying joyousness and affability of disposition. He it was who took charge of their frugal meals; and, a blacksmith by trade, he knew how to manufacture useful articles for the Indians, who gave him in exchange venison, fish, or maple-sugar. Brother Aloysius had been long familiar with the secret which unites prayer with labor. Many a time were the Fathers edified by hearing him singing hymns or saying the Rosary whilst discharging his duties in the kitchen or elsewhere. But let us not think that his was an existence all glowing with sunshine and spiritual joy. By no means. It was under the pressure of grievous temptations and interior trials that our good Brother Aloysius won the crown of perseverance in his holy vocation.

The 15th of August brought an addition to the little American colony in the persons of Fathers Joseph Prost and Peter Czackert, the former of whom came as Visitor and remained as Superior. On his way to Norwalk, Father Prost passed through Rochester, where he was hospitably received by Father Bernard O'Reilly, who entreated him to take compassion on the German Catholics of that place, already very numerous, and give them a little mission during which they might have a chance of going to confession. Father Prost, ever eager to assist souls, cheerfully complied. When the task assigned him by Divine Providence was completed, Father Prost saw himself besieged on all sides by his grateful countrymen, who promised to build him a church and provide for his support if he would only stay and be their pastor.

And so began the Redemptorist mission-house and St. Joseph's congregation, Rochester. Father Prost satisfied the demands made upon him by promising to return as soon as he had consulted his brethren, whom he was even then on his way to join at Norwalk, Ohio. He then departed full of consolation at having been chosen by the Master to fulfil this by-work, as we may call it, in his missionary career.

On reaching his destination, the first whom he met at the residence of the Fathers was Brother Aloysius who, in a linen coat, was just emerging from the stable, where he had been feeding its only occupant, the cow. Let us hear Father Prost's own account of his first impressions at Norwalk: "I was prepared, indeed, to find things on a poor scale, but the reality far surpassed the picture of my imagination. In the church, rough logs of wood took the place of pews. The Fathers' residence was a wretched log-cabin containing only one large room, which was divided off into sleeping compartments. The Brothers slept in the garret, the flooring of which consisted of single planks laid side by side over the rafters. One had to be careful in stepping from one to the other. If Brother Aloysius had happened to fall out of bed some night, he would have pursued his downward career to the lower story, though not, thank God! to the lower regions."

Bishop Rézé, of Detroit, made a special visit to Norwalk, to engage the Redemptorists to make a foundation in his diocese. His offer was accepted, and Father Sänderl returned with the prelate.

When Father Prost was informed of the Bishop's offer and its acceptance, he hastily transacted the business on hand, and hurried off to Detroit, hoping to find Father Sänderl there. He was not disappointed, as the Father had not yet left the city. After discussing the subject of the projected foundation, they embarked on a sailing-vessel for Green Bay. A storm soon arose which drove the vessel on the foot of a cliff, where it lay embedded in the mud. Before it could be got off, cold weather set in as the captain had predicted, the lake froze, and next morning the ship was ice-bound. There were on board some fanatical Protestants who now began to curse and swear, ascribing their misfortune to the presence of the two priests.

"Put them off, put them off!" they cried. "Put them off on the ice and leave them there."

The captain stood irresolute as to how he should meet these furious demands, when, at last, cowardice prevailed. He was on the point of yielding to the diabolical suggestion,—the sailors, in fact, were about seizing the Fathers,—when a young physician interfered and vigorously opposed the execution of so barbarous a design. He warmly defended the Fathers, upbraided the crew with inhumanity, the captain with injustice and dereliction of duty, and threatened, if they dared lay hands on the two priests, to have them all arrested. The courageous and energetic defence of the young physician overawed the cowardly aggressors, and the Fathers escaped molestation. After two weeks of hard labor amid ever-present dangers, the sailors succeeded in bringing their vessel to within a short distance of Green Bay, but they could not enter the harbor, which was frozen up. The vessel had to be abandoned for the season, and the passengers completed the rest of their journey on foot.

And now let us follow Fathers Prost and Sänderl as they make their way to the locality destined for them by the good Bishop. Surely we shall share their dismay when we find ourselves in the abode offered them for their future convent—a large frame building whose whole interior remained unfinished. To render it even partially habitable would entail great expense; consequently Father Prost determined to leave Green Bay as soon as travelling became practicable and, with God's assistance, seek a foundation elsewhere. A new cross was in store for the good Father. Some time before his departure, he received news that his baggage, which he had left in New York and which could not be forwarded during the winter months, had been destroyed by fire. This was, as we may suppose, something of a loss to one already struggling with poverty both professed and necessitous; but a loving *Fiat* or a *Deo Gratias* sets all things right.

Almighty God satisfied, as it were, with the good-will

evinced by His servants, now opened up a way by which some permanent advantage was to accrue to them. Father Prost received a letter from Bishop Dubois, about this time, inviting him to go to Rochester and there take charge of the German Catholics. This was the most encouraging offer he had as yet received in America; for Rochester would be a far more eligible location for a house of the Congregation than Norwalk, and Green Bay was altogether out of the question. The Bishop's invitation was accepted at once, and Father Prost set out for his new scene of labor. When passing through Detroit, he was pressed by Bishop Rézé to remain in the diocese; but, as the prospect of establishing a house there at that period was very gloomy, Father Prost was forced to decline. He reached Rochester on Sunday, July 10, 1836, and great was the jubilation of those who had been the objects of the zealous Father's former ministrations there. Here he found Father Neumann, who, as we have already mentioned, had that very day celebrated divine service for his (Father Prost's) future parishioners.

With the approbation of Father Bernard O'Reilly, the German congregation had purchased a Methodist meeting-house to be used for religious purposes, and the administration of its affairs was confided to trustees. The building was large, the upper part affording ample space for divine service; consequently Father Prost fitted up the basement to be used as a school and as a temporary dwelling for the pastor. From that time the German portion of the Catholics had regular attendance, and the various ceremonies of our holy religion were conducted with as much solemnity as possible. The schedule for Sundays and holy-days was as follows: first, an early Mass; at half-past ten, High Mass and sermon; at three in the afternoon, Vespers, Catechetical Instructions, and Benediction of the Most Holy Sacrament. To awaken and increase in the hearts of the faithful a loving devotion to the Blessed Mother of God, Father Prost established the Archconfraternity of Mt. Carmel, and introduced, both in the church and in families, the custom of saying the Rosary in common. His zeal extended to the school, and, until a suitable teacher could be procured, Brother Louis Kenning filled that post. He had but lately been admitted as a candidate to the Congregation of the Most Holy Redeemer, and shortly after to the holy habit. He was the first novice received in America, and was ever distinguished as a devoted lay-brother. He was sent to New Orleans, where he rendered invaluable service from the establishment of the house, in 1847, till his saintly death, in 1875.

The Bishop, the clergy, and the laity witnessed with satisfaction the progress made by St. Joseph's congregation, and unanimously congratulated Father Prost on the success of his efforts. But Satan, the opponent of all that is good, the adversary of Jesus Christ, could not endure so happy a beginning for the Redemptorist Fathers. He foresaw that their labors in America would bring forth a rich harvest of souls, would be attended by magnificent results; consequently, an enemy of peace and harmony himself, he began to sow discord and create disturbance among the people. For this end, he made use of the trustees, who seemed determined to do all in their power to counteract their pastor's zealous exertions. They frustrated every attempt at establishing a church and convent to be entrusted to the Fathers for the benefit of the parish. Father Prost, unwilling to face the storm, resolved to leave Rochester for a time, hoping to return under more favorable circumstances. In the spring of 1838 he arrived at Norwalk. He immediately held a consultation with his brethren as to the best place for a foundation of their Congregation. The Fathers all seemed inclined toward Norwalk itself, and Father Prost was seriously thinking of the same.

The fall of 1837 had witnessed Father Hätscher's

return to Vienna. He had labored and suffered much during his four years' apostolic campaign in northern Michigan. To the Indians and the Canadian French he had been a true father. The Protestants regarded him with ill-will; indeed, their enmity manifested itself in a most practical form, as they once set fire to his church and even threatened his life. He was a true-hearted apostle of his Lord, and he is still known in Mackinaw, Green Bay, and Sault Ste. Marie as "le bon Père François."

In this same year, 1838, in which we find Father Prost consulting on the expediency of a foundation in Norwalk, an unforeseen event led to the abandonment of such a design. An order arrived from Vienna directing the Fathers to send some of their force to Illinois, where an Alsatian "Land Company" had purchased a large tract for a Catholic settlement. The Redemptorists were offered here one hundred acres of land for a convent, a church, and a school. The order was promptly obeyed, and Father Czackert set out for the locality designated. On his arrival, however, he found that the company, in order to attract colonists and sell their land to advantage, had set the rumor afloat that there were already in the new settlement a church and a school-house under the charge of the clergy. But what could the Fathers do with a hundred acres of land in those western wilds? To live in such isolation would have been simply impossible, and much less could they follow out the ends of their holy vocation; so the four missionaries again separated to disperse in various districts of Ohio, Illinois, and Michigan. Their labors in these places were not brightened by the faintest shadow of a hope that one day, sooner or later, they would be able to establish a house in any of them. Indeed, both Fathers and Brothers were seriously contemplating a return to Europe when the Vicar-General of the Congregation wrote to console and encourage them to perseverance. He exhorted them to patience, repeating the assurance he had given them in the year 1836, which was to this effect: that the same year which would behold the canonization of the founder of the Congregation, Blessed Alphonsus Maria di Liguori, would also see the foundation of the first Redemptorist convent in America.

Father Passerat was a man of prayer. A disciple of the venerable servant of God, Clement Marie Hofbauer, whom he regarded as his model, he had learned how to practise the prayer of contemplation, in which he was divinely enlightened by God. A child of the Blessed Virgin and her chaste spouse St. Joseph, Father Passerat usually chose their exalted virtues as the subject of his meditation, which practice attracted upon him the choicest lights and graces. As a proof of this, and that not among the least, is the prediction above alluded to, the precise time of the establishment of the Redemptorists in the United States. The year 1839 had taken its place upon the calendar, and in the Old World the month of May was to usher in the solemn canonization of the Blessed Alphonsus; whilst in the New World the prospects of a permanent settlement for his sons seemed as distant and as uncertain as on the day which witnessed their advent to its shores.

CHAPTER II.

St. Philomena's Church, Pittsburg; and St. Alphonsus', Baltimore.

DIVINE PROVIDENCE had wisely ordained that the Congregation of the Most Holy Redeemer should owe its existence in America to Him alone. *Man proposes, but God disposes;* and the greater the distress and discouragement of His servants, the nearer is God with His powerful aid.

A good honest farmer named Adelmann, of Butler County, near Pittsburg, went to Norwalk, Ohio, in 1839, on a visit to his relatives. He witnessed with edification the fruits born of the Redemptorists' labors in that place, and earnestly besought Father Prost to send spiritual assistance to the four or five thousand German Catholics of Pittsburg, who had no clergyman to attend to their spiritual wants. Mr. Adelmann entreated Father Prost to go and see for himself the truth of his words and the religious destitution of those for whom he pleaded. Father Prost both admired and praised the good man's zeal, but explained to him, at the same time, that only an invitation from the Bishop could authorize the Fathers' establishing themselves in any diocese. This last remark was not lost on the good farmer. Three weeks had scarcely elapsed, when Father Prost received a letter from Right Rev. Francis Patrick Kenrick, of Philadelphia, to which diocese Pittsburg then belonged, requesting him to take an interest in the German Catholics of Pittsburg, and appointing St. Patrick's Church as their place of meeting for divine service. In all this, Father Prost saw the finger of Almighty God.

He handed the Norwalk mission over to Father Tschenhens, and on the following Sunday, the first after Easter, set out for his new destination. The second Sunday after Easter saw regular service inaugurated for the German Catholics of Pittsburg.

Father Prost found before him no easy task, as the condition of his new parish was anything but satisfactory. Rev. Father Charles B. M'Guire, a most learned and exemplary ecclesiastic, had been from 1820 to '25 the only priest of the city and country around. He built St. Patrick's, a small edifice, and attended to the spiritual wants of the whole Catholic community until, shortly before his death, two assistant priests shared with him his onerous burden. A word here of this generous apostle of Christ may not be deemed amiss. We cull from Rev. A. A. Lambing's "Catholic Church in Pittsburg and Allegheny," and give, in a somewhat abbreviated form, the following account of Rev. Charles Bonaventure M'Guire, O.S.F. " He made the Church in Pittsburg what it is," said one who knew him. Born in Ireland and educated at Louvain, he exercised the duties of his sacred ministry in various parts of the Netherlands and Germany. During this period he acquired a remarkable knowledge of the German language. He escaped from Louvain during the French Revolution, and made his way to Rome, where he spent six years in the performance of clerical duties. He afterward travelled over the Continent of Europe, reached Brussels just at the time of the memorable battle of Waterloo, and to many of the wounded and dying administered the last rites of the Church. Shortly after he set out for America, and reached our shores in safety, 1817. He was stationed in Westmoreland County until transferred to Pittsburg. With his appearance a new era commenced for the entire Catholic body. Religion found in him an expositor worthy of herself, and the Catholic body gradually assumed and thenceforth maintained a dignity and respectability in the opinion of dissenting Christians not allowed them prior to his coming. As a man, as a priest, as a scholar, none knew Father Charles M'Guire but to respect and love him.

One of the two priests mentioned above as Father M'Guire's assistants was Rev. Father Masquelez, an Alsatian by birth. He manifested unbounded interest in the spiritual welfare of the German portion of his flock, and by his direction a factory belonging to a Mr. Jacob Schneider was rented. Here they assembled for divine worship. But party-spirit crept even into this humble community and created confusion. Fathers Masquelez, Stahl, Baier, Herzog, and a Benedictine, named Father Nicholas Balleis, vainly endeavored to restore harmony. Fathers Herzog and Balleis even separated the factious parties in the hope of removing the causes of discord, and formed two parishes, one of which attended service in what was denominated the "Factory Church," the other in St. Patrick's; but even this measure proved fruitless. Conciliatory means seemed only to increase the feeling of bitterness and widen the breach. Fathers Herzog and Balleis, seeing all their efforts unsuccessful, left Pittsburg, and the Germans were for some months deprived of the assistance of a pastor. It was at this juncture that Divine Providence sent Father Prost to settle difficulties.

After acquainting himself with the existing state of affairs, he set to work energetically to bring about peace. He held public and private interviews, he reasoned, he remonstrated, though apparently in vain; the evil appeared irremediable, the antagonistic parties incorrigible. When affairs seemed at their worst, Almighty God interposed. He inspired Father Prost to address the congregation on a certain Sunday afternoon, at the close of Vespers, and recount the innumerable miracles everywhere wrought through the intercession of the virgin-martyr St. Philomena. He exhorted his hearers to choose her as their patroness and solemnly promise to dedicate the "Factory Church" to her if she would obtain the restoration of peace among them. On that very day the contending parties moderated their demands, and Father Prost was thus enabled to purchase the factory for the sum of fifteen thousand dollars. The building was large, and ample room was found in it for a church and a small convent destined for the abode of the Redemptorist Fathers.

After procuring the furniture absolutely necessary for both, Father Prost directed Fathers Tschenhens and Czackert to join him in Pittsburg. He had in the mean time received from Most Rev. Father Ripoli, Rector at Nocera di Pagani, extensive faculties for the government of the Congregation of the Most Holy Redeemer in America. He was thereby authorized to establish mission-houses, receive novices, etc. The first use Father Prost made of his power was to announce the foundation at Pittsburg as the first house of the Congregation in the New World.

In consequence of this definitive establishment of the Redemptorists in Pittsburg, the missions of Ohio and Michigan had to be abandoned, in the spring of 1839. St. Joseph's parish, Rochester, had now been a whole year without a pastor; they would have been entirely destitute of spiritual assistance, had not Father Neumann's zeal led him to go occasionally from North Bush and hold service for them. He was greatly edified on seeing how much good had been effected during the short stay of the Redemptorist Fathers, and he could find no terms in which to speak their praise.

At their own earnest request, Father Sänderl was again called to Rochester, to take charge of the German Catholics, and it was hoped that a house of the Congregation would soon be established there.

The prophecy of the saintly Father Passerat was now fulfilled. The same year that witnessed the canonization of Alphonsus di Liguori, Founder of the Congregation of the Most Holy Redeemer, beheld also the foundation of the first Redemptorist house in America. After seven years' rude experience and painful uncertainty, three Fathers, with Brothers Aloysius and Louis, were at last enabled to enter upon the conventual life according to the rules and constitutions of their Congregation.

One year later, in May, 1840, Father Prost received an invitation to the Fourth Provincial Council of the Bishops of North America, to be held in Baltimore. The invitation was accepted, and during his stay in Baltimore Father Prost was the guest of Rev. Benedict Bayer, of St. John's German church. He received much encouragement from the assembled prelates, who, in the kindest manner, expressed their appreciation of the zeal that animated the Redemptorists for the salvation of souls. The Council over, Father Prost returned to Pittsburg.

The Congregation of the Most Holy Redeemer, after its innumerable trials and vicissitudes, was at length fairly established, its prospects bright and promising for the future. Father Prost had now held the office of Superior for five years. He thought it his duty to return to Vienna, both to render an account of his administration to his Superior, Rev. Father Passerat, the Vicar-General, and to obtain further help and instructions for the American missions. He intended to take Brother Aloysius with him as his companion. But unforeseen difficulties sprung up to counteract his design. Bishop Kenrick not only refused him the letter of recommendation for which he applied, but endeavored to dissuade him altogether from undertaking the journey. All things could be arranged by letter, said the Bishop. The truth was, Bishop Kenrick feared that the progress which the Congregation was now making would receive another check. His decision was very painful to Father

Prost, who looked upon an interview with his Superior concerning the affairs of the Congregation in America as necessary. He therefore applied to Archbishop Eccleston, of Baltimore, for the letter of approbation, the kind reception tendered him on the occasion of the Provincial Council encouraging him to hope for success in that quarter. The Archbishop expressed his willingness to furnish the desired document, on condition of Father Prost's going to Baltimore and having an interview with him on the matter.

Toward the close of July, 1840, Father Prost, accompanied by Brother Aloysius, arrived in the archiepiscopal city, all necessary preparations for his trip across the ocean having been previously made. But here a fresh obstacle awaited him. The Archbishop laid before him his intention of transferring the Germans of St. John's, Baltimore, to the Redemptorists, strenuously urging upon him the acceptance of the charge. However welcome such an offer might be to Father Prost at any other time, it could not but be a subject of embarrassment at the present moment. The thought of deferring his journey was an unpleasant one; yet consideration for the Archbishop's wishes forced him to change his plans.

It was arranged that Brother Aloysius should accompany Father Bayer, who was about to sail for Europe and make an oral report at Vienna of the state of affairs in America. Father Prost accepted the church and parish offered by Archbishop Eccleston, for which the latter expressed himself most grateful, ever after evincing the highest confidence in the Redemptorist Fathers. Later on, he transferred to them St. James's Church, his own personal property.

Early in August, Father Bayer and Brother Aloysius departed for Europe. During the same month, Father Prost took possession of St. John's Church, which then occupied the site on which was afterward erected the beautiful Gothic church of St. Alphonsus. A few words upon the early history of the first German church in Baltimore will, perhaps, prove interesting to the reader.

In 1800, Baltimore could boast only one Catholic church, St. Peter's, on the northeast corner of Sharp and Saratoga streets. The college of the Christian Brothers now stands on the site, and is known as Calvert Hall. The church alluded to was built during the Revolutionary War, under the protection of the French troops, then the allies of the Americans. Small in the beginning, it was afterward enlarged and raised to the rank of the first metropolitan church in the United States. The constantly increasing number of Catholics soon necessitated the erection of another church, and it was determined to have one exclusively for the use of the Germans, as they would thus be enabled to hear sermons in their own language.

With this view, the German Catholics purchased a lot, 60 by 155 feet, on the northeast corner of Saratoga and Park streets, where they built St. John's Church. Contrary to the will of Archbishop Carroll, the congregation had obtained from the municipal authorities a charter of incorporation. This was a serious step in those days, as the result soon proved; for from that time, in fact—that is, from 1806 until 1839, when the Redemptorists took charge of the church—quarrels were frequent, and acts of violence were perpetrated even in the sacred precincts. A legal decision at last ended the strife. The clergy who ministered to the congregation of St. John's were the following: Rev. F. Brosius, 1804–1805; Rev. C. Reutor, 1806; Rev. Nicholas Merz, December 6, 1805–May, 1820; Rev. Peter Babad, 1820; Rev. P. Beschter, S.J., 1828; Rev. Francis Rolef and Rev. Louis Barth, 1828; Rev. M. P. Gallagher, 1838; and, lastly, Rev. Benedict Bayer.

The last-named reverend gentleman undertook to

remove the source of all party-spirit, viz., the trustee system. His proposal to build a new church on a larger scale gave great offence to many members of the congregation, and disunion and dissatisfaction reigned supreme among them. Their worthy pastor, Father Bayer, conceived the idea of handing the church over to the Redemptorists, and Archbishop Eccleston approved the plan as the best and most efficacious remedy to the long-existing evil. One year later, Father Bayer himself joined the Congregation of the Most Holy Redeemer, in which he died after a faithful fulfilment of his religious obligations. It was at this critical juncture that Father Prost entered upon the pastoral charge of St. John's—no easy task before him, as experience soon proved. But Divine Providence had a great consolation in store to sweeten the bitterness of his chalice, and that was the reception of Father Neumann to the ranks of the rising Congregation. The first time they met in Rochester, Father Prost was favorably impressed by the young missionary's saintly deportment, and conceived for him so great esteem that his petition for admittance to the Congregation was granted without question or difficulty.

CHAPTER III.

Father Neumann a Novice among the Redemptorists.

AFTER due reflection, Father Prost decided upon Pittsburg as the scene of the novice-priest's year of probation. Here he would be under the direction of Father Tschenhens, whose piety and devotedness were well known. But two weeks had scarcely elapsed when the Novice-Master was called to Baltimore to be the assistant at St. John's, whose congregation had increased so rapidly as to render the parochial duties too heavy for one priest. Father Czackert was now the only Redemptorist in Pittsburg; and as he was almost always absent on country missions, the poor novice, Father Neumann, had to be parish-priest, his own Superior, and his own Novice-Master at one and the same time. The Redemptorist Congregation and the training of new subjects had, during these first years of its existence, to depend wholly upon a kind and merciful Providence. On November 29, 1840, Father Prost went to Pittsburg for the purpose of investing Father Neumann with the religious habit. The ceremony took place in the church after High Mass, on the Feast of St. Andrew, Apostle, and was conducted with the utmost solemnity. Very poor was the young colony at this time. It possessed not even a Ceremonial containing the prescribed formula for the occasion, the questions and answers, the prayers and psalms for the clothing. The celebrant, Father Prost, had to trust to his memory in performing the sublime ceremony.

Father Neumann thus speaks in his journal concerning his novitiate: "There was no novitiate in America at that time, and no Novice-Master, but an overwhelming amount of work to be despatched. I daily made two meditations and two examens of conscience with the community, spiritual reading in private, and a visit to the Blessed Sacrament. I recited the Rosary, also, and that was all." But God's all-powerful grace, with which Father Neumann fully and faithfully co-operated, supplied what was wanting. He well understood how to acquire the childlike, submissive spirit expected of him as a novice, as also the peculiar spirit of the Congregation and its saintly founder.

Shortly after his reception to the habit, Father Neumann was called upon, according to a custom generally practised in the evening recreation of the Fathers, to relate something edifying. He began in all simplicity to recount a dream that he had had the previous night. It appeared to him that he was in Baltimore, where some Bishop wished to seize nim and, *nolens volens*, consecrate him, raise him to the episcopal dignity; but the more vigorously the Bishop tried to drag him to the church, the more resolutely did the novice resist. In his struggle to free himself from his assailant's grasp, he awoke.

Father Czackert listened to the recital, and then, with a view to humble the holy novice, he exclaimed, somewhat contemptuously:

"What a silly dream! You had better dismiss such nonsense at once, and aim at your own perfection. When you have made your vows, you will have very different thoughts."

Meanwhile, Father Bayer, who had, as we remember, gone to Vienna at Father Prost's request, was very successful in arranging matters for the Congregation in America. At Vienna, Munich, Lyons, and Rome he collected a considerable sum for the support of the missionaries, and succeeded in obtaining from the Vicar-General, Father Passerat, an additional force for the

American mission. Brother Aloysius had the happiness of returning to America with four Fathers and one professed student. On March 7, 1841, the little company landed in New York. They were Rev. Alexander Czwitkowicz, the future Superior, and Fathers Gabriel Rumpler, Mathias Alig, Louis Cartuyvels, and the student, Frater Joseph Fey. Fathers Alexander and Louis, as they were familiarly termed, parted from the little company in New York and thence proceeded to Baltimore, whilst the rest went on to Pittsburg.

In May, 1841, the novice-priest, Rev. Father Neumann, the student, Frater Fey, and Brother Wenceslaus were summoned to Baltimore. It was soon found that the Fathers' small residence would not afford accommodations for so large an addition to the community, and, after a few days, Father Neumann was sent to New York to assist Father Balleis at St. Nicholas's Church. Scarcely two weeks had passed in the discharge of his new duties, when the novice was summoned to Rochester, there to resume the exercises of the novitiate under the direction of his old Novice-Master, Rev. Father Tschenhens. Thither he repaired at the call of obedience, but only to find his intended Novice-Master on the point of starting for Norwalk, Ohio. A schism had been created in that place, and Father Tschenhens was ordered to set out at once and do all in his power to counteract the evil. Again is the poor novice left to his own guidance. For two months, as once before in Pittsburg, he is Superior and pastor, Novice-Master and novice, at one and the same time. The close of July brought Fathers Prost and Sänderl to Rochester.

Father Pax, of Buffalo, falling ill about this time, begged the Fathers to let him have his former friend and neighbor, Father Neumann, to take his place. The request was granted, and for six weeks the novice rendered service to his old friend at St. Louis' Church.

Thirty years later, Father Pax, then in his venerable

old age, spoke as follows of those days: "I had the happiness to have with me once more my friend, Father Neumann. I was sick, and the Bishop had no priest to send me; but the amiable and obliging Father Neumann, with permission of Superiors, came and spent six or eight weeks with me. I lay sick in bed, whilst he labored indefatigably in my parish. Many a pleasant, confidential hour we spent together. The time passed all to quickly; and his permission having expired, he was obliged to return to his novitiate at Rochester."

Again the novice sets out, hoping that this time, at least, he would be allowed to recommence and continue without interruption his much-desired novitiate. He reached Rochester, but, alas! only to go in pursuit of his Master, who was still in Norwalk. Arrived at this latter place, Father Neumann did, indeed, find a Master, though not the quiet and seclusion of a novitiate. The parochial duties had, by this time, so multiplied that one priest could by no means discharge them all; so the well-tried novice had to turn round and gird himself for work. On him devolved a full share of duty, and he rarely saw his Novice-Master, who was most of the time hunting up the Catholics scattered throughout the northern part of Ohio. Toward the middle of November he received orders to return to Baltimore, not by direct route, but by slow stages, pausing to give missions in the little parishes that lay scattered along the way. He set out without delay, and in an open stage-coach, amid torrents of rain, reached Canton, November 19th. Here he met Right Rev. Bishop Purcell, of Cincinnati, with Father Henni, his Vicar-General. Meanwhile the rumor had spread in Ohio that the Congregation of the Most Holy Redeemer was near its dissolution in America; and, in consequence thereof, no novice could make the religious profession among the Redemptorists. The archenemy made use of this report to subject Father

Neumann to a grievous temptation. Bishop Purcell crediting the rumor, strongly urged our novice-priest to go with him to Cincinnati and there take charge of a parish. But Father Neumann resisted the temptation and decidedly refused the offer.

After a short stay at Canton, he went on to Randolph, where he had been invited to give a mission. Here he found the Catholics, as in so many other places, divided into two parties. They had been at variance for three years. The dispute was at last carried so far that one party, thinking to thwart the other, maliciously set fire to the house of God. This diabolical act, the outcome of implacable animosity, was punished as it deserved: the whole parish was deprived of the Sacraments. The difficult task of bringing about a reconciliation between the offending parties was imposed upon Father Neumann. Confiding in the divine assistance and the intercession of St. Alphonsus, he entered actively upon his delicate undertaking. The mission lasted ten days, during which time the holy missionary's prayers were heard and his confidence rewarded; for, notwithstanding the cold weather, his sermons were well attended and all, without exception, received the Sacraments. The contending factions were reconciled, and peace restored. Encouraged and consoled by the success of his labors, Father Neumann continued his journey to Wheeling. On the way he fell ill, and was forced to seek shelter and assistance at a house on the road, about ten miles from Steubenville. The inmates were Americans wholly indifferent in religious matters; but they were kindhearted, hospitable people, and nursed their poor sick guest with the tenderest care. In a few days he was well enough to travel, and he soon reached Steubenville. He was known to the Catholics of this place, for he had often visited them from Pittsburg and celebrated Mass in their little church. Here he tarried a few days, administering the consolations of religion, and thence proceeded by stage to Wheeling, Cumberland, and Frederick, after which he took the cars for Baltimore.

He was surprised on his arrival to find that his brethren had removed to the neighborhood of St. James's Church, St. John's having been doomed to demolition in order to make way for a more spacious and elegant edifice, under the patronage of the glorious St. Alphonsus. The novice's emotions at this news were those of unmingled satisfaction, for he looked upon the fact as an evident sign of the Redemptorists' firm foothold in Baltimore. Before his departure for Rochester, Father Prost had drawn up the plans for the new church, which were subsequently carried out by his successor, Father Alexander. A lot was purchased on Saratoga Street for the erection of a spacious church and commodious convent. On May 1, 1842, with the Archbishop's approbation and in presence of a numerous concourse of people, the corner-stone was laid by Canon Salzbacher, of Vienna. The building progressed under the most favorable auspices, and was soon completed to the satisfaction of all concerned.

The time now drew near for Father Neumann to make his religious vows, the first made by any Redemptorist in America. The ceremony took place in old St. James's, Baltimore, January 16, 1842, Rev. Father Alexander presiding. The chronicles of the Congregation record the event in the following brief but significant words: "In truth a *new man* [*ein neuer Mann*] for our Congregation."

How earnestly Father Neumann regarded this important act we may gather from a letter to his parents written shortly after his profession. "I belong now," he writes, "body and soul, to the Congregation of the Most Holy Redeemer. The corporal and spiritual aid mutually given and received, the edification and good example which, in a society of this kind, one has around him till death, wonderfully facilitate the life I am now leading, the vocation to which I have been called. I have every reason to hope that death will be more welcome to me in this holy Congregation than it usually is to seculars."

Father Neumann had now attained the object after which he had so long sighed; he had successfully met and overcome the multiplied trials of the novitiate, rendered more difficult in his case by its repeated interruptions. His probation of fourteen months was not without its temptations both interior and exterior. This he tells us himself, fifteen years later, in a letter written, when Bishop of Philadelphia, to encourage his nephew, who had but lately entered the Redemptorist novitiate. He says:

"I myself was never a real novice, for when I entered our beloved Congregation it had neither a Novice-Master nor a novitiate in America. Notwithstanding this disadvantage, I am not without my share of experience; I passed through the numerous temptations with which the evil spirit is accustomed to try the recruits of St. Alphonsus. One poor novice perhaps imagines himself deficient in physical strength; another deludes himself with the notion that the rule is better kept in another Order, or that in it he could possibly do more good than in the one in which he now is. Sadness and dejection seize upon some, whilst others are beset by a love of their own ease. Some are attacked by home-sickness or other temptations born of self-love, disgust for prayer, want of confidence in superiors, etc., etc. The temptations of the soul are, doubtless, as numerous as the disorders of the body; but, to remain steadfast in all this turmoil of spirit, there is no better remedy than prayer to the Blessed Virgin for the grace of perseverance, whilst, at the same time, an immediate disclosure of the temptation to one's director is absolutely necessary."

We will now furnish the reader a few edifying incidents of Father Neumann's novitiate. His perseverance under the most trying circumstances, his exemplary conduct during the period of his probation, must certainly excite our sincere admiration. Constantly travelling from place to place, in order to give assistance in the different houses of his Congregation then in existence; for long intervals left wholly to himself; laboring outside his convent; attending to the innumerable duties of his ministry,—he was, under all circumstances, ever the same, ever in his own estimation what his position made him for the moment, a novice, the last and least of all his brethren, who witnessed with edification the virtues that shone so conspicuously in him. Some of the hardest trials to which he was subjected sprung from his own humble diffidence in self. The following lines will give us an insight into them. When alone on the different missions to which he was appointed, he often desired his Superiors' decision or advice on important cases laid before him, and he frequently wrote to this effect. But Divine Providence generally permitted, doubtless for his greater humiliation, that no answer whatever should be vouchsafed him, or that he should receive such as did not even remotely touch on the question. His doubts were not removed; his trouble and perplexity remained the same. The cool reception his applications met did not, however, lead him to relinquish this submissive mode of acting toward his superiors. Sometimes the answers he received to his letters were more wounding to him than would have been the perfect silence on the part of those to whom they were addressed, being couched in harsh and even bitter terms. From Father Tschenhens, his Novice-Master,—whether to try him or not we do not know,—he often heard the not very encouraging words: "You had better return to your former missions. You will never persevere with us."

Severe as such words may sound, and galling as they must have been, they could not effect Father Neumann's vocation. It was safe in the hands of her to whom he had entrusted it, safe under the protection of his loved Mother, the ever Blessed Virgin Mary. Nor could such treatment lessen his love and veneration for Father Tschenhens, whom he chose for confessor as often as he had an opportunity for doing so. Shortly after his religious profession, he wrote him a most cordial letter, thanking him for the kindness he had received at his hands, and expressing his belief that he, his former Novice-Master, would share in the joy he himself felt on the occasion of making his sacred vows.

Long accustomed to practise the most rigorous poverty, Father Neumann was more than satisfied with whatever fell to his lot in the way of food, clothing, or lodging. Whilst in Rochester he found room for the ordinary furniture of a sleeping apartment, a bed, a stand, etc., under one of the staircases. These were luxurious accommodations compared with some others in his lifetime; but what cared one of his spiritual calibre whether his rest were taken on a hard bench or a soft couch, except, indeed, rather to give preference to the former?

Privations the greatest found him outwardly silent, cheerful, affable; whilst in the depths of his soul he roused his faith and adored the will of the great Father whose mercy apportioned to him those precious little crosses. When humbled, despised, or neglected, an observer might detect that movement of the lips which betokens prayer, and his whole countenance breathed not only interior devotion, but also joy at having something to offer to God. On such occasions he was sometimes heard to murmur, "My dearest Jesus, all for Thee!"

The labors and privations necessarily encountered by a newly-established Congregation were insufficient to satisfy the fervor of our saintly novice; he must needs add to them. When alone at the different stations assigned him, he allowed himself but a scanty share of food, and it was no rare thing for him to fast the whole day long; he wore an iron cincture furnished with points which entered the flesh and made painful wounds; moreover, the frequent use of the discipline and protracted vigils were not unfamiliar to him.

His obedience was exact, childlike, and edifying; the duties entrusted to him were performed with rigorous exactitude and as much perfection as possible. He never meddled in the affairs of others, unless requested to do so. We quote the following incident as an example of the religious fidelity which influenced his every action. It so happened, whilst he was with Father Tschenhens at Norwalk, that a wedding was to take place on a certain day, the parties belonging to the more influential class of society. Father Tschenhens had prepared the bride and groom for the reception of the Holy Sacrament, and he it was who was to perform the ceremony. The appointed hour drew near, the wedding-train had arrived, but the officiating clergyman was still among the missing. He had been giving a mission at a distance and, from some cause or other, failed to make the exact time. The bridal party began to show signs of impatience, and some even went so far as to urge Father Neumann to perform the office of celebrant, assuring him at the same time that Father Tschenhens had in his possession the requisite documents. But no argument could induce Father Neumann to celebrate the marriage without his Superior's permission.

Though so closely engaged in the works of his ministry, Father Neumann found time for numerous occupations conducive to the general good of the community. The number of Fathers was small; consequently they had not as yet an *ordo* for Mass and the Divine Office. Father Neumann undertook the tedious task not only of arranging one, but of sending to each of the Fathers, as a New-Year's gift, a copy made by his own hand. The lines accompanying each contained some cordial and witty remarks like the following: "I doubt not, dear Father, that it will take you a whole year to get through this letter."

The details we have given of Father Neumann's probation may very possibly create astonishment in some minds, as it is well known with what care St. Alphonsus elaborated and defined his rules for the novices of his Congregation, and with what fidelity its members adhere to their founder's regulations on this point, as on all others connected with their institute. But if we attentively consider the circumstances of those times, the spiritual wants of the country, we must admit that, apart from the conscientious observance of the rules of the Congregation, no more suitable training could have been bestowed upon one destined to carry out the spirit of the holy founder in America. We shall admire, also, the admirable workings of Divine Providence in choosing Father Neumann, that great soul whose biography we now write, as the first scion of the Redemptorists in America.

In difficult and extraordinary times Almighty God gives extraordinary graces, as is proved in Father Neumann's case. The Redemptorist chronicles of those early days inform us concerning this first acquisition to their holy Congregation: "The first novice of our American province did not enjoy the advantages found in the regular instruction and careful discipline of a well-regulated novitiate. He was entrusted with duties which usually fall to the charge of professed religious only; nevertheless he distinguished himself by a faithful observance of rules, unaffected love for the congregation, and the practice of eminent virtues."

Many changes took place after Father Neumann's profession. Father Rumpler was nominated to the German church of New York; Father Bayer sent to Rochester; and the Superior, Father Alexander, set out for Europe with the hope of procuring an additional force for the American mission. Fathers Fey and Neumann remained in Baltimore, in which city there were, at that early day, about four thousand German Catholics, though the parish school could muster only ninety children. The pastor's duties were rendered the more arduous by the fact that his flock lived scattered throughout the city and its environs. Sick-calls were frequent, and often from a distance of many miles. The number of converts under instructions was from ten to twenty every day: not a Sunday passed without witnessing the abjuration of several.

The Redemptorists' charge, at that period, was not confined to the Germans of Baltimore alone. Many other places around contained numerous German Catholic families minus a resident priest. The following stations for two years, 1842-44, were regularly attended from Baltimore: Cumberland, Harper's Ferry, Martinsburg, Kingwood, Richmond, Frederick, York, Columbia, Strasburg, and Westminster. Nor were these all. As often as possible, the Fathers visited other towns of Maryland, Virginia, and Pennsylvania, to administer the Sacraments to the faithful. These distant missions usually fell to Father Neumann. However toilsome or dangerous the journey, never did a complaint escape his lips, never did he give expression to annoyance or chagrin. The fatigue consequent on these trips can hardly be estimated nowadays with our numberless modern facilities for travel. If we remember that the only railroad at the time was the one between Baltimore and Frederick, we may perhaps, form some idea of the difficulties attending such excursions. The canal-boat or stage-coach was the only mode of conveyance, and when this failed, as it often did, the missionary was obliged to proceed on horseback or on foot through forests and uninhabited districts, at all seasons, in rain or shine, heat or cold. But Father Neumann's love of mortification and zeal for souls surmounted every obstacle. When, after all his exertions, he received the reward usually bestowed by the world, when his well-intentioned efforts were met by ingratitude, when his laborious undertakings were greeted with scorn and ridicule, then with redoubled earnestness did he press forward in his pursuit of souls. What would have intimidated another, what would have led him to abandon the work altogether or pursue it with dampened ardor, only stimulated Father Neumann to more heroic self-sacrifice. His health now was not what it once was, not what we knew it when he laughingly termed himself a "Bohemian mountain-boy," for he was now a prey to frequent wasting fever which slowly consumed his strength. A letter written thirty years later by his old friend Father Pax gives us the following touching incident.

"In the fall of 1843, before returning to Europe, I visited Baltimore for the purpose of seeing for the last time my very dear friend, Father Neumann. The reception I met from him was most cordial. I found him suffering greatly. His throat was swollen, and fever was wasting his health; yet he still worked hard in the confessional and the pulpit, nor were his accustomed affability and cheerfulness affected by his ill-health. After a very happy day together we parted. The moment was a painful one for both; I shall never forget it. His last words were: 'Farewell for this life and till we meet again in heaven!'"

We have every reason to believe that these two friends and fellow-laborers are now united in the enjoyment of their eternal reward. Father Pax, after living to celebrate his golden jubilee, died at Saargemünd, diocese of Metz, February 18, 1874, aged seventy-six years.

Charity toward the poor and distressed was always a distinguishing trait in Father Neumann's character. Let their misfortunes be what they might, they invariably found a friend in him. On January 12, 1844, he had the consolation of performing the last services of his ministry for a poor criminal condemned to the scaffold. The wretched man had been convicted of the murder of two wives in succession. January 12th, the day appointed for the execution, arrived, and the whole city of Baltimore was alive with excitement. An immense concourse of people had assembled to witness the appalling sight. Suddenly the hum of voices ceased, and silence fell upon the surging mass as the condemned appeared on the gallows with Father Neumann at his side. Holding a crucifix in his hand, he addressed words of encouragement to his penitent, exhorting him to offer to Almighty God his merited punishment in atonement for the crimes he had committed, the scandal he had given. Having made him confess his guilt by an act of contrition, he presented the crucifix to his lips, and remained on the spot till the criminal had paid the penalty of his guilt and his soul had passed to the presence of its Judge.

Father Alexander returned from Europe in 1843, accompanied by eight Fathers, one professed student, Francis Xavier Seelos, and five lay-brothers. About the same time Rev. Joseph Müller and six lay-brothers entered the Congregation.

By order of the Vicar-General, Rev. Father Passerat, the Superior of the Redemptorists in America, was thenceforward provided with two Consultors, Father Neumann being appointed to that responsible post. The Congregation of the Most Holy Redeemer was now perfectly organized in America. Enlarging its field of usefulness, it spread from year to year throughout the vast districts of the New World. It rendered inestimable service to the German Catholics by gathering hundreds of thousands of them into over two hundred parishes, which, with few exceptions, are at the present day in a flourishing condition, attended by their own parish priests. Baltimore, Pittsburg, Rochester, and Philadelphia became the special theatres of its successful ministrations. In fact, the Redemptorist Fathers were almost the only priests who assumed the charge of the German Catholics of those cities.

CHAPTER IV.

Father Neumann Superior of the Redemptorists, Pittsburg.

ON March 5, 1844, Father Neumann was chosen Superior of the Redemptorists in Pittsburg. It will not be out of place to mention here some of the difficulties attendant on the formation of St. Philomena's parish of that city. As we have already seen, its establishment gave rise to much anxiety and frequent contests which lasted many years. Father Prost had, indeed, succeeded in restoring something like harmony; but two years later, in 1841, his successor, Father Alexander, was forced into new altercations with some members of the parish. They had become so infatuated with the mischievous and unchristian trustee system that they could not understand why they should be excluded from a voice in every matter connected with the church. They went so far as to renew their claims upon the property of both church and pastoral residence. Father Alexander called a meeting in which he positively declared that, if they persisted in contesting the right of the Redemptorists to the church-property, the Fathers would leave Pittsburg. His words produced a deep impression upon all present. Voices arose, some for and some against the trustee system. At last, when things were assuming a serious aspect, Jacob Schneider, an honest, well-meaning citizen, the former owner of the property under dispute, arose and addressed the assembly in the following truthful, laconic, though somewhat blunt language: "This is none of your affair, therefore be silent. No one has a right to a word on the subject. All this property was once mine. I sold it to Father Prost; it belongs to him. Now let us say no more." That Mr. Schneider's statement was correct no one could deny; and so the meeting was dissolved without further discussion.

In consequence of this decision Father Louis Cartuyvels began, though under many difficulties, the erection of the new church of St. Philomena.

On May 26, 1842, the Feast of Corpus Christi, the corner-stone was laid in presence of a large concourse of people. Two months later the old factory was taken down and a temporary church and school-house erected. These were used until 1847. During the two years of Father Cartuyvels' term of office he did much for the improvement of the parish; but, even with the best intentions, he found it impossible to remove all difficulties. His successor, Father Fey, feeling unequal to the onerous task, resigned into the hands of Superiors a post which he had held only a few weeks, March 1, 1844.

The building of the temporary chapel and school, together with the laying of the foundation of the new church, had already accumulated a considerable debt. The erection of the latter was still going on: how were funds to be procured? The parish was small, the parishioners were poor.

It was under these apparently most unfavorable circumstances that Father Neumann was appointed Superior of St. Philomena's. The chronicles of the congregation tell us that by his extraordinary confidence in God he accomplished what was, humanly speaking, impossible.

On his arrival in Pittsburg the community gathered around him. All witnessed the struggle it cost him to take the first place, the place due to his office of Superior. The rule was quoted, but even then his countenance betrayed the pain he felt at being forced to take precedence among his brethren.

Shortly before Father Neumann's appointment as

Superior, Pittsburg had been raised to the dignity of a bishopric. In 1843 the pious and learned Father Michael O'Connor, Vicar-General of the diocese of Philadelphia and an intimate friend of Father Neumann, was consecrated its first Bishop.

The erection of the newly-projected church of St. Philomena claimed the first attention of the new Superior. The entire responsibility of the undertaking rested upon him, even to the direction of the work in its minutest details. He began by forming a "Building Society" whose members contributed five cents a week; even the poorest of the parish could command this small sum, and they paid their mite most cheerfully. The common saying was again verified: "It is the poor that build and support our churches." Notwithstanding the readiness of his parishioners to fall in with their good pastor's views, yet, as might be expected, he sometimes found himself in great pecuniary straits. The saintly Father Seelos says: "While Father Neumann was Superior in Pittsburg the beautiful Gothic church of St. Philomena was built. Who can estimate the weight of care and anxiety that then rested upon him with the weekly drain on his slender resources in the shape of laborers' wages, etc.? The whole superintendence of the building devolved upon him, and what, under such circumstances, the holy man endured, God alone knows. On the last great day He will manifest it to the glory of His faithful servant. I shared, in a measure, his anxiety. The workmen had to be paid on Saturday, and it frequently happened that Friday came round and not a cent on hand for the purpose—no prospect even of obtaining money. And yet, wonderful to say, Saturday evening brought with it the requisite sum for paying off the hands."

St. Philomena's is a Gothic structure one hundred and sixty feet long, sixty-five feet wide, and sixty feet high in the middle nave. The steeple rises to the height of two hundred and twenty-five feet. The proportions of the entire building are in harmony, and the effect produced by the whole most pleasing. Father Neumann's stay in Pittsburg was too short to enable him to superintend the frescoing of the interior, but to him belongs the honor of having sketched the outlines for the same. The beautiful altars are works of art; the Stations of the Cross, the richly decorated statues, the stained-glass windows—all tend to inspire the beholder with devotion. The opinion is unanimous that the external structure and the interior finish of St. Philomena's can rarely be surpassed.

Let us now consider Father Neumann in the midst of his flock, for whose spiritual welfare his devotedness knew no bounds. On him devolved the burden of the care of souls. City and country claimed his zeal; and had not his presence been necessary for the building of the church, the latter, as being the more laborious, would have been his by right of preference. In the confessional, in the pulpit, in the school, he was indefatigable. He devoted himself especially to those plain catechetical instructions usually given in the Redemptorist churches on Sunday afternoons; here he signalized himself. With what ease he prepared for his sermons is well known to all who were in any way familiar with him; indeed, we may say that he needed no special preparation, since his life of prayer and study rendered him capable of announcing the Word of God at all times. He ascribed this facility to a little method adopted in youth. When reading he noted down the striking maxims or beautiful sentiments presented by the page before him; whatever he thought might be of benefit to souls he made his own. In this way he laid by an immense amount of material which in his free moments he arranged to use when expedient in sermons, conferences, and catechetical instructions. Did the attendance on a sick-call involve some extra trouble, it was claimed as a right by the devoted Superior, whose eager desire was to spare his subjects as much as possible. Sometimes the latter complained of never being allowed to discharge this most onerous part of their ministry; but they were playfully put off with the words: "You need all the rest you can get. I cannot sleep at night, so I might as well go myself."

Father Neumann was ever ready to lend assistance and to give advice; none ever left him dissatisfied or unconsoled. As in the early days of his missionary life, so now in later years do we find him exhibiting the same affectionate interest in the education of youth. The well-being and progress of the schools were always a primary object with him, for he was firmly convinced that only Christian education can form a good Catholic congregation. He took them under his own special superintendence, bestowing upon them all the time and attention he could possibly spare from other duties. He excelled, as we have before remarked, in catechetical instructions, as he possessed in a high degree the secret of making them pleasing and intelligible to children. The simplicity of his explanations appealed to their understanding, whilst the piety of his own true heart awoke a corresponsive flame in theirs. He was, besides, so affable, so gracious, so condescending toward the little ones of his flock that he found at once a way to their innocent young hearts, he won their whole confidence. When his well-known step was heard entering the school-room, smiles of welcome lit up every face, and great was the disappointment when their good Father Superior was prevented from paying his accustomed visit. Crowds of these little people used to gather round him on the street, touching his hand, pulling at his coat, or asking a blessing. To prepare them for their First Communion was, of all occupations, his chosen one. His care and diligence in this duty was unremitting. He left no means untried to awaken fervor and piety in their youthful breasts, and to impress upon their minds a full understanding of what they were to receive in Holy Communion. He procured, as far as in him lay, that the day on which they approached the Holy Table for the first time should be celebrated with all possible magnificence, that the deep impression made thereby on the young communicants might cause them ever to revert with joy and gratitude to the inestimable favor then bestowed.

A catechism suited to the use of our schools was, at that time, a desideratum. Father Neumann took upon himself the difficult task of compiling one, and its excellence has been very generally acknowledged. The experience of many years had taught him the importance of teaching children something of sacred history, in order to facilitate their memorizing the answers of the catechism; consequently his next step was to write a Bible History for the use of the schools. His day's work over, he used to spend the entire night in such compilations, that the books might be placed as soon as possible in the hands of teachers and scholars. These two little books are magnificent proofs of Father Neumann's abilities as a teacher of youth, and of the high respect in which he held the Holy Scriptures; for, whilst endeavoring to make the sacred narrative intelligible to children, he retained as far as was practicable the words of the text through reverence for the written Word of God.

He also composed manuals for the various confraternities usually established in the Redemptorist churches, in order to make known to the members the graces and privileges in which they might share and the conditions necessary for doing so. He introduced the Confraternity of the Living Rosary, and in those already existing he endeavored to excite greater fervor; for he was convinced that by such societies the love of Jesus Christ and His Blessed Mother would take deeper root in the hearts of the faithful.

Of the special end of his own Congregation, the Missions, he never lost sight, and he availed himself of every opportunity to induce the secular clergy to allow these exercises to be preached in their parishes. Although his parochial duties claimed so large a portion of his time and strength, yet he was ever ready to undertake those apostolic labors, and often directed them himself. They were, too, often fraught with mortifications and humiliations. Father Seelos informs us of an incident which happened on one of Father Neumann's journeys to the scene of one of these missions, and which affords us an insight into his conduct under rebuffs and insults. He writes: "Father Neumann and I were to give a mission at St. Vincent's, where stands at present the great Benedictine abbey. We arrived in the evening at Youngstown, a little village in the neighborhood. Unable to continue our journey as far as St. Vincent's, we were obliged to pass the night in a tavern, so called. Our reception was ungracious enough, and not without difficulty did we succeed in procuring something to eat. After supper, we thought surely a bedroom would be assigned us, but we were disappointed. We sat unnoticed on a bench which was eventually to serve the purpose of a bed. The door was locked, and no alternative left us but to make the best of our situation. 'We shall have to content ourselves with a bed like to that of the Fathers of the Desert,' said Father Neumann good-humoredly; and spreading his cloak on the bench along with my own, he bade me lie down. I did so in obedience, whilst he sat up all night in prayer, to which fact may doubtless be ascribed the rich fruits of our mission." Father Seelos adds: "I could relate many other similar incidents."

In this little trait we behold Father Neumann's paternal care of his subjects. True, it was not always in his power either to prevent or to remedy every evil; but at such times his unbounded confidence in God effected what human means could not. He had recourse to prayer with such ardor, such confidence, such importunity that of him it might be said as formerly of Jacob: "He wrestled with his God, saying, 'I will not let Thee go, except Thou bless me.'"

One subject of deep regret to Father Neumann was the want of laborers in the Lord's vineyard, and we often find him giving expression to it both by word and writing. Behold the following: "The scarcity of German priests is sensibly felt. The few that we have are sadly out of proportion with the ever-increasing wants of the faithful. There are Catholics who have not been to confession for many years, and there are young persons of nineteen or twenty who have nothing of Catholicity about them saving their baptism,—and all this from the want of priests. The longer this need continues, the more difficult will it be to reanimate faith and the fear of God." After forty years, we behold in our own day the sad realization of Father Neumann's prediction. It was his decided opinion that German Catholics should be attended by priests of their own nationality. English-speaking priests do not learn German, and the Germans acquire too little English after coming to this country to understand with profit the truths of faith taught them in that language. Therefore Father Neumann suggests means by which America may be supplied with good German priests. "It cannot be expected," he says, "that the episcopal seminaries should educate German students for the ministry. The best way to provide for this want would be to establish a society of ecclesiastics in Austria on the same plan as the Seminary of Foreign Missions or that of the Holy Ghost in Paris. This association would, then, supply our destitute States with missionaries."

Of the dangers to which youth is exposed, Father Neumann's judgment was as far-seeing and profound as it was true. Speaking of education, he says: "The school-system of the United States is very liberal in theory; but in reality it is most intolerant toward Catholics. Every one has to contribute to the erection and maintenance of the public schools, in which instruction is restricted to reading, writing, and ciphering. As respects religious instruction, which is excluded from those schools, parents are free to have their children reared in whatever religion they please. Notwithstanding these liberal concessions, it cannot be doubted that the young mind is influenced by the irreligious dispositions of the teacher. Even the text-books selected for use are injurious to Catholic children. They are nothing else than heretical extracts from a falsified Bible, and histories which contain the most malicious perversion of truth, the grossest lies against the doctrines and practices of the Catholic Church. The teachers are, for the most part, either Protestants or infidels. Immorality reigns in these schools, especially in those which are in the country.

"These circumstances combine for the spiritual ruin of Catholic children; hence the generality of Catholic priests forbid parents to send their children to such schools. But lukewarm or avaricious parents heed little their prohibitions. They allege that the English language, which is thoroughly taught in the public schools, is necessary for their children's success in life; and, as they are obliged to contribute to the support of these schools, they desire to derive some private advantage from them. Many Catholics, therefore, go to the public schools with immense detriment to both faith and morals." *

---

* Since the above was penned the educational system of the United States has considerably improved, and the number of Catholic schools

Another complaint launched against the Catholics of America by Father Neumann is their custom of sending their children to work in factories or, what is still worse, allowing them to take service in infidel or irreligious families at an age at which they ought to attend school.

"It is also quite common," he goes on to say, "for parents to entrust young children that are a burden to them to respectable and wealthy families by whom they are fed, clothed, and instructed until the age of eighteen or twenty. This is a crying evil. American Protestants are fanatical; they use every means to check the spread of Catholicity. They receive Catholic children into their families with the secret intention of destroying their faith; and, as they make fair promises, the foolish parents think themselves fortunate in having so well provided for their little ones. They will, it is true, one day weep over their own folly, but, alas! it will then be too late. The poor children will have not only forgotten parents, language, and religion, but their education, based on pride, sensuality, and self-sufficiency, leads them to contract the vices of their guardians; they are corrupted for life, they are lost for eternity. Such cases are of frequent occurrence, and, as far as my observation goes, no child thus dealt with has met a better fate. The children of the French and Irish were in the beginning similarly situated, for which reason the Bishops have strained every effort to erect orphan asylums over which, as a general thing, the Sisters of Charity preside. Asylums of the same kind for our German children are necessary. They must be regarded as the best, the only means to wrest them from the grasp of infidelity, and eventually from eternal death."

---

has greatly increased, thus facilitating the attendance of Catholic children. Besides, the Bishops assembled in the Plenary Council expressed their views on this head. They permit the frequentation of the public schools to Catholic children only on certain conditions.

The rapid spread of secret societies was another source of grief to Father Neumann. Let us listen to him expressing himself on this evil:

"Several secret societies have been formed lately among infidels and non-Catholics; for instance, the Freemasons, the Odd-fellows, and the Order of Red Men. All assert that the only object of their association is fraternal benevolence and mutual support. But this is merely a specious cloak. The very oath tendered them, viz., secrecy as to what goes on in their meetings, is a sufficient reason to suspect their intention, and to warn Catholics against communication with them. The show of philanthropy and the temporal advantages they offer their members have induced the major part of German Protestants to swell their ranks. Under pain of exclusion from the Sacraments, the Provincial Council has forbidden Catholics to join such societies. Notwithstanding the prohibition many have been enticed into them, and the sad consequences are that they have fallen away from the faith."

Of the worth or worthlessness of the so-called mixed societies, which are neither religious nor masonic, Father Neumann also speaks. In the character imputed to these associations lies the difficulty of passing a correct judgment upon them. Hence the following opinion, which we reproduce word for word as far as possible, is of special value: "Among Americans," he says, "there exists a peculiar hankering after unions and societies having a political or literary object. The Germans, unable to resist their mania for imitation, have already plunged into the current of these societies. Admission to them is easy and, to swell their numbers, a kind of propagandism is practised, it being incumbent on every member to enlist others. Hence it happens that German Catholics joining these associations, harmless perhaps in themselves, come into closer and more frequent communication with certain men than is expedient for their faith and morals. On many occasions, at funerals, anniversaries, for example, sermons are preached and prayers offered in Protestant churches. Such demonstrations are exceedingly pleasing to the American people despite their infidelity. In these sermons, reason and the biblical knowledge of the audience are set up as arbiters; open criticism of the preacher and his words is not only allowable, but even commendable. Such principles are most hurtful to a Catholic. The childlike faith which the Christian must possess in order to gain salvation hereby sustains great injury. Some of these poor Catholics who, either through stupidity or curiosity or the desire to please acquaintances, have been present at such sermons end by wishing their priests no longer to treat the Word of God as a revelation of divine truth, but as a scientific subject which they themselves may freely discuss and decide. Sermons, they say, should flatter their whims and views; anything else is distasteful.

"To counteract these evils, to eradicate them, or, at least, to neutralize their pernicious effects, the German Catholic missionary must be endued with extraordinary prudence and constancy. That his parishioners may be restrained from joining secret societies, from too intimate intercourse with heretics, from the reading of Protestant and immoral books, etc., a very discreet zeal is needed. The proper remedies must be applied to these evils. The following appear the most suitable: in our churches divine service must be conducted with as much solemnity as possible; solid and popular sermons and instructions must be preached on Sundays and holydays; confraternities must be introduced; newspapers and good books must be diffused; but, above all, prayer and the frequentation of the Sacraments must be insisted upon."

Prejudice against our Holy Church was in those days

both bitter and wide-spread. Catholics were looked upon as ignorant and superstitious, taught by their priests that all who differed from them in faith should with fire and sword be swept from the face of the earth. The feeling thus engendered against the ministers of religion led to their being ridiculed, insulted, and sometimes even pelted with stones. It was only by patience and perseverance, the erection of imposing churches, schoolhouses, and charitable institutions that these odious prejudices gradually disappeared.

In a letter to the Archbishop of Vienna Father Neumann thus describes the condition of Protestantism in America at that period: "The delusions of the Methodists, whose numbers are constantly on the increase in the United States, are like the action of nitric acid on marble; they dissolve the older sects of Protestantism into a thousand different fragments. The erroneous doctrines of these new American denominations are closely allied to those of the ancient Gnostics and Manicheans. As regards the knowledge of what is holiest in heaven or upon earth, of the eternal weal or woe of immortal souls, nothing is more ridiculous than the confused reveries of these new sects. The terrible punishments of God are visibly afflicting these proud, unfortunate men who, shamefully heedless of the voice of Jesus Christ in His Church, have separated from the unity of that spiritual body in which alone life and holiness are found. These sects which have sprung up here within the last hundred years are all eagerness to begin the millennium, or the thousand years of Christ's reign upon earth, whilst others imagine themselves already in it. The best-known sect in these States are the Shakers, who claim that the millennium has already begun for them; that they all possess apostolic gifts; that baptism and the Holy Eucharist, being only for the first ages, are no longer necessary. They deny the eternity of hell, torments, excepting in the case of unfortunate apostates from their own sect. They say that Christ will not come again, since He has already come in His *Saints* (*the Shakers*) They affirm that even now, in our own time, the Last Judgment has begun; the books are opened, the dead are rising from their graves and coming to be judged by them. They reject marriage because they are now in eternity, their old earthly Adam is destroyed; and, according to them, they are already in the splendor of the bright and celestial intuition of God. They pretend that every sin against God is a sin against each individual member of their sect also, and the sinner to obtain forgiveness must confess his crimes to them. They likewise affirm that their leaders have free access to the spirit-world, etc.

"Their religious rites are mysterious and varied. Sometimes they assemble on a mountain and, on the supposition that the time for the spiritual harvest has arrived, they gravely and silently imitate the movements of reapers at work. At a given sign all make a motion with their hands, as if weeding, then as if threshing and putting wheat into the mill. Then they mimic bakers and cooks, and lastly prepare a meal at which all partake of invisible food and drink, accompanied by signs of hearty relish. Dancing forms another feature in their religious ceremonies. The dancers, men and women, in a costume for the occasion, jump up and down about four inches from the ground, interspersing their leaps with various extravagant movements of the limbs. Then they sing, now high, now low, their appearance leading one to imagine them bewitched. The violent efforts that they make bring on a relaxation of nerves, and they begin to tremble as if with chills. Some clap their hands, and others spring up so high into the air that they end by tumbling headlong to the ground. This sect came to America from England in 1774, and settled in New York, Pennsylvania, and Maryland. The

Shakers have, however, earned a good name for their peaceable disposition, and they are, moreover, excellent farmers."

Not so harmless were many of the other sects which, in their fanaticism, aimed at injuring the Catholic Church wherever they could. Apostasy from her fold they rewarded by temporal advantages; in fact, they supported whole families who had been thus seduced from their faith. Strange as it may appear, there were not wanting cases in which impoverished Catholics were willing to barter their eternal salvation for a little temporal interest. We give the following singular fact as an illustration of this lamentable blindness. A German family, all Catholics, lived for some time in a state of great destitution; starvation stared them in the face. One of these sectarian proselytizers asked the father one day to join his church, promising, in the event of his doing so, to get him plenty of work at high wages, and to furnish him at once with a sum sufficient to help him out of his needy circumstances. The poor fellow hesitated; he found himself in a most embarrassing position. What answer should he give? He was unwilling to jeopardize his own and his children's salvation, yet could he longer behold his little ones pleading for that bread which he was unable give them? What should he do? It was, indeed, a fearful stratagem of the enemy of souls. At last the poor man hit upon an expedient. Forgetful of the sin he was thereby incurring, he resolved to feign apostasy and so obtain the needed help. He communicated his intention to his wife in the following words: "Let us join the heretics outwardly, but in our heart let us still belong to the Catholic Church. Let us accept both the money and the work. As soon as we shall have relieved our distress, we shall live again as Catholics." The wife fully comprehended the magnitude of the crime such dissimulation would entail, and not without a heavy heart did she agree to her husband's proposal.

But hunger pressed; she saw no alternative. The poor creatures received the promised relief, but remorse gnawed like a worm at their heart. Shortly after the wretched father had occasion to go to Pittsburg. It was Sunday morning, and he was passing St. Philomena's Church just as the High Mass began. He hears the familiar sounds of the organ, and the magnificent strains of the "Kyrie" strike on his ear. "Lord, have mercy on us! Lord, have mercy on us!"—the words re-echo in the depths of his soul, and, obedient to some powerful interior impulse, he enters the house of God. And why does he not pause there at the door? Where is he going—he, the apostate? Urged on by the same invisible power that bade him enter, he goes on and on—he pauses not until he reaches the sanctuary-rail, and there he stands. Motionless, breathless, supporting himself on his stick, he stands and gazes at the sacred scene before him. Father Neumann, the Superior, is at the altar; he it is who is about to offer the propitiatory sacrifice. The more solemn parts of the Mass draw near,—the offertory, the sanctus, the consecration,—and still the man stands spell-bound outside the rail. The celebrant divides the Sacred Host over the chalice, the Communion approaches, when—hark!—a cry, a groan, and the unhappy but now contrite apostate falls on his knees in an agony of tears and repentance. What had he seen? What had he heard? What forced that cry of bitter anguish from his breast? Let us hear his own account: "When the priest broke the Sacred Host, I saw drops of blood trickling from It!" For the salvation of that one poor soul, Almighty God had deigned to work a stupendous miracle. Oh, how surpassingly good is God toward the stray soul in whom He can discover one spark of faith, one feeling of sorrow! At the same instant in which with his corporal eyes the poor man saw the blood, he seemed to hear in his soul a voice, saying, "This blood hast thou forced from Me by thy apostasy!" Need we say that his conversion was accomplished? After Mass he hurried to the sacristy, where he related to Father Neumann all that had happened, made a contrite confession, and in a short time led his whole family back to the bosom of the Church.

Innumerable similar conversions were wrought through the instrumentality of the Fathers, though unattended by the external miraculous evidences accompanying that just narrated; consequently we must not wonder at their attracting upon themselves the malevolence of Satan and his emissaries. Their hatred fell principally upon Father Neumann, against whom insults and annoyances of all sorts were directed. One day a drunkard presented himself at the residence of the Fathers. It so happened that the first one whom he met was Father Neumann, the Superior, and upon him was poured out the wrath of the inebriate. The vilest abuse, torrents of threats and imprecations, flowed from his foam-covered lips. Father Neumann listened calmly, and, after the storm had somewhat abated, asked in a gentle tone, "Have you anything more to say?" The fellow had sense enough left to wonder at such meekness, and answered, "No, I have said all that I have to say." "Well, then," said Father Neumann, "you had better go home and sleep off the effects of liquor;" and he gently but resolutely led him to the door. Not long after, the unfortunate victim of drink acknowledged his error and asked pardon with many signs of confusion. His violence was intended for Father Joseph Müller, but it fell upon Father Neumann. The latter failed not to detect the mistake. "Take care," said he to Father Müller, "take care not to encounter ——. He is greatly incensed against you."

One night an abandoned wretch set fire to the school-house, which, like the temporary church and the pastoral residence, was only of wood. Everything would have been consumed had not Almighty God frustrated the diabolical design. A Catholic gentleman, happening to drive down Penn Street about midnight, was interiorly urged to turn into the narrow street in which the schoolhouse stood. He discovered the fire, promptly gave the alarm, and thus the property was saved.

On the first Sunday of October, 1846, the Feast of the Holy Rosary, the beautiful church of St. Philomena was solemnly blessed and opened for divine service by Right Rev. Michael O'Connor. This much of the great work was accomplished; but not yet was it permitted Father Neumann to sing his "Nunc dimittis," not yet was it his to say, "Now, O Lord, Thou dost dismiss Thy servant in peace," since his beloved little community was still unprovided with a suitable abode. This, also, was to be his task, the erection of a convent for the Fathers. Active as ever, hopeful as ever, trustful as ever in that Providence which never yet had failed him, he set to work. He wished the building to correspond, as far as possible, to the style of the church, and to furnish accommodations not only for the resident Fathers and Brothers, but also for whatever novices or students might in the future make Pittsburg their home. In its interior and exterior arrangements the new convent was to be modelled according to the requirements of the rule. These plans Father Neumann happily carried out. The convent attached to St. Philomena's Church is the most commodious house of the Congregation, and up to the present it has undergone no material change.

So far we have followed Father Neumann in his exertions for the well-being of others, for the welfare of all confided to his care. Let us now turn our attention to the life led by him in the seclusion of the convent.

The innumerable cares attendant on a large parish, besides those entailed by the erection of the buildings of which we have spoken, never interfered with Father Neumann's conscientious discharge of his duties as a religious whether as subject or Superior. The punctual observance of the rules and customs of the Congregation in all their minutiæ was his conscientious study, and of his subjects he required a similar exactitude. The difficult circumstances with which the Fathers had to contend in those early days of their missionary career in America rendered such exactitude no easy matter; but, by mildness and firmness joined to his own example, he succeeded in maintaining regular observance in the community. He was convinced that religious attract upon themselves and their labors the fulness of divine grace only by strictly observing the rules of their Order, and acquire its spirit by walking in the footsteps of their founder. Besides, Father Neumann required nothing of his brethren as Superior that he was not ready to practise himself. He shone a model of all virtues common to the religious life; therefore did he always find his subjects ready for any sacrifice demanded by the honor of God, their own sanctification, or the salvation of their neighbor. Fathers Tschenhens, Cronenberg, Joseph Müller, Schäffler, Hotz, and Seelos, who had the happiness to live under his direction at the period of which we write, unanimously declare that in him they never failed to find a vigilant Superior, a loving Father, a kind and obliging confrère. Nothing escaped his watchful eye. The trifling faults common in a community, and the wants of its individual members, were equally detected by him. The former fell under the ban of gentle reproof; the latter were speedily and lovingly supplied. His paternal solicitude extended to everything, for his only desire was to see the religious committed to his care living happy and contented in the faithful observance of the rule and according to the spirit of St. Alphonsus. That his efforts were successful we can judge from their results; for, amid poverty, distress, and arduous labors, the home of the Redemptorist Fathers was ever the abode of holy joy. We have the foregoing from the saintly Father Seelos, who, fifteen years later, wrote as follows: "The years of 1845 and '46 I spent in Pittsburg, where Father

Neumann held to me the place of Superior. I was his subject, nay, rather his son. I had just left the novitiate, and the more inexperienced I was, the greater need had I of his direction. And, indeed, he was to me in every respect a father whom I can never forget. He taught me how to act, how to direct my steps in the practical walks of life; he was my confessor and spiritual guide; he cared for me in every way. The remembrance of his good example, his extreme modesty, his deep humility, and his patience that overcame all difficulties, will ever be mine. Our poor abode was so wretched that one night, during a severe thunder-storm, the rain poured down upon our beds. We had to leave our room and seek shelter in another part of the house. I say *our* room, since we were obliged to share one between us, a curtain being our only partition. I often heard Father Neumann saying his prayers till late in the night. He generally slept so little that I wondered how he could live and labor with so little rest. As he was accustomed to rise before the appointed hour, he used to kindle the fire, often bringing up the fuel himself, that the room might be warm before I arose."

His sincere humility and charity toward his subjects rendered his spiritual guidance easy and delightful. Was there something disagreeable or difficult to be done, that was his by right; the easy or the honorable he left to his companions. His modesty was at all times so unaffected, so natural, that neither in word nor in act could an observer discover the least indication of his office as Superior. From the rule he claimed no exemption, never absenting himself when avoidable from community exercises; even if up the greater part of the night on a distant sick-call, the morning meditation found him in his accustomed place in the oratory.

He made the monthly and the annual retreat prescribed by the rule with scrupulous exactness; never was he known to omit them. Although engaged in superintending the buildings, yet he never failed to announce to his brethren the evening before his intention of making his monthly retreat the next day.

The habit of recollection seemed to have become a second nature to him. His observance of silence was truly exemplary and according to the spirit of the rule. He never spoke at prohibited hours except for real necessity; and, in the true spirit of that holy and sanctifying virtue, he carefully avoided all kinds of noise. But if duty or charity required him to speak, he did so, and in such a manner that neither silence nor cordiality suffered thereby.

A secular priest was for some time a guest in our convent. As he had heard so much of Father Neumann's piety, he determined to watch him narrowly. He did so, and afterward informed the Fathers both of his resolution and his inability to discover the least fault in their saintly Superior.

In the summer of 1845, Very Rev. Father de Held, Provincial of the Belgian Province, to which the Redemptorists in America at that time belonged, arrived from Europe, accompanied by Rev. Father Bernard. His object was to make the visitation of the different houses in the United States. After it was over, the Very Reverend Provincial expressed his opinion of Father Neumann in the following terms: "The Superior, Father Neumann, is a great man. He unites eminent prudence and firmness of character with true piety. Were it not that I have already appointed Father Czackert as my representative in America, I would choose Father Neumann for that post."

The Reverend Visitor's intentions respecting Father Neumann were, however, soon to be realized. But before his appointment as Provincial of the Redemptorists in America, we shall behold Father Neumann undergoing a severe trial. Almighty God willed to purify him for the responsible office to which He destined him by a very serious illness which brought with it grave thoughts of death. The mental and physical strain to which he had so long been subjected at last began to tell upon him; his strength gave way, and serious apprehensions were entertained that his days were drawing to a close. A constant cough, accompanied by spitting of blood, were looked upon as sure indications of pulmonary troubles. He who had been ever solicitous for the well-being of others now forgot himself. The Fathers repeatedly urged him to spare himself and to take the advice of a physician, but all in vain. He answered with a smile, "It is nothing. I shall soon be well."

At last his brethren believed themselves in duty bound to procure an order from the Provincial for Father Neumann to submit to medical treatment. A physician was consulted, and, after a thorough examination of the sick man, he declared his lungs involved: the worst results were to be feared if remedies were not promptly administered. The invalid submitted to the physician in a spirit of obedience, and after a few weeks was pronounced out of danger. "But," added Dr. N——, "if he wishes to be restored to health, Father Neumann must leave Pittsburg."

At this announcement, Father Czackert, the Vice-Provincial, summoned Father Neumann to Baltimore, January 27, 1847. The latter obeyed, leaving the convent attached to St. Philomena's, and which had progressed most satisfactorily, to be completed by his successor.

CHAPTER V.

Father Neumann Vice-Provincial of the Redemptorists in America.

FATHER NEUMANN was destined not long to enjoy the rest he so much needed. At the end of two weeks, February 9, 1847, he received a letter bearing date December 15, 1846, in which Father de Held appointed him Superior of the American Province.* Great was Father Neumann's surprise on receipt of this news. In his humility and love of retirement, his only desire was to live and die as a simple religious, and he had flattered himself that his present state of health would necessarily contribute to the fulfilment of his wishes. But Divine Providence had ordained otherwise: the more important the more onerous position of Vice-Provincial, was now laid upon him. Again must he put his hand to the plough, and again shall we behold him neither faltering nor looking back; but, strong in the strength of confidence in the All-Powerful, with St. Paul he stretches forward to the things before him. The larger the field opened up to his labors, the more brightly glowed his zeal for the glory of God, the welfare of his brethren, and the salvation of souls.

To form a correct estimate of Father Neumann in his new position, it is fitting that we cast a retrospective glance at the formation of some parishes which were, at that time, in the hands of the Congregation of the Most Holy Redeemer.

---

* Father Frederick de Held died April 20, 1881, at Vaals, in Holland, at the advanced age of eighty years, in the sixtieth of his religious profession and the fifty-eighth of his priesthood.

The early history of St. Alphonsus' and St. James's, Baltimore, we have already sufficiently dwelt upon, as also that of St. Philomena's, Pittsburg. Let us, therefore, turn our attention to St. Joseph's, Rochester. We remember that Father Prost left here in 1838, from which date till the close of 1839, almost a year, the German Catholics were without a pastor; Father Sänderl was then sent to take charge of them.

In spite of manifold difficulties and contradictions, the building of the new church went on without interruption. Father Bayer, having been appointed Superior at Rochester, so energetically pushed forward the work, that on August 15, 1843, the Feast of Our Lady's Assumption, the corner-stone was laid. The following January he went to Europe, leaving his place to be supplied by Father Beranek, who had just laid the foundations of St. Peter's, Philadelphia. He arrived in Rochester to find the new church there just as far advanced as the one he had left. Two years and a half later, July 26, 1846, the Feast of St. Ann, St. Joseph's Church, Rochester, was dedicated.

We shall now glance at the most important establishment of the Congregation of the Most Holy Redeemer in America, viz., that of New York. The Fathers had received an invitation to settle in New York City, under pretty much the same circumstances as those recorded of Pittsburg and Baltimore. Until 1833, the German Catholics of New York had no priest of their own nationality. About this time Father Raffeiner, as before stated, arrived in that city with the intention of joining the Redemptorists. But changing his mind, he devoted himself to the spiritual welfare of the Germans whom he found there. Renting a blacksmith-shop at the corner of Pitt and Delancy streets, he there held divine service.

Two years later, 1835, he purchased a Protestant meeting-house, and finally built the little church of St. Nicholas in Second Street. Father Raffeiner had labored among the Germans for about six years, when, worn out by the continued opposition of the trustees, he sought another field of action in Williamsburg, opposite the city of New York.

Several other priests successively endeavored to guide the parish of St. Nicholas, but all found it impossible to cope with the difficulties of their position. Finally, Right Rev. Bishop Hughes called the Redemptorist Fathers to New York. On August 21, 1842, Father Rumpler took charge of the German Catholics, and three months later Father Joseph Müller joined him as assistant. No sooner was the change effected than the Fathers saw themselves confronted by the opposition of the trustees, who managed to embitter and render still more difficult their already onerous duties. It is almost incredible to what petty annoyances these men condescended to stoop. They wished to control everything: even the number of candles on the altar was to be determined by them.

Despite these bitter animosities and persecutions, Father Rumpler courageously persevered in laboring for the souls confided to him, and energetically carried out his plan for the erection of a second church for the German Catholics of New York. His efforts were more than successful. The very next year he purchased for two thousand dollars a lot in Third Street; and on September 19, 1843, he announced to his congregation that, with the Bishop's approbation, he intended to form a new parish. On Ash-Wednesday of 1844 the corner-stone of a temporary church was laid, and on Easter Sunday, April 20th, the Church of the Most Holy Redeemer was dedicated and opened for service. Several Fathers were sent to Father Rumpler's assistance, and service was regularly held in both churches. The formation of a second German parish created much opposition at first on the part of the trustees mentioned above; but by degrees minds became calm, and the Church of the Most Holy Redeemer proved a source of the richest blessings to Catholics at large. In June, 1844, the Capuchin Fathers Ambrose Buchmeyer and Felician Krebes assumed the care of St. Nicholas' parish, and the Redemptorists were enabled to devote their undivided energies to the welfare of the new parish. God blessed their labors. They had begun modestly—a temporary frame church, with a school-room capable of accommodating about one hundred children. Ten years later, on that very site, Archbishop Hughes consecrated the present beautiful Church of the Most Holy Redeemer, and the little school-room has given place to a building whither fourteen hundred children flock for instruction. Besides their own churches in New York City, the Fathers attended to over twenty country missions throughout the State.

The next Redemptorist foundation took place in Philadelphia. The various parishes of which the Fathers had hitherto accepted the charge were, without exception, disorganized and divided by party-spirit; now, however, we find one deviation from this general rule, and that was St. Peter's, Philadelphia. Apart from the difficulties inseparably connected with every new foundation, the most amicable relations here existed between the parishioners and their pastors, the former faithfully co-operating with the latter. This happy state of things was owing in part, no doubt, to the sad experience connected with the church of the Holy Trinity, which had up to that time been the only German Catholic church in Philadelphia.

Provided with a letter from Bishop Kenrick, then Bishop of Philadelphia, to the Redemptorist Fathers, a deputation proceeded to Baltimore in order to present a petition to the Provincial, Father Alexander, begging him to take charge of St. Peter's parish. After mature deliberation with his counsellors, Father Alexander granted the request, and promised to visit Philadelphia himself for the purpose of making all necessary arrangements. On the site where now stands the large and beautiful school-house, three old frame houses were turned into a temporary church. The commencement was, indeed, poor enough; but it was favorable, and God's blessing rested visibly upon it. The reader may form some idea of the poverty of this young parish from the fact that the collection during the first solemn services held in the church amounted to *one dollar and forty cents!* About one hundred children attended the school during the first year. Father Sänderl, the first pastor, was succeeded in June of the same year by Rev. Father Beranek, who laid, as we have elsewhere remarked, the foundations of the present church. He was unexpectedly removed to Rochester in 1843, and his successor, Father Louis Cartuyvels, continued the work as vigorously as his means would allow.

About this time, Philadelphia was the scene of certain lawless transactions disgraceful alike to society and humanity, viz., the violent persecution of Catholics by the so-called Native American Party. This fanatical mob, composed of sectarians of every stripe, roamed the streets, burning down churches and dwellings, and murdering inoffensive citizens. Many Catholics fell victims to these cruel proceedings on May 7, 1844, in the northern and eastern section of the city near St. Peter's Church. On the 8th, St. Michael's, with the convent of the Sisters of Charity hard by, was consigned to the flames; whilst in another direction, St. Augustine's, together with the pastoral residence, was similarly destroyed. Strange that St. Peter's, situated about midway between these two churches, should have been spared! Yet so it was. Divine Providence had manifestly cast around this humble germ of a new parish the mail of Its mighty protection. Under the direction of Father Fey, the present edifice was completed and opened for divine service, December 29, 1844. On February 14, 1847, it was consecrated by Right Rev. Francis Patrick Kenrick.

One among the most memorable of the Redemptorist foundations was that of St. Mary's (Marienstadt) among the mountains of Pennsylvania, destined to be handed over at a later period to the Benedictines. A company of German Catholics had purchased here an immense tract of land, forty-eight thousand acres, with the design of establishing a colony. Father Sänderl had several times visited the district from Pittsburg, and administered the Sacraments to the colonists; but only in 1843 did Father Alexander accept the offer to take permanent charge of their spiritual welfare. He it was who gave to the colony the name of St. Mary's. To Father Cartuyvels and Brother Louis, the latter an expert builder, was assigned the care of erecting in the wilderness a temporary church, together with a school and dwelling. In 1845 Father Alexander arrived in capacity of Superior. His interest was enlisted in the welfare of the little colony, and he exerted himself in every way to further it. To ameliorate the poverty existing among the colonists, he tried to engage them in agriculture. He also put up a larger church, convent, and school. The first of these, a frame structure, sixty by thirty feet, was made to serve three purposes. The school was at first attended by only thirty children, whom Brother Xavier instructed; but immigration soon swelled its numbers, so that by 1847 the pupils counted one hundred and sixty-two, the colonists having increased to two thousand souls. The poverty of the immigrants was extreme; the majority had come without any means of subsistence, and even the necessaries of life were wanting. Whence were food and clothing to be procured for them? Very little could be expected from the rude, uncultivated soil. The Fathers shared their bread with the hungry, and the contributions received from their brethren in the different cities were freely distributed to the poverty-stricken multitude. A daily allowance of soup was given to the poor children of the school from the convent-kitchen;

and it was truly a touching sight, these miserably clad little ones kneeling during Holy Mass, their tiny hands folded and clasping the spoon soon to be put to good use. Louis I. of Bavaria, his chaplain Father Müller, and the Most Reverend Archbishop of Munich sent generous donations to the sufferers, whilst Father Alexander himself was not deterred from incurring debt in order to assist them. But it was not in accordance with the designs of God that the Redemptorists should establish themselves at St. Mary's. The labors of agriculture entered not into their special vocation, and Superiors resolved to transfer the colony to an Order one of whose particular ends is the cultivation of the soil. In 1848, therefore, St. Mary's was handed over to the Benedictines.

Before resuming the thread of Father Neumann's life, we shall mention briefly some other foundations established previously to the time of his appointment as Provincial. In 1844 the Fathers were invited to Buffalo by Bishop Hughes; and here the oft-told tale was repeated, troubles arising from the trustee-system. The stubborn resistance of the trustees belonging to the church of St. Louis against lawful authority obliged the Bishop to place it under interdict. But, not to leave the well-disposed members of the congregation destitute of a pastor, he transferred the parish to the Redemptorists, assigning to them provisionally the church of St. Patrick as a place of service for the German Catholics. The Fathers readily assented to the Bishop's arrangements, and during that same year built a temporary church for their large congregation on the corner of Batavia and Pine streets. This site is now that of the spacious and beautiful St. Mary's.

Bishop Timon, who had meantime been made first Bishop of Buffalo, speaks, in his work entitled "The Missions of the Western Part of the State of New York," of the labors of the Fathers in the temporary church.

He makes use of the following words: "The Redemptorists had already begun a house in Buffalo, where they were laboring most successfully. They resided in a wretched dwelling, and had to labor in a church that scarcely deserved the name of church. Yet at every service it was crowded with the faithful. The zealous Fathers did an extraordinary amount of good."

During the same year, 1844, the Redemptorists gave a mission in Monroe, Michigan, to a congregation at that time without a pastor. At its close, Bishop Lefevre, of Detroit, expressed his desire to leave the parish in the hands of the Fathers, that they might there establish a mission-house. To this he was impelled by the conviction of the good that would emanate from this most powerful means of salvation. Father Neumann, the Vice-Provincial, was not the man to put obstacles in the way of any such design; consequently, in June of that year, the Fathers took charge of the parish. Under their administration it increased so rapidly that the church had to be enlarged the following year. On December 8, 1845, it was solemnly consecrated by Bishop Lefevre, under the title of the Immaculate Conception. We may judge of the success of the Fathers at Monroe from the annals of the above-mentioned church, which record four thousand members as belonging to its Temperance Society.

In 1846 the Redemptorists took charge of St. Mary's Church, Detroit, under circumstances similar to those that influenced their installation among the German Catholics of Buffalo. The parish under trustee government had lapsed into the direst confusion. Bishop Lefevre engaged the Fathers to give a mission to the congregation, after which he handed the church over to them.

During the same year the German Catholics of Washington, D. C., were also provided for by the Redemptorists, and St. Mary's Church built for their use.

CHAPTER VI.

Father Neumann's Labors as Vice-Provincial.

WHEN Father Neumann entered upon his duties as Vice-Provincial, he found ten houses of the Congregation in America, with about thirty Fathers, a number totally inadequate to the work devolving on them. Besides the care of their own extensive parishes, many mission-stations were depending upon them at this time. The German Catholics scattered throughout the country districts would meet together, sometimes from a distance of over one hundred miles, and build a little log-church hardly suitable for divine service. Thither a Redemptorist would make his way, sometimes on horseback, again on foot (for railways, we may believe, were not common in those parts at that remote period), to preach the Word of God, celebrate the Holy Sacrifice, and administer the Sacraments to the faithful.

Father Neumann had from the first rightly appreciated the immensity of the work assigned the Congregation of the Most Holy Redeemer in America; he understood the difficulties that the Fathers would encounter in their respective establishments; he was well aware that the labor surpassed the strength of the laborers; he was practically acquainted with their poverty; and he had felt the pressure of debt. He was conscious that the major part of the labors and contradictions consequent upon such a situation had been laid on his own shoulders; but the full measure of the sufferings, the persecutions, the humiliations that fell to his share during the short term of his office as Vice-Provincial, he certainly could not foresee.

Does it not seem as if God willed that this new dignity, to which in His wisdom He had raised His faithful servant, should serve as a novitiate for the honor and burden of the episcopacy? We have every reason to believe that this was, indeed, the design of Divine Providence, when we behold Father Neumann passing through this trying ordeal ; and we marvel at the resignation with which he shouldered the burden and began the discharge of the arduous duties attached thereto. We may, perhaps, search for the secret of his strength : we shall find it in his unbounded confidence in God, his humble diffidence of self.

During the short period of his Provincialship he effected extraordinary and lasting results for the good of the Congregation of the Most Holy Redeemer.

The establishment of the Redemptorists at New Orleans was principally owing to his energy.

In the fall of 1843 Father Czackert went to New Orleans to collect for the building of St. Philomena's Church, Pittsburg. Archbishop Blanc received him most cordially, offered him the hospitality of the archiepiscopal mansion, and entreated him to take an interest in the spiritual concerns of the German Catholics of the city. Father Czackert willingly assented to the wishes of the Archbishop, earnestly hoping, at the same time, that Superiors would at some future day consent to make a foundation there.

Service for the Germans was held at first in the French chapel of St. Vincent de Paul. But soon after Father Czackert removed to that part of the city which is called Lafayette, where he hired a hall from the Protestants and fitted it up for a chapel. On December 3, 1843, he bought near Josephine Street some lots on which to erect a temporary church. The building materials were collected and the work about to be begun when Father Czackert was called away by his Superiors. But as the Archbishop was fully determined that the post should be held by the Redemptorists, Father Kundek continued the building of the church in their name. On January 14, 1844, the corner-stone was laid, and on April 14th of the same year the church was solemnly dedicated under the title of the Assumption of the Blessed Virgin. In 1847 Father Czackert's hopes for the foundation of a house of his Congregation in New Orleans were realized, and he was deputed by his Superiors to begin the work. He started on his mission with Louis Kenning, a lay-brother, who proved himself a most faithful companion.

The Archbishop was greatly rejoiced at the success of his enterprise. He installed Father Czackert himself as pastor of the German church, and expressed his wish for the Fathers to take charge also of the English and the French parishes in the same part of the city.

Shortly after, Father Neumann sent two Fathers and two lay-brothers to New Orleans to assist those already there. In the summer of 1848 Brother Louis opened a school with only fourteen scholars on the first day; at the end of a month the number had increased to forty.

The early foundation of this house was marked by great trials. Poverty, added to hardships and contradictions of all kinds here, as in other places, fell to the lot of the sons of St. Alphonsus. In addition to all this, yellow fever, that terrible scourge of New Orleans, raged in the city. In September both the Fathers and Brothers were stricken down by the disease. Not one was left to nurse his brethren. The Vicar-General of the diocese and other members of the clergy magnanimously offered them every relief; they nursed the sick and attended to their pastoral duties. But alas! despite the care bestowed upon him, good Father Czackert succumbed to the violence of the disease. He, the zealous founder of the Redemptorists in New Orleans was the first in the long line of victims to the dreadful, scourge recorded in the annals of the Congregation.

His death occurred September 2, 1848, just five years after his first visit to New Orleans.

Father Petesch now stood alone in the midst of an overwhelming amount of labor. He longed for assistance, but none could be granted, as Superiors could not conscientiously send a Father to New Orleans whilst the fever was raging. Father Neumann's kind heart was torn by the thought of the good Father's isolated position. He consoled and encouraged him by his letters, and that was all he could then do. One of his letters ran thus:

"I am truly concerned about you, dear Father, not only on account of the immense weight of duty that now devolves upon you, but also for your health and your life. Your heroic resolution to remain and, if needs be, die at your post is, indeed, a subject of consolation to all your brethren, as well as to myself. It would, however, be a heavy blow to us to lose you. May God's holy will be done!" Father Neumann goes on to express his deep regret at being unable to send Fathers to New Orleans whilst the epidemic was raging, since one not acclimated would surely fall a victim to its attacks.

About this period, Father Neumann turned his eyes toward Cumberland, a flourishing town in the northwestern part of Maryland, wherein to establish a new foundation. For years the Redemptorist Fathers from Baltimore had visited the German Catholics of Cumberland, and administered to them the consolations of religion. Father Neumann when in Baltimore had himself often made the journey of one hundred and eighty miles—a journey long enough in those days—for the same purpose; and the beautiful situation of the little town was not lost on him. He now set about realizing his plan of a foundation, deputing Father Urbanzek and Brother Adam to begin the good work. His first care was for the church, which he resolved should be spacious enough to accommodate a large congregation. On June 4, 1848, the corner-stone of the present church of Sts. Peter and Paul was laid by Archbishop Eccleston, of Baltimore. September 23d of the following year beheld the dedication of the same by Rev. Father Bernard, who had succeeded Father Neumann as Provincial. The magnificent site of the convent, perched as it is on a hill, joined to the healthfulness of the locality, suggested, even at that early date, the idea of establishing there the novitiate and House of Studies. This project was carried out at a later period.

The early history of the Cumberland foundation records its share of crosses and difficulties; but it prospered in the end and soon became the favorite spot of the Redemptorists, who for many years attended the faithful far and near and formed them into parishes. At the present day, these various stations, the fruits of the zeal and labors of the Redemptorist Fathers, can boast their own churches and pastors.

The same period beheld Father Neumann's energies directed to a second undertaking similar to the one above recorded, viz., the foundation of a convent in Buffalo. In October, 1847, a new church, one hundred and eighty by eighty feet, was begun. On April 9th of the following year, which happened to fall on Easter-Monday, Bishop Timon laid the corner-stone of St. Mary's of the Immaculate Conception. On the last Sunday of July, 1850, the church was consecrated.

Another important foundation made under Father Neumann's direction was that of St. Alphonsus, in the southwestern part of New York City. Father Rumpler, a man burning with zeal for souls, had long felt the necessity of providing a church for the German Catholics of that quarter. Father Neumann took a lively interest in the project, and aided Father Rumpler to carry out his plans. On September 18, 1847, the corner-stone was laid, and two months later, November 25th, the church of St. Alphonsus was dedicated. The first pastor of the new congregation was Father Tappert, whose chief object was to provide a school-house for the children. The blessing of God rested on the whole undertaking; for on the site of the old church has since arisen a spacious and magnificent edifice in the Romanesque style. The sons of St. Alphonsus have here as elsewhere developed great and successful results for the glory of God and the salvation of souls.

Father Neumann did not restrict his zeal to the government of the houses of the Congregation entrusted to his care as Provincial. He also promoted with special predilection and personal activity the great work of the missions, a work which forms the principal end of the Congregation. Through his instrumentality, Bishop Rappe, of Cleveland, petitioned for missions throughout all the parishes of his diocese. During these missions, Father Neumann, in his humility and modesty, always chose for himself the less conspicuous and more wearying part, such as early morning instruction and the recitation of the Rosary before the evening sermon. In the confessional he was indefatigable; the whole day long, from dawn till late at night, found him at his post.

Father Neumann understood equally well the great importance of retreats for priests and religious; therefore he devoted special attention to such exercises. From their priests the people imbibe faith and piety. If the priest is a man of faith and prayer, he will infuse his own spirit into the souls committed to his care. Such gifts and graces are communicated to the clergy in a special manner by means of retreats. These life-giving exercises Father Neumann frequently conducted himself with equal facility in German, French, and English. His humble bearing in presence of the clergy and religious was the source of great edification, a silent sermon in itself, whilst the lively faith, the ardent love of God, embodied in his discourses moved the hearts of his hearers and produced much fruit.

His exertions were not confined to works at a distance; he took an active part in the ministry among his own parishioners of Baltimore, where, as Vice-Provincial, he was also local Superior. In 1847 he made such changes in the house adjoining St. Alphonsus' Church as would render it suitable for a convent, and he gathered around him a large community whose members led a truly edifying religious life. The present beautiful Gothic church was built under the superintendence of Father Alexander, and on March 14, 1845, was dedicated by Archbishop Eccleston. It is a spacious edifice crowned by a steeple two hundred and twenty feet in height—an ornament to the neighborhood in which it stands.

The pulpit, the confessional, the schools, the sick—all were special objects of Father Neumann's zeal. Austere toward himself, condescending toward others, affable and obliging toward those with whom he came in contact, he won his way with all; he was beloved by his own brethren, by the secular clergy, and by the faithful at large. The most difficult and trying duties, and those attended by the least *éclat* were his by right of choice. The Sunday explanation of the Christian Doctrine, sick-calls at night, catechetical instructions to converts late in the evening—all such duties he reserved for himself. It was a touching and edifying sight—the crowds, young and old, that flocked on Sunday afternoons to hear the divine truths from the lips of him who so well understood how to speak to both mind and heart in a clear, practical, apostolic way.

The training of the students of the Congregation was another work dear to Father Neumann's heart. "The novitiate and the House of Studies," he used to say, "are the seminaries of the Congregation; from them are our missionaries to go forth. If the students are educated according to the spirit of St. Alphonsus, the Congregation will continue to correspond to the end for which it was established."

The house attached to St. James's, Baltimore, was in course of time found too small for the purposes originally intended. The novitiate was therefore transferred to Pittsburg. Father Seelos, a pious and enlightened religious, was appointed Novice-Master, an office for which he was eminently qualified. The professed students were retained in Baltimore, that, under Father Neumann's watchful care, they might dispose themselves for their sublime vocation. For their special accommodation, he erected a house adjoining St. Alphonsus'.

On September 26, 1847, Father Neumann wrote to his family in Bohemia. We give his letter almost entire, as from it we glean some particulars connected with his labors in Baltimore. He writes:

"MY VERY DEAR PARENTS AND SISTERS:

"The reason of my long silence is that nothing new has occurred either to brother Wenceslaus or myself. The former is now in Pittsburg and I am in Baltimore. Our German parish is always on the increase. Before I went to Pittsburg, two priests could more easily accomplish here what it now requires seven to perform. We have charge of three schools, and Protestants are constantly coming for instruction in our holy religion. They generally end by entering the Church, after which many of them show their gratitude to God by leading a Christian life such as is seldom witnessed in Europe. Eighty-five adults, one third of them negroes, were last year received into the Church.

"It would give me great pleasure to hear from Prachatitz and my old schoolmates. I occasionally receive books and money from the Society of St. Leopold, but who the benefactors are I do not know. Since brother Wenceslaus' arrival I have no news from home.

"As we now have a house and church in New Orleans,

Louisiana, I have begun to study Spanish. At thirty-six I have again become a child and am learning grammar. But this is of little importance."

This letter rouses our admiration of the writer's deep humility. Not one word in reference to the responsible post he then occupied as Vice-Provincial.

The schools again came in for a large share of Father Neumann's attention. For four months, from July to November, he was busy with the building of a new school-house opposite the Redemptorist convent, Baltimore. It was known later as St. Alphonsus' Hall, and was in 1873 totally destroyed by fire.

It may be interesting to insert here the testimony of an eye-witness respecting the influence Father Neumann brought to bear upon the work so dear to his heart, the mental and moral training of the young. A Sister of the Order of Notre Dame speaks as follows of this period:

"When Father Neumann was Superior of St. Alphonsus' in Baltimore, I had charge of the girls' school; consequently I had ample opportunity to admire his virtues and eminent qualities. He was an accomplished catechist and a great lover of children. His gentleness, meekness, and perseverance in communicating religious instruction to the children often awoke my astonishment, and the salutary impression he made upon even the most faulty and troublesome of our little people was quite remarkable. The young delinquents would freely avow to him their faults, their deviations from the truth, their petty thefts, etc. His mere glance seemed to contain in it something of the all-seeing attribute of God, so did it penetrate their souls. They often said to me, 'Sister, Father Neumann looked right into my heart.'

"I had the bad habit," the same Sister continues, "of speaking in a high tone and of losing patience whilst teaching; but after Father Neumann had surprised me in this fault once or twice, I learned how to correct. He used to enter the school-room so quietly, so modestly, that sometimes I did not perceive him until greeted with the words, 'Sister, I thought I heard you screaming just now,' and then he would fix his large, expressive eyes upon me so earnestly that there was no mistaking his meaning."

Wherever the honor of God and the salvation of souls could be promoted, Father Neumann was ready for any sacrifice. A new field for his zeal was soon opened before him. The Sisters of Providence (colored) occupied at this period a convent on North Park Street. They exercised the same vocation then as they do now in their new and more commodious convent, viz., the care of an orphan asylum and a boarding-school for colored children. The worthy Sisters accomplished much good, but from lack of funds, and still more on account of the want of spiritual assistance, the community was in danger of being dissolved. God raised up for them a true friend in the person of Father Neumann, who in all things connected with them manifested a lively interest. In 1847 he took charge of them, held divine service in their chapel for the benefit of the colored people, instructed the orphans, and rendered every assistance in his power. Under his wise and holy direction their institution prospered, the number of religious increased from three to sixteen, and their pupils from fifteen to one hundred and thirteen. When, later on, his zeal was directed to the establishment of other similar institutions, he transferred the care of this community to Father Anwander, C.SS.R., who earnestly contributed to the maintenance of its prosperity.

As confessor of the Carmelite Nuns, Baltimore, Father Neumann led these daughters of St. Teresa onward in the path of perfection. The survivors among those that had the happiness to share his wise direction speak of him in the following terms: "Rev. Father Neumann contributed largely to the perfection of our Sisters.

His exhortations and instructions were animated by his own enthusiasm for the honor of God, the sublime end of the religious state. They inflamed our heart with an ardent desire for religious perfection, for a total oblation to God."

The year 1847 afforded Father Neumann an opportunity for calling into existence another great work, one whose wide-spread and lasting influence has done much in behalf of Christian education in America. In August of this year there arrived in Baltimore from Munich, Bavaria, five School-Sisters of Notre Dame, who came to seek in the United States a new field for their labors. Rev. Mother Teresa, Superioress-General of the Sisters, headed the little band. She wished to see for herself whether America could supply the kind of work suitable to the vocation of her religious. The coming of these Sisters was wholly unexpected, and therefore no preparations had been made for their reception. But Father Neumann actively bestirred himself in their behalf, gave them advice, and furnished them with whatever they needed. He procured hospitality for them in the different convents of the city until they could obtain employment in some school. For this they had not long to wait, as he entrusted to them the schools attached to St. James's Church, giving them for their convent the commodious dwelling adjoining the same. A short time after, St. Alphonsus' school also was transferred to their management. Father Neumann did not, however, content himself with appointing them to the charge of the three female schools under his own jurisdiction in Baltimore; he recommended them likewise to the Bishops of various dioceses as exemplary religious and excellent teachers.

In the fall of 1848 Rev. Mother Teresa was to return to Munich; but before taking leave of the United States she deemed it expedient to visit some of the more important cities, that she might be able to decide which would be most suitable for foundations of her Congregation. Sister Mary Caroline accompanied her as companion, and Father Neumann resolved to make one of the party himself on their long and wearisome trip. Sister Caroline, now Mother Caroline, is at present Superioress of the Sisters of Notre Dame in America. During her tour through the States she had many opportunities for observing the virtues of her reverend guide and patron—opportunities that she failed not to improve, and that afforded her room to admire his saintly qualities. We shall record a few of the edifying incidents she relates in connection with that journey. She says:

"We visited Pittsburg, Cleveland, Milwaukee, New York, and Philadelphia. We travelled by land and by water, by steamboat and stage-coach, Father Neumann perseveringly embracing every opportunity to give me lessons in English.

"He was one of the most patient of men, contented with anything and everything. I often saw him buy some biscuits for a few cents and make them serve for a meal. He would sit apart quietly eating them. I also noticed that, even during the greatest heat of the day, he never took a glass of water.

"On one occasion a rude fellow who was on the same boat with us called the Father an 'accursed priest;' but the only answer he received was a friendly glance and gentle smile. The man slunk away, apparently ashamed of his rudeness.

"Our progress on one of the steamboats was retarded by low water. Father Neumann was sitting on deck, and, being overcome by weariness, he fell asleep. Some mischievous boys were near, and they no sooner beheld the reverend gentleman dozing than they began to play pranks upon him. With a piece of chalk they covered his back with little crosses. I saw what the young scamps had done, and when the Father awoke I offered to brush them off. But, not in the least disturbed by the trick played upon him, he quietly replied, 'Oh, it is not necessary; they will rub off of themselves.'

"This man of God was, in truth, the instrument of Divine Providence in spreading and firmly establishing the Congregation of the School-Sisters in the United States. We may justly regard him as our founder in America. We were, besides, so happy as to have him for five years as our confessor and spiritual adviser. We had ample time and opportunity for discovering his learning, his kind-heartedness, and his sanctity. He was our spiritual director till his elevation to the episcopate. Between the years 1847 and '52 he must have trodden the road from St. Alphonsus' to St. James's at least a thousand times to hear our confessions and to give us conferences, retreats, etc. Like Bishop Wittman, he understood the art of fostering in others that true religious spirit which had become a second nature to himself. His zeal for souls was simply indefatigable. He showed the deepest interest in our ceremonies, particularly those of reception to the habit and the profession of vows. We were extremely happy under his wise and paternal direction. We have indeed every reason to revere him as our founder in America."

Up to the present we have closely observed and no less ardently admired Father Neumann's unrelenting zeal in the practice of those virtues that go to make up the perfect religious. But if we contemplate his life with a view of discovering what virtue most distinguished him, we shall find it difficult to decide. He had formed the resolution, and he kept it inviolably, of sedulously imitating the virtues of his holy founder, St. Alphonsus, especially his unremitting ardor for the glory of God, his spirit of prayer, his humility, meekness, self-denial, and disinterestedness. Of all these virtues, any single one of which practised for the love of God would form a saint, it seems to us that Father Neumann excelled in the most difficult—humility. This virtue was in him truly unfeigned. Occasionally it gave rise to amusing incidents. One morning, at an unusually early hour, he arrived in New York and sought admittance at the Redemptorist convent. The porter, a postulant lately come to the house, answered the bell. When he saw a little man in the garb of a priest, and rather shabby withal, standing at the door, his first thought was, "This must be the sacristan from Bloomingdale. He has come early to borrow our dalmatics." Then addressing the stranger, he said, "Well, what do you want?"

"I should like to see the Superior, Father Rumpler. Is he at home?"

"Yes," answered the Brother. "He is at home."

"What is your name, Brother?" asked the stranger with a smile.

"I am Brother N——," answered the postulant, as he turned into the house to call the Superior. Father Neumann made a move as if to follow him, when the Brother stopped short, exclaiming, "Stay here, if you please. Take a seat on that bench, whilst I go call the Superior." And as he went he muttered to himself quite loud enough for the stranger's ears, "This sacristan is inquisitive. He asks my name, and even wants to enter the cloister."

Father Neumann smiled, and seated himself where he had been directed. After the lapse of a few minutes, Brother N—— again appeared, this time with the inquiry,

"Who are you? What is your name?"

"I am Father Neumann," was the gentle answer.

"Father Neumann!" repeated the astonished porter. "Oh, if you are one of the Fathers, pray come in."

Father Neumann entered and followed Brother N—— to the Superior's room, where, to his amazement, he beheld Father Rumpler fall on his knees before the stranger and ask a blessing.

The poor Brother was quite bewildered. Ashamed of the reception he had given the Father Provincial and a little in dread of the result to himself, he avoided meeting him. But Father Neumann sent for him, spoke to him kindly, and set him entirely at his ease by telling him that he had faithfully performed his duty as porter. "However," added he with a significant smile, "do not get into the habit of thinking aloud."

Father Neumann sought occasions of humbling himself and of being humbled as eagerly as others try to shun them. It is customary for Superiors in Redemptorist communities to kiss the feet of their brethren on Thursdays and publicly accuse themselves of their faults. Such acts of self-abasement were dear to the heart of our humble Father, who performed them with so great fervor and holy joy as to leave their impress on his countenance. Kind-hearted and gentle in his intercourse with his brethren, as we have before remarked, he knew how to detect and to banish their temptations in a manner peculiar to himself. No one ever addressed himself to him under the pressure of interior trial without finding consolation, instruction, and support.

A venerable old Father relates that in 1847 he asked Father Neumann's permission to make a pilgrimage to Jerusalem. To lend weight to the arguments he brought forward in support of his cause, he quoted a passage from the writings of St. Alphonsus, and related the following example from the Middle Ages: "Once upon a time there lived in France a good old monk who conceived a desire similar to that which now urged him, viz., to make a pilgrimage to the Holy Places. He made known his wishes to his Abbot, who not only accorded him permission to do so, but even supplied him with money for the journey—forty bright gold pieces. Moreover, to show their appreciation of their confrère's undertaking, several of his brethren accompanied him barefoot for some days, singing psalms and reciting prayers as they went." But as in our own days this style of making pilgrimages is no longer feasible, the Father declared that he would content himself with the permission of his Superior, dispensing with the accompanying features—the barefooted monks, the psalms, and the prayers. Father Neumann listened quietly to the projected journey, praised the good old Father's fervor and piety which suggested a visit to the Holy Sepulchre, and expressed his interest in the story of the old French monk. He ended, however, by advising the Father to pray for some time that God would make known to him whether his desire proceeded from Him or was a delusion of the evil one. And so the pilgrimage ended. Far from taxing the good old Father with imprudence or extravagance, Father Neumann thus kindly and considerately dissipated what he knew to be merely an idle temptation.

In important affairs Father Neumann ever refrained from a decision founded merely upon his own opinions and sentiments. Though a man of vast erudition and great experience, he constantly mistrusted his own strength, and in every question submitted to him he betook himself to prayer. Following in the footsteps of the wise and spiritual men that had gone before him, he sought the advice of the Consultors assigned him by his rule. Then whatever resolution had, after mature deliberation, been adopted, he carried out in his own quiet though resolute manner.

Above all things else he had at heart the preservation and increase of the religious spirit; for his principle of action was this, that whatever labors were undertaken in behalf of souls, must, to be pleasing to God and conducive to the end in view, spring from a pure intention and a true love of His Divine Majesty. Therefore he insisted on self-sanctification as the first requisite in the sublime work of the ministry, and required of all under his charge the acquisition of holiness chiefly by the exact observance of rule. This he could all the more lawfully exact as he himself was a model of every virtue, a living exemplification of every rule, of every custom, of the Congregation. As Vice-Provincial no more than as a simple subject would he allow the least exception in his own favor. His superiority entitled him to no privileges excepting that of choosing whatever was most difficult and unpleasant for himself.

Defects which could not at once be remedied contributed not a little to increase the care and anxiety of so conscientious a Superior as was Father Neumann. In his solicitude for exact observance he undertook the translation of the rule from the Italian, and he employed every means in his power, mildness and earnestness, kindness and firmness, to restore regular discipline wherever it had suffered. We find this translation among his manuscripts. It is a leather-back book, pocket size, copied out most carefully in his own handwriting. Its appearance indicates its having been carried about with him, and the ornamentation of the title-page bespeaks the childlike love and reverence he entertained for its contents. In another book of the same kind he copied all the prayers and acts of devotion usually recited by the members of the Congregation.

Nor was less zeal displayed by Father Neumann in the annual visitation of the houses under his charge. He entered into the minutest details on such occasions, and used every means to supply whatever deficiencies might be at the time existing. In one house he found a want for which he at once provided, viz., the tablet on which, as the rule prescribes, are recorded the annual patrons, with the virtues and prayers assigned by lot to every member of the Congregation. Nothing escaped his vigilance: the least shared with the greatest his serious attention. In word and in writing he exhorted Superiors to procure, as far as possible, books the most suitable for the promotion of science and the advancement of the spirit of the Congregation, and many a donation of this kind he himself made to houses of limited means.

In perusing the lives of the greatest servants of God we are often impressed by the extraordinary sufferings and persecutions endured by them, sometimes even at the hands of their nearest friends, sometimes from those bound to them by special ties of love and gratitude. St. Alphonsus, as we know, was no exception to this almost general rule; and do we not hear the Apostle to the Gentiles enumerating among his trials those he was called upon to endure from "false brethren"? Almighty God permits His chosen ones to suffer in this way that they may heap up treasures of merit, may seek for nothing outside of Himself. Through this ordeal, so bitter, so galling, to a soul sensitive as his, Father Neumann had to pass. But like unto the palm-tree, which raises its stately head in bolder grandeur "the more the winds beat and the more the rains fall," his beautiful soul grew nobler, stronger; his virtue was perfected in the fiery furnace of tribulation.

The time drew near for Father Neumann to be relieved of the burden of the Vice-Provincialship; but it came not quickly enough to satisfy the craving of his soul after the humble station of an inferior.

On January 9, 1849, Father Bernard Hafkenscheid arrived from Europe in quality of Vice-Provincial, the Consultors appointed him being Father Neumann and Father Rumpler. We shall not follow Father Bernard in the discharge of his new office. Suffice it to say, that he governed with a firm and secure hand the convents which he received in a flourishing condition from his predecessor.

Relieved from the responsibilities of office, Father Neumann once more breathed freely. His cell was his favorite resort, the practice of obedience his joy, and to be able to devote himself unreservedly to the work of the ministry his highest aim in life.

On August 28, 1850, Father Bernard sailed for Europe to be present at a meeting of the Superiors of the Congregation, leaving Father Neumann to hold his place during his absence—a period of six months. By this mark of confidence Father Bernard clearly manifested his own private opinion of Father Neumann. He regarded the complaints made of the ex-Vice-Provincial as wholly unfounded, and by this public act he vindicated his saintly predecessor. In a letter to New Orleans, dated January 10, 1851, Father Neumann makes these remarks: "God be praised we have more work than we can do! Numerous missions are called for; we are putting forth every effort to meet them all. New Orleans will soon be attended to. Father C—— is very anxious to take part in that mission, and so too is your humble servant."

In the government of the Congregation a great change had taken place. Rev. Father Passerat was succeeded, July 1, 1850, by Father Smetena as Vicar-General. The Congregation in America was definitively raised to a province, and the houses of St. Alphonsus in Baltimore, of St. Philomena in Pittsburg, and of the Most Holy Redeemer in New York, were made Rectorates. Father Bernard returned, March 20, 1851, as the first Provincial of the Redemptorists in America.

Father Neumann received his appointment as first Rector of St. Alphonsus, Baltimore, discharging at the same time the office of Consultor to the Provincial. As Rector, he chose for himself the smallest cell in the house—a room unpleasantly located near to the entrance. This he did to be at hand for any disagreeable or difficult duty that might present itself; for, esteeming himself the servant of all, he held himself in readiness for every emergency. His love for his brethren was truly paternal; his solicitude was akin to that of a tender mother for her child. Did a Father fail to return home at the appointed hour, Father Neumann was all anxiety on his account. He would refuse to retire on such occasions, so great was his fear for the safety of the absent one. A certain Father relates that once only did he receive a severe reprimand, and that was from the gentle Father Neumann. He, the Father that tells this incident of himself, had been on duty at one of the neighboring stations, from which he returned toward midnight. "Father Rector," he says, "met me at the door, whither he had repeatedly gone during the evening to make inquiries of the Brother-Porter concerning me."

In the spring and fall he used to examine the clothing of the community himself, in order to supply promptly whatever might be needed. It was with a true father's joy that he sought to surprise his subjects by causing to be laid in their cells some new article of clothing instead of the well-worn garment accustomed to be found there. He insisted earnestly upon the strict observance of poverty; for instance, carelessly to allow crumbs to fall on the floor, to cut bread on the table-cloth thereby endangering the latter, he designated as faults against this holy vow.

He sought both by word and example to maintain the community-life among his subjects, whilst at the same time he was watchful to make things as pleasant as possible to them. In his weekly conferences he often repeated the words, "Fraternal charity and love for the Congregation must be the bonds by which its members will be united into one blessed family." In this, as in all other things, his own manner of acting afforded an example for imitation. Always cheerful in recreation, he entertained his companions with useful and interesting conversation. He spoke in rather a low tone, and nothing in his manner could in the least betray a consciousness of superior knowledge or mark him out as holding the first place among his brethren. His intercourse with the learned and the unlearned was therefore most pleasing and enlivening. Sometimes he would sing a hymn softly, accompanying himself on the piano.

If in scientific discussions the Fathers happened to differ in opinion,—and indeed this was often the case,—Father Neumann would keep silence until each had delivered his opinion freely. Then, taking up the thread of discourse, he would consider the question in its every bearing and draw conclusions satisfactory to all. His judgment was received as trustworthy, and in difficult cases his opinions were held as conclusive. His mildness, his gentle considerateness, exhibited in such disputes were really admirable; his conversation and writings breathed naught but benevolence. In 1851 he wrote several letters to his relatives in Bohemia, which are all expressive of his characteristic gentleness. For some years he had received no letters from his family. Now he begs them in the most affectionate terms to write to him, whilst he thanks for the letters last received. We subjoin a few passages:

"MY BELOVED FATHER AND VERY DEAR SISTERS:

"Brother Wenceslaus and I had given up all hope of ever hearing again from our dear home, when we were most unexpectedly rejoiced by the arrival of a letter from our dear cousin, George Zahn, and another, a short time ago, from sister Caroline. We had been long anxiously desiring to hear from home. I cannot conceive how your letters could have gone astray. It would be a great consolation to us to know the date of dear mother's death, also that of our sister Veronica and all our other friends and relatives lately deceased, that we may be able to celebrate their anniversaries.

"We thank the Lord our God for having called us to this holy Congregation of St. Alphonsus. With the exception of some slight indisposition, my health has been excellent; and notwithstanding my constant journeying by sea and by land, in steam-cars and on horseback, I have never met with an accident. This special mark of God's protection I ascribe chiefly to your prayers. Although no day passes without my longing to be among my dear relatives and friends, yet I never regret having devoted myself to the missionary work here. I recognize it as my vocation to labor for the honor of God among our poor Germans of North America. The labors of all my brethren are visibly blessed by Almighty God, and I confidently hope and trust that God will keep us, each and all, in His holy grace, and give us after death the reward promised to those that have left earthly things to follow Him. In this reward our dear parents will participate, since they made the sacrifice of allowing us to leave them. That I should leave you was, without doubt, the will of God. I trust He will unite us all in heaven, where there will be no separation."

In December, 1851, he again wrote to his father:

"The two churches of which we now have charge in Baltimore are crowded every Sunday, especially at High Mass. In about six weeks the third church for the Germans will be finished, and it, too, will be filled on Sundays. That God has protected us in every danger and blessed all our labors, we must no doubt ascribe to your prayers and those of all the friends of the missions. The world is converted more by fervent and continued prayer than by any other means. We beg you, therefore, and all our friends and relatives in Prachatitz and its neighborhood, to offer fervent petitions to the Lord, along with the Holy Sacrifice of the Mass, that He may continue to bless our labors."

The inward peace and happiness that Father Neumann tasted in his vocation may be detected in the following words addressed by him one evening in recreation to a good lay-brother:

"Oh what a blessing it is to live in the Congregation, especially here in America! Here we can really love

God. We can labor much for Him, and all so quietly, quite unnoticed by the world."

In the fall of 1851, about six months previously to Father Neumann's elevation to the episcopacy, Brother Athanasius, a very pious and edifying lay-brother living in the Redemptorist convent of Pittsburg, asserted that he had had a vision in which he saw Father Neumann habited in the episcopal robes and environed with splendor. Father Seelos, Brother Athanasius' Superior, and himself a disciple of Father Neumann, writing to the latter about the same time, mentioned it casually, with a few pleasant words on the same. Father Neumann's humility took fright at the mere thought of such a thing coupled with his name. In his answer to Father Seelos' letter he says, "Tell that good Brother that, if he is not already crazed, to pray that he may not become so." Severe words from the gentle Father Neumann! The event, however, soon proved the good Brother's sanity.

During Father Neumann's rectorship at St. Alphonsus', Baltimore, Archbishop Kenrick was in the habit of paying a weekly visit to the convent. With that heavenly intuition which springs from nearness to God, the holy Archbishop had not failed to recognize in the humble Redemptorist a soul bearing the same genuine stamp as his own; he saw in him the saint, and chose him for his confessor. In one of his visits he communicated to Father Neumann a piece of intelligence that had come to him privately, viz., that he, Father Neumann, had been preconized Bishop of Philadelphia. He added jokingly, "My dear Father, you had better see about getting yourself a mitre."

We can imagine Father Neumann's consternation. Throwing himself on his knees, he begged the Archbishop with tears to have compassion on him, to avert from him a dignity for which he was wholly unsuited. Moved by his deep humility and unaffected distress, the

Archbishop promised to use his influence to prevent the episcopal dignity's being imposed upon him. But Father Neumann was only half reassured by the Archbishop's promise. He wrote at once to Father Queloz, the Procurator-General of the Congregation in Rome, beseeching him to exert every means in his power to prevent the appointment. He did not rest here; he had recourse to prayer, the efficacy of which he had so often tested, and sought to prevail upon Almighty God to spare him so heavy a trial. Any other cross, any other burden, seemed preferable to the one impending over him. He begged the Divine Spirit to enlighten those who had been guilty of so grave an error as to fix their eyes upon his lowliness in connection with so exalted an office. He appealed to all the holy souls in the circle of his acquaintance, and they were not few, to unite their prayers with his to avert so great a calamity from the Church and from himself. He had novenas made in religious houses to ward off, as he told them, a great danger from one of the dioceses of America. The Fathers of his own convent said daily the seven penitential psalms for the same end. But Almighty God's designs were not to be thwarted. He had marked out this His favored servant for one of the highest stations in the Church, and the time had come for the accomplishment of the Divine Will. The light of this humble, faithful son of St. Alphonsus had shone for many years with a lustre not to be ignored by any one of those with whom the duties of his ministry brought him in contact: now, however, this light was to acquire new brilliancy; now it was to shed its beams over a still wider field of action—it was to be set upon a still more honorable candlestick.

On March 19, 1852, the feast of the glorious patriarch St. Joseph, Father Neumann after a short absence entered his little cell about dusk. As he stepped toward the small table at which he was accustomed to read and write, his glance discovered something on it sparkling and glistening in the dim evening light. He drew near, and found lying there an episcopal ring and pectoral cross. Perplexed, and not daring to collect his thoughts, he hurried to the Brother-Porter to know who had entered his room during his absence. "Reverend Father," said the Brother, "the Archbishop was here, and went up to your room as usual to make his confession." This was enough for poor Father Neumann. The truth dawned upon his mind; he understood only too well the meaning of the episcopal insignia laid upon his table. Without a word he hastened with a faltering step back to his room, locked the door, and threw himself on his knees. Morning came and found him still kneeling in the same spot where, in the agony of his soul, he had wrestled with God through the long hours of night. He had prayed, and he was heard—but not according to his desires. He had prayed, and Almighty God, in conformity with His own eternal designs, granted him the strength to carry the burden it was His gracious pleasure to lay upon him —to carry it nobly and generously for the honor of that same good God, for his own sanctification, and for the salvation of many souls.

Next morning the Archbishop presented Father Neumann the Bulls of his appointment, together with the formal command of the Holy Father enjoining his acceptance of the see of Philadelphia.

Father Neumann was a true son of St. Alphonsus; a Redemptorist heart and soul, his only desire was to live and die a Redemptorist. Honors and dignities, be they even ecclesiastical, were thoroughly distasteful to him. We have not followed him thus far in his saintly career without arriving at such a conviction; but Rome had spoken. There was now nothing left to her obedient son but to recognize in the command of the Holy Father the declared will of God, and to submit to that adorable will at any cost.

In compliance with Father Neumann's urgent and reiterated requests, every effort had been made in Rome to procure his escape from the dreaded dignity, but all in vain. Father Queloz, the Procurator-General of the Congregation of the Most Holy Redeemer, wrote to the Provincial at Vienna as follows:

"The news of Father Neumann's nomination to a Bishopric will doubtless cause you pain. All our efforts were fruitless. His Eminence Cardinal Altieri, with the papers in his hands, defended our cause before the Congregation of the Propaganda. He had four of the Cardinals on his side, but the majority voted for Father Neumann, whom the American Bishops had placed second on the list. Monsignore Barnabo, Secretary of the Congregation, communicated to His Holiness the result of the election, and made use of the occasion to say a word in our behalf. But Pius IX. replied, 'I bear the Redemptorist Fathers in my heart. They have done in this matter what God willed they should do. I am confident that He will not refuse me the light to discern what the good of the Church in general and of the Congregation in particular demands of me. Therefore I sanction the choice of the Cardinals, and I command Father Neumann under formal obedience (*sub obedientiâ formali*) to accept the diocese of Philadelphia without further appeal.'"

The Bulls were expedited on February 1, 1852, and reached the Archbishop of Baltimore on the evening of March 19th. After an interview with Father Neumann the Archbishop fixed upon the 28th of the same month as the day for the consecration. This date was doubly memorable in the life of the young Bishop-elect as being the day of his birth as well as that of his baptism. On the next anniversary he would complete his forty-first year. A remarkable coincidence in these dates, and one not without deep significance, is the fact that Good Friday of the year 1811, the year of Father Neumann's birth, fell upon the 28th of March. The same date fell in 1852, the year of his episcopal consecration, upon Passion-Sunday. It was, as we have remarked, a concurrence of dates and feasts that failed not to make an impression upon him, in whose life they stand out with noticeable prominence. Father Neumann recognized in it an expression of God's designs over him—trials and sufferings were to be the portion of the cup now presented to his lips. Following out the thoughts thereby suggested, he chose for his device the words, "*Passio Christi, conforta me!*—Passion of Christ, strengthen me!"

The Provincial of the Congregation, Father Bernard, resolved that the consecration of this, one of its most humble and most worthy sons, should be attended by all due pomp and solemnity. He took charge of the preparations himself, and directed all things connected with it on a liberal and becoming scale. Meanwhile he for whom all this stir was being made entered upon a retreat of eight days, glad to shut himself away for even that short period from the thought of the break about to be made in the loved tenor of his conventual life.

On the Sunday preceding the great solemnity, Father Bernard announced from the pulpit of St. Alphonsus' that one week from that day, Passion-Sunday, the Rector, Father Neumann, would be consecrated in that church. He also recommended the Bishop-elect to the prayers of the faithful. "If," said he, "you were at this moment to search for Father Rector you would find him on his knees in prayer, begging from God the strength and grace necessary for the new and onerous charge laid upon him."

Father Bernard addressed the community in the same strain. After holding Father Neumann up to them as a model of every virtue, as a true Redemptorist, he emphasized the fact that only by the express command of the Holy Father had he been induced to accept the episcopal dignity; that as he had ever been an obedient son of

St. Alphonsus, he now humbly submitted to the Holy Father, whatever pain such submission might cost him.

The news of Father Neumann the Redemptorist's appointment as Bishop of Philadelphia soon spread throughout Europe and America. It created, of course, its own share of excitement, and gave rise to varied and contradictory remarks. Some held that to fill so important a see as Philadelphia a Bishop of American birth should have been chosen; that he should be conspicuous for his eloquence and fine address; that a religious wedded to prayer and the seclusion of his convent, who shrunk from ecclesiastical honors and distinctions, was entirely unsuited for so elevated a dignity. Others, on the contrary, regarded the new appointment with favor, and expected much from the Bishop-elect. King Louis of Bavaria wrote as follows to his chaplain, Rev. Father Müller: "Father Neumann the Redemptorist has been appointed Bishop of Philadelphia, and the appointment has been confirmed by the Holy Father. This is a subject for joy. It will exert a powerful and beneficial influence not only on the interests of the Church at large, but it will contribute also in a very particular manner to the promotion of Christian education, to true culture."

In Philadelphia itself private opinion ran in countercurrents. Many were in favor of the new appointment; others (and such are ever to be found), with very little, perhaps no knowledge of the merits or demerits of the new incumbent, adopted opposite views; yet all were edified at the fact of Father Neumann's having been constrained by a formal obedience from the Holy Father to accept the dignity.

The Cathedral of Philadelphia was not at this period completed; it had in fact but just been commenced. The Congregation attended the churches in their nearest vicinity—St. Patrick's, St. John's, etc. But two of the parlors in the episcopal residence had been fitted up as a chapel. Here the Holy Sacrifice was offered, the parishioners free to attend if they wished, and the children were assembled for catechetical instructions. The pastor of this little temporary chapel wrote to the Bishop-elect a letter filled with expressions of the kindest sentiments. He described the good-will of his future flock, their devotedness to their diocesan, and ended with the hope that, with the blessing of God, he would effect grand results in behalf of souls. Father Neumann answered in the same cordial strain, remarking pleasantly that he feared his correspondent would be greatly disappointed in the expectations he had formed of him; that he viewed him in far too favorable a light.

It will not be uninteresting to hear how old Mr. Philip Neumann, the Bishop-elect's sole surviving parent, received the intelligence of the honor conferred on his son. The first intimation of it was from a priest who had seen the appointment in one of the newspapers. He proceeded to offer his congratulations, when the simple-hearted old gentleman interrupted him with the words, "Father A——, how can you believe such a thing? Who has dared to ridicule us in this way?" Shortly after an official entered with the same glad tidings, but Mr. Neumann would not listen to him. He cut short every attempt at explanation with the words, "Don't bring me such news!" Next came the Reverend Dean on the same errand, but he too was met with the reproof, "Reverend Father, are you also so credulous as to put faith in such rumors?"

It was not till Father Neumann himself wrote to acquaint his father of the dignity to which he had been raised that the venerable old gentleman would credit what to him seemed utterly incredible.

Very Rev. Father Bernard desired Father Neumann to write before his consecration a sketch of his own life, to be handed over to the Congregation. Father Neumann complied with his Provincial's command, and wrote four quarto pages, dated March 27, 1852. He concludes with these words: "To-morrow, March 28th, my birthday, which this year falls on Passion-Sunday, I shall, if nothing prevents, be consecrated Bishop in St. Alphonsus' Church, by Most Rev. Archbishop Kenrick. But do Thou, O Lord, have mercy on us! Jesus and Mary, pity me! Passion of Christ, strengthen me!"

On the eve of this most eventful day in a life so crowded with high and noble deeds in God's interests, the day on which Father Neumann's consecration was to take place, numbers of Redemptorist Fathers arrived in Baltimore from their different houses. They came to express by their presence the love and respect they entertained for the object of the unusual solemnity. One of them to whom Father Neumann's humility was well known, one who fully appreciated the painful emotions his appointment must have excited, gave utterance to some words of sympathy and questioned him as to his feelings upon the occasion. Father Neumann answered, "If our Lord gave me the choice either to die or to accept this dignity, I should prefer to lay down my life to-morrow rather than be consecrated Bishop; for my salvation would be more secure at the judgment-seat of God than it will be if I appear before it burdened with the responsibility of a bishopric."

CHAPTER VII.

Father Neumann is raised to the Episcopate.

EARLY on the morning of Passion-Sunday the faithful flocked from far and near to St. Alphonsus' to witness the sublime ceremony of an episcopal consecration. Hours before the appointed time the spacious edifice was already densely crowded. The Catholic societies of the city assembled to join in the demonstration offered to Father Neumann. A procession was formed headed by the children of the schools under the charge of the Redemptorists, and closed by the reverend clergy surrounded by a guard of honor. The procession moved in silence through Saratoga, Howard, Franklin, and Charles streets, as far as the archiepiscopal residence. Here it was joined by the Archbishop and other dignitaries, when it returned through Charles and Saratoga streets to St. Alphonsus' Church, where the young Bishop-elect knelt at the foot of the altar. The consecrating prelate, Archbishop Francis Patrick Kenrick, was assisted by Bishop O'Reilly of Hartford, and Father L'Homme, Superior of St. Mary's Seminary, Baltimore. Father William Elder, Professor at Mount St. Mary's, Emmittsburg (afterward Archbishop of Cincinnati), and Father Coudenhove acted as Deacons of Honor. Besides those mentioned, there were over thirty members of the clergy present in the sanctuary. Rev. Father Sourin, administrator of the diocese of Philadelphia, preached on the occasion, and addressed the new Bishop in the most cordial terms. His words and the imposing ceremonies made a deep impression on all present. But when, at the close, the twenty-four Redemptorist scholastics intoned the solemn *Te Deum* whilst the newly-consecrated Bishop passed down the aisle, giving the episcopal blessing to his beloved parishioners, over whom he had so lovingly and faithfully presided for years, the whole congregation melted into tears.

That evening, the evening of a day so memorable for St. Alphonsus' Church, Bishop Neumann preached his farewell sermon. In feeling terms he thanked his hearers for the confidence they had always reposed in him as their pastor, encouraged them to perseverance in the way of God, and bequeathed to them as his parting gift a child-like devotion to Mary, ever blessed.

Service over, the German Catholics of Baltimore presented the new Bishop with an address, embodying thanks for all the good he had effected in their behalf and regrets at being called upon to part from him. They congratulated themselves on having had a guide for whom the common Father of the Faithful had entertained so great esteem as to raise him to the dignity of the episcopate. Deeply moved, Bishop Neumann returned thanks for their sentiments in his regard, and promised ever to be mindful in prayer of the Catholics of Baltimore.

Not merely by words did his former parishioners express their respectful and grateful love for their pastor: they manifested the sincerity of their devotedness to him by deeds. On March 22d it was resolved in general meeting to give the Bishop a grand serenade before his departure to his diocese, and to present him a handsome chalice, a ring, a pectoral cross and chain, all of gold, together with other episcopal ornaments.

St. Philomena's congregation, Pittsburg, was not unmindful of the good that the Bishop had done among them. A delegation from its members waited upon him to offer congratulations and to present him with a beautiful ostensorium.

The day following his consecration the Bishop visited the schools and earnestly exhorted the children to lifelong fidelity to their God.

And now the voice of duty, that powerful underlying principle of John Neumann's life, called. He must away to the new scene of future labors in his Lord's vineyard. The call was heard and obeyed. Unhesitatingly, his heart filled with that deep, abiding trust in God which we have so often seen and reverently admired in him he set out on Tuesday morning, March 30th, for his episcopal city of Philadelphia.

The burden so dreaded was upon him. He took up his cross and followed *Him*, "the Way, the Truth, and the Life."

PART IV.

FATHER NEUMANN AS BISHOP OF PHILADELPHIA.

1852–1860.

CHAPTER I.

The Diocese of Philadelphia.

THE diocese of Philadelphia is one of the oldest and largest in the United States, as a brief glance at its history will show. In 1852, when Father Neumann entered upon its government as its fourth Bishop, it embraced two thirds of the State of Pennsylvania, the western part of New Jersey, and the whole of Delaware. We may form an idea of the extent of its territory when we remember that since 1868 five new dioceses have been formed out of it, leaving it still one of the largest in the States.

At a remote period Catholic missionaries made their way to Pennsylvania to administer to the settlers the consolations of our holy religion. But the first mention made of the existence of Catholicity in Philadelphia we find in a letter written by the founder of the State, William Penn. According to it, an aged priest in 1686 held divine service for the Catholic settlers in a frame building on the northwest corner of Front and Walnut streets. It is certain that in the year 1708 the Holy Sacrifice of the Mass was celebrated in Philadelphia, since in that year complaints were launched against Governor James Logan that, in spite of the rigid laws of England, he had permitted Catholics to hold divine service. In 1733 Governor Gordon disapproved the building of St. Joseph's Church which Father Greaton had erected in Fourth Street. The governor stigmatized it as a "Popish Mass-house." Yet in the decrees of Divine Providence the time had been determined for the fetters placed by England upon the Church in America to be removed. This was effected by the Revolutionary War of 1775. The freedom of the States from the English yoke brought with it also the independence of the Church. The French and the Spanish soldiers, our Catholic allies, had with them their chaplains, who, little heeding the laws of England against the Church, held public service for full congregations of both soldiers and officers. This, as a contemporary writer remarks, was a novel sight for American sectarians. Partly from curiosity, partly through politeness, the officers of the Federal troops accompanied their allies to divine service, and this contributed in no small degree to awaken among the masses a disposition more favorable to Catholicity.

After the successful close of the war, a solemn *Te Deum* was sung in St. Joseph's, in thanksgiving to the Lord of Hosts for the victory granted the Federal arms. The Holy Sacrifice was offered on the same occasion, and Rev. Father Beduale, chaplain of the Spanish Embassy, delivered a most eloquent sermon. The Marquis de la Lucerne had invited to the solemnity the members of the United States Congress and the highest officers of the State of Pennsylvania. The invitation was accepted; even Generals Washington and La Fayette were present. A public recognition was thereby given to such Catholics as Carroll, Barr, Moylan, Fitzsimmons, who had sacrificed much for their country, and also to the brave soldiers of the same holy faith who had ventured their all for liberty. After the independence of the United States had been proclaimed and the free exercise of Catholic worship secured by the new Constitution, the Catholics, ever ready to make sacrifices, began to erect churches for the exercise of their holy religion. The Germans, though few in number at that early period, were not behind in their efforts to uphold the faith. In 1787 they erected on the corner of Sixth and Spruce streets the church of the Holy Trinity, which was dedicated on November 20, 1789. A few years later the Augustinian Fathers built St. Augustine's in Fourth Street. At the beginning of the present century, therefore, four Catholic churches were already in existence within the precincts of Philadelphia.

When, in 1808, Baltimore was raised to an archiepiscopal see, Boston, New York, Philadelphia, and Bardstown, respectively, became new dioceses. The first Bishop of Philadelphia, Rev. Michael Egan, was consecrated October 28, 1810, by Archbishop Carroll, in St. Peter's Church, Baltimore. The Baltimore diocese comprised an extensive territory, but numbered only fourteen priests, of whom seven belonged to the Society of Jesus and four were Augustinians. Bishop Egan was succeeded by Bishop Conwell, who died April 22, 1842, at the advanced age of ninety-five.

On June 6, 1830, Rev. Francis Patrick Kenrick was made Coadjutor of the aged Bishop, with the right of succession. As Coadjutor and, later on, as the third Bishop of Philadelphia he was most active and zealous in the government of his large diocese. The great learning of this prelate, which has been characterized as *exhaustive*, together with his eminent holiness, has elicited for him unanimous and well-deserved praise.

August 19, 1851, saw Bishop Kenrick transferred to the archiepiscopal see of Baltimore. He was succeeded, as we have already seen, by Father Neumann, C.SS.R., the subject of this biography.

CHAPTER II.

Bishop Neumann's Arrival in Philadelphia.

THE fame of Bishop Neumann's eminent virtues had long preceded his entrance into his diocese; and when the clergy of Philadelphia met in council to determine upon the worthy reception of their new Bishop, one of the gentlemen arose and spoke as follows: "Reverend sirs, I am acquainted with the humility and modesty of our new Bishop. He is no friend to worldly pomp, or splendor, or public demonstrations; in fact, such a reception would annoy him exceedingly. I therefore propose, as a fitting demonstration of our cordial welcome to him, to establish a new school, and explain to him on his arrival that in doing so we sought to give expression to our joy at his appointment as Bishop of Philadelphia."

The proposal was esteemed highly judicious and met with unanimous approval. The work was begun at once. When Bishop Neumann arrived in the city and found a number of the clergy assembled at the railway station to escort him to his residence, his countenance beamed with joy, and he exclaimed, "Oh, how I thank you, gentlemen, for this quiet but cordial reception! It is just what I wished."

Again was his happiness augmented when, in a short address, he learned that the establishment of a new school, and not external pomp, was to celebrate his entrance into his diocese. In a few cordial words the Bishop acknowledged their kindly interest, and declared that they had rightly estimated his heart's desires; that works such as they now proposed would greatly lighten for him the cares of his office. On that same evening the German Catholic societies of St. Peter's assembled before the episcopal residence and welcomed their Bishop with music and addresses. He thanked them for their expressions of love and respect, exhorted them to live as true children of Holy Church, and dismissed them, pleased and gratified, with his paternal benediction.

One of Bishop Neumann's first acts in his new capacity was to visit the prison in which two brothers were awaiting the execution of their condign sentence for murder. The fatal day was drawing near, but the unfortunate men still obstinately refused every spiritual assistance. Hour after hour did the zealous prelate remain in the cell of the condemned, until at last, by his meekness and prayers, those hard hearts were softened, and he was made glad by hearing them ask for the Sacraments, which they received with sincere sorrow and devotion on the very day of their execution.

The sentiments and intentions that animated the young Bishop we may learn from his first Pastoral Letter, which he issued the second week after his consecration. It reads as follows:

"JOHN NEPOMUCENE, *by the grace of God and favor of the Apostolic See Bishop of Philadelphia, to the Clergy and Faithful of the diocese of Philadelphia.*

"Grace be to you and peace from God our Father, and from the Lord Jesus Christ.

"Venerable Brethren of the Clergy and dearly beloved Children of the Laity: When it was first announced to us that our Holy Father Pius IX. had appointed us to the pastoral care and government of this important portion of the flock of Christ, we must confess that the heavy charge filled our heart with anxiety. To leave those from whom we had experienced for many years the most cordial affection; to enter upon an entirely new sphere of duty; to assume the government of so vast a number of souls, who would look to us to lead them on to our heavenly home—all this urged us to implore the Lord to remove the chalice from us. We have, however, been compelled to bow in obedience to the successor of St. Peter, knowing that whatsoever he binds on earth shall be bound also in heaven; and submitting to the will of God, we humbly hope that He who hath commenced in us what the Apostle St. Paul calls "a good work" will graciously grant us that sufficiency which is required to bring it to perfection. This our trust in God has been much strengthened by the kind encouragement we have received from the Most Rev. Archbishop Francis Patrick Kenrick, who through so many years of untiring labor endeared himself to you all. He has repeatedly assured us of the zeal and attachment he had experienced on the part of your reverend pastors. Often has he spoken in terms of praise of the piety by which you had consoled him in the midst of his toils; of your liberality, which had called into existence and supported so many charitable institutions, and erected edifices to the glory of the living God which will bear testimony to future generations of your lively faith, prompt generosity, and practical charity, when you are enjoying in His presence the eternal rewards He has in store for those who love Him.

"Since we have occupied our episcopal see we have daily received unequivocal marks of attachment and obedience. The former administrator of the diocese, the Very Rev. Edward J. Sourin, has accepted the office of our Vicar-General, much to our satisfaction. The cordial welcome we have met in the different religious houses and congregations we have visited, has confirmed our happiest anticipation as to the faith, piety, and zeal of the flock committed to our care by the Divine Pastor and Bishop of our souls. For all His mercies we return thanks to Him, 'the Holy One and the True, who hath the key of David, who hath given before us a door opened,' which, we trust in God, no man will be able to shut.

"Venerable brethren, we beseech you most earnestly to assist us always by your prayers for us, that we may finish our course and the ministry of the Word which we have received from Jesus Christ; that we may take heed to ourselves and to all the flock over which the Holy Ghost has placed us, a Bishop, to rule the Church of God, which He has purchased with His own precious blood; and that we may use without fear or wavering that power which the Lord hath given us to the edification of His Church. On our part, we shall not cease to entreat the Good Shepherd to increase His grace in your hearts, that as men of God you 'may fly all worldly desires and pursue justice, piety, faith, charity, patience, meekness; that you may keep the commandments without spot, blameless unto the coming of our Lord Jesus Christ.'

"And those amongst you, beloved children, who, listening to the invitation of the Most Holy, have left father, mother, brethren, and sisters to dedicate yourselves to the service of Jesus Christ in poverty, chastity, and obedience, truly have ye chosen the better part. Strive, therefore, fervently to render yourselves ever more pleasing to your Divine Spouse, for your life is hidden with Christ in God. Put ye on, therefore, as the elect of God, holy and beloved, mercy, benignity, humility, modesty, patience; bearing with one another, and forgiving one another if any have a complaint against another. But above all these things have charity, which is the bond of perfection. And when Christ shall appear, who is your life, then shall you also appear with Him in glory.

"Beloved children of the laity, my joy and my crown, if you be faithful in those things which ye have both learned and received, we exhort you with the great

Apostle that you 'may be blameless and sincere children of God, without reproof in the midst of this world; hating that which is evil, cleaving to that which is good; loving one another with the charity of brotherhood; in spirit fervent, serving the Lord; to no man rendering evil for evil; providing good things not only in the sight of God, but also in the sight of all men. And whosoever shall follow this rule, may peace be upon them and mercy; and may my God supply all your wants, according to His riches, in glory in Christ Jesus!

"On your zeal and charity, next to the good pleasure of the Almighty, we must continue to rely for the completion of several important works commenced by our most reverend predecessor. Among them, not only on account of the grandeur of the work, but even more in consequence of the heavy expense we must incur while it remains in its present unfinished state, we especially commend to your attention the Cathedral of SS. Peter and Paul. We are not unmindful, beloved brethren, of your many sacrifices for the sake of your religion. We cannot be insensible how greatly your generous devotion has contributed to the diffusion of truth and virtue, and to the relief of suffering humanity. But whilst the gradual increase of wealth on every side, the accumulation of all the comforts and luxuries of life, attest the prosperity to which this favored country has already attained, in which prosperity many of you participate, let us beware lest the reproaches of the prophet should prove well founded in our regard: 'This people saith, The time is not yet come to build the house of the Lord. And the word of the Lord came by the hand of Aggeus the Prophet, saying, Is it time for you to dwell in ceiled houses and this house be desolate? And now thus saith the Lord of hosts: Set your hearts to consider your ways. You have sowed much and brought in little; you have looked for more, and behold, it came less; and you brought it home, and I blowed it away: why? saith the Lord of Hosts. Because my house is desolate, and you make haste, every man to his own house.' To these complaints of the Holy Spirit what answer did Israel give? With zealous emulation, they went in and did the work of the Lord of Hosts, their God; and the temple was not yet finished, when they heard—'From this day I will bless you. Take courage, all ye people of the land, and perform: fear not, for I am with you—and my spirit in the midst of you, saith the Lord of Hosts.'

"Though circumstances do not now allow us to dwell at length on the subject, we avail ourselves of this earliest opportunity to express our approbation of the efforts which have lately been made in several congregations to organize parochial schools. We exhort the pastors, and all who have at heart the best interests of youth, to spare no efforts to ensure success. Whatever difficulties may at first attend, and even obstruct, this most desirable undertaking will be gradually overcome by mutual good-will and co-operation.

"It is with grateful joy we make known to you that our Holy Father has again offered to the faithful throughout the world a plenary indulgence in the form of a jubilee; the most salutary effects, both for the Church and society, having resulted from that proclaimed within the last few years. Amid the many trials and profound sorrows which have marked his pontificate, he has been consoled by the accounts that have reached him from every part of Christendom of the multitudes who, with humble and contrite hearts, have thronged our churches to hear the Word of God, to purify their souls in the sacrament of reconciliation and receive the Holy Eucharist; performing, meanwhile, with humble and devout obedience the other spiritual exercises which, as the Vicar of Jesus Christ, he had enjoined upon them. Thousands in every country, who had been for years astray from the way of truth and salvation, have been enlightened by the grace of God to forsake the shadows of death and to commence a truly Christian life.

"Notwithstanding this happy result, our chief Pastor is not without apprehension for the future welfare of the Church and of society. He beholds the dangers which threaten both; the designs of men who, deceived by a vain philosophy and their false ideas of liberty, despise all lawful authority, whether civil or ecclesiastical, pervert the minds of inexperienced youth, and expose to contempt the most sacred rites and institutions of religion. Aware that from no quarter can they expect more determined and constant opposition than from the Apostolic See, it is therefore against this venerable authority that they direct their most violent attacks. In these dangers, what other course remains for the friends of order, justice, and virtue than to recur to the Almighty, who is our hope and our salvation, and to pray without ceasing that He would deign to look down upon the nations, to enlighten their erring minds, to purify their hearts, and subdue that rebellious will which now leads them to revolt against Him and His Church, 'that, being delivered from the hand of our enemies, we may serve Him without fear, in holiness and justice, all the days of our life'?

[Here the Bishop mentions the conditions for gaining the indulgence of the jubilee, and recommends in the following words to the prayers of the faithful the Council which the Bishops of the United States were to hold in Baltimore:]

"You are probably aware, beloved brethren, that the First National Council will soon be held in Baltimore, its opening being fixed for the fourth Sunday after Easter. Every faithful member of the Church in the United States will regard it as an imperative duty to invoke the Holy Spirit—the Spirit of truth, wisdom, and piety— to preside over its deliberations, that all its proceedings and enactments may tend to the glory of Jesus Christ and the more perfect establishment of His kingdom in all hearts. To this end, we direct that the collect, *De Spiritu Sancto*, be added in the Mass whenever the rubrics allow it; the religious communities will recite daily the Litany of the Blessed Virgin; and the same or other prayers for this object we exhort the faithful of our diocese to offer to God until the close of the Council.

"And now, brethren, commending you to God and to the word of His grace, our daily prayer for you is 'that your charity may more and more abound in knowledge and in all understanding; that you may approve the better things; that you may be sincere and without offence unto the day of Christ, replenished with the fruit of justice, through Jesus Christ, unto the glory and praise of God.' May our dear Mother Mary and her Divine Son bless you all! Amen."

CHAPTER III.

Bishop Neumann's Pastoral Charge.

RICHARD H. CLARKE says, in his work entitled "Lives of the Deceased Bishops of the Catholic Church in the United States," "Bishop Neumann chiefly distinguished his administration by continuing and increasing the work of his predecessor; in new and important undertakings of his own; in promoting piety and faith amongst his people."

The Bishop's first care for the judicious government of his vast diocese was to examine closely into its condition. In this examination he was successful, as his subsequent regulations prove. On the very first Sunday after his installation, he performed the ceremony of blessing the palm and preached in St. John's, his pro-Cathedral. That afternoon he administered the Sacrament of Confirmation at St. Patrick's, and preached again that night at St. Joseph's. No Sunday or holy-day passed without his preaching in one or several churches. During the first weeks of his residence in Philadelphia he visited all the religious communities, the orphan asylums, the hospitals, etc., informing himself as to their spiritual and temporal condition. Everywhere was he received with respect and treated with confidence. His whole demeanor bespoke him a true father who sought only the good of every member of his large family. Both clergy and laity called on him frequently for advice and consolation in their doubts and difficulties.

Well aware that not the city of Philadelphia alone claimed his care, Bishop Neumann set out as soon as possible to make his pastoral visitation, in which he included (this being the first time he performed the duty) the smallest and most distant country stations. His custom ever after was to visit the larger places of his diocese every year, the smaller at least once in two years. He remained several days in each parish, instituting a minute inquiry into their actual condition, in order to remedy as far as practicable any abuses or evils that might exist. His pastoral visit was, at the same time, something of a mission for the people, for he preached to them and gave special instructions to the children. The daily exercises he mapped out for such occasions were like those of a spiritual retreat. From early morn till late at night he was open to all—all were at liberty to communicate to him, their good pastor, whatever they might have on their mind. The confessional was the chosen theatre of his activity. The faithful rejoiced to be able to confess to their Bishop, to lay open to him the wounds of their soul, and to draw consolation from his paternal heart. And there was yet another reason why they should exult. In all parts of his diocese he found some who could not confess to their pastors in their native tongue; but the Bishop, it was generally known, was conversant in almost every language spoken. If he met with some scandal in a parish, he left no means untried to remove it, and his efforts were generally crowned with success. In this way did the young Bishop spend his days. His labors were so rich in blessings that even during the first years of his administration he acquired a perfect insight into the state of every parish under his jurisdiction. He himself drew up a map on which every one was properly located. The fervor of his flock was so great, that wherever twenty or twenty-five Catholic families were found, there they petitioned to build a church. But prudence often obliged the Bishop to moderate their zeal and defer the fulfilment of their generous design. During the first five years of his episcopacy he opened over fifty churches. In 1853 he wrote to his venerable father:

"The past summer was spent, for the most part, in making the visitation of my diocese, a work not unaccompanied by fatigue and privation, but which, nevertheless, affords abundant consolation. Our Catholics continue to increase in numbers, and they exhibit a fervent love for their holy religion. Last summer twenty churches were built and paid for out of the collections taken up in their respective parishes. Six of these churches are for the Germans. Here in Philadelphia four other churches are now being erected. The Cathedral will be of stone, the others of brick."

The Bishop's designs for the welfare of his flock were not, however, always seconded; sorrow and vexation, caused by certain self-opinionated individuals, were not unknown to him. But his patient kindness, his gentleness, above all his intercession at the throne of grace, generally overcame the obstinacy of those that had been blinded by passion. On taking charge of the see of Philadelphia, Bishop Neumann found Trinity Church under interdict, and the feeling of a certain party in this the oldest German parish in the city against ecclesiastical authority running high. The prudence and firmness evinced by the Bishop in the unhappy affair soon brought things to a crisis. The most unruly members were justly dealt with by the highest court in the land, whilst the better disposed made their peace with their lawful superiors.

As in the past when only a simple missionary, so now as chief pastor of one of the principal sees of the United States, Bishop Neumann showed forth the same burning zeal for the work of the missions. He procured them for many churches of his diocese during the first years of his episcopate, and sought by his own presence at the exercises, joined to his prayers for their success, to animate the faithful to profit by them for their souls' salvation. Nothing could equal his joy and consolation on beholding them well attended. The sight of the wonderful and persevering assiduity of the crowds that thronged the churches early and late was a blessed one for him, thirsting as he did for souls.

In one of the larger parishes of the city there existed, unhappily, an unusual number of mixed marriages which had been contracted before Protestant ministers. The pastor of said parish was very severe toward these careless Catholics whose indifference and disobedience to Holy Church had rendered their reconciliation with God most difficult. To bring back these stray sheep into the fold of the Lord and Master, the Bishop went himself during the mission, to the church in question, and requested the Fathers to send him all the delinquents of this class. He was obeyed; and this faithful imitator of the Good Shepherd had the consolation of reconciling many repentant sinners to their God.

If the good Bishop were wholly powerless in the prevention of an evil, he did what he could to diminish it as much as possible. A father whose daughter would not abandon her intention to marry her Protestant suitor came to the Bishop and imparted to him his trouble. The Bishop sent for the deluded girl, reminded her of the innumerable evils likely to result from such unions, and ended by laying before her the formal prohibition of the Church. The girl listened, but the paternal admonitions addressed to her were without effect; she remained obstinately resolved on her first purpose. The Bishop, seeing that further remonstrances would be unavailing, reluctantly accorded her a dispensation, warning her, however, that many trials were in store for her, and that she would live to repent of her rash step. The prediction was, alas! literally fulfilled. The unhappy girl did, indeed, live to expiate by years of bitter sorrow her act of disobedience to both parent and ecclesiastical superior.

True shepherd as he was, Bishop Neumann was ever ready to sympathize with any member of his flock in misfortune. Witness the following fact. It has long been an established custom for the children belonging to the different parishes to make an annual excursion into the country, there to spend a day in cheerful and innocent recreation of mind and body. In 1850 the young people of St. Michael's Church had long looked forward to July 17th, the day appointed for their picnic. They started at an early hour for Fort Washington, about fourteen miles from the city. The pastor of the church, Rev. Daniel Sheridan, the teachers of the school, and many of the parents and friends of the children formed part of the happy band, and they were determined to make it a gala-day for their innocent young charges. The children numbered seven hundred, and ten cars had been chartered to bear them to their destination. Smiles played on every countenance; young hearts beat high with expectation of fun and frolic and freedom from restraint for one day, at least. And older hearts, hearts chastened by the cares and strife of busy life, were scarcely less jubilant, for theirs was to be the pleasing task of contributing to the enjoyment of the little ones. But, alas! a sudden check, a fearful silencing of innocent mirth and gleeful prattle! As they neared their destination, shortly after six o'clock, an appalling accident occurred. The excursion-train ran into another coming from an opposite direction, and that with such force as to dash both locomotives to pieces. The cars caught fire. Sixty-four killed, among them the lamented Father Sheridan, and seventy-nine wounded were dragged from the burning débris. Consternation seized upon the community at large; sorrow clouded once happy firesides. The lamentations of grief-stricken relatives and friends can better be imagined than expressed. Bishop Neumann was absent from the city at the time, administering the Sacrament of Confirmation in distant quarters of his diocese. No sooner was he informed of the dire catastrophe than he returned in haste to Philadelphia, to offer assistance and consolation to his bereaved flock. He visited the wounded in the hospitals, tenderly exhorting them to patience and resignation, instructing them how to unite their sufferings with those of the Man-God in atonement for sin and in return for His infinite love toward us. He consoled the afflicted parents and relatives by his paternal sympathy, sweetly suggesting powerful motives for resignation to the Divine Will. His affectionate heart bled at the thought of the sorrowful ending of that long-expected, long-to-be-remembered 17th of July.

It is needless for us to say what every reader may glean from the foregoing pages, that the saintly Bishop Neumann lived entirely for his diocese. When at home, the following was the order of his day: At five o'clock he made meditation in his own room, and at the half-hour repaired to his chapel, to which part of the first floor of the episcopal residence was devoted. There, at six, he celebrated Mass served by two of the seminarians. During the Mass which followed he made his thanksgiving, then heard confessions, recited the Divine Office, and partook of his frugal breakfast. The whole day after this, often till late at night, was given up to the business of his diocese and to visits from both clergy and laity. Nor was this all: the hours of rest were often broken in upon, in order to attend to his correspondence and perform his accustomed devotions.

Toward the close of 1853 he wrote to Rev. Father Holba, one of his fellow-students:

"My present position is indeed laborious, as I have no one to help me; but such is the case with all Bishops in America. God will assist me, since He bestows so many blessings on the Church in this country. This confidence helps me to bear my trials, and even makes them a source of joy to me, as they contribute to His greater honor and glory."

When occupied with the visitation of his diocese

the days were too short for his zeal, for he was then Bishop, pastor, missionary, all at the same time. He preached daily at stated hours, gave familiar instructions, and heard confessions from early in the morning till late at night. In the "Lives of the Deceased Bishops" we read: "No priest spent more time in the confessional than Bishop Neumann." In his solicitude for every member of his flock, he learned the Irish language, as there were many of that nationality unable to make their confession in English, and even Irish priests were not familiar with their native tongue. There is a pleasing little incident connected with the above. A good old Irishwoman had vainly sought for one to hear her confession in her own language; but again and again was she dismissed with the discouraging information that the priest did not understand Irish. At last Divine Providence led the good old woman to Bishop Neumann. He received her with his accustomed kindness and, to her intense satisfaction, heard her confession in her own dear tongue. "Thanks be to God!" cried she, as she wended her way homeward, "thanks be to God! We now have an *Irish Bishop.*"

Bishop Neumann claimed no distinctions; the crosier and mitre made no change in him. Simple and humble, he never dictated; and when making his visitation, his Mass was always celebrated at the hour appointed by the pastor of whatever church he might happen to be at. When administering Confirmation, he usually addressed his audience on the means to preserve and increase the grace then received. His great anxiety was that the candidates for this Sacrament of the strong should be well instructed and sufficiently prepared for its worthy reception. On the eve of the day appointed for its administration he generally gave instructions himself, and if he found the candidates ignorant of what they ought to know, he postponed the ceremony. In such cases he would not hesitate to employ several days in giving instructions, at which he desired the pastor to attend. The people everywhere showed the greatest confidence in their Bishop. They approached him without constraint, and communicated to him their wishes and their sorrows. The pastors of the different stations usually accompanied him to the next on his route, and faithfully seconded him in his efforts for the welfare of his flock.

CHAPTER IV.

The Establishment of Catholic Schools in the Diocese of Philadelphia.

BISHOP NEUMANN'S first care on taking possession of his see was to erect Catholic schools in every parish. Even previously to their Bishop's arrival, the Catholic community of Philadelphia were aware that their new Bishop directed special attention to the promotion of Catholic education. All eagerly awaited his first Pastoral Letter, and they were not disappointed. The Bishop clearly expressed his sentiments. "Our Catholic youth," he said, "can be saved only by Catholic schools:" which words were embodied also in his first sermon after his installation. A reverend gentleman present says: "The Bishop's sermon respecting St. Joseph clearly unfolded to his hearers his views on Catholic education. He openly declared his firm resolution, with God's help, to begin and carry out that work of vital importance, the establishment of Catholic schools. Persuasively and emphatically he exhorted parents to give their children Catholic training, to enforce their attendance at Mass and the other services of religion, to educate them at home both by word and example, but above all to send them to schools in which they would be taught under the eye of the Church.

"These words are for us a sign," continues the same reverend gentleman, "that the day is not far distant when in Philadelphia there will be no church without its school in which the children of the parish may receive a Christian education."

After mature reflection upon the means suited to the

end in view, the Bishop at once set to work. On April 28, 1852, he invited the pastors of the various congregations and several prominent members of the laity to assemble at the episcopal residence for a conference touching the interests of the question in hand. He opened the meeting himself with an animated discourse explanatory of its object. He laid down as his unshaken conviction that for Catholic children Catholic schools are an absolute necessity in order to educate them in the faith, form them into good and useful members of the Church and of society, and secure their eternal salvation. The Bishop's sentiments were heartily approved by the assembly, several of whom, both priests and laymen, arose and expressed their concurrence in his views. All agreed as to the indispensability of Catholic schools, and declared that no sacrifice could be too great for the furtherance of the Bishop's designs. A committee was appointed to consult on the best means to use, and the secretary was directed to notify all absent pastors of the resolutions adopted and invite them to the next meeting.

This was held a few days later, May 5th, and, to the Bishop's satisfaction, it was a full one. The resolutions drawn up by the committee were read and unanimously adopted; a central "Committee for the Education of Catholic Youth" was appointed. It consisted of the reverend pastors of the different congregations and two of the laity from each. The Bishop, as president, was to give his sanction to all resolutions.

The business of this committee was twofold: first, to deliberate upon some practical method of instruction without, however, interfering with the finances of the different schools, the appointment of teachers, or the introduction of text-books, etc.; secondly, by the collection of monthly contributions it was likewise to assist in the maintenance of such schools as might be unable to support themselves.

These meetings were held every month at the Bishop's residence, and the proceedings forwarded to every priest in the diocese. The Bishop, as president, was never absent from his post, unless prevented by his pastoral visitation or other pressing affairs. In such cases he was careful to notify his Vicar-general to preside as vice-president. Should it happen that Bishops or prominent laymen from other dioceses were staying in the city at the time, Bishop Neumann never failed to solicit their presence. He used to introduce them himself to the gentlemen assembled, and invite them to say a few words in favor of the good cause. In this way he sought to win friends and supporters for the noble enterprise of Catholic education.

The Bishop lent his encouragement not only in a general way, but he also embraced every opportunity of manifesting his interest even in minor details. The parochial schools claimed his special attention. On his visitations he would gather round him the children of the various parishes, to give them instructions; and if there was a school attached to the church, he always visited it to encourage both pastors and parents, as well as the little ones themselves, to renewed exertions. He often attended the public examinations and questioned the pupils himself. His presence drew thither their parents and friends, the halls were filled, and all were animated with new zeal. That the reader may form some idea of Bishop Neumann's fatherly deportment on such occasions, we shall here cite one from among the many such examinations which he thus honored. After addressing the children a few kind words calculated to inspire confidence, they were questioned in catechism and the other branches usually taught. The children, encouraged by the gentleness and the manifest interest of their good Bishop, answered well and satisfactorily; the most proficient received premiums from his hand, after which he arose and pronounced an impressive discourse which embraced the parents' even more than the children's instruction. At its conclusion, one of the lads stepped forward and, in the name of his companions, presented the Bishop a beautiful crucifix, begging him to accept it as a token of their filial reverence, and to pray for them as often as his glance rested upon it. The good Bishop was visibly touched by this innocent expression of respect; he graciously accepted it as a valued offering from the little ones of his flock. In making his acknowledgments, he expatiated upon the pleasure he felt at receiving the image of our Lord from the hands of his children. He expressed the hope that throughout their whole life they would remain faithful to the wholesome Catholic instruction received at school, and persevere till death in the practice of the lessons there inculcated; thus they would become useful members of society, worthy children of the Church, and insure their claims to the kingdom of eternal life. He remarked that he had heard a very good account of their school, but now he was convinced of its truth, having seen for himself the progress it had made under its worthy pastor and efficient teachers. All bore evidence to the solid Christian education there bestowed. The pupils had given satisfaction in catechism, in vocal and instrumental music, in declamation, etc. He saw that their mind was being cultivated, their memory exercised, and he doubted not that the culture of the precious soul far surpassed that of which external signs had just been given. Turning to the parents, the Bishop once more exhorted them to watch over their children, to follow up the instructions received at school by setting their little ones a good example in the home-circle. In conclusion, he again thanked the children for their beautiful present, and assured them that he would not only think of them when he looked upon it, but that he would remember them also at the Holy Sacrifice of the Mass.

The schools increased year by year. In the last

months of his life the holy Bishop could say: "Almighty God has so wonderfully blessed the work of Catholic education that nearly every church of my diocese has now its school." Emulation arose among the teachers from the well-known fact of the Bishop's deriving unbounded pleasure from his visits to the parochial schools. Such emulation was beneficial and led to gratifying results on all sides.

The falling off in attendance at the public schools of the city became remarkable; vacant seats might be counted by thousands. The circumstance was so noticeable as to attract the attention of the press. The following lines appeared in one of the dailies: "We regret to see that the most esteemed denomination in this city has withdrawn its confidence from the public schools. Serious defects must exist in our school-system; authorities should therefore investigate and improve the condition of the said schools."

We must not conclude, however, that Bishop Neumann encountered no difficulties in his work for Catholic education; to this undertaking, as to every other destined to rob hell of its prey, obstacles were not wanting. But Bishop Neumann's was a nature that knew how to pray and bide God's own time. When apparently insurmountable barriers arose between him and the accomplishment of his laudable projects, he could calmly lay the latter aside and wait for more propitious days. If dread of labor and expense stood in the way, his wonderful prudence and energy of will soon discovered some means to overcome both. He had repeatedly enjoined upon the pastor of one of the largest parishes in Philadelphia the duty of erecting a school, but his admonitions fell unheeded. The invariable reply was: "It is impossible just now." At last the Bishop said to the dilatory clergyman: "If it is indeed impossible for you to establish a school, I shall have to look for another to fill your place. He will perhaps find it possible to secure a Christian education for the children of that parish." This was enough. The reverend gentleman promised to fulfil the Bishop's injunctions. He set to work, built a school-house, and opened with a thousand children the very first day.

"The parochial schools of the whole diocese of Philadelphia, and especially of the city itself," says Clarke, "increased wonderfully in numbers, in attendance, and in efficiency during his administration, and became a crowning glory of his work. The boys' schools he confided to the Christian Brothers, and those of the girls to the Sisters of St. Joseph, the Sisters of Charity, the Sisters of Notre Dame, and other female Orders. There were two parochial schools in Philadelphia when he went there in 1852; and at the time of his death, 1860, he had increased the number to nearly one hundred."

Besides the parochial schools, Bishop Neumann devoted his attention to the industrial schools already in existence, to the colleges and academies established by various religious Orders, and he encouraged the establishment of others. In 1852 there were three Catholic colleges in the diocese: one at Villanova, under the charge of the Augustinians; St. Joseph's College, Philadelphia; and St. Mary's College, at Wilmington. For young ladies there were also three institutions: one in Philadelphia in connection with the convent of the Visitation; the two others at Holmesburg and McSherrytown, conducted by the Ladies of the Sacred Heart.

Under the Bishop's fostering care there were established: St. Joseph's College, in Susquehanna County; three academies for girls, one in the above-mentioned county, the others in Philadelphia and Reading; an Industrial School for girls, directed by the Sisters of the Holy Cross; St. Vincent's Home, for orphans under four years of age, in the Cathedral parish; St. Vincent's Orphan Asylum, for the German parishes of the city, presided over by the Sisters of Notre Dame; and a

German hospital, under the care of the Franciscan Sisters.

Bishop Neumann did not neglect the higher educational establishments. Himself a lover of the sciences, he endeavored by all means in his power to promote in these institutions a great zeal for study. He visited them often, showed his deep interest in every branch of science, and awoke in the pupils a thirst for knowledge. They loved to propose their scientific difficulties to him and hear his solution of them. One day he entered a certain institution and found teacher and pupils in quite an animated discussion over what they thought a discrepancy between their text-book of astronomy and their own telescopic observations. They turned eagerly to the Bishop. He soon discovered the cause of the apparent discrepancy, and smilingly explained away the difficulty.

The pupils of another institution showed him a plant whose order and species they were unable to find in their text-book of botany. He examined the plant attentively for a few moments, and then mentioned its name and order, as well as the work in which they might find it described.

The orphans were the dear objects of his solicitude; he was to them a true father. A Sister of a religious community says: "When Bishop Neumann visited an orphan asylum he appeared the very counterpart of our Lord, the Friend of children. He went among them like a tender, loving father. He never came with empty pockets. He always brought some presents, such as books, pictures, toys, etc. The little ones would gather round him and listen attentively whilst he told them of God's love for them, or explained the different parts of a flower, or some other wonder of nature suited to their young mind. He knew how to use plain and simple language, such as would chain the attention of even the most frolicsome. He led them, as far as their capacity permitted, from the meditation of created things up to the contemplation of God Himself. Their multiplied questions never annoyed him."

He lost no opportunity to rescue a child from moral ruin. We know his predilection for the hardest work in the sacred ministry. His elevation to the episcopal dignity made no change in this respect, and he still claimed as his own the attending to sick-calls at night. In the exercise of this function he often found a dying parent to whom the thought of leaving a helpless orphan rendered the bitterness of death doubly bitter. In such cases his kind heart grew glad at being able to soothe and resign the dying soul to the holy will of God with the promise that he would himself take charge of the orphaned child. One day he made his appearance at the asylum holding by the hand a little tot of three years, for whom he sought admittance. His kindness so won the little creature's heart that ever after it called him by the endearing name of father.

Another work in which Bishop Neumann's gentle heart delighted was the visiting of hospitals. It was his joy to alleviate the sufferings of the poor sick by loving words and tender sympathy. A certain religious says: "When the Bishop visited the sick he went from bed to bed, lingering ateach as if loath to leave. He had words of comfort and encouragement for every poor sufferer of whatever age, rank, or faith. He used earnestly to remind the Sisters in charge to look upon the sick as the suffering members of Jesus Christ, and as such to bestow upon them conscientious care.

CHAPTER V.

Bishop Neumann's Solicitude for his Clergy.

WHEN Bishop Neumann took possession of his see in 1852, he found in it about one hundred priests engaged in the sacred ministry a force wholly insufficient for so large a diocese, and for the ever-increasing number of Catholics. He was therefore obliged to turn his attention to the supplying of this want as promptly as possible, by appointing zealous young priests to vacancies. The seminary of the diocese counted only forty students of philosophy and theology, among whom were very few Germans, notwithstanding the special need for priests of that nationality. In his distress the Bishop applied to his old friends, the Superior of the seminary in Prague, and to Rev. Hermann Dichtl, requesting them to send him some worthy priests or theological students who had finished their studies. In May, 1853, he was able to report as follows to Father Dichtl:

"I thank God for His rich blessings upon your efforts in behalf of this diocese. Father R—— is laboring with great fervor and self-devotedness at his mission among the miners. He will soon finish his little log-church. Mr. W—— is still at the seminary. He will be ordained deacon to-morrow. As he has finished his studies and his conduct is exemplary, I shall ordain him this summer. I hope our poor Germans may have reason to thank God for his arrival in America. Of those mentioned in your letter, none have, as yet, arrived. I am anxiously expecting them, for scarcely a week passes that I am not asked by petitions and deputations to send a German priest some place or other. So far, I have not been able to do anything more than exhort such applicants to pray God to send us good priests, and then to wait in patience."

Bishop Neumann never lost an opportunity of impressing on his clergy the necessity of devoting special attention to boys who manifested a vocation for the priesthood. He exhorted them to watch over their conduct; to instruct them how to lead a pious life; and, in case there was good reason to believe that they would eventually enter the ranks of the ministry, to present them to him as candidates. He sent numbers of such boys to college at his own expense, that they might prepare for the higher studies. From the very beginning of his administration, he entertained a lively desire of establishing his own preparatory seminary as a safeguard for youth and a means of implanting in their tender minds the virtues necessary for the sacerdotal state. Seven years were, however, to roll by ere he was to see the fulfilment of his judicious plan. It was not till the year 1859 that he rejoiced in its realization. A Pastoral Letter upon this subject gives us his views respecting the training of candidates for the priesthood. It runs as follows:

"*To the Clergy and the Laity of the Diocese of Philadelphia:*

"Grace be to you, and peace, from God our Father, and from the Lord Jesus Christ.

"The great and happy progress made by our holy religion in the United States fills us with joy, and we offer continual thanksgivings to the Almighty for the graces which He so abundantly pours out upon our country.

"The trials of the young Church of this country were, in the beginning, most severe, and the first laborers were encompassed by poverty and difficulties of every kind; but they confided in God and, through Him, obtained the grace of laboring perseveringly in the vineyard of the widely scattered faithful.

"Even at the beginning of this century our Church received notable increase from all parts of Europe; and still every month brings thousands to our shores. In a short time the number of Catholics has grown beyond computation.

"We see numbers of churches filled with worshippers, and hundreds of children flocking to our spacious parochial schools. Every year witnesses the opening of new colleges and academies, the erection of asylums, hospitals, and convents. The poor wanderer, far away from the home and scenes of childhood, no longer feels himself *a stranger in a strange land;* for he beholds on all sides majestic temples before whose altars he can worship his God. Yet whilst religion is thus making rapid strides, there is a great want felt, that of laborers in the vineyard—a want which grows more urgent day by day.

"It is, indeed, true that during the last fifty years many priests have come to our shores from Europe. They had heard of our spiritual distress; and, actuated by holy zeal and in imitation of the Apostles, they left home and friends to labor in God's house here in America. Many young men, also, not yet in orders, but who had chosen the Lord for their inheritance, found their way to our land, and offered themselves to the Bishops; being accepted, they entered our seminaries, completed their studies, and were admitted to the ranks of the priesthood. In this way our prelates have been able to supply the most important missions with good priests. Since the beginning of the mission-work in our diocese, one hundred and seventy priests have been engaged in it. Of these, forty-seven were native-born, and one hundred and fifty-seven finished their studies in our diocesan seminary. But we cannot depend entirely on such sources. During the last two or three years applications have been less numerous. We shall therefore soon sensibly experience the want of priests; our work will not advance. The clergy are subject to the same evils as their fellow-mortals: sickness and death seek victims among them.

"But God, who in His infinite wisdom orders all things well, will provide for our wants. He already points out the way by which we can supply them, viz., by the co-operation of those whose duty it is to instruct you and to sanctify your souls. The way shown us by Divine Providence is the education of our young men to the priesthood in institutions established for this purpose. Through them we shall have constant and abundant sources from which to procure good and able ministers for our holy Church. The lively faith manifesting itself in so many Catholic families, the grandeur and solemnity of our services, the holy influence of religion on our parochial schools, must naturally inspire numbers of our young men with a love for the sacerdotal state Even during these last years we have perceived in our youth a growing inclination for the priesthood. Year after year, applications are made to us from young men of our diocese to be admitted into different educational establishments with a view to the clerical state. Not many years ago no fewer than twenty were received by us at one time. They have now been studying for three years at the preparatory seminary of St. Charles, Maryland. It gives us great pleasure to be able to state that to their progress in learning, as well as to their good conduct, we can testify.

"This is also a manifest sign that Almighty God desires that we should carry out without delay the decree of the Council of Trent, by establishing a preparatory seminary within the precincts of our own diocese. This institution, in connection with our theological seminary of St. Charles Borromeo, will, with the blessing of God and our own co-operation, supply us with pious and learned priests to aid in the fulfilment of our pastoral duties.

"The holy Council of Trent (Sess. 23, chap. 18) issued

the following decree: 'As young men, if not rightly directed, give themselves up to the pleasures of the world and, if not trained from their tender age in piety and virtue, will never submit to ecclesiastical discipline, the holy synod decrees that all cathedral churches are obliged according to their ability to support gratuitously a certain number of young men of the city and diocese, to train them religiously, and to form them in ecclesiastical discipline. The youth who wish to be received for this end must not be under twelve years of age; they must have been born of lawful wedlock; must be able to read and write; and their moral character must justify the hope that they will devote themselves to the service of the Church. Especially should poor children be chosen for gratuitous education. The rich are not to be excluded, though they should be supported at their own expense. The Bishop should divide these young men into as many classes as appears advisable with respect to age, number, and intelligence in ecclesiastical affairs. From these he chooses those who are fit, and again selects others to take their place, so that the institution will continually furnish him servants for the Church. In order that young persons may be better kept in ecclesiastical discipline, they should wear the clerical dress; they should learn grammar, church-music, and other useful sciences; they should, moreover, be instructed in Holy Scripture, and in the homilies of the saints.'

"The establishment of these diocesan seminaries according to the plan of the Fathers of the Council of Trent was deemed necessary for the restoration of church-discipline. We doubt not for a moment that this plan will be carried out in our diocese also, and be accompanied by the most gratifying results. The guardianship of parents is certainly the best nursery for good Christians; the blessing of the marriage-sacrament, even under less favorable circumstances, produces more powerful, more efficacious results under the parental roof than the most brilliant scientific educational system in a foreign institution, however richly the latter may be endowed, however distinguished by the learning and talents of its professors. But if Christian youth are to be educated for the service of the Almighty, all contact with what would withdraw them from their holy vocation must be avoided. Parental influence occasionally makes an undue impression on the mind of youth, sometimes turns their thoughts away from the things of God.

"It is true, the hearts of these young men are still innocent, yet they are susceptible of good and bad. Their natural waywardness, their want of experience, and the unfortunate striving after the imitation of whatever they foolishly admire in others can very easily tarnish the purity of the soul, sadden the Holy Ghost, and deprive them of the grace of their vocation. It is a great boon which the Church grants to her future servant if she opportunely snatches him from the noxious influences of the world, shelters and fosters him in the salutary atmosphere of her secluded sanctuary, till his character has developed and he has grown up in the wisdom of God.

"A period of ten or twelve years devoted to scientific branches, especially ecclesiastical science, qualifies him to instruct the ignorant, strengthen the doubting and wavering, guide the faithful, preach and defend fearlessly the truths of our holy faith.

"The character of the priesthood elevates him to a high dignity, even above the angels, and to this dignity must correspond his virtues that he may be a worthy servant of God, possessed of Christian holiness in so eminent a degree as to be able to discharge the duties of his high office in a manner pleasing to God and salutary to the souls of men.

"The time which a seminarian spends at college gives him sufficient opportunity to ascend from virtue to virtue until he reaches the perfection required by the

Church of her priests. The Holy Sacrifice of the Mass, meditations in common, prayers daily recited by all, the good example of fellow-students, frequent Holy Communion, and the dwelling under the same roof with our Lord in the Blessed Sacrament, impose upon him the happy necessity not only of avoiding every wilful sin, but aid him to prepare his heart for every virtue.

"We were therefore highly satisfied when informed last spring that a piece of land with suitable buildings, situated in a healthful region, had been offered for sale. Trusting in God's help and your generosity, we bought it without delay, and made the necessary improvements for the reception of young students. With pleasure we announce for your consolation that there are now twenty-six students and four professors in the institution.

"As this institution is connected with our large seminary, we think it advisable to recommend to you their united claims. We do not deem it necessary to exhort you to contribute to them. We know well that our appeal will meet a hearty response, and that every parish priest will do his best to make these establishments successful; neither do we wish to change our plan for raising funds. It has proved itself effective. But we should like to see a more general co-operation on the part of the faithful; therefore we request the reverend clergy to read this Pastoral from the pulpit on the first Sunday after its receipt, and to appoint as many of the faithful as are willing to gather subscriptions, in order that the seminaries may be freed from their heavy debts.

"The collection is to continue from October until the middle of November.

"Yet, dear brethren, not gifts alone laid on the altar will secure for us good priests, but humble prayer with fasting is necessary.

"Particularly during the ember-days should the

faithful not omit to pray, to receive Holy Communion, and to practise works of self-denial, in order that the Pastor of our soul may send worthy laborers into His vineyard, and that we may enter undefiled into the possession of the inheritance reserved for us in heaven.

"✠ JOHN NEPOMUCENE,
"Bishop of Philadelphia."
"PHILADELPHIA, October 2, 1859,
"Feast of the Holy Rosary.

As the time approached for the seminaries to attain the end at which they had been aiming, the greater became their good Bishop's zeal that they should be worthily prepared for so high a dignity. When at home, no day passed without his visiting the seminary. He used to give the theological students discourses on pastoral theology, into which he knew how to weave excellent remarks on moral theology, canon law, and church-history. Clarke says: "The seminary during Bishop Neumann's administration attained a reputation such as it had never had before." The Holy Father bestowed upon it the privilege of conferring the doctorate.

The priests of Bishop Neumann's diocese found in him a friend and father. If one called at his residence, he might on admission walk up to his room, knock at the door, and enter without previous announcement. Once in the Bishop's presence, he could freely and leisurely communicate to him his business or difficulties. He was heard with interest, and never dismissed without a decision or a word of good advice or encouragement, as the case might require. The Bishop was invariably kind and affable to all whom he met, and, like the holy patriarch Abraham, he delighted in the exercise of the virtue of hospitality. Apartments were always in readiness for the reception of ecclesiastics who might happen to be in the city from a distance. Yet with all his remarkable meekness, Bishop Neumann kept a vigilant eye upon the conduct of his priests. With paternal love, yet with truly apostolic zeal, he conscientiously saw to the faithful fulfilment of their duties, as is sufficiently proved by the regulations of his synods. Among other things, he ordained that the clergy of his diocese should wear the ecclesiastical dress and avoid sea-side resorts.

For the regulation of the temporal affairs of the different parishes, and for the safeguard of the honor of the priesthood, he made several wise rules to be observed in the whole diocese. In ten chapters of these rules, the administration of church-property of the parishes was regulated, and provision made for difficult cases that might arise.

In his anxiety to remove abuses, Bishop Neumann occasionally met opposition; but his calmness, his purity of intention, which sought only the honor of God and the salvation of souls, usually effected his purpose. In one of his synods he spoke of the disadvantages of taking up a forced collection at the door of the church, a practice usual in some places, and pointed out the fact that this was frequently the cause of many persons not hearing Mass. When the reverend gentlemen present were asked to give their opinion for or against this practice, several arose and warmly opposed the innovation, as they were pleased to term it, which the Bishop wished to introduce. "By cutting off these sure revenues for the churches," they said, "a great injury would be done, and whoever would abolish the custom would plainly show that he knew very little about a certain class of people," etc.

The listeners fully expected the Bishop to resent authoritatively the personal attacks made upon him, or at least give his opponents a severe lesson. But no: the humble Bishop exhibited no sign of displeasure. He quietly asked whether any one else desired to express his opinion on the question. All sat silent, conscious of the affront offered their good prelate by the passionate language just uttered in his presence. They were, in truth, not a little astonished at his meekness and forbearance. At last, after a few moments of painful suspense on the part of the clergy and of expectant waiting on that of the Bishop, the latter, receiving no response to his invitation, closed the meeting with these words: "Gentlemen, some of you appear to differ on this matter, and the reasons you have urged for the same I regard as weak. I, too, have reasons—very grave reasons—for my opinions. Since we do not agree, we must allow the Holy See to decide in the matter, and submit to whatever decision may be given."

The synod was at an end. The priests, as they dispersed, spoke only of the unfortunate occurrence, which they very much deplored, whilst they admired their Bishop's humility. His most zealous opponent, deeply mortified at his own indiscretion, gave expression to his thoughts in the following words: "We have, indeed, a saintly Bishop."

We may style Bishop Neumann's interest in his clergy a truly paternal love, since he saw to both their spiritual and temporal well-being. He pressed them to apply to him in all their difficulties, to make known to him all their wants. If they wrote to him, he answered promptly; he spared no pains in his efforts to oblige them.

The annual spiritual exercises he sometimes conducted for them himself, or chose one from the religious Orders for that purpose. In the former case, his own exemplary observance of the order of the day conveyed to them almost as much instruction and edification as his words.

Long before his elevation to the episcopacy, Bishop Neumann was noted for the lively interest he manifested in those unfortunate priests whose faults had incurred suspension. He earnestly sought to lead them back to a sense of their duty. If they consented to enter upon a few days' retreat, he aided them all in his power, and when he saw signs of thorough amendment, he wrote to their Bishop begging him to receive once more the repentant clerics. When raised to the mitre, he devoted himself even more zealously to this work, and his paternal interest was all alive was there question of one of his own priests. His natural kind-heartedness was ever ready to assert its rights when he believed repentance sincere. Toward the close of his life, however, grown wiser by experience, he placed but little confidence in those unfortunates, that suspended in their own dioceses, asked admission into his.

His respect and affection for good, earnest priests were unbounded. How often were not poor clergymen, though not having made known their wants, been unexpectedly relieved by their Bishop with money, vestments, or sacred vessels! Even articles of clothing, received as donations from charitable friends for his own use, frequently found their way to distressed ecclesiastics.

CHAPTER VI.

Bishop Neumann's Solicitude for the Religious of his Diocese.

THE welfare of religious Orders was another object near to Bishop Neumann's heart. In them he took the liveliest interest; for what concerned them he was as solicitous as a father for his well-beloved family. His affections naturally clung to the Congregation of which he formed so bright an ornament, the Congregation of the Most Holy Redeemer: and who would blame him for this? Before his elevation to the episcopate, he had been, as we have said, one of its most active members, a witness of the great work it was accomplishing, a co-laborer in the same. A true son of St. Alphonsus, burning with the same untiring zeal that urged his founder on in his career of devotedness to God's glory, we have seen how Bishop Neumann bore the burden of the apostolate in by-gone years. A thorough Redemptorist at heart, he found the necessity to which he was condemned by the episcopal office a hard and bitter one. He repeatedly petitioned to have a Father of the Congregation and a lay-brother, or at least one of them, as a member of his household; but the state of things at that time would not permit his request to be granted. This refusal did not, however, prevent the Bishop's choosing the seal of the Congregation of the Most Holy Redeemer as his episcopal coat-of-arms, and he continued for a time to wear the Redemptorist habit. But when he perceived that this wearing the habit was misunderstood and unfavorably commented upon, he appeared in public clothed in the episcopal robes. When, however, he found himself for a few days a guest at any of the Redemptorist convents, he gladly donned his beloved habit again : he was once more the Redemptorist Father.

To Bishop Neumann's great annoyance, it was asserted by some individuals that his episcopal consecration had cut him off from membership with the Congregation which he loved so much. In his doubt and anxiety, he recurred to the Holy Father, requesting him to decide the mater, urging that it would cause him great pain if, after having rendered obedience to the Chief Pastor of the Church, he should now be deprived of the graces and privileges of his dear Congregation. The answer of the Holy Father removed all doubt on that head. Here are the words of His Holiness :

"Because you, my beloved son, have united the virtues of a religious with the burden of a Bishop, you shall remain a religious ; and even if you were no longer a full member of the Congregation, I would, by virtue of my power, receive you as such."

For the removal of further scruples, the Holy Father added a few regulations as to the manner of his keeping the vows of poverty and obedience.

Every week he went on foot to the convent at St. Peter's, to confer with his confessor ; he spent one day there every month in retreat, and the ten successive days of his annual retreat as prescribed by the rules of the Congregation of the Most Holy Redeemer. His name headed the list of the community ; and on New-Year's eve, when patron saints, virtues, and particular prayers are allotted to each for the coming year, the Bishop, like all the rest, received his. When with his brethren, he always sought the last place among the lay-brothers and very reluctantly accepted the highest. Let us cite here the following incident which happened in Cumberland, whither the Bishop had gone to confer minor orders on some of the Redemptorist students. It is customary in Redemptorist convents to visit the Blessed Sacrament after dinner and there recite the psalm *De profundis*. The lay-brothers, leaving the refectory first, go processionally followed by the Fathers in order to the sanctuary, where they range round the altar. The Superior walks last; but when the Bishop happened to be present, this post of honor was assigned him. On such occasions there was always placed before the altar a kneeling-stool for the use of His Lordship; but he, instead of proceeding to the place assigned him, would take his station behind the lay-brothers, thus securing for himself the necessity of going out directly after them at the close of the prayers. If we follow him, it will be to the kitchen, where we shall find him chuckling over the success of his well-executed plan whilst girding himself with a huge apron preparatory to helping with the dishes. To be sure, we shall not have to wait long before good Father Superior makes his appearance, insisting on the Bishop's going with him at once to the recreation-room, where the Fathers are assembled for their after-dinner chat. And now behold a scene blessed in the sight of Him who was "meek and humble of heart"! Father Superior's earnestness to lead him back in triumph, and the good Bishop gently pleading to be allowed to perform the lowly act, to feel that he is still a Redemptorist. O Humility, golden virtue, pride itself must bow down before thee!

It is usual among the Redemptorists for the Fathers sometimes to assist in such offices for the sake of practising humility.

When the Sacrament of Confirmation was to be administered or any other episcopal function to be performed in the Redemptorist convents out of his own diocese, Bishop Neumann was always ready, with the permission of the Ordinary, to offer his services. Such opportunities of obliging his brethren afforded him the highest gratification. He went to New York to be present at the consecration of the Church of the Most Holy Redeemer, which took place with great solemnity on November 28, 1852, and he willingly accepted the invitation to preach the same evening. In the Redemptorist parishes of Baltimore and Pittsburg he frequently administered the Sacrament of Confirmation, performed the ceremonies of ordination, of laying the corner-stones of churches and schools, and of blessing bells, etc. Archbishop Kenrick and Bishop O'Connor, being personal friends of Bishop Neumann, were well aware of what could afford him gratification; consequently each gladly accorded to him a general permission to perform episcopal functions in his diocese. He sung Pontifical Mass at St. Peter's, Philadelphia, several times a year, and graciously responded to every invitation to exercise his faculties as Bishop.

His deep attachment to his own beloved Congregation was no hindrance to his loving kindness for all other religious Orders. He entertained for each and all the highest esteem, nay, even reverence, being convinced that their pious labors drew down upon his diocese the richest blessings of Heaven. Animated by this spirit, he strove to improve the condition of those already within its precincts, and to introduce others. During the first year of his episcopate he wrote his sister Mary Caroline, a Sister of Charity of St. Charles Borromeo, Bohemia:

"As soon as I can procure means, I intend to open an Infant Asylum for a class of children of which hundreds have hitherto been lost to the Church; and I hope that in a short time a hospital will be established for sick immigrants. As soon as things are ready, I shall not fail to apply to you. I had this thought on the Feast of St. Charles Borromeo. It can very easily be realized, since the various religious communities in the United States are always in need of subjects."

Again he wrote to Father Dichtl: "God be praised, religious institutions are increasing in the diocese! The Jesuit Fathers in Philadelphia are opening their college in a new and much larger building; the Sisters of the Holy Cross from the diocese of Le Mans, France, will open an industrial school for poor girls; and the Sisters of Notre Dame from Namur, Belgium, are daily expecting to take charge of a parochial school. However gratifying this news, the difficulties connected with the introduction of religious Orders are indescribable. I have had an offer of eight acres near the city. I intended to accept it and retain the property for the Sisters of St. Charles Borromeo, to be used by them as a hospital and mother-house; but the gentleman that made the offer has since lost forty thousand dollars by fire, and I know not whether he can now carry out his benevolent intentions."

The Sisters of the Immaculate Heart of Mary, first established in the diocese of Detroit, had many difficulties to overcome in the foundation of their Congregation. Bishop Neumann lent them assistance, and received them into his diocese. They are at present laboring successfully as teachers in several other dioceses.

The Sisters of the Third Order of St. Francis, owe their existence as an Order to Bishop Neumann, and justly honor him as their father and founder. These are the Sisters of St. Francis who first formed a community, April 9, 1855, under the following circumstances. During his stay in Rome, the Bishop communicated to the Holy Father his desire to introduce into his diocese, and that at an early date, the Sisters of St. Dominic, who might supply such wants as could not be met by other Orders. His Holiness, Pius IX., advised him to train the daughters of the Seraphic St. Francis for this purpose. Regarding the Holy Father's advice as the declared will of God, the Bishop began at once to organize the first Franciscan sisterhood in America. To this end he sent for some Fathers of the Order, called Conventuals, to train these daughters of St. Francis in the spirit of their holy founder. He appointed Mother Mary Francis Superioress of the little community, which then consisted of only five members, and gave them a rule written by his own hand. No one could peruse its contents without feeling himself deeply impressed by the rare wisdom and prudence of the author. Notwithstanding his multiplied occupations, he found time to instruct the Sisters in monastic discipline by means of conferences, and to lead them forward on the road of perfection. Like all the works of God, the new institute had to contend against innumerable contradictions and difficulties; but under the Bishop's fostering care it gradually grew and flourished. Following out his views, the Sisters were to unite to the active life that of prayer and meditation, their principal object being the care of the sick, whom they both visited and nursed. As long as their small domicile afforded accommodations for only a limited number of patients, the Sisters devoted themselves more freely to the care of the sick in their own homes. When, however, postulants were received and the community increased, they began the second object of their mission, viz., the education of youth.

Scarcely four years after their establishment the Sisterhood counted four houses in which the virtues of the Seraphic St. Francis were fervently imitated, the love of God and the neighbor practised. At the present date this Congregation numbers about twenty-five convents, with two hundred professed Sisters, all unceasingly active in the several works enumerated above. These convents are in Philadelphia, Buffalo, New York, Baltimore, Pittsburg, etc.

One of the strongest proofs of Bishop Neumann's high appreciation of the religious life lies in the fact of his repeatedly directing the attention of his seminarians to that sublime vocation, and unhesitatingly encouraging them to manifest to him any desire they might entertain to enter it. "I shall cheerfully give you my permission and blessing, should you wish to take such a step." Such was the language of this most disinterested Bishop, who nevertheless left no means untried to supply his diocese with good recruits for the secular clergy.

Bishop Neumann, as might be judged from the foregoing pages, delighted in acting as celebrant in the ceremonies of religious receptions and professions. An observer could not fail to mark the joy that lit up his countenance on such occasions, a joy mingled with devotion. His earnest and soul-inspiring discourses at such times evidenced his own lively faith, his interior piety, and his high esteem of the religious state. When unable to attend these ceremonies, his regrets were couched in terms so humble and cordial as to compensate, in some degree, for his absence. Once he wrote to a certain Superioress by whom he had been invited to take part in the ceremony of receiving a novice to the habit: "It would afford me real pleasure to witness the reception of a new member to your community; yet this time I must content myself with being present in spirit. I shall, on the day of the ceremony, offer up the Holy Sacrifice for the welfare of your novitiate."

His solicitude for his religious extended to whatever interested their well-being. He wished to be informed of the most trifling circumstances, that he might furnish counsel and assistance when necessary; indeed, he frequently exhorted Superiors by letter not to fail to apply to him in all their necessities. "In whatever distress you may be," he wrote to one, "I beg you to let me know, and I will help you according to my ability. I am poor myself, yet I know that God will not forget us in our poverty."

One day he called at a convent whose poverty was so great that its inmates often wanted the necessaries of life. "Right Reverend Bishop," said one of the Sisters ingenuously, "we can scarcely get along. Sometimes we have no coal to make a fire; and when we have coal, we often have nothing to cook."

The Bishop looked at her thoughtfully, then, pointing to a crucifix that hung near, he said: "There, dear Sisters, there is a book. Read it, meditate upon it. It will lighten your trials, it will help you to bear your crosses."

But not to mere words was the good Bishop's sympathy confined. With a smile full of sweetness and benevolence, he turned to the Superioress and said: "As I usually distribute medals among the Sisters, I must not omit to do so now; but to-day I am going to give you Yankee medals," and he handed her fifty dollars in gold to procure necessaries for the house. When relating this incident, the Sisters remarked: "His tone of voice when pointing to the crucifix, his whole manner, made a deep impression upon us. We felt encouraged, and we resolved to bear our privations with patience."

To the Superioress of another convent newly-founded, he wrote: "I foresee that you will have to struggle with many difficulties, especially with great poverty. But I am full of confidence in God, who always supports what is undertaken for His own greater glory. Do not waver in your hope. The greater your distress, the greater should be your trust in help from on high. Let us pray, and God will show us what we must do."

But above every other care was that which he entertained for the spiritual good of his religious. He appointed their confessors only after mature reflection, since to them chiefly appertains the noble task of leading these souls along the path of perfection. The regular observance was a point on which he displayed untiring vigilance; his tact for discovering whatever evils existed in a religious community was truly wonderful. He applied a remedy without delay, insisting especially upon strict enclosure for nuns. He did not wish to see the spouses of Jesus Christ encouraging unnecessary intercourse with seculars. In a letter to a certain Superioress he says: "I beg you to introduce as soon as possible all the spiritual exercises prescribed by the rules of your Order, for I wish your house to be a model of religious observance. I am not solicitous about its temporalities. Divine Providence will see that you always have what is necessary, if the Sisters faithfully observe their rule and by their mutual love and harmony attract His blessing upon themselves. I exceedingly dislike that religious houses should depend on the favor of creditors. Let us trust in God and St. Joseph. In God's own good time things will come right. Procure whatever is necessary. Be satisfied with what is needed for the present day, and confide the future to God. This, I know well, exacts great self-denial, but it is the surest way of acting."

On another occasion he wrote to the same Superioress, who was laboring under severe trials: "I am doing what I can, but patience is necessary. Such crosses God sends that we may learn how displeasing it is to Him to oblige Him to wait for our confidence in Him and for the observance of our rule, since to all this He is justly entitled at every moment of our life."

Although Bishop Neumann was a man of vast erudition and one who highly valued science, yet he preferred virtue to learning. "Your chief study," said he to the Sisters of a certain academy, "is your rule. If you observe it faithfully and conscientiously, God will bless your work. Our labors are crowned not so much by our own efforts as by God's blessing. I am fully convinced that a Sister who possesses comparatively less learning, yet who is faithful to God, will have more success than others who are perhaps better educated, but who do not observe the rules faithfully."

The Superioress-General of a certain Order often wrote to Bishop Neumann for advice in matters of importance. In one of her letters she incidentally complained of the burden and responsibility of her office, remarking that for such a post she was too young and altogether unfit. The Bishop's reply was as dignified as it was paternal. "My dear Sister," he wrote, "God strengthens and enlightens even young and weak Sisters in such offices. Reconcile yourself to your position in all humility. Every Superior has his faults. There has never yet been a man, never a Superior, that has not sometimes made mistakes, that has not sometimes erred." The young Superioress to whom the above was addressed afterward declared that the Bishop's words quieted her, whilst at the same time they afforded her salutary humiliation.

These and similar expressions he often used for the peace or consolation of others. They always produced a soothing effect upon the mind of those to whom they were directed and stimulated them to the practice of virtue. Upon one of his visits to a convent he found the Sisters occupied in laborious household duties. They wore a look of fatigue, which the kind-hearted Bishop noticing, said: "Remember, dear Sisters, your labors are similar to those of the Blessed Virgin. If you unite them to hers, you will find them less wearisome."

On another occasion he said: "This is the season commemorative of our Lord's sufferings. We must carry our cross with Him." His uninterrupted intercourse with God produced a most beneficial impression upon all that conversed with him. His most frequent expression was, "For God alone!" or "For God, the Almighty!"—words uttered with so much earnestness, with so much faith, that the hearers felt persuaded that they sprung from the depths of his own upright soul.

CHAPTER VII.

Bishop Neumann's Reverence and Devotion in the Performance of Sacred Functions.

IF Bishop Neumann's habitual recollectedness exercised so salutary an influence upon those that came in daily contact with him, his faith and love of God shone out still more clearly when engaged in the performance of sacred functions. When administering the Sacrament of Confirmation, of holy orders, or performing other ceremonies peculiar to the episcopal office, his whole countenance was radiant with devotion, whilst his every word and movement was stamped with unaffected dignity. On such occasions he carefully observed every formula; not a rubric was neglected. Dr. Richard Clarke says: "Bishop Neumann distinguished himself by his exact observance of all the prescribed ceremonies of the Church;" and one of his clergy remarks on the same point: "I shall never forget the time that I was present with him at the laying of the corner-stone of St. Alphonsus' Church, Philadelphia. To have been near him on such an occasion is to retain an impression full of admiration for his faith, his reverence, his childlike fidelity to the Church in the observance of her sacred ceremonies."

In the performance of such functions Bishop Neumann was indefatigable. On Holy Saturday of 1853 he officiated in St. Peter's, Philadelphia. At six in the morning service began with the blessing of the new fire and the paschal candle, followed by that of the baptismal font and the baptism of several adults. After the singing of the Litanies came High Mass, during which the

Bishop conferred the tonsure, the four minor orders, the diaconate and subdiaconate on several candidates for the ranks of the secular and regular clergy, besides ordaining others. The ceremonies were long and fatiguing; yet the Bishop looked upon this part of Almighty God's service as a joy, yes, even a recreation.

The Bishop was as great a stickler for the reverential performance of sacred duties and adherence to rubrics in the case of his priests as in his own. He made excellent rules on these points in his diocesan synods; and at the quarterly conferences he caused one or other of the reverend gentlemen to practise certain ceremonies according to the rules laid down in the Ritual and Ceremonial. He was, above all, deeply interested in the exact and respectful celebration of the Holy Sacrifice of the Mass, and he frequently instructed the theological students himself how to offer up the Holy Mysteries in the spirit of the Church. On this subject he once wrote to Rev. Father Dichtl: "Last month I assembled all the priests of my diocese, and gave them the spiritual exercises; then followed a synod: and I have reason to rejoice over the success of both. These synods are especially needed in the United States, in order to secure uniformity in the performance of clerical functions. As missionaries come here from all parts of Christendom, each bringing with him the peculiarities of his own nation, discord may thereby be engendered. I know of no better means than these synods to settle things at once, as is done in the Eternal City. Besides several statutes enacted upon various points of discipline, it was also proposed to introduce into the larger churches of the diocese the devotion of the Forty Hours, so that there might be no week in the year in which the Blessed Sacrament would not be exposed for the adoration of the faithful."

In the Blessed Sacrament Bishop Neumann found the sweet object of his lively faith, his firm hope, his tender love. His devotion to Jesus hidden under the Eucharistic veils was earnest and edifying; and intense was his desire to enkindle the same among his flock. He longed for them to share largely in the rich blessings flowing from this source of grace. The best means to accomplish this lay, as he thought, in the devotion of the Forty Hours; and the thought of introducing it into his diocese, of celebrating it with all possible pomp and splendor, was one that constantly recurred to his mind.

During the last diocesan synod, as we have read above, the introduction of the devotion had been proposed, but nothing definitive connected with it agreed upon. The Bishop did not desire to be the sole originator of the movement, so he communicated his inspiration to a few of his confidential and most experienced friends among the clergy. But his wishes met with no response from them. They were of opinion that the time had not yet arrived for the worthy celebration of the devotion in this country; that the faithful were not ripe for it; that our Lord Jesus Christ would receive more dishonor than honor in those long hours of exposition. The good Bishop, though a little disappointed at not finding himself supported, yet did not consider the hesitation of the persons consulted a sufficient reason for abandoning his cherished design. He would, on the one hand, gladly have been influenced by the opinion of prudent men; but, on the other, his intense love for Jesus in the Blessed Sacrament constantly urged him to the execution of his design. Whilst thus undecided, the following incident occurred, in which our Lord appears to have encouraged him by a miracle in the accomplishment of what was to be so fruitful in glory to His hidden Majesty and blessings to His redeemed ones.

Late one evening, Bishop Neumann sat in his room busy inditing answers to innumerable letters that lay before him. Midnight sounded and found him still at work. The candle that he used in sealing his letters had well-nigh burned out, and he vainly tried to steady the only remaining piece at hand in the candlestick. Not being able to succeed, and preoccupied with the thought that had so long pursued him, that of the Forty Hours, he rather carelessly,—we should perhaps say providentially,—stood the piece of lighted candle on the table, placing around it as a support some letters and writing-paper. Wearied by so many hours of close application, he fell into a light sleep, from which he suddenly awoke in alarm to find the candle consumed and his table covered with smouldering paper. He gazed in astonishment at the glowing sheets, many of them burnt and charred, though the writing they contained remained untouched and legible. Overcome by what he saw, and heedless of quenching the glowing sparks, the servant of God sank on his knees. As he knelt in silent gratitude for this apparently miraculous interposition of Divine Providence, it seemed to him that he heard an interior voice saying: "As the flames are here burning without consuming or even injuring the writing, so shall I pour out My grace in the Blessed Sacrament without prejudice to My honor. Fear not profanation, therefore; hesitate no longer to carry out your designs for My glory."

The Bishop was confirmed in his resolution. At that very hour he expedited the order for all the parish churches of his diocese to celebrate the devotion of the Forty Hours. This was in the year 1853.

He caused a pamphlet containing the history of the devotion, the manner of conducting it, and the prayers for the same to be printed in Latin. In 1855 the Pope granted to all the faithful of the diocese of Philadelphia the same indulgences as are gained in Rome on such occasions.

The church of St. Philip Neri was the first in Philadelphia to celebrate the devotion. The Bishop himself inaugurated and directed the solemnity; he scarcely left the church during the three days of its continuance. His soul overflowed with heavenly consolation, and his countenance beamed with joy at the sight of this blissful realization of his long-cherished scheme. The clergy and laity alike were deeply edified at his ardent love for Jesus in the Holy Eucharist. For the worthy celebration of the devotion, he gladly lent his own magnificent ostensorium and his richest vestments. It was his greatest happiness to contribute in every way to the glory of his hidden God: magnificent ornaments, rare flowers, innumerable lights—all that the wealth of earth could afford or the skill of man devise he wished to lay in homage upon the altar of his Lord. Whenever it was possible, he opened the Forty Hours with Pontifical High Mass, took part in the procession, or closed the solemnities.

The faithful flocked to the churches in crowds, both for public and private devotions, during the three days of exposition—a fact which affords the most striking proof that the introduction of the Forty Hours in this country was entirely opportune. Bishop Neumann's example was soon followed by his brother-Bishops, even by those who withheld the weight of their encouragement when the question was first mooted. At the present day there are few dioceses in the United States that do not gratefully share in the blessings emanating from this public homage to Jesus in the Most Blessed Sacrament.

The feelings that animated Bishop Neumann's heart for this Mystery of Love led him, in 1855, to establish the Archconfraternity of the Blessed Sacrament in St. Alphonsus' Church, Philadelphia. He himself drew up the rules and arranged the order of devotions. The members bind themselves to honor their Lord and Saviour in a special manner by faithful compliance with the duties of their state, and by appropriate devotions before the Blessed Sacrament. Exposition follows Vespers of every Sunday and holy-day, when a short sermon on the Holy Eucharist is delivered, and the Litany of the Holy Name of Jesus or that of the Blessed Virgin is recited by the officiating clergyman, the congregation answering. This is followed by a hymn, to which succeed indulgenced prayers in honor of the Five Sacred Wounds, offered in reparation for the ingratitude, indifference, and profanations which Jesus endures in the Most Blessed Sacrament. The veneration of each Wound concludes with the short act of adoration: "Praised and blessed forever be the Most Holy Sacrament of the altar!" The devotions terminate with Benediction. On the second Sunday of each month the Blessed Sacrament is borne in solemn procession through the church.

To excite and nourish among the faithful an effective and grateful remembrance of the sufferings of our Lord, Bishop Neumann prescribed special Lenten services throughout his diocese. On one day of the week the Way of the Cross was to be made by the priest and the people together, and on another a sermon was to be preached on the Passion, Benediction of the Blessed Sacrament to be given at the close of each devotion. Where there were several churches, he so arranged that these devotions took place on different evenings, thus affording the faithful an opportunity for more frequent attendance.

Bishop Neumann was of opinion that confraternities are an excellent means to foster true piety among the faithful; consequently he introduced several into his diocese. To a prominent ecclesiastic in Bohemia he wrote as follows: "Please to give the enclosed picture of the scapular to Mr. N——, and tell him to make use of it as an incentive to greater veneration toward the Blessed Virgin. The Mother of God will obtain many graces for him at the hour of death, if he is faithful in asking her for them. I hope he will not forget me in his prayers. During the visitation of my diocese this year I had the consolation of witnessing the happy fruits produced by the missions. The Fathers have introduced into many congregations the Confraternities of the Scapular, the Rosary, and the Immaculate Heart of Mary. All this, with God's help, will serve to foster the spirit of faith and piety, an end so important in the United States, where faith is exposed to greater danger than elsewhere."

Bishop Neumann made regulations also for the careful and respectful preservation of everything appertaining to the service of the altar, sacred vessels, vestments, etc. All were to be preserved in good condition and in proper places. As no suitable vessel had as yet been devised for the holy oils, he had one made according to his own directions. It has been found most convenient, both as to material and form, and it is now in general use.

The following incident will present to the reader some idea of the highly refined and artistic bent of Bishop Neumann's religious soul. We have seen, in treating of the Forty Hours, his eagerness to place whatever treasures our earth can afford at the feet of his God. The circumstance of the famous ivory crucifix we may adduce in proof of the same. As soon as his eyes rested upon this masterpiece of more than human skill, he conceived so tender an affection for the Crucified as there represented, he expressed his admiration in terms so enthusiastic, so indicative of the artist's soul burning within him, that the owner, though fully conscious of the prize he possessed, could not refuse to let him have it. The Bishop lost no time in securing for his Cathedral this treasure of art, this product of heavenly inspiration.

A sketch of this crucifix and its carver will, doubtless, be of interest to the reader.

Carlo Antonio Pesenti was born February 23, 1801, in the valley of Brembana, Italy. He received from his parents a good Christian education, and was remarkable even in childhood for piety. His greatest delight was to fashion the images of Mary and of his patrons, Saints

Charles and Anthony, out of wood. Thus did he grow up from boyhood to manhood, the years bringing with them naught to mar the beauty and freshness of his innocent soul. At the age of twenty-two, he conceived the design of carrying out a long-cherished desire, that of visiting the Holy Places in Rome. God favored the youth, and things fell out propitiously for Antonio. On his homeward journey he resolved to turn aside a little in order to visit the monastery of St. Nicholas Tolentino, not far from Genoa. Here he sought shelter for the night, and here it was that Almighty God made known to him his vocation to the religious life. Touched and edified by the prayers and canticles of the good monks, Antonio obeyed the secret inspiration which urged him to ask to be received among them. His request was favored; he entered the novitiate, and in due time made his vows as a laybrother. His virtuous life soon made him a model for the whole community. Fifteen years passed, and Fra Antonio lived on in fervor, in prayer, and in deeds of charity, carving rude images of the saints, studying their lives and striving to imitate their virtues. Especially was he devout to the Sacred Passion of Christ, from the uninterrupted contemplation of which his very countenance had caught a seraphic glow. Once, whilst absorbed in such meditation, a vision unfolded itself before his enraptured gaze—a vision of his Lord hanging on the Wood of Redemption, His sacred features breathing love and peace. In an ecstasy of grief and love, the monk gazed on the wondrous spectacle, and as he gazed there sprung up in his soul a longing to represent in some visible form what he then saw. But how was this to be accomplished? What could he, a simple laybrother, do? Everything was wanting to him—materials, implements, and, more than all, knowledge of that art whose rules would direct him to the end. But He who had engraven this picture of His sufferings so deeply in

Antonio's heart guided the unskilled hand in the use of hammer and chisel.

In the storeroom of the old convent lay a massive block of ivory, measuring over three feet in length, fourteen inches in thickness, and weighing about one hundred and twenty-five pounds. The prior's permission being readily obtained, Fra Antonio removed the block to his cell and with steady purpose set about his task of love. Layer after layer of discolored crust was carefully and patiently removed ere the pure white ivory was reached.

Four years rolled by, and still were hammer and chisel busily plied, fashioning the rough mass into the image of the Crucified such as He had deigned to show Himself to Fra Antonio's ravished eyes. Oftentimes the monk grew weary, temptations to abandon his design seized upon him. Was it not, to say the least of it, rash and foolish after all—this undertaking of his? How could he, ignorant of the sculptor's art, hope to succeed in so bold an enterprise? And what did Fra Antonio at such moments? He *prayed*, he invoked Our Lady's help, and he *fainted not.*

Twenty-four, even thirty, consecutive hours often found the monk still bending over his work. Tears and prayers mingled with the hammer's blows and the chisel's strokes; visitors, drawn by the fame of the work and the workman, crowded the secluded cell: and still the monk toiled on.

At last a day came on which the hammer was silent and the chisel was laid aside. The monk's task of love was finished, and he gazed with tearful eyes upon the embodiment of the vision of ravishing beauty that had once been his.

The work was pronounced a masterpiece, a marvel of art, by the most distinguished connoisseurs who came from far and near to behold the production of that untrained hand.

In 1843, Mr. E. Lester, United States Consul at Genoa, visited the convent to see for himself the crucifix so admired, so praised even, by eminent artists. He saw, and he longed to possess. The convent was poor; Mr. Lester's offer was large: and need we say that he soon found himself the fortunate owner of the wondrously beautiful object? He transferred it to the Academy of Fine Arts in Genoa, whither, as to the humble cell of its carver, it soon attracted numbers of visitors. The most celebrated artists declared it inimitable; and it is indeed in every respect, even in the minutest details, a perfect work. The Divine Countenance unites an expression of exquisite suffering with a smile of ineffable sweetness.

From Genoa it was, at the suggestion of Mr. Power, the great American sculptor, taken to Florence, and afterward exhibited in many of the cities of Europe and America. The Cosmopolitan Art Association purchased it from Mr. Lester for ten thousand dollars; thence it passed into the hands of a gentleman of Pennsylvania, and from him into the possession of Bishop Neumann, through whom it was to reach its fitting destination. Encased in glass, it is now exposed in the Cathedral of Philadelphia, an object of devout admiration to the visitor.

Bishop Neumann's fondness for articles of devotion had in it something remarkably childlike. He greatly venerated holy relics, numbers of which he always had in his possession. These he used to exhibit to his visitors as precious treasures, relating the while some beautiful traits from the lives of the saints to whom they belonged. He often divided them himself into small particles, enclosed them in reliquaries, sealed them, and affixed thereto a certificate of authenticity. He delighted in presenting them to his priests and religious, with an injunction to value them highly and venerate them lovingly.

CHAPTER VIII.

The Building of the Cathedral.

WE have seen that the Cathedral of Bishop Neumann's episcopal city was but recently commenced at the period of his taking possession of it; but in its progress and completion he took the liveliest interest. That he was endowed with qualifications for carrying on the great work we may learn from a remark made by Bishop O'Connor, of Pittsburg. When the prelates of the Baltimore Province assembled in 1851 to propose three candidates for the vacant see of Philadelphia, the learned and saintly Bishop O'Connor, on giving his vote, spoke as follows: "Philadelphia must have a Bishop that can build the Cathedral. Since the Redemptorist Father Neumann knows how to erect fine churches with small means, I give him my vote." Bishop O'Connor here made allusion to the beautiful church of St. Philomena built by Father Neumann during the period of his rectorship in Pittsburg.

The foundation of the Cathedral, Philadelphia, had been laid by Bishop Neumann's predecessor, Most Rev. Archbishop Kenrick, on September 9, 1846.

In his first Pastoral the new Bishop reminded the faithful of their obligation to contribute according to their means to the erection of a temple worthy of the Lord. On May 4, 1852, he issued a circular exhorting his flock to renewed exertions in this so important matter, and inviting their attendance at a meeting to be held for the purpose of taking measures for its completion. A committee was appointed to aid the Bishop. In his opening address Bishop Neumann made known his resolve to go on with the building only as long as he could command the funds necessary for it, only when he had money in hand; for the Cathedral, he said, should have no debts. The want of means had caused the discontinuance of the work, but it should be resumed as soon as the contributions of the faithful authorized such a step. The Bishop made the following proposal to the committee, which was readily accepted:

"In every parish throughout the diocese let collectors keep a list of contributors' names, together with the amount subscribed, the money to be handed over to the pastor, who will forward it to the treasurer."

The annual mass-meeting for the benefit of the Cathedral was always well attended, and at it the Bishop generally presided. A remarkable feature of these grand meetings was their unbroken peace and harmony. At one of them the Bishop spoke as follows: "The report that Rev. Mr. Waldron will read to us presently proves that the erection of the Cathedral has been continued with the same zeal and earnestness as it was begun under the direction of my most reverend predecessor. We are hopeful that a similar zeal will bring the great work to a happy completion. The circumstances, however, of its progressing slowly ought not to discourage any one, nor should any be tempted to doubt of its ever being finished. Such an assertion would offend Divine Providence. The old saying holds good here: 'What is to last long must be built slowly.' Our principal object in moving thus slowly is that the faithful may not be taxed too heavily, since every parish has its own institutions to support.

"If we make the same progress in the future that we have done in the past, this beautiful house of the Lord will certainly be finished. It will be not only an ornament to the city, but a monument of the fervent piety and self-sacrificing spirit of the faithful of this diocese. The contributions received in the past, with the names of the contributors, are a certain proof that all with few exceptions have done their duty. This knowledge must be a new stimulus for the future." (Applause.)

After the secretary had read the amount of receipts and expenditures during the preceding year, several prominent members of the clergy and laity addressed the meeting in terms expressive of their approval of the Bishop's suggestions.

At the meeting of the following year, 1857, Bishop Neumann remarked that the Catholics in the diocese amounted to three hundred thousand souls, of whom one half belonged to Philadelphia. So large a number was an additional reason why the Cathedral should soon be completed.

In 1858 the walls were up, and on September 13, 1859, the keystone was set and the cross placed in position. This event was commemorated by a celebration in which several prelates and a large number of the clergy participated. Right Rev. Martin John Spalding, Bishop of Louisville, preached to an immense concourse of people, taking for the subject of his discourse the signification of the cross. The ceremony of blessing was performed by Right Rev. Bishop Wood, Bishop Neumann's coadjutor.

Bishop Neumann presided, his heart overflowing with gratitude to the Almighty for the success thus far attained in the great undertaking. He had the joy and consolation of seeing the exterior of his Cathedral finished. He was richly compensated for the weight of care that had rested upon him, for the efforts he had made in the past seven years to bring it to its present advanced state.

The style of the Philadelphia Cathedral is the modern Roman cruciform. It is one of the largest sacred edifices in the United States, being one hundred and thirty-six feet wide, two hundred and sixteen long, two hundred and ten feet high to the roof of the dome, which latter measures seventy-one feet in diameter. The middle nave is fifty feet wide, and is separated from the two side aisles by massive fluted columns of the Corinthian order. The side aisles are seventy-two feet in width, and nearly equal in height to the central nave. The sanctuary is fifty feet broad and forty-four feet long, affording ample space for the performance of ceremonies on grand festivals and other occasions. The two side-aisle chapels are each twenty-two by twenty-four feet, and surmounted by domes of smaller dimensions than the central one. The grand entrance is supported by four pillars sixty feet high, and, like the entire building, is of the richest and purest Corinthian style. Over this entrance is read the inscription, "*Ad majorem Dei gloriam*"—"For the greater glory of God."

Despite the Bishop's energy and the support he received from the faithful, the construction of the Cathedral proceeded slowly, owing to the fact that the work was carried on only when funds for the same were on hand. Foreseeing that many years would elapse before it would be ready for service, the Bishop, for the accommodation of the parishioners, erected in 1857, on a lot adjoining his residence, a large chapel so constructed as to answer the purposes of a school-house at some future day.

The Bishop viewed with horror that want of foresight which here in America so often involves church-property in debt; and he frequently raised his voice against such rashness in the erection of churches, schools, etc. He admonished his clergy never to embark in these undertakings without his special permission. This wise and judicious command could not, however, prevent ecclesiastical property from sometimes being thus placed in jeopardy. Certain unfortunate circumstances combined at one time to embarrass the finances of St. Alphonsus' Church, Philadelphia. The sacred edifice was on the point of being put up at sale in order to satisfy the demands of its creditors. The Bishop heard of it, and hastened to adopt suitable measures to relieve the church of its debts. Some prominent citizens advised him to leave the church in the hands of the creditors for a public sale, at which he could buy it in himself for less than its amount of indebtedness. But the Bishop could not reconcile such a proceeding to his own ideas of justice. Discarding the well-meant advice, he set about using such means as he deemed prudent and necessary to raise the requisite funds. His efforts were successful, and he was enabled to satisfy the creditors without sacrificing the property. Almighty God manifestly lent a blessing to the good Bishop's conscientiousness, for the church is now free from debt.

CHAPTER IX.

Bishop Neumann visits Rome and his Native Place.

IN October, 1854, Bishop Neumann received from the Holy Father, Pius IX., a formal invitation to the Eternal City, to be present at the solemn promulgation of the dogma of the Immaculate Conception of the Mother of God. The heart of the holy Bishop beat with joy. A devoted client of the Queen of Heaven, the triumph of his Lady was happiness to him, and to be able to join with the Head of the Church in celebrating her glorious prerogative was a favor not to be discarded. He had, besides, long desired to make a pilgrimage to the tomb of the Apostles, and to give to the Holy Father a verbal account of the state of his diocese. The thought that his absence might be detrimental to his flock had made him waive his desires on this head; now, however, at the call of Peter, hesitation vanished, and he at once set about arrangements for his journey. On October 21st he sailed from New York in the steamer Union. Before his departure he issued a Pastoral whose every word, filled with unction and piety, breathes the sentiments of his own filial heart for the Mother of God. The portion relating to the Immaculate Conception runs as follows:

"And since one of the principal intentions of the reigning Pontiff in proclaiming this jubilee has been by means of your united suffrages to obtain the grace of the Holy Spirit in giving a decision on the subject of the Immaculate Conception of the ever-venerable Virgin Mother of Jesus Christ, shall we not confidently believe that abundant light will be imparted to him and to the prelates now convened around his throne in the Eternal City? As the long-wished-for day approaches, let us pray still more fervently, attentive to the invitation of the Church we so often hear, '*Sursum Corda!*' *Let us lift up our hearts* in frequent, earnest prayer that the decision may be such as will redound to the praise of the adorable Trinity, the salvation of man, and to the honor of her who, next to God, is indeed the

*Æterna Cæli Gloria,
Beata Spes Mortalium,*

the eternal joy and glory of the heavens, the ever-blessed hope of fallen man. If such be the will of God and your piety deserves it, before the close of this year we may hear again the voice of Peter, as when the days of Pentecost were accomplished, making known by the lips of Pius IX. to the assembled representatives of every nation under heaven that from henceforth and forever all generations of true believers shall invoke Mary, Mother of God, as THE EVER-IMMACULATE VIRGIN, CONCEIVED WITHOUT STAIN OF ORIGINAL SIN.

"Such appears to be the expectation of the whole Catholic world. The looking forward for the 'coming of the Messias,' her Divine Son, Christ Jesus, was not more general in the time before His advent than is this universal expectation that the Vicegerent of that same Divine Son, our Holy Father, will decide that the Blessed Virgin was *never* stained by original sin; that by a special privilege, which the Almighty could certainly grant, Mary was *always* exempt from that law to which all the other children of Adam are subject; that, from the first moment of her existence, Mary was perfect purity itself in the sight of God; and that, therefore, the words of Holy Writ and of Christian antiquity are to be understood in their literal sense when it is said, 'Thou art all-beautiful, O Virgin Mary!

and there is not a spot in thee. In thee no spot of sin either is, or ever was, or ever will be.' '*Tota pulchra es, Virgo Maria! et macula non est in te; macula peccati non est in te, neque unquam fuit nec erit.*'

"Although the Church has not yet declared the Immaculate Conception to be an article of faith, nevertheless it is evident she cherishes this most just and pious belief with a loving constancy second only to that infallible certainty with which she maintains the truth of all those doctrines the acceptance of which is necessary for salvation. With a zeal probably never surpassed in former ages, the subject has been investigated by many of the most gifted and holy men now living; and with such a munificent outlay of ancient and modern learning, of profound argument and soul-stirring eloquence have they treated it, as to leave not only the more devout clients of Mary, but every unbiassed mind convinced beyond the possibility of doubt, that if there be anything certainly true, next to the defined doctrines of faith, it is this apostolic and therefore ancient and beautiful belief.

"Hence it is not surprising that, wherever enlightened piety exists, hardly a moment's hesitation on this subject will be entertained. '*Caro Jesu! Caro Mariæ!*'—'The flesh of Jesus is the flesh of Mary!'—they will at once exclaim with the great St. Augustine. How can it be that the God of all purity, to whom even the least shadow of sin is an object of eternal abhorrence, should have suffered His Virgin Mother to be, even for an instant, such an object in His sight? From her He received that flesh and blood—that human nature in which, made one with the Divinity, He redeemed the world: and can we believe that the same in Mary's person, in any possible degree, was ever sullied by the demon's breath, dishonored by the taint of guilt? Or, again, with St. Cyril the pious Catholic will ask, 'Who hath ever heard that an architect built a glorious dwelling for himself and at once gave it over to be possessed by his most cruel and hated enemy?'

"If there were no other words of Holy Writ on this topic than these—'Mary, of whom was born Jesus, who is called Christ' (St. Matt. i. 16.)—they would be amply sufficient. Behold the divine fact that overthrows every difficulty, the inspired oracle that sweeps away every objection!

"Never, Christian brethren, never can we admit that she was for one moment the slave of the devil;—the Virgin who was destined to be the Mother of God, the Spouse of the Holy Spirit, the Ark of the New Covenant, the Mediatrix of Mankind, the Terror of the Powers of Darkness, the Queen of all the Heavenly Hosts.

"Purer than heaven's purest angel, brighter than its brightest seraph, Mary, after her Creator, God,—who made and gave her all,—is the most perfect of beings, the masterpiece of Infinite Wisdom, Almighty Power, and Eternal Love.

"To such a being we cannot reasonably suppose that a perfection was denied which had been already gratuitously bestowed on inferior creatures—on the Angelic Spirits, for example, some of whom afterward fell away from God and are lost forever. And again, the first man and the first woman were created sinless—pure as the virgin world on which the Almighty had just looked down with infinite delight and declared it to be '*valde bona!*'—*exceeding good!* How just and natural, therefore, —may we not add, how unavoidable?—is the conclusion that this sublime privilege was not withheld from Mary, set apart as she was from all eternity for an office and for honors in the kingdom of God, to which no other created being ever will or can be exalted! The more so since profound divines do not hesitate to assert that, rather than be without the grace conferred upon her in her Immaculate Conception, and thus, though only for an instant, an object of God's displeasure, Mary would have preferred to forfeit forever the infinite dignity of being the Mother of Jesus Christ.

"Gladly would we dwell more at length on the subject, but as you may yourselves observe the occasion does not allow it. The few thoughts we have uttered are but the echo of Christian antiquity, of the faith, the filial love, the confidence in Mary, when apostles and evangelists were still on earth and revered her name.

"How profound should be our gratitude in being able to say, that name we also reverence, their confidence in Mary we cherish, their filial love we share, their faith is ours! Could the Martyrs and Virgins, the heroic confessors of the faith, the renowned Fathers and Doctors of the Church, 'beloved of God and men, and whose memory is in benediction' (Eccles. xlv.)—could these arise and unite their voices to those of their successors now around the Chair of Peter, what would be their testimony? They would point to their immortal writings, and in the language of St. Augustine, so worthy a representative of the genius, wisdom, and piety of the primitive Church, they would remind us that when they speak of the law by which all the children of Adam are born children of wrath, '*they speak not of Mary*,' with regard to whom, on account of the honor due to our Lord, when they discourse of sin they wish to raise no question whatsoever. (*Lib. de nat. et grat.*) Nay, with an *Amen*, loud as that which St. Jerome tells us rolled through the magnificent churches of Rome like the thunder of heaven, they would respond to the following declaration of the Council of Trent (Sess. V.): 'This Holy Synod declares that it is not its intention to include in this decree, where original sin is spoken of, the Blessed and Immaculate Mother of God.'

"May the day soon dawn upon the world—whether it be in our unhappy times or not—when with one mind and heart Christendom will acknowledge and proclaim this her most honorable privilege! Meanwhile, submitting every thought, word, and wish to the judgment of the Church, we shall continue to confess her power, regarding Mary as that 'great sign' which St. John saw in heaven—a woman so resplendent with light, grace, and dignity that he describes her as 'a woman clothed with the sun; with the moon beneath her feet, and on her head a crown of twelve stars; whose Son shall rule the nations with an iron rod: and her Son was taken up to God, and to His throne.' (Apoc. xii.)

"And should the Dragon of Impiety spoken of in the same mysterious vision, whose power to seduce the nations is but too evident, still continue to make war on God and His Church; should the fearful days of wide-spread unbelief foretold by the Apostles prove to be *our own*, when men will no longer endure sound doctrine, but, according to their own desires, will heap up to themselves teachers having lying lips; turning away their hearing from the truth to give heed to fables; speaking proud words of vain philosophy; despising government and all majesty; audacious, self-willed; fearing not to bring in sects; promising their followers *liberty*, whereas they themselves are the slaves of corruption—days of calamity in which, the same inspired teachers warn us, men will blaspheme whatever things they know not, that is, the unsearchable ways of God and mysteries of religion; and what things soever they naturally do know, in these they will be corrupted mockers, murmurers, full of complaints, inventors of evil things; disobedient to parents; without affection, without fidelity; walking according to their own desires in ungodliness; filled with avarice and envy; counting for a pleasure the delights of a day; sporting themselves to excess; rioting in their feasts with you, having their eyes full of adultery and never-ceasing sin; alluring unstable souls who have lost their faith and, leaving the right way, will in the end discover that they have been following 'wandering stars to whom the storm of darkness is reserved forever;'—Christian brethren, if these be the times in store for the already afflicted Church of Jesus Christ, in the midst of which, with fear and trembling, we her children are to work out our salvation, to whom can we turn with more confidence than to His Divine Mother, whom the Church has never invoked in vain?

"Hail! Holy Queen, Mother of Mercy! Guard the kingdom of the Christ-loving Pius, our chief Bishop. Pray for the people. Intercede for the clergy. Protect the consecrated virgins. Unto us all give strength against our enemies and thine, courage to the fearful, joy to those that mourn, peace to the contrite of heart, perseverance to the just. Let all experience thy protection, Virgin and Mother! through whom the nations are brought to penitence, the demons are put to flight, and they that sit in darkness and the shadow of death are filled with the knowledge and the love of thy Son!

"Given under our hand, at our residence in Philadelphia, on the Feast of St. Charles Borromeo, in the year of our Lord eighteen hundred and fifty-four.

"✠ JOHN NEPOMUCENE,
"*Bishop of Philadelphia.*"

The above, though somewhat lengthy, we have thought well to insert because of its intrinsic beauty, as well as the knowledge it affords of Bishop Neumann's sentiments on the question at issue, the Immaculate Conception of the ever Blessed Virgin.

After a rough voyage of seventeen days, the Bishop landed safe at Havre on the morning of the 7th of November. Eager to reach the Eternal City, he hurried on to Marseilles, where he embarked for Civita Vecchia.

He had written to his aged father from Paris to inform him of his arrival in Europe, and also of his intention to visit him on his return from Rome. Great was the joy of that little household in Prachatitz. Father and sisters exulted in the thought of having again among them, after an absence of over eighteen years, him who had left them under far different circumstances. This journey to Rome furnished an occasion for old Mr. Neumann to give emphatic utterance to his own stanch belief in the doctrine of the Immaculate Conception. "But why," said the old gentleman, "why must the Bishops be summoned from America to Rome to tell us that the Most Blessed Virgin was conceived without sin? Have we not always believed that?"

While in Rome, Bishop Neumann stayed at Monterone, a convent of the Redemptorist Fathers, where his religious bearing delighted and edified his brethren.

The Fathers remarked in him two virtues especially, viz., humility and poverty. He traversed the streets of Rome divested of every external sign of his ecclesiastical dignity; and, unless when obliged to appear in them at public meetings of the prelates, or when visiting the Holy Father and his cardinals, he never assumed the episcopal insignia. The most inclement weather could not deter him from going on foot, as he was unwilling to incur useless expense. His extraordinary humility and poverty often exacted of him a solitary walk, as he could find no one willing to bear him companionship; but, "never less alone than when alone," the good Bishop thought little of such a privation. Intent on satisfying the devotion that consumed him, he was, we may believe, well pleased to be allowed to do so observed by none save God and His holy angels. His spirit of retirement and mortification, joined to the strict observance of the rules, won for him golden opinions among the inmates of Monterone. Rome furnished ample food for his piety. He visited the Holy Places, and gazed upon those objects of devotion with which the city abounds, as we have learned from his own words. But, humble and retired as he was, the saintly Bishop could not escape notice. The attention of the Cardinals and of the Holy Father himself was soon turned upon him, and he was more than once summoned to private audiences with the highest dignitaries of the papal court, who conferred many marks of distinction upon him. When first presented to the pope, His Holiness graciously addressed him in these words: "Bishop Neumann of Philadelphia! Is not obedience better than sacrifice?"—thus recalling the formal command he had received to accept the bishopric of the above-named city. Pius IX. listened with interest to the Bishop's report of his diocese, gave some decisions highly satisfactory to the prelate, and conferred upon him numerous privileges and faculties for the benefit of his flock.

Each of the prelates then assembled in Rome received from the Holy Father a silver medal commemorative of the great day on which the dogma of the Immaculate Conception was solemnly defined. On one side is an image of Pope Pius IX., on the reverse the interior of St. Peter's, representing the scene in which the Holy Father, as the Vicar of Jesus Christ, surrounded by Cardinals and Bishops, solemnly declared the Immaculate Conception of the Mother of God to be an article of faith.

In a letter from Rome to a priest in Bohemia, under date December 17, 1854, Bishop Neumann says: "To describe the solemnity of the 8th instant would be greatly beyond my power, even had I time to do so. You may see from the programme enclosed the ceremonies of that glorious occasion. I thank God that, to the multiplied graces already bestowed upon me, He has added this of having been present in Rome on that day."

We shall now follow the good Bishop to the home of his childhood, the little town of Prachatitz, toward which filial piety and fraternal affection drew him. He set out like a poor religious, pausing on the way to satisfy his devotion at various places of religious veneration. A pilgrim who had become acquainted with him in Rome met him again at Ancona, in the garb of a simple cleric; he was astonished at the plainness exhibited in his dress and in his whole manner of living. This careful concealment of everything that could betray his rank caused the Bishop no little inconvenience on one occasion. He was travelling through Austria. One night whilst riding in a stage-coach, a gendarme demanded their passports of the passengers. The Bishop produced his; but as it was in English, with which language the official was unfamiliar, he refused to receive it. Despite the cold and the lateness of the hour, for it was night, he ordered the Bishop to follow him on foot to the next station. The snow lay deep on the ground; so, to escape this unpleasant alternative, the Bishop had no other resource than to produce his episcopal cross and ring. At sight of these the gendarme was satisfied and withdrew without further remark.

Bishop Neumann's profound reverence for the mystery of the Incarnation and his ardent love for the Infant Jesus drew him to the Holy House of Loretto. With indescribable devotion he offered here the Holy Sacrifice, and placed in Mary's hands his hopes, his desires, and his intentions.

On reaching Vienna he visited his former fellow-student, Rev. Adalbert Schmid, who had for many years been discharging the functions of the priestly office in the seminary of Graz, Styria. Several days were here spent, the two friends renewing the sweet ties of friendship formed long ago in early youth, and communicating to each other the joys and sorrows that marked the life of each in that long separation of eighteen years.

Whilst in Vienna, Bishop Neumann tarried some days with his brethren in their convent of "Maria Stiegen." On Saturday he preached a moving discourse on devotion to the Mother of God and her high prerogatives, dwelling especially upon her Immaculate Conception. His animation and fervor, his lively faith and, childlike love toward the Queen of Heaven, deeply impressed his hearers.

On his journey to Vienna the Bishop lost a small trunk, containing all the relics he had procured, not without considerable trouble, in Rome, Loretto, and other places. The loss was a grievous one to him. He telegraphed to every station at which there was any likelihood of its having been left, but from all he received the same return: "No trunk of that description here." Deeply lamenting the loss of his sacred treasures, the Bishop paced up and down the railway station, reflecting upon some means of obtaining a clue to their whereabouts. Suddenly he remembered St. Anthony of Padua. He vowed to say Mass the next day in his honor, and, if put in possession of the missing property, to expose the picture of the saint to public veneration in one of the churches of his diocese. Scarcely was the vow uttered, when a young man approached and accosted him: "Right Reverend Bishop, here is your trunk." With an exclamation of glad surprise, the Bishop gazed at the object of his anxious search, as if to assure himself of its identity, whilst the thought flashed through his mind, How did the stranger know that he was a Bishop, since nothing in his dress indicated his rank? He raised his eyes to question the youth, but, lo! he was gone. He looked right and left, but nowhere was he to be seen; he had disappeared as suddenly as he had come. With a heart full of thanksgiving for this miraculous intervention of the saint, the Bishop fulfilled his vow. The full-length portrait of the saint which he had painted on this occasion may still be seen in what was once the Cathedral Chapel, Philadelphia. It occupies the same position as during the Bishop's lifetime.

From Vienna the Bishop pursued his way to Prague, where he visited his sister Johanna, who for the last fourteen years had led the religious life among the Sisters of Charity of St. Charles Borromeo. Her name in religion was Sister Mary Caroline. This was indeed a joyful meeting. Sister Mary Caroline was next in age to her holy brother, and similarity of vocation had strengthened the bonds of family affection between them. The Bishop visited the churches of Prague on foot in order to venerate the relics of the saints, in which the city is rich. His friend Rev. Hermann Dichtl introduced him to the pious Emperor Ferdinand, who received him cordially and invited him to the imperial table. The most welcome part of the entertainment was the dessert, at which the Emperor caused a handsome sum, all in the gold coin of the United States, to be laid on a plate and presented to the Bishop, as an offering toward his new Cathedral.

At Budweis, the episcopal see of his native place, Bishop Neumann was hospitably received by Right Rev. Bishop Valentine Iirsik, who took a lively interest in all that concerned the diocese of Philadelphia. Here our traveller stayed some days. One morning he unexpectedly informed his host of his intention to depart the next hour for Prachatitz, his native city. Bishop Iirsik, surprised at the announcement, inquired his reasons for so sudden a departure. "I wish to enter Prachatitz unnoticed," answered his guest. The humble Bishop, by forestalling the time of his arrival, wished to make anything like a public reception impossible. Bishop Valentine urged him to defer his departure for some days, at least; but, finding him resolved upon starting at once, he begged him to accept the use of his carriage. This, too, the lowly follower of a lowly Saviour declined, saying playfully, "Every child on the road might then cry out, 'There goes the Bishop of Budweis!'"

On February 2d, shortly after dinner, he left Budweis in a close sleigh, expecting to reach his home unnoticed and take his family by surprise that evening. Not so, however, reckoned the good people of Prachatitz. They had resolved upon receiving the Bishop of Philadelphia in grand style, and they were not to be defeated in their design. Aware of his great humility, they instinctively knew that their looked-for guest would endeavor to shun any demonstration in his honor, and they had, accordingly, provided for such a contingency. One of their number had been appointed to take notes at Budweis, and to find out the exact time of the Bishop's departure for Prachatitz. No sooner had good Adalbert Benesch, the messenger in question, obtained the desired information, than he set out on foot and, in true courier fashion, announced at every house on the road that Bishop Neumann would soon pass that way.

Alas for the poor Bishop! His well-arranged plans were all frustrated. Scarcely was he well on his journey, when out flocked whole families to receive the episcopal blessing. In the little town of Nettolitz, midway between Budweis and Prachatitz, the humility of the Bishop met a still greater shock. When the sleigh came in sight, the bells of the town rang out a peal of welcome, and all the good folks, the clergy at their head, turned out in procession and escorted him to the church. Here he gave them his episcopal benediction and addressed to them a few words. How was his arrival known? what did it all mean? were questions that puzzled the disappointed traveller. They were soon solved; and great was his dread that all his care to enter Prachatitz quietly would meet with a similar result. "Ah!" said he to his young nephew, who had gone forward to meet him; "we must try to slip out of this place as quietly as possible. If they find out that we are going, they will pass the word to Prachatitz, and all our plans will be vain. Let us send the sleigh back to Budweis, and walk the rest of the way. It is only a journey of three hours. I know the road well. Many a time I travelled it when a student. We can enter the city in a direction opposite that by which they will expect us."

Scarcely were the words uttered, when the clergy and town officials gathered around him, begging him not to refuse them the honor of remaining till the next morning. The Bishop, thus urged, was forced to yield. He remained, celebrated Mass in the parish church at eight o'clock, and by half-past nine was ready to depart. The large square before the church was crowded by those who had come to see the Bishop and receive his blessing. At last, amid hearty cheers and the ringing of bells, he escaped from their noisy adieus. "Alas!" sighed he, "what have these good people done? May God forgive them for having led me into the temptation of vanity!" The crowds that surrounded him at the moment of starting prevented his noticing that, instead of the ordinary sleigh in which he had come, the magnificent equipage of the Prince of Schwarzenberg had been substituted. The Prince had given orders to his steward to offer his own sleigh for Bishop Neumann's accommodation as far as Prachatitz. True to his character, the Bishop shrank from such a display, and declined with expressions of gratitude and appreciation the kind offer of the Prince. The steward, however, was not to be baffled. He gave orders for the sleigh to be kept in readiness for the Bishop and his nephew; and long before the appointed hour, with its four spirited horses and liveried attendants, it took up a position so near to the pastor's residence that the Bishop's poor equipage could not approach.

Lightly they bounded over the crisp snow in the direction of Prachatitz amid the pealing of bells and the firing of signal-guns. Clerics, town-officials, and private citizens, in sleighs, met them at a short distance from the town, and welcomed the Bishop in the name of the city. After the ceremony of kissing the episcopal ring, the sleighs moved on in procession. At the little village called Old Prachatitz a crowd had assembled. The civic guard, headed by a magnificent band, stood in line on both sides of the street, and, when the Bishop approached, saluted him with military honors. The drums sounded, the musicians united in one grand chorus, and the cheers of the multitude rent the air. After this demonstration the band struck up a lively march, the city bells began to ring, and the procession moved forward. The scene was one of triumph. It was a reception such as might have been extended to a conqueror returning with well-earned laurels.

The ancient city-gate was richly decorated with appropriate emblems and inscriptions, conspicuous among them the episcopal insignia. Was it through this same old gateway, eighteen years before, that, as a young man, he whom we have followed with so much interest had passed at the call of God? Friendless, companionless, almost penniless, he had gone to battle for the cause of God, to win numberless victories over the powers of darkness, and to snatch myriads of souls from the enemy's grasp. And this return, this ovation despite his own efforts at concealment—surely, the judgments of the Lord are incomprehensible and His ways past finding out!

On entering the city, the Bishop was greeted by the imperial officers ranged on either side of the gateway, whilst the street, as far as the eye could reach, was lined with people who knelt devoutly as he passed. Next came the children of the schools to welcome him in a short address; and then followed the Dean, Rev. Father Fucik, surrounded by the clergy. The Bishop was conducted to the church, where, before the high altar, was intoned a solemn *Te Deum*, which the choir and orchestra continued. What were the Bishop's emotions as he knelt before that altar where eighteen years before, February 9, 1836, he had prayed God in the Holy Eucharist to help and guide him in his new career! His heart overflowed with love and gratitude at the thought of the innumerable blessings showered upon him. He arose and, ascending the steps of the sanctuary, addressed the crowd in stirring accents. He told them of the mercies of the Lord during the past eighteen years, of the work of God in the far-off land from which he had come; and he referred all the glory to the Most High, who had led him back once more to his native place. He thanked his fellow-citizens for their gracious reception; by their zeal to honor the episcopal dignity in his person they evinced, he said, their love for Holy Church and for her Founder, Jesus Christ. After these and other remarks of a like nature, the Bishop gave the assembled multitude his solemn benediction.

And now drew near the moment for the meeting between the saintly son and the venerable father. His advanced age and the unfavorable weather prevented Mr. Neumann's leaving the house. The Bishop had received an invitation to make the deanery his home during his stay in Prachatitz; but this he thankfully declined. "The few days of my stay in my native place," he said, "I must spend with my old father. Filial affection exacts this of me." In the same spirit he refused, also, to enter the Prince's sleigh again. He was as well able now to go on foot to his father's house as he was in his youth, he said; and so he set out surrounded by priests and officials.

A vast crowd had already assembled around Mr. Neumann's dwelling, eager to witness the meeting between father and son. The hum of voices gradually died away as the Bishop drew near; silence reigned throughout the crowd, and all eyes turned in fixed attention to the venerable figure standing in trembling expectancy in the doorway. One moment, and the long-absent son is clasped to the father's heart! Tears bedewed every cheek, and words of thanksgiving arose on all sides for this happy reunion, this foretaste of eternal bliss. One of the bystanders exclaimed, "Oh, that his mother were alive to share in this happiness!" To which the Bishop quickly replied: "She sees us, she sees us! My good mother is looking down upon us; she is rejoicing with us."

The Bishop, narrating this circumstance afterward, remarked: "My good old father actually bore me in his arms up the stairs. My feet never once touched the steps."

Relatives and friends and the companions of his youth pressed around to kiss his hand and receive his blessing. It was long past noon, and still, despite the cold, hundreds besieged the house eager to approach the man of God. At last, Mr. Neumann, seeing no other way of procuring for his son the rest and refreshment he so greatly needed, ordered the doors to be closed, and begged him to dismiss the crowd with a blessing from the window. But not even this could induce the good people to disperse, so great was their fear of losing an opportunity to catch a glimpse of him of whom they were so justly proud. Crowds came and went from early morn till late at night during those six days of his stay in Prachatitz. People flocked from the country around to see the Bishop from America and to get his blessing. Indeed, so great was the concourse that the good Bishop's safety was, at times, endangered. Strong arms had to be stretched forth to protect him from the eagerness of indiscreet admirers who, unmindful of all save the gratification of their own desires, stumbled over chairs and upset tables, in their onward course. This account may to some wear the semblance of exaggeration; but when we reflect that Bishop Neumann's reputation for holiness had long before spread among those who had known him in his boyhood and youth, and who, in turn, transmitted their knowledge to their children, we shall readily comprehend why they flocked in crowds to receive his blessing and some pious token of remembrance from his hand. There he stood, calm, meek, recollected amidst the honors heaped upon him, affable and kind to all. Not one went away disappointed. All without exception were allowed to kiss his hand, receiving from him at the same moment a medal of the Immaculate Conception, a picture, or a rosary.

Every morning at eight o'clock he said Mass in the parish church, which was crowded as on a grand festival. On Sunday, moreover, he assisted at the High Mass and preached, we may say, to the entire city, for all turned out to hear him. In burning and convincing words he addressed his hearers upon the inestimable benefits bestowed upon us by our holy faith, and of our strict obligation to live in accordance with it. His apostolic zeal and unfeigned humility produced a powerful impression. Years have passed since that memorable visit to Prachatitz, and yet the words he then uttered still live in the memory of many of his hearers. The negligent, who rarely darkened the church-door, went on that occasion through a motive of curiosity; but, as they afterward acknowledged, the earnest words of the saintly Bishop powerfully stimulated them to a more fervent Christian life. A famous scoffer at religion was among the number who listened to the apostolic Bishop. After the sermon he remarked, "Ah! were I often to hear that Bishop, I feel that, whether or not, I should have to be converted."

On the second day of his stay in Prachatitz a formal reception was tendered him in the town-hall. The most spacious apartment was tastefully decorated for the occasion with festive wreaths, inscriptions, and the episcopal insignia. The orchestra executed several fine pieces composed expressly for the occasion; the imperial and the civil officials addressed the Bishop in befitting terms expressive of their appreciation of the honor conferred on their city by his visit. After this, a little girl in white stepped forward and, in a short address, presented the Bishop, in the name of the citizens of Prachatitz, a magnificent album.

The album was of Parisian make, artistically bound in different kinds of foreign wood. It had been ordered for this joyous occasion. On the first three leaves, in illuminated colors and gold, is the dedication of the memorial; then follows a poem with the autograph signatures of the most prominent citizens. We subjoin a translation of both, though we warn the reader not to judge the original by it. The harmony and flow of the German rhythm can ill be reproduced in English.

" *To His Lordship the Right Rev. Bishop*
JOHN NEPOMUCENE NEUMANN,
Bishop of Philadelphia, etc.,

The best of sons, the pride and honor of his native place, this memorial is respectfully dedicated, as a slight token of esteem, by the representatives of the city in commemoration of his happy return to the home of his infancy, and in memory of his departure thence.

"PRACHATITZ, the year of our Lord 1855.

" God hath not given thee in vain
  A noble soul, a spirit choice.
Regardless of all toil and pain,
  Go forth, obedient to His voice!
For thou hast heard the call divine
  Unto a life of toil and care;
But, fired with love, that soul of thine
  Shrinks not to labor everywhere.
Like to the fishermen of old,
  Obedient to the Master's call,
With hearts sincere, with spirits bold,
  Who left their nets, who gave their all,
Thou, too, hast gladly cast aside
  The glittering fetters of the heart
And all that flatters human pride,
  To choose the nobler, '*better part.*'
Led on by God's protecting hand,
  Across Atlantic's billows far,
Unto a strange, benighted land,
  The holy cross, thy guiding star,

That standard of our saving faith,
   In triumph there thou didst display—
Thou'lt grasp it faithful unto death,
   Loyal and true thou'lt own its sway.
Thy God watched o'er thee when alone
   On arid plain, in forest dim,
Where thou the seed of faith hath sown,
   And nourished well for love of Him,
Who well repaid thy toil and pain,
   Since thou didst labor for thy God;—
Lo! it sprang up as golden grain,
   And idols sank beneath the sod.
Because a faithful servant thou
   In *lesser things* hath been, thy Lord
Hath set thee over *greater* now,
   And glorious shall be thy reward.
Hail, faithful shepherd! to thy fame
   Thy Lord hath added honors new,
Far, far beyond all earthly claim,
   Rich guerdon of the '*chosen few.*'
Off in the West, where thy flock feeds,
   The Lord of Hosts bestowed on thee,
For noble acts, heroic deeds,
   In Holy Church high dignity.
Thee hath the Lord most kindly led
   To view once more thy childhood's home,
To greet loved friends, whose hearts oft sped
   In anxious thought where thou didst roam.
O'er prairies vast, through forests grand
   That teem with Nature's riches rare,—
Yes, in that strange and distant land
   Our spirit traced thee everywhere.
Permit us, then, most honored guest,
   Our welcomes at thy feet to lay,
By which the joy that swells our breast
   In trembling accents we would say.
Accept the heart-felt salutation,
   Feeble though the tribute be,—
Accept the love and veneration
   Thy native city brings to thee!
And, noblest of her sons and best,
   Whose virtues magnify her fame,

>   List graciously to our request:
>   When'er thy glance rests on these names,
>   Think kindly of thy home of yore.
>   May God be with thee evermore!
>   Amen."

The presentation over, the Bishop arose and expressed his gratitude for these reiterated proofs of affection from his fellow-citizens. It was his most earnest desire, he said, and he would ever pray God for its fulfilment, to see them remain true and faithful children of Holy Mother Church. He rejoiced that this opportunity had been afforded him to give utterance in their presence to his heart-felt appreciation of the pious Christian education that had been bestowed upon him by his worthy parents, one of whom was now enjoying the reward of the same in the kingdom of heaven. To Rev. Peter Schmidt, also, he tendered his sincere thanks, since to him, as Catechist and Director, he felt chiefly indebted for his present position in the sacred hierarchy.

One afternoon was devoted to his relatives. They were overjoyed at being allowed to entertain their honored kinsman as a guest in their own homes. Those eighteen years of absence, we may well believe, had wrought their own changes around those firesides. Many who had presided there in the Bishop's time were now resting peacefully in the little cemetery outside the city; and many others, the little ones of long ago, had grown up to take their place. They, too, knew their saintly relative through the oft-told tales of the elders, and now that he stood before them, his unaffected kindness and affability won all hearts.

The next visit was to the hallowed home of the dead, the resting-place of the loved and lost, among them the Bishop's own noble, true-hearted mother. She it was whose lively faith, firm trust in Divine Providence, and deep love for her gifted boy had made him what he now was. The distance was great, the weather inclement;

but go he must, and on foot, too, to kneel at the spot so sacred to him, the grave of that venerated mother. And long did he kneel in earnest prayer, his soul communing with the spirit of the loved departed. Slowly he passed from mound to mound. Those eighteen years had dotted that little enclosure with many a stone and cross unseen before.

Strangers came, priests and friends from a distance, to pay their respects to Bishop Neumann. The thought of the episcopal dignity with which he was clothed somewhat overawed them at first; but his humble demeanor, his frank and cordial manners, quickly dispelled all feelings of embarrassment, and the most shrinking entered freely into the general joy. The respectful attention with which every word the prelate uttered was received was something remarkable. But in vain did they listen to catch some word connected with his own labors, when he spoke of affairs in America. Not one word about himself. If, at times, some such allusion in passing was unavoidable, it was always accompanied by a word of disparagement; for instance, he often reverted to the equestrian adventures, recorded in one of our first chapters, that betrayed his own unskilful horsemanship. When one of his visitors remarked to him that Prachatitz could lay claim to many distinguished men, but that he was the first Bishop of whom it could boast, he replied, "If any priest had accompanied me to America, he would, without doubt, have been made Bishop instead of me." Another remark of similar import was met with the laughing rejoinder, "Oh, even a blind hen will sometimes find a grain of corn!"

The good people of Prachatitz delight in their social gatherings, even at the present day, to recall expressions heard from the Bishop's lips, and which only his unfeigned humility could have made him utter. One day he was engaged to dine with a Mr. Spinka. The hospitable host noticed that his honored guest was not doing justice to the choice viands before him, that, in fact, he had not even touched some of them. Mr. Spinka made use of the rights of hospitality and urged him to taste, at least, of the various dishes. The Bishop complied with his customary affability, but said with a smile, "Mr. Spinka, do you want me to earn a long purgatory for myself at your grand dinner?"

Six days had quickly sped, and this memorable visit was drawing to a close. February 9th was the day appointed for his departure, but the Bishop wished it to be kept secret for two reasons: first, to escape the demonstrations that would certainly attend a public farewell; and secondly, to spare himself and his friends the mutual pain of leave-taking, for the ties of nature held strong sway in his loyal heart. Grown wary from experience, perhaps, he was more successful in this than in his preceding plans; he managed things so cleverly that not even his nearest relatives suspected his intention. Late on the evening of February 8th he ordered through one of the clergy, whom he had bound to secrecy, a sleigh for the next morning; but with all his precaution he could not prevent the members of his father's household from having some inkling of his design. And now arose a storm of questions and remonstrances. His aged father joined with the rest of the family in begging him to defer his departure, if only for a few hours; but no—he must go. Gently and lovingly he reasoned with the good old gentleman, arguing that he could not in conscience remain longer, that duty called him back to his diocese. At last Mr. Neumann yielded to his son's arguments and consented to see him depart. Before daybreak, therefore, on the appointed day, February 9th, Bishop Neumann, quietly and unobserved, left his father's house, accompanied by his friend Rev. Joseph Brunner, who had faithfully kept the secret confided to him.

On reaching the parish church—that church around

which clustered tender recollections of childhood and boyhood—he alighted from the sleigh to kneel for some moments before its closed doors. Then rising with a swelling heart, he left his home for the second time, and this time forever.

The morning dawn, as usual, brought a crowd before the dwelling of the Neumann family, all anxious to see and speak with the Bishop; and at eight o'clock the church was filled, as on the preceding days, with devout worshippers expecting to hear his Mass. Great was the general disappointment and dismay when the news spread that Bishop Neumann had left the city before daybreak.

Rev. Father Brunner afterward related many incidents connected with this secret departure. The Bishop, he said, restrained his feelings not without difficulty. When the sleigh reached the mountain-ridge whence a view of the little city could be had, he turned to take a farewell glance at its familiar scenes, at his father's house, and the tears rolled down his cheeks. A four hours' ride brought them to the celebrated shrine of Gojau, to which, it will be remembered, he had made a pilgrimage before setting out the first time for America. Here he said Mass. In a letter to his father he speaks as follows:

"On February 9th, four hours after our separation, I said Mass in Gojau with the intention of drawing down the protection of God on my homeward journey. I then visited the Right Reverend Prelate in Krumau, and met several of our relatives and some of my old fellow-students. The Bishop of Budweis had repeatedly entertained me with generous hospitality and more than fraternal charity. I called on him and bade him good-by, as I intended to be at the collegiate church in Hohenfurt on the 14th, where the Prelate was to celebrate his patronal feast."

To be able thus to return thanks in person to his former professors at the Cistercian college for the favors and benefits received from them in his student-days was a great satisfaction to Bishop Neumann. He had received through Rev. Waldemar Wiesner, a native of Prachatitz, an invitation to visit the venerable monks. It was a pleasure for him to accept, and, in order to give a more lively expression to his gratitude, he chose, as he tells us in his letter, the reverend prelate's feast-day for his visit. The secretary of the institute, Mr. Leopold Wackar, also a native of Prachatitz, rode as far as Kaplitz, a distance of twenty miles, to meet and escort him to Hohenfurt, where he received a most cordial reception. Here he spent two days to the great satisfaction of both professors and people. Thence his journey led through Linz to Alt-Oetting. A violent snow-storm had rendered the road through the Bohemian forest almost impassable, even dangerous in some places. The right reverend prelate tried to persuade him to defer his departure for a few days, but Bishop Neumann, believing that he had fully complied with the claims of gratitude, could not longer be detained. He recommended himself to the Mother of God, whose shrine at Alt-Oetting is regarded as miraculous, and, trusting to her protection, continued his journey. His confidence was rewarded. He arrived at his destination without accident. In a second letter to his father he says:

"On February 18th I arrived at Alt-Oetting in Bavaria. The snow was so deep that I was forced to remain three days with my brethren, which detention, however, caused me more joy than regret. By it I was enabled to offer the Holy Sacrifice in that ancient chapel where so many graces are constantly obtained. You, all my loved ones, and the whole city of Prachatitz, I recommended to Our Lady's maternal care. I reached Munich only on the 21st, when I hastened to finish up, as speedily as possible, all business connected with my diocese. I was everywhere received with such kindness as to lead me to hope for the success of my affairs here."

Business detained the Bishop in Munich for several days, during which he was the honored and welcome guest of Mr. Stiessberger, a highly respectable merchant of the city, brother of Father Stiessberger, C.SS.R. We need scarcely repeat that the unobtrusive manners of the holy Bishop secured the admiration and esteem of every member of this worthy household, and awoke in all profound veneration for his sanctity. We shall here record an incident illustrative of his humility and modesty. During his stay in Munich there were celebrated in St. Mary's Cathedral the solemn obsequies of the recently deceased Archbishop Anselm. A little before the services began, a plainly dressed ecclesiastic was seen entering the sacristy, a travelling-bag in hand. The stranger was scarcely noticed in the crowd of priests assembled to do honor to the late Archbishop. He slipped into a retired corner and began saying his Rosary. After a short time had passed, some one present remarked that Bishop Neumann, of Philadelphia, had accepted an invitation to the funeral, and that it was almost time for him to make his appearance. With that the little priest who all this time had been sitting unnoticed in a corner arose, announced himself as Bishop Neumann, and, to the surprise of all, donned the episcopal robes. The ceremonies over, a contention began among the reverend gentlemen as to who should escort the Bishop to his lodgings. Some who had noticed with feelings of admiration the extraordinary humility of the Bishop's bearing had already seized his travelling-bag, and for a moment there was a struggle as to who should be allowed to carry it. The Bishop interposed, begging to be permitted to do so himself. He was vanquished, however, and forced not only to relinquish for a time all right to his property, but also to accept an honorable escort home. On another occasion, he returned to Mr. Stiessberger's after transacting some important business. The weather was stormy, and the Bishop's shoes were wet. When some one suggested the propriety of changing them, he smilingly replied, "Were I to change, it would only be from one foot to the other, as I have only one pair."

Whilst in Munich, the humility of the saintly prelate was put to a severe test, and a pious artifice was resorted to in order to induce him to have his portrait taken. During his travels he had been frequently asked for his likeness. His invariable reply was, "Surely, I am not so important a personage that you should desire my portrait." The same request was repeated in Munich, but this time it was couched in a form which his pious heart could not refuse. Let him have his portrait taken, they said; it might afterward be lithographed and copies sold for the benefit of the poor of his native place. "Charity dealeth not perversely," least of all Bishop Neumann's charity; so he was photographed, holding in his hand the memorial album which the good people of Prachatitz had presented him. The likeness was an excellent one, and several were struck from it after his death. So far as we know, there exist only three portraits of him: the first is an oil-painting, representing him a little boy of six years; the second, a photograph taken in Baltimore, in obedience to the Provincial, Father Bernard, who, when he heard that Father Neumann was to be made Bishop, lost no time in giving him a command to leave this memento to his Congregation; the third is the one whose history we have just recorded.

From Munich, Bishop Neumann travelled with Bishop Timon, of Buffalo, through Augsburg, Stuttgard, Spire, etc., of which journey he thus writes:

"In Spire we were kindly received by Right Rev. Bishop Weis, who accompanied us to the Cathedral, which had been recently repaired and beautified. This church, in which St. Bernard once preached and, in his holy enthusiasm, added the exquisite closing salutations of the 'Salve Regina,' is, for its size and the magnificence of its frescos, one of the grandest in the world. It is a lasting monument to the liberality and artistic taste of the recent Bavarian kings, and especially of good King Louis. By it they have acquired merit before Almighty God whom it is designed to honor, and to whose glory all the arts and treasures of this world should be made subservient."

On arriving in Paris, Bishop Neumann found that the next steamer would not sail from Havre till the 14th of March, which information made a change in his plans. He resolved to go to Liverpool *via* London, desiring, if possible, to reach his diocese by Palm-Sunday. On March 10th he sailed from Europe in the steamer Atlantic, in company with the Archbishop of New York and Bishop Timon, of Buffalo.

After an uneventful voyage of seventeen days our travellers landed in New York, March 27th, at ten o'clock in the forenoon. Bishop Neumann proceeded at once to the nearest church, where he offered up the Holy Sacrifice in thanksgiving for their safe arrival. The next day, the 28th, his birthday and the anniversary of his consecration, he was anxious to spend in his own episcopal city; consequently he left New York that same evening, and reached Philadelphia by ten that night.

As his return voyage had been an unusually lengthy one, fears were beginning to be entertained for his safety, especially as several steamers had lately been lost on the American coast. But when assured of their prelate's happy arrival, joy became universal, and the reception he everywhere met proved the estimation in which he was held by his flock.

CHAPTER X.

Bishop Neumann is Assigned a Coadjutor.

WE again find Bishop Neumann actively engaged in the extensive field of the Catholic Church in America. The first Plenary Council was held in Baltimore, May 9-20, 1852. It was attended by six Archbishops, twenty-six Bishops, and twelve Superiors of religious Orders. It tended greatly to promote the welfare of the Church in America; important points of discipline were discussed, and excellent regulations were made. Conspicuous by his reputation for learning and piety, Bishop Neumann held a prominent position in this imposing assemblage of Churchmen. A certain distinguished prelate made the following remark when, some time after, conversing upon the saintly Neumann:

"I had an opportunity during the Council in Baltimore to admire Bishop Neumann's wonderful memory and extraordinary theological attainments. He had a solution for every question proposed. What edified me most of all was his unruffled composure, which betokened deep humility and perfect self-control. I always regarded him as a saint."

Bishop Neumann's two catechisms were highly extolled and commended by the Bishops of the Council. The smaller one, for beginners, has reached its thirtieth edition; the larger, its eighteenth.

The Bishop, writing to his old friend, Father Dichtl, thus refers to the Plenary Council: "We have been holding a Plenary Council in Baltimore, during which the erection of new dioceses was proposed. Such steps are, however, generally accompanied by so many unpleasant things that few priests are willing to assume the trouble and responsibility of them. As for myself, my long years of missionary work have made such hardships pleasant to me. I should prefer the direction of such a diocese to that of Philadelphia. Though I cannot say that the latter has degenerated since confided to my charge, yet not a day passes that I do not long to be once more in those vast forests which, for so many years, I used to traverse every week in my mission to the log-huts of the Catholics scattered here and there throughout the country. Feeling that my present position could be more easily filled than a new see provided for, I proposed to the Council my willingness to take charge of one of the projected dioceses, if it seemed good to the Holy See to transfer me thither.

"The Acts and Decrees of the Council were sent more than a year ago to the Propaganda, but the illness and subsequent death of the Cardinal-Prefect have prevented our receiving a decision as yet. May the holy will of God be done!"

Bishop Neumann's tender solicitude in the discharge of his duties weighed heavily upon his highly sensitive soul. Again and again, with childlike sincerity, did he complain to his confessor that his episcopal office was an insupportable burden; that he felt every morning as if he were to be executed that day; that with his whole heart he longed to return to the midst of his beloved brethren. He had, in fact, twice drawn up a petition to the Holy Father in which he urged every possible reason for a release from his position; but his confessor, without whose approval he did nothing in which the affairs of his conscience were involved, commanded him each time to burn it.

Toward the close of 1856 he wrote to one of his friends in Bohemia: "The labors of my diocese are daily on the increase; their number and kind render them ever more and more difficult. My cares multiply in the same ratio as our Catholics. Oh, if the faithful only advanced as rapidly in the love of God as they do in numbers! I am still alone; for, as the Cathedral is not yet sufficiently advanced for service, I could not, at present, support or find occupation for several priests. I am therefore obliged to attend to all my correspondence myself, give dispensations, and settle business of all kinds for both clergy and laity. From séven in the morning till nine at night I am occupied in this way almost without interruption. By that time I am, it is true, exceedingly fatigued, but my health is good, and I fear Almighty God will not soon relieve me of my burden."

Let us not misunderstand the holy Bishop's so-called complaints. The dread of not being equal to his responsible position, and not the arduous duties of his office, forced from him that cry to be relieved. His offer to resign his post to another and, as he termed it, a more competent person, in order to take charge of a new and more difficult one with the approbation of the Holy See, was not accepted in Rome, nor was it thought advisable to divide the diocese of Philadelphia. A Coadjutor was, however, given to the Bishop. Rev. James Frederick Wood, at that time pastor of one of the churches in Cincinnati, had just been appointed President of the American College in Rome. He was making preparations for entering upon his new position, when he received the Bulls appointing him Bishop of Antigonia, "in partibus infidelium," and Coadjutor of the Bishop of Philadelphia, with the right of succession.

The *Catholic Herald* of April 11, 1857, noticed the nomination in the following words:

"Bishop Neumann, in his great humility, has most earnestly requested the Holy Father to free him from the responsibility of administering so large a diocese; but the Pope was too well instructed in regard to the ardent zeal, and untiring solicitude of our revered Prelate, the effects of which are seen in the erection of so many churches and institutions. For this reason the Holy Father did not grant his request, though the Bishop's health is suffering from the unceasing labors of his episcopal office.

"The diocese of Philadelphia surpasses every other of this continent, as well in extent of territory as in the number of priests and people. Under these circumstances many were of opinion that the diocese should be divided. His Holiness, however, after mature deliberation, has decided that the diocese is not for the present to be divided, but he has assigned to our Right Reverend Bishop, John Nepomucene Neumann, a Coadjutor in the person of Rev. James Frederick Wood. The latter was born in Philadelphia, in 1813. He was educated in this city, and devoted himself to a commercial course of study. He afterward obtained a situation in a bank in Cincinnati. This state of life, however, did not please him; he felt that the security of his eternal salvation was more important than all earthly gain. He went in search of the truth, and the grace of God led him to the knowledge of it, and to the conviction that only in the Catholic Church, as the institution established by Jesus Christ for the salvation of man, could he save his soul. In the year 1836 he was received into the Church by Archbishop Purcell, of Cincinnati; in the following year he went to Rome to study for the priesthood. On the 1st of October, 1844, he came as a priest to Cincinnati, and after having served faithfully as curate and pastor till the year 1857, he will on the 26th of April be consecrated Bishop of Antigonia and Coadjutor of Bishop Neumann, with the right of succession."

Bishop Neumann, accompanied by the Rev. Father Kleineidam, rector of St. Peter's Church, Philadelphia, set out for Cincinnati to be present at the consecration of his Coadjutor and to escort him to his future home. On the return journey, all three visited the

Redemptorist House of Studies in Cumberland, Maryland, on which occasion Bishop Neumann conferred the order of deacon on seven of the students, and minor orders on a still larger number.

From this period the two Bishops labored conjointly in the extensive diocese over which they watched "as being to render an account." Bishop Wood gave efficient service in the administration of episcopal functions, Bishop Neumann having entrusted to him the temporal affairs of the diocese.

This assistance was very much needed by Bishop Neumann, since, besides the innumerable cares devolving upon him at home, his services were often demanded in other dioceses. He was frequently called upon for retreats, and his well-known kindness of heart and unbounded zeal for souls never suffered him to discard such requests. We have the following testimony from a reverend gentleman who had the happiness of making the spiritual exercises under his direction in one of the retreats to the clergy of Buffalo. This same reverend gentleman was afterward raised to the episcopal dignity.

"Bishop Neumann," he says, "gave to the clergy of the Buffalo diocese a retreat which I attended. On the second day he was told that there were several Germans making the exercises who did not understand English well enough to profit by instructions in that language. What did he do? Every day he gave two meditations in English and a corresponding number in German; also a conference in English once a day, and another in German. He preached six times a day! His courteous and affable bearing won the confidence of the priests; all wished to go to confession to him. His discourses were powerful and attractive. He never reproached, he admonished. His sermons excited our admiration all the more as we knew that Bishop Timon had invited him to give the retreat so short a time

Bishop Neumann is Assigned a Coadjutor.

before it began as to leave him no chance to prepare for it."

Letters from the clergy and the laity poured in upon the Bishop; some asking his advice in perplexing affairs, others requesting a solution of difficult questions. His kind-heartedness would never permit him to leave any unanswered. His first impulse on the receipt of a letter was to answer at once, or, if that were impossible, he did so at his first free moment. Day brought its own load of care; the night was given up to satisfying these outside calls. The good Bishop's obligingness of disposition was generally known, and everywhere looked upon as an effect of his eminent holiness. A priest belonging to another diocese once remarked: "I wrote to the late Bishop Neumann upon a matter whose solution was not clear to me, in fact I could give no explanation concerning it. What was my astonishment on receiving from him a few days after a most satisfactory answer which dispelled all doubts! He sent me at the same time the subjects of the clerical conferences held in his diocese, and also the last Decree of the Holy See in reference to the Odd-fellows. I was the more pleased and impressed by his prompt attention, as I was a perfect stranger to him."

CHAPTER XI.

Some Traits of Bishop Neumann's Saintly Character.

WE have in preceding chapters alluded to Bishop Neumann's affability, modesty, and discretion. His whole demeanor breathed these virtues; even passing intercourse with him could not fail to impress the stranger with the fact of their existence. A certain lady who had frequent recourse to him on business affairs renders the following beautiful testimony on this point: "I had occasion to call on Bishop Neumann very often, but in no one of my visits did I ever see him fix his eyes on me. He smiled, and his expression then was truly heavenly, but he never raised his eyes. And yet his downcast glance had nothing forced or repulsive in it. No one could feel offended at it; on the contrary, all left his presence edified and with the consciousness of having spoken to a saint."

During a mission given by the Redemptorist Fathers in the Cathedral Chapel, October, 1858, the Bishop might be seen every morning at four o'clock, opening the door to admit the crowd already assembled outside. He would stand at the entrance a moment, salute the faithful as they passed in, and exhort them to pray devoutly until the sermon began. Whilst the mission lasted the episcopal residence was open all day long to any who might wish to speak to the missionaries; and it was no rare sight to see the Bishop himself exercising the office of janitor, so great was his solicitude that no one wishing to see one of the Fathers should leave the house disappointed. He neglected nothing that might facilitate easy communication between the pastors of souls and those that came to seek from them advice or consolation. He had a bell hung in his residence for the purpose of calling any of the reverend gentlemen of his household who might happen to be wanted; and, in his humility, he would never dispense himself from the same regulation. When the bell sounded *one*, he promptly answered; when *two*, his Right Reverend Coadjutor; and so on, each member having a certain number of strokes.

One day several ladies called and asked for Rev. Mr. N——, who had, they said, promised to show them the beautiful ivory crucifix described in a previous chapter. Rev. Mr. N—— was out; but by some happy chance the Bishop became aware of the circumstance and the ladies' disappointment. Down he hurried to the parlor, saying: "Come with me, my children, come with me. I will show you that masterpiece of art. I will tell you the history of the Genoese crucifix." The invitation was gladly accepted. We shall allow one of the fair visitors to finish the story. "The Bishop," she said, "showed us his sacred treasures, his numerous relics of the saints, the silver medal commemorative of the day on which the Immaculate Conception was declared a dogma of the Church, and many other things besides, not forgetting the chief object of interest, the exquisite crucifix. When he noticed that two of us were daughters of the Emerald Isle, he became enthusiastic over St. Patrick, whose feast happened to fall on that very day. He told us many wonderful facts connected with our saint which we had never before heard. In a casket with a glass top lay a life-size figure in wax. It looked so natural that for an instant I drew back. 'Bishop, what is this? Whom does this figure represent?' I ventured to ask. The Bishop answered, with one of his gracious smiles: 'That represents my patron, St. John Nepomucene. It will, one of these days, find a suitable resting-place under an altar which is to be erected to his honor in the new Cathedral.'"

Bishop Neumann understood well how to treat with persons of wealth and culture. Holiness imparts to its possessor a sort of intuitive knowledge of what is demanded in intercourse with the neighbor, be he high or low, rich or poor. Blessed Henry Suso well expressed this when he said: "Purity, intelligence, and virtue give a feeling of wealth to those that possess them," which *feeling of wealth* flows in an exuberance of kind and gentle words and deeds over all with whom it comes in contact. Such was the *wealth* of him of whom we now speak; and yet, though so well calculated to win his way with the rich and great of this world, he never felt himself at home among them. After the example of his Divine Master, he sought out the lowly that he might do them good; he condescended to the rich for the same godlike end. On some occasions he was constrained to accept invitations to social gatherings and formal dinners oftentimes given in his own honor. He invariably tried to escape such attentions, but this was not always possible. Speaking of one instance in particular when, after repeatedly declining, he had been forced to take tea with a family moving in the highest circle of society, he said: "I was obliged to accept; special reasons forbade an absolute refusal. But the formalities attendant on such occasions are diametrically opposed to my tastes: they are empty, meaningless ceremonies. I would rather fast than be present at such banquets. But a greater good which I had in view obliged me to accept that invitation."

The good Bishop shrunk with equal distaste from those dinners which social custom and propriety constrained him to give in his own mansion. It often happened on these occasions that he would contrive to have some urgent business on hand, when, leaving his place to be supplied by his Coadjutor, he would slip quietly away, inwardly congratulating himself on his escape from what was ever to him the most irksome of the duties imposed by his high position. Sometimes he did not even make his appearance among his guests; a gracious message of welcome to them, and of apology for his own absence, satisfied the demands of etiquette. His housekeeper declares that she has known the Bishop, at such times, on returning before the close of the entertainment, to slip into a side apartment, take a mouthful of bread and wine, and hurry up to his room, intent only upon escaping notice. Once within its sheltering precincts, he would resume his work, reading, writing, or whatever it might be. She says that she actually had to watch him to see that he got his meals. From the same informant we learn that for whole weeks at a time the bed in his room presented no appearance of having been used. Morning found it in the same condition as upon the preceding evening. He usually took his short rest of about two or three hours sitting in a chair at his writing-desk.

Whilst treating this point, we must not omit the striking and characteristic account given by one of his clergymen who often accompanied the Bishop on his episcopal visitations. "When," says the reverend gentleman, "I accompanied Bishop Neumann on his visitation, I often sat at table with him, and I had a very good opportunity to observe him. To-day, perhaps, we would dine in style; to-morrow, very likely, we would sit down to a rustic meal served in the most primitive manner. But I always remarked that these latter had the effect of calling into play the Bishop's highest powers of humor and sociability. He would indulge in little pleasantries, he was the life of the circle around him. But if, on the contrary, we found ourselves feasted in style, at a table laden with delicacies, the poor Bishop was out of his element, he had very little to say, and would manage to escape as quietly and quickly as possible. One day we were obliged to dine at the house of a very rich Catholic. The guests were numerous and the appointments brilliant. The Bishop was more than ordinarily serious, and he scarcely touched the rich meats and wines before him. The very next day brought us quite a change of circumstances, for we dined in a log-cabin, off simple fare, our only beverage pure water. But this was seasoned with the precious wine of Christian cordiality; and the childlike pleasure evinced by our good host in attending to the Bishop's wants, more than supplied for the sumptuous entertainment of of the preceding day. What a difference between the Bishop of yesterday and the Bishop of to-day!—yesterday serious, constrained; to-day all affability and condescension, even prolonging the repast beyond the usual time. On taking leave, he presented every member of the family with some little object of devotion. When out of the house, he remarked: 'What a difference between yesterday and to-day! Yesterday we were treated to a well-filled table, empty forms of politeness, and useless conversation; but to-day we were surrounded by the charming simplicity of a pious Catholic home.'"

With all his gentleness, Bishop Neumann knew how to answer to the point when he deemed it fitting, or when the spiritual welfare of his neighbor seemed to call for it. One day, whilst superintending the work on his Cathedral and talking familiarly with the men who were preparing the immense blocks of stone for the front, a respectable-looking person whose speech proclaimed him a Quaker approached the Bishop and said, "Friend, does thee not think that it would be better to give the money to the poor instead of spending it on this grand building?" "That," retorted the Bishop, "is just what we are doing. These poor men do the work, and every Saturday evening they get their good wages. Is it not better to spend in this way than to bestow alms upon such as do not, or who are often unwilling to labor?" The Quaker, somewhat abashed, turned off with the words, "Oh, if thee view it in that light, thee may be right."

Although dispensed from the obligations of the vow, he loved and practised the virtue of poverty in a high degree. He had a skilful way of slipping his purse into the hands of the poor. After thus relieving his pocket, it was no unusual thing for him, upon the next demand made on his charity, to search in vain for a few cents. But he was never at a loss. When he found himself in such straits, he would seize the first article upon which he could lawfully lay his hands and give it to the beggar. Clothes, linen, shoes — all in turn found their way to the poor. For himself he reserved barely what was necessary. Such liberality (excessive and indiscreet, some might style it) threw him at times into the greatest embarrassment. On a certain Sunday he was on his way to one of the churches in the city, in which the devotion of the Forty Hours was to commence. A priest belonging to a neighboring church happened to meet him. Shocked at the Bishop's shabby appearance, he could not forbear exclaiming, "Right Reverend Bishop, you are in a wretched condition! This is Sunday! Will you not change that coat for a better one?" "What shall I do?" answered the Bishop, smiling; "I have no other." This was actually true. He had just given his best coat to a poor fellow asking alms.

When preparations were being made for the reception of his Coadjutor, the good Bishop was informed that the room destined for the expected stranger was without a wardrobe, and, what was worse, there was no money in the purse to buy one. "Then," said the Bishop, with a smile, "we must think of another way to get one. I know: take the one from my room and put it into Bishop Wood's; I can easily do without it."

When a simple religious, Bishop Neumann had always appeared in worn and patched clothing. His brethren were so accustomed to see him shabbily dressed that the change he was forced to make in this respect on the day of his consecration was a subject of amusement to many of them. One Father jokingly addressed him: "To-day, at least, I shall have the pleasure of seeing you well dressed." "Ah!" replied the object of his bantering, with a sigh, "Holy Mother Church treats us as parents do their children. To encourage the child to perform its task, the parent promises it some new article of dress."

After his elevation to the episcopal dignity, Bishop Neumann changed nothing in his conduct, his dress, or his sentiments, nor could he become accustomed to his new title. Toward the close of his life, he said jestingly on this subject to one of his friends: "Whenever I hear myself addressed 'Right Reverend Sir' or 'Right Reverend Bishop,' I imagine behind me some distinguished personage to whom the title belongs."

His plain, even shabby appearance often gave rise to amusing blunders. One day he was visiting his brethren in their convent at St. Peter's, Philadelphia. The community was gathered around him in the general recreation-room, pleasantly chatting, when a certain Father who had but recently arrived from Europe, and who had not yet been presented to His Lordship, entered unobserved and joined the little group. "How singular!" he thought. "Is this the way they do here in America? Do they allow strangers and people of no account to enter the cloister and communicate so familiarly with the community?" Here a break in the conversation afforded an opportunity for an introduction between the newly-arrived Father and the poorly-clad individual whose presence had given rise to his indignant strictures. What was his amazement to find himself face to face with Bishop Neumann of whom he had heard so much—Bishop Neumann of whom, as a Redemptorist, he might be so justly proud!

True to his principles in the smallest as well as in the

greatest circumstances of life, the Bishop would never suffer himself to be waited upon by a servant. He brushed his own clothes, polished his own shoes, arranged his own room himself. He would never allow his breakfast to be brought to him. He used to go down to the dining-room, take a slice of bread and butter and a glass of water, and return to his own room without having been seen even by the servants. His greatest care was to give trouble to no one. The Redemptorist custom not to ask for anything at table he continued to observe as Bishop. He took simply what was offered him, but he asked for nothing. As to whether his food were pleasing to his taste or otherwise, that appeared to be a matter of indifference to him; indeed, it was sometimes said of him that he had lost the sense of taste. Tobacco he never used in any form.

A reverend gentlemen going to the Bishop's room one day, found him sick. He was lying on a bare plank and apparently suffering intensely. Alarmed at the sight and moved with compassion for his comfortless position, the priest exclaimed, "Bishop, you are sick, very sick. You ought to go to bed." "To bed?" echoed the Bishop. "Why, I am just as comfortable here." "No, no," rejoined the good priest; "you are not as comfortable there, and you have no right under these circumstances to do as you please. You are a Bishop; you belong to your diocese." This was enough. The Bishop arose from his hard couch with, "Well, whatever you say."

Soon after, his obedience was again severely tested. A hot drink was brought him and recommended as an excellent remedy. The Bishop took it in silence, raised it to his lips, but instantly withdrew it, saying, "Why, this is wine!" "No, it is soup; it will cure you," was the reply. The Bishop again raised the goblet to his lips, and in a spirit of obedience drained its contents, though the effort to swallow it cost him a struggle against nausea.

Next day, however, the patient found himself considerably better, and in answer to the anxious inquiries of his reverend nurse, he said laughingly, "Your soup did me good, after all."

After the holy prelate's demise, his spiritual director rendered of him the following beautiful testimony: "Bishop Neumann was unrelenting in the practice of the virtues of self-denial and mortification, but so prudently, so modestly did he act in this respect that such practices never attracted attention, never rendered him burdensome to any one. He wore a girdle of iron wire that penetrated the flesh; he chastised his innocent body with a scourge which he had armed with a sharp nail; by interior recollection and constant vigilance over his eyes he shut out every temptation that could sully the purity of his heart. His virginal soul uninterruptedly communed with God; he had attained a high degree of prayer. After the example of St. Alphonsus, he had made a vow never to lose a moment of time, which vow he kept till death. Even when travelling, he either read or spoke about the things of God."

When obliged to go to distant country stations to administer Confirmation, he always, as we have before stated, combined the duties of a missionary priest with those of a Bishop, giving instructions, hearing confessions, etc. His thanksgiving after Mass could not be prolonged, as the faithful had to return to their daily avocations and many of them had come from a considerable distance. This necessity of shortening his devotions troubled the good Bishop's tender conscience. He mentioned the circumstance to his confessor, adding that the thanksgiving prayers of the Roman Missal he knew by heart and always said after his Mass. These prayers consist of the "Canticle of the Three Children," the "Laudate Dominum," Psalm 150, the prayers of St. Thomas, St. Bonaventure, and St. Augustine, together with versicles and responses, etc. His confessor, hearing this, bade him have no scruple, as his missionary duties and the administration of the Sacraments are in themselves acts of thanksgiving. What an insight these lines afford into the interior workings of this blessed soul! What a lesson they convey for the careful utilizing of those moments which contribute so largely to the work of sanctification, the precious moments following Holy Communion! Ah, truly a beautiful mirror of all virtues, this life of our venerable Bishop—life worthy of a saint!

Bishop Neumann seems to have had a presentiment of his approaching death. A few days before the sad event that was to rob the diocese of one of the brightest stars that ever gleamed in its episcopal hierarchy, he went to the Redemptorist convent of St. Peter's and, whilst awaiting the arrival of the Superior, he engaged in conversation with one of the lay-brothers. "Brother," said he abruptly after a pause, "which would you prefer, a sudden death or one preceded by a long illness?" The Brother thought that the latter would be an excellent preparation for the passage to eternity; whereupon the Bishop replied: "A Christian, still more a religious, should always be prepared for a good death, and in that case a sudden one is not without its advantages. It spares us, as well as our attendants, many a temptation to impatience; and besides, the devil has not so much time to trouble us. In either case, however, the death that God sends is the best for us."

This apparent premonition of his own demise was soon, alas! to become a reality for the saintly speaker. Farther on we shall record another and a very striking remark made by him to his reverend nephew on the same subject.

CHAPTER XII.

Death and Obsequies of Bishop Neumann.

ON Thursday, January 5, 1860, Bishop Neumann showed symptoms of unusual suffering, though he continued to work on uncomplainingly and unremittingly. At the dinner-table he endeavored to conceal his condition from the members of his household by relating an amusing anecdote of his early life. We give it as we had it from the lips of his Coadjutor, the late Archbishop Wood:

"As we sat at dinner that last day of his life, Bishop Neumann, though evidently suffering, told us the following story. 'How simple-hearted,' he began, 'are the good people in the Old Country! When, having finished my studies, I was making preparations for my journey to America, the report of my intended departure spread throughout the little town. Neighbors and relatives flocked to say farewell and to wish me a safe voyage. One of my friends from the country drew me aside and, in a low voice, said: "John, you are going on a long and dangerous voyage. Now, take my advice. Here are two gold pieces. When you go on board the ship, just slip them into the captain's hand and say, 'Captain, here are two gold pieces for you, on condition that you always steer the ship in shallow water near the land.' For you see," continued my friend, "if anything should happen to the ship, you could save yourself by swimming."' We laughed heartily at this piece of simplicity, little thinking that it was the last anecdote we should hear from the lips of our beloved Bishop."

Dinner over, Father Urbanczek, C.SS.R., was announced; and, to the surprise of the reverend visitor, Bishop Neumann, his former confrère, appeared at first hardly to recognize him. Approaching nearer and gazing steadily at the Bishop's countenance, Father Urbanczek noticed that his eyes wore a glassy appearance. He inquired whether he was sick; to which the Bishop answered: "I have a strange feeling to-day; I never felt so before. I have to go out on a little business, and the fresh air will do me good."

The Father, thinking nothing serious the matter, took his leave, and the Bishop went to have a deed connected with some church-property legally signed. Returning home, he took the north side of Vine Street. On reaching Tenth, he met an acquaintance, one of his flock, who saluted him in passing, but noticed a certain unsteadiness in his gait like that produced by vertigo. Three squares above, near Thirteenth Street, the Bishop suddenly staggered and fell on the steps of one of the private residences. He was immediately borne into the house and stretched on the floor, a pillow supporting his head. Physicians were summoned in haste, efforts were made to restore him, but all in vain. A few deep-drawn sighs, and the beautiful soul had abandoned its earthly tenement.

Meanwhile the gentleman who had seen the Bishop fall hastened at full speed to give the alarm. The episcopal residence was only about six squares off, and the Bishop's secretary was soon on the spot with the holy oils. But too late: the noble, saintly soul had departed to a better, brighter world. Loosened from the things of earth, it had flown to that resting-place to which it had so often risen in prayerful desire, the bosom of its God. It was just three o'clock in the afternoon when the servant of God appeared before his Lord and his Judge, in whom he had believed and hoped, whom he had so devotedly loved, whom he had so faithfully served during his short career.

No relative, no friend, no one of all those laborers in "the vineyard" whom a word from him could have assembled in scores, stood by that death-scene. Alone, unaided, abandoned we might almost say, his life went out. Had he prayed for this? Doubtless he had. We know of his deep love and devotion toward the Sacred Passion of his Lord; we know the device of his own choosing when raised to the episcopate—"*Passio Christi, conforta me!*"—and, if we do not know for a certainty, we have reason to believe ourselves not far from the truth when we say that, like unto his Divine Master in life, he had prayed to resemble Him also in death. And so closed that life of scarcely forty-nine years—so short in days, so full in works! Truly may it be said of him, "He fulfilled a long course in a short time."

The news of the calamity that had befallen the diocese spread like wildfire through the city, and was telegraphed in all directions. The announcement was not credited: Bishop Neumann had not been ill; on the contrary, he was regarded as a man of robust health. But alas! the painful truth soon forced itself upon even the most incredulous. The next day, Friday, was the Feast of the Epiphany. The pastors of the different churches announced to their congregations that their holy prelate had died suddenly the evening before of apoplexy, and recommended him to their prayers. On the Sunday following, the loss the diocese had sustained was again announced by the officiating clergymen in all the churches, and was made the theme of many touching remarks. In St. John's, Rev. E. J. Sourin, now of the Society of Jesus, preached, embodying in his sermon the following beautiful tribute to the deceased Bishop's memory:

"This church is the pro-Cathedral, and this is, properly speaking, the Bishop's congregation. Hence I deem it well to remind you that one of the last acts of that truly learned, devoted, and saintly prelate was to invoke, during the Pontifical Mass which he celebrated here a few days ago, a last blessing upon you all. The last time I visited him I noticed that he was very unwell, and I begged to be allowed to call in a physician for him. But he answered, with a smile: 'I shall be well enough to-morrow.' The following day he went on one of his usual errands for the benefit of the diocese, and did not again return.

"Having been closely associated with the Bishop as Vicar-General, I can testify that upon many occasions he was unable when retiring at midnight to utter a word to any one, so exhausted was he with the arduous labors of the day. It has been remarked that it is strange that he died so suddenly, so strong and robust did he always appear,—and indeed he seemed to have an iron constitution. Yet such labors as he underwent would, sooner or later, weigh down the strongest man. It is now eight years since the Bishop came among us. From the first day to the moment of his death, the period has been one of labor and suffering. He knew very well, my dear brethren, that in this city there were many who wished, as an occupant for the episcopate of this diocese, a man more according to the judgment and tastes of the world. He therefore tried to avoid the cross laid upon him, and to shun the dignity. It was only when he had reason to believe that it was the will of God, manifested to him through the Pope, that he should accept that mitre and that crozier, that he consented to do so. It was with the same spirit of self-sacrifice that he dwelt among us. He labored through every part of the diocese, and, undoubtedly, did more for its better organization and for the spread of piety through the various congregations than might have been done by another in even ten or twenty years. He was a providential man for this diocese. He spared himself in nothing. He has, therefore, received the noblest, highest recompense that a priest or Bishop can desire—to fall laboring in his Master's service. He was called away in the midst of his toils, his duties, and his sufferings. There was not in the United States a priest or a Bishop his superior in zeal for souls. Besides his literary acquirements he was a profound theologian. When any one of us was in doubt respecting some subject in theology, he could go to him for advice and at once receive the desired explanation. . . ."

On Saturday morning, January 7th, the remains of the right reverend prelate were laid in state in the sanctuary of the Cathedral Chapel, the coffin surrounded by lighted tapers, at the head the famous Genoese crucifix. The chapel was heavily draped, and thronged from morn till night by the faithful anxious for a last look at their beloved Bishop. For three days there was one continuous procession in the direction of the Cathedral. The members of the Conference of St. Vincent de Paul attached to the parish acted day and night as a guard of honor around the venerated remains.

At an early hour on Monday morning, January 9th, the Catholic community of Philadelphia was astir and moving toward the Cathedral. At nine o'clock six venerable priests took up the remains and bore them to the magnificent funeral-car with its sable plumes. The funeral-procession was the largest ever witnessed in Philadelphia. It moved slowly down Eighteenth Street to Chestnut, down Chestnut to Thirteenth, and up Thirteenth to St. John's, the pro-Cathedral. The order of the funeral-cortege was as follows: a body of city police; military company with band; eight literary societies; twenty-seven beneficial societies and conferences; thirteen societies from Baltimore in full regalia; the orphans; the students of the ecclesiastical seminaries; and one hundred reverend gentlemen of the clergy. Although the weather was unfavorable, yet the streets were thronged to witness these last sad honors to the illustrious dead. The police with difficulty opened a way for the procession. Roofs in every direction were covered, and every window was filled with spectators, who gazed with emotion upon the calm face of their deceased prelate. The grand funeral-car formed the centre of interest; to it all eyes were turned. But perhaps the most touching feature in this mournful pageant was that presented by the two imposing figures directly behind the car, Rev. Fathers Egidius Smulders and Henry Giesen, C.SS.R., whose true hearts mourned the loss of him who lay before them with folded hands and peaceful smile. Faithful to him in life and loved by him in life with the tender love of a child for a mother, the Congregation of the Most Holy Redeemer abandoned not in death him of whom they have every right to boast. They surrounded his remains with all the expressions of affection and honor that loyal hearts could suggest. His memory is held by them in benediction, his virtues as models for imitation.

When the funeral-train reached St. John's, six of the clergy again acted as pall-bearers and bore the remains from the hearse to the richly adorned catafalque prepared before the high altar. The body was so placed as to leave the features of the deceased plainly visible. The whole interior of the church was heavily draped, pillars and ceiling, sanctuary and nave, all shrouded in the sombre hue of mourning. The scene was indescribably solemn.

On the right of the catafalque stood the walnut coffin with its rich purple lining and covering of black cloth, at the head a cushion of purple satin with silver tassels and trimmings. A heavy silver plate and cross on the coffin-lid bore the inscription: "John Nepomucene Neumann, Fourth Bishop of Philadelphia, died January 5, 1860."

As soon as the body had been placed in position, Right Rev. Bishop Wood celebrated the solemn Requiem, and the clergy and seminarians recited the Office of the

Dead. Most Rev. Archbishop Kenrick of Baltimore, Right Rev. Bishop Wood of Philadelphia, Right Rev. Bishop McGill of Richmond, Right Rev. Bishop Loughlin of Brooklyn, and Right Rev. Boniface Wimmer, mitred Abbot of St. Vincent's Abbey, Pa., officiated at the Libera. The funeral-oration was delivered by Most Rev. Archbishop Kenrick of Baltimore. The newspaper report of this oration was very defective, but, fortunately, the original was found among the Archbishop's manuscripts after his death. Like all his other productions, it is simple in style and moderate in expression. It is a document well worthy of preservation, one that forms an interesting chapter in our ecclesiastical history. Two circumstances combine to clothe the obsequies of Bishop Neumann with more than ordinary interest. Of the two distinguished prelates, one the lately deceased, the other the orator of the occasion, one was from Bohemia, the other from Ireland. Both, like the Apostles, had left all to follow Christ, to devote themselves heart and soul to the American missions, "the charity of Christ" urging them. From remote parts of Europe, living under widely different governments and institutions, speaking different languages, with nothing in common but their faith and their charity, they had been brought together on this distant continent, and had zealously labored side by side in the cause of Christ. Their faith had made them brothers. Only the Catholic Church with its world-wide sympathies growing out of its blended unity and catholicity can present such a spectacle as this. Faith levels distinctions, and makes one common brotherhood of all that are willing to come under its blessed influence. The second circumstance referred to is, perhaps, still more striking. The orator that pronounced this eulogy over a brother so suddenly called away from the scene of his labors was himself destined, little more than three years later, to be summoned to the bar of the Just Judge in a manner no less sudden. It would almost seem that the saintly Kenrick was foreshadowing his own death whilst portraying the awful suddenness of that of his deceased brother-Bishop; and we readily and vividly apply to his own end those warning words of his which, doubtless, he himself heeded in their fullest import and most solemn signification: "*Remember that heaven is your home. Be mindful of the uncertainty of life, and live with a deep consciousness that every day may be your last.* WHEN YOU GO OUT TO ATTEND TO YOUR AFFAIRS, UNDERSTAND WELL THAT YOU MAY NOT RETURN TO YOUR HOME ALIVE. WHEN YOU LIE DOWN TO REST, BE FULLY SENSIBLE THAT THE MORNING MAY FIND YOU A CORPSE." Of the last two sentences, the former describes the manner of Bishop Neumann's death; the latter that of the holy Archbishop himself, for he was found one morning dead in his bed. The coincidence is striking. It would almost seem that he had a presentiment of his own end.

The following is the Archbishop's sermon as we have it in the first rough draft:

"When our Lord gave the solemn warning to be ready for His coming, because the day or hour could not be known, Peter inquired of Him whether it was designed for His select disciples or for all men in general. The Divine Teacher, without directly answering the question proposed, proceeded to describe the faithful and wise steward to whom the care of the household is entrusted, that he may distribute to the domestics their allowance in due time. Such a one is the type of an apostle or a disciple called by the Lord to preside over His family, who should discharge the duties of his office with fidelity, in daily expectation of being surprised by the arrival of his Master. The suddenness of the visitation is not to be feared by the faithful and wise servant, since he is happy because found engaged in the discharge of the duties of his charge, and is rewarded with higher gifts and greater proofs of confidence. This instruction is specially applicable to the prelates of the Church, although it is not confined to them exclusively. It is for all.

"You must perceive, brethren, the force of the warning, and the illustration in reference to the prelate whose obsequies we are celebrating. He was truly a faithful and wise steward, set over the family of the Lord by divine appointment, to distribute and to dispense the means of sanctification and salvation. He was not unmindful that his Lord might come at any time, on a day and at an hour least expected, as in fact He did come. But although suddenly snatched away, the good prelate was blessed, because his Lord found him doing the duties of his sacred office, and rewarded him, we may well presume, with admission to a participation of the divine glory and happiness. For my part, I have no fears or misgivings on this subject. From my intimate knowledge of his virtues and labors, I entertain full confidence that he has found acceptance. Yet the Church wisely offers up prayers and sacrifice for him, and for every one however holy and perfect he may appear, because the divine judgments are different from those of men. Imperfection is found in actions which win our admiration, and even saints are not wholly without blemish, since the heavens are not stainless in the divine sight. The Pontiff who already occupies the chair so recently left vacant begins his ministry by offering the Divine Victim for his lamented predecessor. The clergy, assembled in great numbers around the altar, join in the solemn oblation for the repose of their venerated Father in Christ. The pious associations which he fostered fill the church to unite in earnest supplication. Many members of similar institutes from Baltimore are present, mingling their fervent orisons for their former pastor with those of his late children. Notwithstanding the confidence inspired by the recollection of his virtues, we dare not rest on his merits, but, awed by the consideration of the divine judgments, we repeat the supplication of the Psalmist: 'Enter not into judgment with Thy servant, O Lord, for no man living shall be justified in Thy sight.'

"Brethren, although our chief duty is to pray for the soul of the departed prelate, yet it is permitted me to say some words in his praise for your edification. I feel the delicacy and the danger of eulogizing a frail mortal in this sanctuary, before this altar, in the presence of God, who wills not that flesh be glorified in His sight. Yet I do not fear that anything exaggerated shall escape my lips on this occasion—anything that might be censured by those intimately acquainted with the deceased.

"He was born in Bohemia, on the 28th of March, 1811, which was Good-Friday. I know nothing of his early life, but that he made his studies with marked success, and attained high literary honors in the University of Prague. From his subsequent career it is fair to judge that piety and innocence characterized his youth. Divine Providence led him forth from the house of his father, who even now survives, and from his fatherland, to these distant shores. The late venerable Bishop of New York, John Dubois, being satisfied with the testimonials which he presented, and with the proofs of piety which he gave during the short time of special preparation, ordained him priest in June, 1836. His ministry was exercised for some years in the western part of the State of New York. Either from an apprehension of the dangers incidental to the secular priesthood or from a desire of religious perfection, he joined the Order of the Redemptorists, founded in Italy about a century before by St. Alphonsus Liguori. But few members of it were in this country, scattered in various places; and though having scarcely any facilities for practising the duties of a conventual life, yet he entered into it with so great fervor that he became thoroughly imbued with the spirit of the holy founder, and was appointed Superior of his brethren, to lead them onward in the sublime ways of perfection. While applying himself with intense ardor to the interior and contemplative life, he did not neglect those external functions which are directed to the conversion of sinners, the favorite object of the institute. His apostolical labors in Pittsburg, Baltimore, and various other cities and in country missions were constant, zealous, and marked with great fruit. He was the chief projector and builder of the beautiful church of St. Philomena in Pittsburg. It is impossible to relate in detail his successful efforts to establish pious confraternities, schools, and asylums; his incessant preaching; his assiduous attendance at the confessional, accompanied with a supernatural influence in the guidance of souls. While thus pursuing his course with no ambition but that of gaining souls to God, an event occurred which gave occasion to his promotion to the episcopate, and placed as it were on the candlestick of the Church the light which lay concealed, or which was observable only by a comparatively small number.

"My translation from this see to the metropolitan church of Baltimore imposed on me the duty of proposing to the Holy See, with the advice and consent of my colleagues, three candidates, that one of the number might be appointed to replace me. The high commendation given by the distinguished Bishop of Pittsburg of Father Neumann, whom he had intimately known, induced me to place his name second on the list. I do not mean to insinuate that the Bishop recommended that he should be proposed; but as I deemed the knowledge of the German language an important qualification for a prelate in a diocese containing so large a population speaking that tongue, he named him as a priest of eminent merit. It pleased the Holy Father to appoint the humble Redemptorist to this high office, and, in order to prevent disappointment, he enjoined on him under obedience to submit to the Divine Will. Thus all hesitation was removed, and the consecration of the

Bishop-elect took place in the church of St. Alphonsus, Baltimore, on Passion-Sunday, which by a remarkable coincidence fell in the year 1852 on the 28th of March, his birthday. The sacrifice of his feelings in this circumstance can only be estimated by those who knew his deep humility and great love of the religious state. He felt as if he were torn from his loved retreat, and from the society of his brethren, to be exposed to the gaze of a proud world, likely to scorn the lowliness of his appearance and the simplicity of his manners. He dreaded the responsibility of governing a flock so vast, and of managing interests so complicated, for which his retired habits had not prepared him. He feared lest the difference of nationalities might impede and embarrass his efforts, if not wholly defeat them. But, as he had not sought or desired the post, he went forward, relying not on himself, but on God, who strengthens the weak and effects His high counsels by the instruments of His own choice, to show forth His power and mercy.

"Brethren, I may well appeal to you as to the manner in which the venerable prelate fulfilled the duties of his high office during the period which has since elapsed, almost eight years. You will testify to his blameless life and unfeigned piety. The constant visitation of his diocese, throughout almost the whole year, marked him as the good shepherd anxious to afford his sheep the pastures of life eternal. He usually spent three days in each congregation, preaching, hearing confessions, enrolling applicants in religious confraternities, and otherwise laboring to render permanent the fruits of his visitation. The conferences and synods which he held with his clergy disclosed to them treasures of ecclesiastical learning which filled them with astonishment. The introduction of the devotion of the Forty Hours in honor of the Divine Eucharist enlivened the faith and excited the piety of his flock, while it stimulated other prelates to encourage the same pious exercises. The earnestness with which he promoted Catholic schools showed how deeply impressed he was with the necessity of religious education in order to secure the perseverance of the rising generation in faith and virtue. The many religious institutions which he established attest his untiring zeal and charity. Truly he has been an active and devoted prelate, living only for his flock. To his clergy he has been full of tenderness. With those whom he ordained he was as a father with his children; and to all he was just and kind, teaching them more by example than by word to be in all things without offence, that our ministry may not be blamed. His solicitude for their sanctification appeared in the annual retreats to which he invited them. Their affections were daily more and more won by him, without effort on his part beyond the constant exhibition of paternal kindness. To the laity he was a devoted pastor, always accessible and ready to discharge the duties of his office, although his habits of retirement gave him, in the early part of his episcopate, an appearance of reserve which estranged from him the more fashionable classes. The poor, the humble, always found him kind, condescending, indulgent. His charities were abundant. In order to be serviceable to all, he studied various modern tongues besides the learned languages which he had mastered in his university course, and he actually acquired some of the most difficult, with the least means for attaining to their knowledge. He had, indeed, great natural aptitude for learning, and his literary taste manifested itself not merely in theological pursuits, but in astronomy, botany, chemistry, and various sciences directed to improve and delight the mind. The treasures of learning concealed under his humble exterior are scarcely credible to those who did not know him intimately. We prize him, however, for his piety and devotion far more than for his literary and scientific endowments, and value more the humility of his deportment, the purity of his life, the zeal with which he sought the salvation of souls, than the honors which crowned his studies in the university.

"It is as a pastor watching over his flock that he is specially worthy of our veneration. Among the means employed by him to promote their spiritual welfare are the missions given by members of the religious Order to which he had belonged. The preaching of the Divine Word by those zealous missionaries, with various exercises of piety, during one or two weeks, in various parishes of this city and diocese, have brought thousands upon thousands of neglectful souls to the Sacraments after years of delinquency.

"While he discharged all the duties of his sacred office with fidelity and success, he always remained detached from its honors and eager to return to the privacy of the cloister, where his heart still was. He tendered at various times his resignation, judging himself incompetent to preside in so eminent a diocese, which he was ready to abandon for a country town if his desire for seclusion could not be gratified. If he appeared in any circumstance tenacious of his prerogative, it was only under a sense of duty.

"Brethren, it may be a matter of surprise, as it is of regret, that so holy a prelate should be so suddenly snatched out of life, without a moment's warning save some symptoms which, although strange, did not excite alarm. Just after he had attended to a legal transaction by acknowledging some instrument before a magistrate, in apparent health, leaving the office he crossed the street, sat down on the steps of a house, fell, and died. How melancholy an end! Without the comforts of home, the aid of physicians, the solace of friends, the consolations of religion, as a houseless stranger he expired. But what matters it, brethren? He was prepared to die at any moment, for he lived by faith and walked with God. Each year of his life he passed ten days in retreat preparing for death; each month he observed a day of special recollection in the same spirit; each morning he meditated on heavenly things; each hour, and almost each moment, his soul communed with God. The death of such a man could not be unhappy. What matters it that God knocked not at the door of his heart to apprise him of His coming? He was busy doing his Master's will: and 'blessed is that servant whom his Lord, when he shall come, shall find so doing.' The prisoner who sighs for liberty loses nothing of satisfaction by the sudden opening of the door of his dungeon at a time when he thinks not that his liberation is at hand. We have reason to believe that, after the few sighs and groans which nature gave as tokens of departing life, the spirit of the good prelate joyously soared aloft, to commingle with the holy pastors who in every age ruled well the respective portions of the flock, and now triumphant wear the unfading crown with which the Prince of the shepherds has rewarded their fidelity. His soul now communes with the Ambroses, the Augustines, the Gregories, and especially with the sainted Alphonsus, whom he imitated so diligently. With them he praises God for the multitude of His mercies, and gives Him homage.

"Brethren, the sudden death of your Bishop is a solemn warning for us and for all. We are admonished to be always ready, for we know not the day nor the hour when the Lord will come. We are warned never to remain in a state of sin, never to falter in the performance of our religious duties. It is an intimation given to us that we may receive a hasty summons, which we should be prepared to meet. Be careful, then, to fulfil well the duties of your respective stations, to correspond faithfully with every grace divinely imparted, to walk before God in fear and love, in the observance of His commandments. Live as strangers and pilgrims; abstain from carnal lusts, which war against the soul. Remember that heaven is your home. Be mindful of the uncertainty of life, and live with a deep consciousness that every day may be your last. When you go out to attend to your affairs, understand well that you may not return alive to your home. When you lie down to rest, be fully sensible that the morning may find you a corpse. Commend your souls to God, and implore Him to forgive you your manifold faults and transgressions. Ask of Him to guard you against the many dangers which beset you. Ask of Him to bestow His grace abundantly upon you, that, in whatever circumstances you may die, your soul may be received into that kingdom into which nothing defiled can enter. Ask of Him that you may be found doing His will, and be admitted with His faithful servants to share their happiness."

Bishop Neumann's remains were to have been interred at St. John's, as it had the honor of being the pro-Cathedral, and to this end preparations had already been begun. But when Archbishop Kenrick arrived, other arrangements were made. Very Rev. Father de Dycker, C.SS.R., Provincial of the Redemptorists, petitioned the Archbishop to allow the remains to be taken to St. Peter's, the Redemptorist church. Archbishop Kenrick granted the request in these words: "I gladly consent to Bishop Neumann's finding after death a resting-place where he sought it in life but could not find it."

The services over at St. John's, the body was again conveyed in solemn procession to St. Peter's. The distance was great, and the journey tedious. The procession did not reach St. Peter's till four that afternoon. Whilst the remains were being placed on the catafalque, the faithful entered the church in such crowds that fears were entertained of some disturbance. All were animated by one desire, that of looking once more on the countenance of the deceased. With the aid of the different societies connected with the church, order was enforced. The crowds moved up the middle aisle, gazed upon the beloved remains, and left the church by the side aisles. The tide of visitors lasted until late into the night. At eight o'clock the Office of the Dead was recited by upward of fifty clergymen, and the different societies took turns as guards of honor till the next morning. On the following day, Tuesday, the church was again crowded. At eight o'clock a solemn Requiem was celebrated by Right Rev. Bishop Wood, the new incumbent by right of succession, whilst the sanctuary was filled by a large body of the clergy belonging to the city. Before the *Libera*, Rev. Father Beranek, C.SS.R., of New York, pronounced in German a beautiful and touching eulogy upon the deceased. He alluded to the great affection the lamented Bishop always entertained for the congregation he was now addressing. Here it was that he had made his retreats, here he had frequently administered the Sacrament of Holy Orders and performed other episcopal functions. Here, only a few days previously, on the hallowed feast of Christmas, he had celebrated Pontifical High Mass at midnight. The Father then spoke of the heroic virtues the Bishop had practised as a secular priest, when, forgetful of self, he thought little of a long and difficult journey if he could thereby carry the consolations of religion to even a few souls. The reverend speaker portrayed, likewise, the vast and manifold labors in which the saintly prelate had engaged for the glory of God, and touched upon the innumerable trials he had endured till death heroically, patiently, submissively. He then made a practical application of the foregoing reflections, and encouraged his hearers to a true, active, and disinterested love of God. He closed with the remark that not only the united voices of friends and brethren were now rendering homage to the servant of God, but that God Himself seemed to lend His approval to this general triumph, since the appearance of the deceased presented no change: the body was as flexible as in life, although they reckoned the sixth day since his demise.

The grand tones of the *Libera* now resounded through the sacred edifice; the body was placed in the coffin and, followed by a long train of ecclesiastics, borne in solemn state to the chapel below, into which the laity was not allowed to enter. The altar of this chapel lies under the sanctuary of the church. In front of it a small vault had been prepared, into which the body of the saintly Bishop was lowered. Tears filled the eyes of the reverend bystanders; expressions of sincere regret were heard on all sides, and the words, "I feel as if my own father were being laid to rest," escaped the lips of many.

Solemn funeral-services were offered for the deceased not only in the diocese of Philadelphia and all the convents of his Congregation, but by Bishops, priests, and religious throughout the whole country, so generally was the sainted dead loved and revered. We must not fail to mention the sorrow caused by the news of the Bishop's death in his native city far away in Bohemia.

As his visit to his fatherland, five years before, had been hailed by demonstrations of the liveliest joy, so now the news of his sudden death cast a gloom over Prachatitz and its surroundings. It was resolved in a general assembly to celebrate his obsequies in his native city with the solemnity due his exalted rank in the Church, March 2d being fixed upon for the same. A magnificent catafalque was erected and adorned with the episcopal insignia, and around it burned numberless wax-lights. The services began on the eve with the chanting of the Office of the Dead by the clergy of the city. The large church was crowded. Next morning with the same thronged attendance the solemn Requiem and *Libera* were sung. All the societies and confraternities of the city were present with lighted torches, the imperial and civic officers were in attendance—in short, the whole affair was a magnificent tribute to the deceased prelate's memory, a grand evidence of the veneration in which he was held by his countrymen.

The same feelings animated the discourse pronounced by the Director of the Schools, Rev. Joseph Brunner. His eloquent sermon made a deep impression on his hearers.

Nor were these the only marks of esteem paid the saintly Bishop in his native city. Friends and relatives wished to honor him by some lasting tribute to his memory. After mature deliberation it was resolved to erect in the cemetery of Prachatitz, in the lot belonging to the Neumann family, a metal statue of the Blessed Virgin under the title of the Immaculate Conception. On the pedestal, in gold on a black ground, are inscribed the words: "Mary conceived without sin, pray for us and for the souls of our friends here at rest in the peace of Christ." Lower down are the memorial words:

"To the True Servant
of God,
JOHN NEPOMUCENE NEUMANN,
Born at Prachatitz, March 28, 1811,
Died
January 5, 1860,
as
Bishop of Philadelphia,
This monument was erected by his
Faithful Friends."

The statue of Our Lady is twelve feet in height, and is a handsome specimen of art. It is surrounded by trees, which form for it a protecting arbor, and furnished with two tall lamps, one on either side. This beautiful and generous tribute to the worth of the deceased was not sufficient to satisfy the good people of Prachatitz. They devised another means of perpetuating the noble and saintly prelate's memory. By a resolution of the municipal authorities, the street in which the Neumann family resided was thenceforward to be known as Neumann Street. The Bishop had, with the consent of his brother and sisters, bequeathed his patrimony to the Sisters of Charity. With it they erected a school and orphanage, to the great and permanent advantage of the city of Prachatitz.

CHAPTER XIII.

Bishop Neumann's Reputation for Sanctity. Extraordinary Effects of his Intercession.

IF, at the close of this biography, we cast a retrospective glance at the virtuous life, the labors, the struggles, and sufferings of the servant of God, we shall find realized in him the words of the Holy Ghost: "The path of the just as a shining light goeth forwards and increaseth even to perfect day" (Prov. iv. 18).

In Bishop Neumann's case this light of the just shone forth in the pious child and in the aspiring youth; it was resplendent in the apostolic priest and in the God-loving religious; but when, by a special providence of God, he was placed on the episcopal candlestick, its lustre acquired new brilliancy, its rays penetrated all parts of his diocese and reflected far beyond. With the Apostle to the Gentiles, this shepherd could say to both the clergy and laity of his flock, "*Imitatores mei estote, sicut et ego Jesu Christi*"—"Be ye followers of me, as I am also a follower of Jesus Christ." The servant of God was, in truth, a burning and shining light which enlightened and inflamed with the love of God all that approached him.

It is not surprising, therefore, that Almighty God has glorified His servant both in life and in death by a reputation for sanctity, by extraordinary gifts of grace, and by remarkable favors granted to his intercession.

We shall mention a few facts gathered from reliable sources. We shall, however, premise our account by declaring that we have neither desire nor intention to anticipate thereby the authority of Holy Church. She alone has a right to decide in such matters.

The opinion entertained of Bishop Neumann by the public at large is in the highest degree honorable to him. All look upon him as a saint. We shall first adduce in support of our statement the written testimony in our possession from the pen of creditable authorities.

The Superioress-General of a numerous Sisterhood writes: "Bishop Neumann was a saint. Aside from his special acts of heroic virtue, his every action, his every word, his whole demeanor, even the tone of his voice, bore the unmistakable character of sanctity. Whenever he came to any of our convents, his first visit was to his dear Lord in the Blessed Sacrament; and whilst before the altar, his whole soul was so absorbed in God that he appeared to be no longer of this world. Our Sisters agree with me in what I say. All have had opportunities to be convinced of its truth."

A pious prelate closes his communication in reference to the deceased with these words: "May God be merciful to me through the manifold merits of this apostolic man who, many years ago, occupied my room for a few days!"

Rev. Father Sourin, S.J., writes: "The distinguished and highly esteemed Bishop Neumann deserves to have his life written, on account of his eminent sanctity, his learning, and his labors for the Church of God in America. He was always my best and truest friend. I daily invoke his aid that during the last years of my earthly career he may assist me by his intercession and lead me to a happy eternity."

Even during his lifetime, pictures and relics received from his hand were carefully preserved, and scraps of his garments appropriated as precious relics. After his death, however, the desire to possess articles belonging to him was so great that the eagerness of the faithful had to be checked. Whilst his body was resting on the catafalque, many devoutly kissed his feet—those blessed feet that had so ardently trodden in the ways of God; others touched his hands with their pictures and rosaries which they afterward kept as relics.

The gift of prophecy has been ascribed to Bishop Neumann. One day a poor mother presented herself before him, a sickly-looking babe in her arms. She was in dread of losing the little creature, and she told the Bishop so in tearful accents. "My boy is not yet two years old," she said, "and he suffers agonizing pains along with dropsy of the head. They tell me he must die soon;" and the poor woman wept. The Bishop's tender heart was moved. Laying his hand gently on the child's head, he said: "This child will not die. He will grow up to manhood; he will be your consolation and your joy." And so it turned out. The child became a model youth, the support of his widowed mother and his younger brothers and sisters.

The servant of God likewise foretold the time of his own passage from this world. Walking out one day with his reverend nephew in the summer of 1857, he remarked: "My father is reaching a very advanced age; he is now eighty. But I shall not see fifty." His nephew replied that not only his father but his mother, also, had attained old age (the latter was seventy-three at the time of her death); that all the members of their family were, as a general thing, long-lived; therefore he (the Bishop) might look forward to the same. But the latter repeated, in still more decided tones: "You will see that I shall not see fifty." And in fact, Bishop Neumann was only forty-eight years, nine months, and seven days old at the period of his demise.

On the thirtieth day after the holy Bishop's death, the vault in which he had been laid was opened and the coffin raised. On examination the body was found perfectly incorrupt. Articles of devotion were again touched to the remains, and all present desired to possess themselves of some little scrap of his clothing to keep as a relic. Ten months later the coffin was again opened, when it was found that decomposition had begun its work.

The opinion prevalent among the faithful that Bishop Neumann's life had been that of a saint gave rise to great confidence in him, as well as to the conviction that he had already received the reward of his virtues: that he was in the blissful enjoyment of the vision of God. Numbers of the faithful might be seen kneeling reverently near his grave; there they sought and often found help in their spiritual and temporal necessities. Of the prayers thus answered we have innumerable accounts attested by trustworthy witnesses. Many ascribe to his intercession the relief experienced in trials, temptations, and scruples of conscience. A person of influence and eminent for piety gives the following testimony: "In prayer I often confided my troubles to the saintly Bishop Neumann, and to glorify the truth I must acknowledge that my supplications have frequently and speedily been heard." Similar statements have been sent us by numerous others, both priests and religious.

We have been informed, also, of many wonderful cures effected through the holy Bishop's intercession. Sore breasts, wounds of long standing, were healed in a marvellously short time without leaving even a scar, and epileptics were freed of their malady at his grave.

Mother Mary Caroline, of the School-Sisters of Notre Dame, says: "To Bishop Neumann's intercession we are indebted for the favorable and remarkable answers to many of our petitions. We were also the witnesses of what we may denominate a standing miracle, since it was repeated daily for five consecutive years. Sister Anselma, who was so deaf that she could scarcely understand what we said to her, received daily for five years, through the intercession of Bishop Neumann, whom she had invoked, the wonderful faculty of being able to direct the boys' school. The room in which she taught was situated in the basement of St. Peter's, near the grave of the holy Bishop. In obedience and childlike confidence, Sister Anselma daily invoked his aid before school began, and daily received the grace to hear her scholars. They understood her perfectly, and she conducted her class to the satisfaction of all. She had one hundred and seventy little ones under her charge, among whom silence and attention always reigned during her hours of instruction."

Mrs. Ann Baker writes as follows:

"PHILADELPHIA, September 29, 1872.

"I had been suffering for over a year from open wounds on my feet. I had had the services of several physicians, but the evil, instead of diminishing, gradually grew worse, and for several months I was unable to leave the house. When I heard of the wonderful cures wrought at Bishop Neumann's grave I was at once filled with confidence, and I conceived an intense desire to visit the resting-place of the servant of God, there to implore my cure. Not being able to walk, I went in a carriage accompanied by my aunt. The distance from my home in St. John's parish to the Redemptorist church, St. Peter's, is considerable. On alighting from the carriage, I walked painfully, my aunt assisting me, into the chapel and up to the holy grave. This was on Saturday afternoon, the eve of Passion-Sunday. With lively faith I drew near the grave, and fell on my knees at the sanctuary rail, which cuts it off from the nave of the chapel, when behold! the little gate in the rail opened of itself, as if inviting my entrance. Yielding to an interior impulse, I passed in and knelt on the slab that covers the vault, and there I prayed. I implored the saintly Bishop, if in possession of the vision of God, to help me in my present need, and I recited a few, I know not how many, Paters and Aves. Relief, immediate relief, followed my prayer. I arose and left the chapel without assistance. On entering the carriage, we drove straight to St. John's, as I wished to go to confession to Rev. Father Dunn. He was at the time in his confessional. He knew me well; he knew of my helpless condition, as he had often brought me Holy Communion in my own house. Happening to see me in the church, he left the confessional in astonishment to ask an explanation and to hear my confession in the sacristy. I was somewhat fatigued on returing home, but was able to mount the stairs without help. I at once discarded the use of remedies, and in a short time my feet were entirely well. I have been in excellent health ever since."

Mary Hunneker, a little girl of thirteen, was threatened with blindness, the nerves of both eyes being painfully affected. The best oculists were consulted, but after six months' medical treatment there was no improvement. Then the child began a novena at the Bishop's grave, in which she was joined by her aunt She prayed with childlike confidence, repeating the words: "O holy Bishop, do help me that I may soon be able to go to school again!" Her simple faith was rewarded. In a few days her eyes were perfectly well, and that without the use of the doctor's remedies. When he paid his next visit to his little patient, great was his amazement to find her perfectly restored. He immediately accorded her permission to resume her schoolduties.

In consequence of a nervous shock, Elizabeth O'Driscoll lost her voice, August 25, 1868. Several physicians of Mobile, Ala., and others of Philadelphia, whither she had removed, prescribed for her, but without success. On February 1, 1869, she received Holy Communion in St. Peter's, and whilst praying at the grave of the holy Bishop her voice was perfectly restored.

Joseph Hartmann and Mary Barbara, his wife, were very anxious about their child, which, though three years and a half old, had as yet made no attempt to walk. They promised that if their child, through the intercession of Bishop Neumann, would begin to walk, they would have a High Mass sung in thanksgiving. Shortly after their vow they were amazed at seeing the child running about the yard and playing with the other children. The parents praised God that through the holy Bishop's intercession their sorrow had been changed into joy. Soon after, however, the little one relapsed into its former state: it could not stand; its feet refused to carry it around. The parents looked on with grief and consternation, and suddenly the father bethought him of his promise. It had not been fulfilled. Then he renewed his vow to have a solemn High Mass celebrated for the glory of God and in honor of his faithful servant. The child again began to run around without the slightest trace of its former weakness. We need hardly state that this time the vow was accomplished.

With such facts before us, facts well authenticated, and which occurred so recently after his death, must we not entertain the firm belief that the servant of God has entered into the joys of his Lord, has received his eternal reward? Glorious must have been his triumphal entrance into heaven, heralded by the rich fruits of his apostolic labors, clothed with his heroic virtues, his consecrated hands filled with well-earned merits! What numbers of the redeemed had not his untiring zeal sent thither during his short, full life! With what songs of jubilation they thronged the pearly gates of the Heavenly Jerusalem to welcome in canticles of joy the coming of their benefactor, to lead him to the feet of Mary, his Mother, to the arms of Jesus, the one sole love and desire of his noble heart!

May this biography prove to our times that the age of sanctity is not confined to the past; that there are saints in our own day as eminent for holiness as in any that have preceded us! May it excite in the hearts of clergy and laity an earnest desire to attain perfection in their respective states!

We trust that Bishop Neumann, by his intercession before the throne of God, will continue his apostolate in behalf of the Church Militant in general, and particularly of the portion for which he himself so generously labored, the Church in the United States, to which he sacrificed talents and strength, home and country—yea, even life itself.

In conclusion we must acknowledge our conviction that in the foregoing pages we have paid but a small tribute to the saintly Bishop's deserts. It may be that some master-pen will, after perusing this work, be incited to portray in vivid colors the heroic deeds and virtues of the great servant of God. Hoping such may be among the fruits produced by it, we venture to present it to the public, imploring upon its pages and their readers the blessing of Almighty God, Father, Son, and Holy Ghost.

THE END.